SPACE EXPLORATION

TRIUMPHS AND TRAGEDIES

ISSN 1551-210X

SPACE EXPLORATION
TRIUMPHS AND TRAGEDIES

Kim Masters Evans

INFORMATION PLUS® REFERENCE SERIES
Formerly Published by Information Plus, Wylie, Texas

GALE
CENGAGE Learning·

Detroit • New York • San Francisco • New Haven, Conn • Waterville, Maine • London

GALE
CENGAGE Learning™

Space Exploration: Triumphs and Tragedies

Kim Masters Evans
Paula Kepos, Series Editor

Project Editors: Kathleen J. Edgar, Elizabeth Manar

Rights Acquisition and Management: Margaret Chamberlain-Gaston, Kelly Quin, Sara Teller

Composition: Evi Abou-El-Seoud, Mary Beth Trimper

Manufacturing: Cynde Bishop

Product Management: Carol Nagel

Gale
27500 Drake Rd.
Farmington Hills, MI 48331-3535

ISBN-13: 978-0-7876-5103-9 (set)   ISBN-10: 0-7876-5103-6 (set)
ISBN-13: 978-1-4144-0778-4   ISBN-10: 1-4144-0778-5

ISSN 1551-210X

This title is also available as an e-book.
ISBN-13: 978-1-4144-3819-1 (set)
ISBN-10: 1-4144-3819-2 (set)
Contact your Gale sales representative for ordering information.

38124000838130

629.435
EVANS
2008

Printed in the United States of America
1 2 3 4 5 6 7 12 11 10 09 08

TABLE OF CONTENTS

PREFACE

Space Exploration: Triumphs and Tragedies is part of the *Information Plus Reference Series*. The purpose of each volume of the series is to present the latest facts on a topic of pressing concern in modern American life. These topics include today's most controversial and studied social issues: abortion, capital punishment, care for the elderly, crime, health care, the environment, immigration, minorities, social welfare, women, youth, and many more. Even though this series is written especially for high school and undergraduate students, it is an excellent resource for anyone in need of factual information on current affairs.

By presenting the facts, it is the intention of Gale, a part of Cengage Learning, to provide its readers with everything they need to reach an informed opinion on current issues. To that end, there is a particular emphasis in this series on the presentation of scientific studies, surveys, and statistics. These data are generally presented in the form of tables, charts, and other graphics placed within the text of each book. Every graphic is directly referred to and carefully explained in the text. The source of each graphic is presented within the graphic itself. The data used in these graphics are drawn from the most reputable and reliable sources, in particular from the various branches of the U.S. government and from major independent polling organizations. Every effort has been made to secure the most recent information available. Readers should bear in mind that many major studies take years to conduct, and that additional years often pass before the data from these studies are made available to the public. Therefore, in many cases the most recent information available in 2008 is dated from 2005 or 2006. Older statistics are sometimes presented as well, if they are of particular interest and no more-recent information exists.

Even though statistics are a major focus of the *Information Plus Reference Series*, they are by no means its only content. Each book also presents the widely held positions and important ideas that shape how the book's subject is discussed in the United States. These positions are explained in detail and, where possible, in the words of their proponents. Some of the other material to be found in these books includes historical background; descriptions of major events related to the subject; relevant laws and court cases; and examples of how these issues play out in American life. Some books also feature primary documents, or have pro and con debate sections giving the words and opinions of prominent Americans on both sides of a controversial topic. All material is presented in an even-handed and unbiased manner; readers will never be encouraged to accept one view of an issue over another.

HOW TO USE THIS BOOK

The achievements of the National Aeronautics and Space Administration (NASA) and its counterparts in other nations are widely admired. Yet humankind's space exploration efforts have been expensive, and include some disturbing failures and tragic accidents. As a result, space exploration is at the center of numerous controversies. This volume presents the facts on space exploration's successes and failures, and the questions that surround them. How can tragedies such as the *Columbia* disaster be prevented? Why did they happen in the first place? Are manned missions necessary or are robotic probes more cost-effective? What do we gain from space exploration? Where should our priorities lie? Should we continue to explore space at all?

Space Exploration: Triumphs and Tragedies consists of nine chapters and three appendixes. Each chapter is devoted to a particular aspect of space exploration. For a summary of the information covered in each chapter, please see the synopses provided in the Table of Contents at the front of the book. Chapters generally begin with an overview of the basic facts and background information on the chapter's topic, then proceed to examine subtopics of particular interest. For example, Chapter 5: The *International Space Station* begins with an examination of the early visions of a space station. The development and designs of the *Skylab* by the United States and the *Salyut* and *Mir* space stations by the Soviet Union are discussed. This is followed by a description of how the United States and the Russian Federation decided to design and build the *International Space Station* (*ISS*) and how the effort came to include many different nations. Next, this chapter details many of the problems that have come about while building the *ISS*. The chapter concludes with information on some of the science experiments that are conducted on the station. Readers can find their way through a chapter by looking for the section and subsection headings, which are clearly set off from the text. Or, they can refer to the book's extensive index if they already know what they are looking for.

Statistical Information

The tables and figures featured throughout *Space Exploration: Triumphs and Tragedies* will be of particular use to readers in learning about this issue. The tables and figures represent an extensive collection of the most recent and important statistics on space exploration, as well as related issues—for example, graphics in the book depict breakdowns of NASA's budget and workforce; public opinion about NASA and space exploration in general; a listing of every mission humankind has sent to Mars and its outcome; the plaque mounted on the *Pioneer* spacecraft; and diagrams of dozens of spacecraft and other equipment. Gale, a part of Cengage Learning, believes that making this information available to readers is the most important way to fulfill the goal of this book: to help readers understand the issues and controversies surrounding space exploration and reach their own conclusions about them.

Each table or figure has a unique identifier appearing above it, for ease of identification and reference. Titles for the tables and figures explain their purpose. At the end of each table or figure, the original source of the data is provided.

To help readers understand these often complicated statistics, all tables and figures are explained in the text. References in the text direct readers to the relevant statistics. Furthermore, the contents of all tables and figures are fully indexed. Please see the opening section of the index at the back of this volume for a description of how to find tables and figures within it.

Appendixes

Besides the main body text and images, *Space Exploration: Triumphs and Tragedies* has three appendixes. The first is the Important Names and Addresses directory. Here readers will find contact information for a number of government and private organizations that can provide further information on aspects of space exploration. The second appendix is the Resources section, which can also assist readers in conducting their own research. In this section, the author and editors of *Space Exploration: Triumphs and Tragedies* describe some of the sources that were most useful during the compilation of this book. The final appendix is the index.

ADVISORY BOARD CONTRIBUTIONS

The staff of Information Plus would like to extend its heartfelt appreciation to the Information Plus Advisory Board. This dedicated group of media professionals provides feedback on the series on an ongoing basis. Their comments allow the editorial staff who work on the project to continually make the series better and more user-friendly. Our top priorities are to produce the highest-quality and most useful books possible, and the Advisory Board's contributions to this process are invaluable.

The members of the Information Plus Advisory Board are:

- Kathleen R. Bonn, Librarian, Newbury Park High School, Newbury Park, California

- Madelyn Garner, Librarian, San Jacinto College–North Campus, Houston, Texas

- Anne Oxenrider, Media Specialist, Dundee High School, Dundee, Michigan

- Charles R. Rodgers, Director of Libraries, Pasco-Hernando Community College, Dade City, Florida

- James N. Zitzelsberger, Library Media Department Chairman, Oshkosh West High School, Oshkosh, Wisconsin

COMMENTS AND SUGGESTIONS

The editors of the *Information Plus Reference Series* welcome your feedback on *Space Exploration: Triumphs and Tragedies*. Please direct all correspondence to:

Editors
Information Plus Reference Series
27500 Drake Rd.
Farmington Hills, MI 48331-3535

CHAPTER 1

INTRODUCTION TO SPACE EXPLORATION

Mankind will migrate into space, and will cross the airless Saharas which separate planet from planet and sun from sun.

—Winwood Reade, *The Martyrdom of Man* (1872)

Humans have always been explorers. When ancient humans stumbled across unknown lands or seas, they were compelled to explore them. They were driven by a desire to dare and conquer new frontiers and by a thirst for knowledge, wealth, and prestige. These are the same motivations that drove people of the twentieth century to venture into space.

By definition, space begins at the edge of Earth's atmosphere, just beyond the protective blanket of air and heat that surrounds the planet. This blanket is thick and dense near the surface and light and wispy farther away from the planet. About sixty-two miles (one hundred kilometers) above Earth the atmosphere becomes quite thin. According to the Fédération Aéronautique Internationale, in "The 100 km Boundary for Astronautics" (June 25, 2004, http://www.fai.org/press_releases/2004/documents/12-04_100km_astronautics.doc), this altitude is considered the first feathery edge of outer space.

The very idea of space exploration has a sense of mystery and excitement about it. Americans call their space explorers astronauts. The term *astronaut* is a combination of two Greek words: *astron* (star) and *nautes* (sailor). Thus, astronauts are those who sail among the stars. This romantic imagery adds to the allure of space travel.

The truth is that space holds many dangers to humans. Space is an inhospitable environment, devoid of air, food, or water. Everywhere it is either too hot or too cold for human life. Potentially harmful radiation flows in the form of cosmic rays from deep space and electromagnetic waves that emanate from the Sun and other stars. Tiny bits of rock and ice hurtle around in space at high velocities, like miniature missiles.

Space is not readily accessible. It takes a tremendous amount of power and thrust to hurl something off the surface of Earth. It is a fight against the force of Earth's gravity and the heavy drag of an air-filled atmosphere.

Getting into space is not easy, and getting back to Earth safely is even tougher. Returning to Earth from space requires conquering another mighty force: friction. Any object penetrating Earth's atmosphere from space encounters layers and layers of dense air molecules. Traveling at high speed and rubbing against these molecules produces a fiery blaze that can rip apart most objects.

It was not until the 1950s that the proper combination of skills and technology existed to overcome the obstacles of space travel. The political climate was also just right. Two rich and powerful nations (the Soviet Union and the United States) devoted their resources to besting one another in space instead of on the battlefield. It was this spirit of competition that pushed humans off the planet and onto the Moon in 1969.

Once that race was over, space priorities changed. In the twenty-first century, computerized machines do most of the exploring. They investigate planets, asteroids, comets, and the Sun. Human explorers stay much closer to Earth. They visit and live aboard space stations in orbit a couple hundred miles above the planet. On Earth people dream of longer journeys because most of space is still an unknown sea, just waiting to be explored.

ANCIENT PERSPECTIVES ON SPACE

Since the earliest days people have looked up at the heavens and dreamed of flying there. In ancient Greek and Roman mythology gods and goddesses rode chariots through the skies or had wings of their own. In Greek mythology these included Eros (god of love), Nike (goddess of victory), Hermes (the messenger to the gods), and Apollo (god of the arts). In Roman mythology they were called Cupid, Victoria, Mercury, and Apollo, respectively.

One famous Greek tale concerned Icarus and his father, Daedalus. Imprisoned on an island, they decide to escape by building wings of feathers and wax for themselves and flying to freedom. However, Icarus disregards his father's warning against flying too close to the Sun, and the heat melts the wax in his wings. When Icarus's wings fall apart, he plunges to his death in the sea.

In about A.D. 160 the Greek writer Lucian of Samosata (125?–200?) wrote the story *True History* about a sailing ship whisked to the Moon by a giant waterspout. The sailors find the Moon inhabited by strange creatures that are at war with beings living on the Sun. In a later story, *Icaromenippus*, an adventurer more successful than Icarus uses eagle and vulture wings to fly to the Moon.

ENLIGHTENED OBSERVATIONS

Centuries later the great Italian painter and engineer Leonardo da Vinci (1452–1519) foresaw the day that humans would fly. He wrote, "There shall be wings! If the accomplishment be not for me, 'tis for some other." Leonardo made several sketches of human-powered flying machines and gliders with birdlike wings.

At the time, astronomical knowledge was limited, and it was widely believed that Earth was the center of the universe and everything else revolved around it. The Polish astronomer Nicolaus Copernicus (1473–1543) studied the motion of the heavens and drew different conclusions. In 1543 he published the famous book *De Revolutionibus Orbium Coelestium* (*On the Revolutions of the Heavenly Spheres*). Copernicus insisted that Earth and the other planets orbit the Sun. He said, "At the middle of all things lies the sun."

The first telescopes appeared in Europe during the early 1600s. Even though historians are not sure who invented the telescope, they know that the Italian astronomer Galileo Galilei (1564–1642) popularized their use. Galileo also improved the design and power of the telescope. He used several to study the cosmos and published his findings in the 1610 book *Sidereus Nuncius* (*Starry Messenger*).

At about the same time the German astronomer Johannes Kepler (1571–1630) was also studying the solar system. He discovered that planets move according to mathematical rhythms, and he derived laws of planetary motion from these rhythms that are still being studied. In 1593 Kepler wrote Galileo a letter in which he said, "Provide ships or sails adapted to the heavenly breezes, and there will be some who will not fear even that void."

The mechanics of spaceflight were explored by the English physicist Sir Isaac Newton (1642–1727). Newton first unraveled the mysteries of gravity on Earth and then extended his findings into space. He was the first to explain how a satellite (an orbiting body) could be put into orbit around Earth.

Newton's thought experiment, as it was called, proposed a cannon atop a tall mountain as a theoretical means for putting an object into orbit around Earth. The cannon shoots out projectiles one after another, using more gunpowder with each successive firing. Newton said each projectile would travel farther horizontally than the previous one before falling. Finally, there would be a projectile shot with enough gunpowder that it would travel very far horizontally and when it began to fall toward Earth, its path would have the same curvature as Earth's surface. The projectile would not fall to Earth's surface but continue to circle around the planet. It would be another two centuries before humans could prove Newton's theory.

It was only a few decades after Newton's death that humans began to fly on earthly breezes. During the late 1700s the French brothers Joseph-Michel Montgolfier (1740–1810) and Jacques-Étienne Montgolfier (1745–1799) built the first hot-air balloons. On November 21, 1783, the two brothers ascended to five hundred feet and sailed across the city of Paris. They landed safely miles from the city and offered champagne to the terrified villagers there. The age of flight had begun.

SPACE TRAVEL IN EARLY SCIENCE FICTION

Science fiction is a category of literature in which an imaginative story is told that incorporates at least some scientific principles to give it a sense of authenticity and believability. It is a mixture of science and imagination. The term *science fiction* is generally credited to the writer Hugo Gernsback (1884–1967), who published a magazine devoted to such stories and started book clubs for science-fiction fans. His legacy lives on in the Hugo Award, a literary award given each year by the World Science Fiction Society.

Jules Verne

The French author Jules Verne (1828–1905) was one of the earliest science-fiction writers to incorporate space travel in his stories. In 1865 he wrote *De la terre à la lune: Trajet direct en 97 heures 20 minutes* (*From Earth to the Moon: Passage Direct in Ninety-seven Hours and Twenty Minutes*), a tale of an ambitious gun club in the United States. The men build a massive cannon in Florida and shoot a metal sphere toward the Moon. Inside are three astronauts who plan to explore the lunar surface. Their target misses the mark, and they wind up orbiting the Moon instead. It was the first space travel story based on physics, rather than on pure fantasy.

Five years later Verne published the sequel *Autour de la lune* (*All around the Moon*). The astronauts use small onboard rockets to propel their sphere safely back to

Earth, where it splashes down and floats in the ocean. A nearby ship rescues the men and takes them home to a heroes' welcome. The similarities are striking between these stories and the actual events of the Apollo flights one hundred years later.

Edward Everett Hale

In 1869 the American writer Edward Everett Hale (1822–1909) published a remarkable science-fiction tale in the *Atlantic Monthly*. His tale "The Brick Moon" describes the work of some clever American inventors who decide to build a large beacon to sit in the sky and glow as a constant reference point for ships at sea. To accomplish this goal, the men build a large brick sphere set atop a hill. A track leads down the hill to two giant spinning wheels that are set in a gorge and turned by water from a rushing river. The wheels are to catapult the brick moon into space.

One day the brick moon accidentally rolls away from its restraints and is flung into space with some of the workers and their families aboard. For months their friends on the ground search the night skies with telescopes until finally they spot the satellite in Earth orbit. They are amazed to see its occupants living happily on the satellite surface. On occasion the occupants send signals back to Earth by forming a long line and simultaneously making large and small jumps into the air to spell out messages in Morse code.

The story is prophetic in one interesting respect: during the construction of the brick moon the inventors are plagued by constant design changes, funding problems, and criticism from the public and the press. These difficulties would become common ones for the space programs that later developed.

H. G. Wells

Around the turn of the twentieth century the English author Herbert George Wells (1866–1946) wrote popular space travel stories including *The War of the Worlds* (1898) and *The First Men on the Moon* (1901).

The *War of the Worlds* featured Martian invaders landing spacecraft near London and terrorizing the population with destructive machines and poisonous gas. In the end the humans prevail when a common germ kills the Martians. During the 1930s the story was made into a radio play and rewritten for an American audience. On October 30, 1938, the play was broadcast as a mock newscast. Some listeners thought the "news" was real, which created scattered incidents of panic.

The *First Men on the Moon* also included unfriendly aliens, this time on the Moon. Some daring explorers from Earth travel to the Moon and are captured by antlike creatures called Selenites. The name is derived from Selene, the mythical Greek goddess of the Moon. The story features little actual science and is generally considered more of a romantic adventure tale set in space.

Georges Méliès

In 1902 the French director Georges Méliès (1861–1938) created the first-known science-fiction motion picture. *Le voyage dans la lune* (*The Trip to the Moon*) is an eleven-minute silent film very loosely based on the Verne stories about Moon travel.

This time five brave Frenchmen are catapulted to the Moon, where their rocket actually lands in the giant right eye of the "man in the Moon." The astronauts begin exploring, but are captured by unfriendly Selenites. The explorers manage to escape back to their spacecraft and push it off the edge of the Moon to fall back to Earth. They splash down in the sea and return to France as heroes.

THE WRIGHT STUFF

On December 17, 1903, the American brothers Orville Wright (1871–1948) and Wilbur Wright (1867–1912) made history at Kitty Hawk, North Carolina, with the first sustained flights of a powered aircraft. Each brother took two flights that day. The longest flight covered about 850 feet and lasted just under one minute. The modern age of aviation had begun.

In 1905 the Fédération Aéronautique Internationale (FAI; http://www.fai.org/) was formed in Europe by representatives from Belgium, France, Germany, Great Britain, Italy, Spain, Switzerland, and the United States. The FAI became the official organization for cataloging and verifying aeronautical feats around the world.

Aviation got off to a slow start in the United States. The earliest planes were notoriously dangerous, and several aspiring adventurers were killed flying them. Neither the American public nor the federal government was convinced that airplanes were safe and effective. The mood in Europe was much different. Engineers in France, England, and Germany produced their own versions of reliable and versatile aircraft.

FLYING TAKES OFF

When World War I began in Europe in 1914, the power of aerial warfare became apparent immediately. The United States realized that it was behind its European counterparts in aviation expertise, and in an effort to correct the situation the U.S. government formed the Advisory Committee for Aeronautics (ACA) in 1915. Later, the word *national* was tacked on, and the agency became known as the NACA. The NACA began an ambitious campaign of research and development into aircraft design and flight theory.

By the end of the war in 1918 the United States had made great progress in the field of aviation, including the development of commercial airlines and postal air services. In addition, public attitudes about flying were beginning to change. The daring feats of World War I pilots such as the American ace Eddie Rickenbacker (1890–1973) and the German legend Manfred von Richthofen (1882–1918) had brought an air of excitement to flying.

In 1919 the New York City hotel owner Raymond Orteig (1870–1939) offered a $25,000 prize to the first aviator who could fly nonstop from New York to Paris or from Paris to New York. The Orteig Prize inspired one of the greatest flying feats of the century. A young man named Charles A. Lindbergh Jr. (1902–1974) convinced businessmen in St. Louis, Missouri, to finance his attempt to win the prize. Lindbergh had earned his flying reputation as a successful airmail pilot and barnstormer (one who performs flying stunts at air shows). On the morning of May 20, 1927, he took off from Long Island, New York, in his monoplane the *Spirit of St. Louis*. Thirty-three and a half hours later he landed on a Parisian airstrip amid throngs of cheering spectators. Lindbergh was an instant hero, and flying was suddenly of vital interest to Americans, who thrilled to the adventures of pilots such as Amelia Earhart (1897–1937), Wiley Post (1899–1935), Howard Hughes (1905–1976), and Douglas "Wrong-Way" Corrigan (1907–1995).

Meanwhile, the NACA continued its work in aviation science. Orville Wright joined the organization and remained a member until his death in 1948. During these decades the NACA drove many developments within the field of aeronautics, except for one: rockets.

PIONEERS OF ROCKET SCIENCE

There are four men in history who are considered the founders of modern rocket science: Konstantin Tsiolkovsky of Russia, Hermann Oberth of Austria-Hungary, Robert Goddard of the United States, and Wernher von Braun of Germany. All four were working on rocket science during the early years of the twentieth century. Even though they were scattered around the world, they reached similar conclusions at about the same time.

Konstantin Tsiolkovsky

Konstantin Tsiolkovsky (1857–1935), a Russian schoolteacher, was inspired by a love of science and by Verne's stories, and he even tried his hand at science fiction, before and after becoming a scientist. Tsiolkovsky studied the theoretical concepts of rocket flight, such as gravity effects, escape velocity, and fuel needs. He developed a simple mathematical equation relating the final velocity of a rocket to the initial velocity, the starting and ending mass of the rocket, and the velocity of the rocket exhaust gases. Tsiolkovsky's equation became a fundamental concept of rocket science and is still taught in the twenty-first century.

FIGURE 1.1

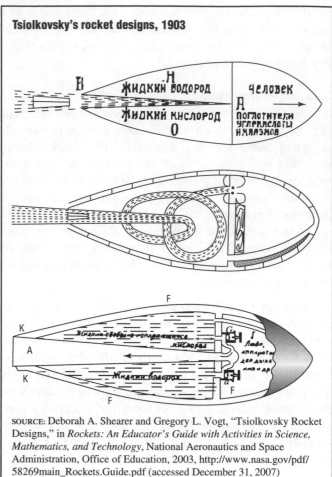

Tsiolkovsky's rocket designs, 1903

SOURCE: Deborah A. Shearer and Gregory L. Vogt, "Tsiolkovsky Rocket Designs," in *Rockets: An Educator's Guide with Activities in Science, Mathematics, and Technology*, National Aeronautics and Space Administration, Office of Education, 2003, http://www.nasa.gov/pdf/58269main_Rockets.Guide.pdf (accessed December 31, 2007)

In 1895 Tsiolkovsky wrote *Dreams of Earth and Sky*. The book described how a satellite could be launched into an orbit around Earth. Later publications included *Exploration of the Universe with Reaction Machines* and *Research into Interplanetary Space by Means of Rocket Power*, both published in 1903. Figure 1.1 shows some of Tsiolkovsky's designs for liquid-propelled rockets. Two decades later, he wrote *Plan of Space Exploration* (1926) and *The Space Rocket Trains* (1929).

Tsiolkovsky believed that rockets launched into space would have to include multiple stages. That is, instead of having one big cylinder loaded with fuel, the fuel must be divided up among smaller rocket stages linked together. As each stage uses up its fuel, it could be jettisoned away so the remainder does not have to carry dead weight. Tsiolkovsky reasoned that this was the only way for the mass of a rocket to be reduced as its fuel supply was depleted.

Tsiolkovsky predicted in a 1911 letter, "Mankind will not remain on Earth forever, but in its quest for light and space will at first timidly penetrate beyond the confines of the atmosphere, and later will conquer for itself all the space near the Sun."

Hermann Oberth

Hermann Oberth (1894–1989) was born in Transylvania, Romania, which was part of the Austro-Hungarian Empire. As a teenager, Oberth studied mathematics and began developing sophisticated rocket theories. He studied medicine and physics at the University of Munich. During the 1920s he wrote two important papers: "Die Rakete zu den Planetenräumen" ("The Rocket into Interplanetary Space") and "Wege zur Raumschiffart" ("Methods of Achieving Space Flight").

In 1923 Oberth predicted that rockets "can be built so powerfully that they could be capable of carrying a man aloft." He proposed bullet-shaped rockets for manned missions to Mars and an Earth-orbiting space station for refueling rockets. Like his Russian counterpart, Oberth advocated multistage rockets fueled by liquid propellants.

Oberth's writings were hugely popular and influenced the movie producer Fritz Lang (1860–1976) to make a movie about space travel called *Die Frau im Mond* (*The Woman in the Moon*) in 1929. Oberth served as a technical adviser on the film. He also inspired the German rocket club known as Verein für Raumschiffahrt (VfR; Society for Spaceship Travel). The VfR put Oberth's theories into practice by building and launching rockets based on his designs.

As World War II (1939–1945) drew near during the 1930s, the Nazi government put Oberth and other VfR members to work developing rockets for warfare, rather than for space flight.

Robert Goddard

Robert Goddard (1882–1945) was an American physicist born in Worcester, Massachusetts. In a speech made in 1904 he said, "It is difficult to say what is impossible, for the dream of yesterday is the hope of today and the reality of tomorrow," and Goddard spent the rest of his life making rocket flight a reality. After graduating from college, he taught physics at Clark University in his hometown. He also spent time on a relative's farm experimenting with explosive rocket propellants. Unlike his Russian and Austro-Hungarian counterparts, Goddard's rocket science was more experimental than theoretical. In all, he was granted seventy patents for his inventions. The first two came in 1914 for a liquid-fuel gun rocket and a multistage step rocket. He is believed to be the first person to prove experimentally that a rocket can provide thrust in a vacuum.

Much of Goddard's research was funded by the Smithsonian Institution and the Guggenheim Foundation. The U.S. government showed little interest in rocket science except for its possible use in warfare. Late in World War I Goddard presented the military with the concept for a new rocket weapon, later called the bazooka. After the war Goddard worked part time as a weapons consultant to the U.S. armed forces.

In 1920 the Smithsonian published Goddard's famous paper "A Method of Attaining Extreme Altitudes," in which he described how a rocket could be sent to the Moon. The idea was greeted with skepticism from scientists and derision from the media. The *New York Times* published a scornful editorial ridiculing Goddard for this fanciful notion. Goddard was stung by the criticism and spent the rest of his life avoiding publicity. His low-profile approach kept his work from being well known for many years. The one person who did take a keen interest in him was Charles Lindbergh, who played a key role in securing funding for Goddard's rocket research from the Guggenheim Foundation.

On March 16, 1926, Goddard achieved the first-known successful flight of a liquid-propelled rocket. (See Figure 1.2.) Throughout the next decade he labored quietly in the desert near Roswell, New Mexico, developing increasingly more powerful rockets. In 1935 Goddard launched the first supersonic liquid-fuel rocket. (Supersonic means faster than the speed of sound. Sound waves travel at about seven hundred miles per hour, depending on the air temperature.) A year later Goddard's achievements finally received recognition when the Smithsonian published another of his papers, "Liquid Propellant Rocket Development."

He continued his work until 1941, when the United States entered World War II. Until his death in 1945, Goddard worked with the military to develop rocket applications for aircraft. Three decades later the *New York Times* finally issued an apology for its 1920 editorial about him. The date was July 17, 1969, and three American astronauts were on their way to the Moon. The newspaper admitted that Goddard had been right after all. The Goddard Space Flight Center near Washington, D.C., and the Goddard crater on the Moon are both named after him.

Wernher von Braun

World War II ushered in the rocket age. The Nazi government of Germany was eager to use rockets against its enemies. The great talents and minds of the VfR were directed to forget about space travel and concentrate on warfare. During the early 1940s Germany developed the most sophisticated rocket program in the world. At its helm was the brilliant young Wernher von Braun (1912–1977).

Von Braun had been Oberth's assistant during the 1930s and an active member of the VfR. He was put in charge of developing a rocket weapon to terrorize the British population. Von Braun's team included Oberth and hundreds of people who worked on the remote island Peenemünde. They developed the rocket-powered *Vergeltungswaffens* (weapons of vengeance), which were called V weapons for short.

FIGURE 1.2

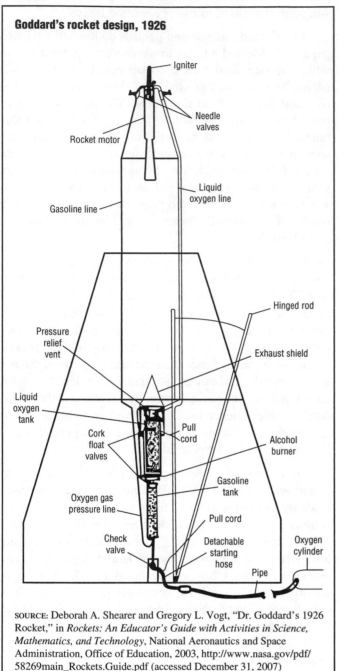

Goddard's rocket design, 1926

Igniter

Needle valves

Rocket motor

Liquid oxygen line

Gasoline line

Hinged rod

Pressure relief vent

Exhaust shield

Liquid oxygen tank

Cork float valves

Pull cord

Alcohol burner

Oxygen gas pressure line

Gasoline tank

Pull cord

Check valve

Detachable starting hose

Oxygen cylinder

Pipe

SOURCE: Deborah A. Shearer and Gregory L. Vogt, "Dr. Goddard's 1926 Rocket," in *Rockets: An Educator's Guide with Activities in Science, Mathematics, and Technology*, National Aeronautics and Space Administration, Office of Education, 2003, http://www.nasa.gov/pdf/ 58269main_Rockets.Guide.pdf (accessed December 31, 2007).

There were two series of V weapons. The V-1 carried a ton of explosives and traveled at a top speed of about four hundred miles per hour. This was slow enough that British gunners could blow apart the V-1s as they descended through the air. Thousands of V-1s were launched against England, but roughly half never impacted the ground.

Far more lethal was the V-2. This was truly a rocket with a top speed around two thousand miles per hour. The V-2s traveled far too fast to be shot down and terrified the British public. In "V-2: Hitler's Last Weapon of Terror" (BBC News, September 7, 2004), Paul Rincon reports that

over 1,300 V-2s were launched against England during World War II, killing 2,724 people.

On September 8, 1944, the first V-2 rocket fell on London. The National Aeronautics and Space Administration (NASA) notes in "The Robotic Exploration of Space" (June 30, 2004, http://solarsystem.nasa.gov/history/ timeline .cfm?Section=1) that von Braun reportedly turned to his colleagues and said, "The rocket worked perfectly, except for landing on the wrong planet." The tide had already turned against Germany. By early 1945 the country was being invaded by the Soviets from the east and the Allies from the west. To be in position to surrender to U.S. forces, von Braun moved his team near the German-Swiss border.

A negotiated surrender was worked out in which von Braun turned over himself, people on his team, and vital plans, drawings, rocket parts, and documents. In exchange, the U.S. Army agreed to transport the team to the United States and fund its work on a U.S. rocket program. The army called the agreement Operation Paperclip. It had no way of knowing that this move was going to put Americans on the Moon.

THE X-SERIES

Even before World War II ended the United States began developing rocket-powered planes. In 1943 the NACA initiated the research program in conjunction with the air force and navy. Because the planes were experimental, they were given the name X-aircraft. In 1944 a company called Bell Aircraft began work on the XS-1, with the "S" standing for supersonic. Later, the "S" was dropped, and the plane became the X-1.

On October 14, 1947, the U.S. Air Force captain Charles (Chuck) Yeager (1923–) flew the X-1 at the speed of sound, which is known as Mach 1. The X-1 was only the first of many high-performance planes tested in the program. Eventually, X-planes flew at hypersonic speeds, that is, speeds greater than Mach 5 (five times the speed of sound). In "X-15: Hypersonic Research at the Edge of Space" (February 24, 2000, http://history.nasa.gov/x15/cover.html), NASA explains that the X-15 was a rocket-fueled plane tested during the late 1950s and early 1960s. It was taken up to an altitude of approximately forty-five thousand feet by a carrier plane, a B-52 aircraft, and released. A rocket engine was then fired to propel the X-15 to incredible speeds and heights. On November 9, 1961, an X-15 flew at Mach 6.04, the fastest suborbital speed ever reached. On August 22, 1963, an X-15 soared across the boundary into space to an altitude of sixty-seven miles. This record would remain unbroken for more than four decades.

The X-series were high-speed, high-altitude planes unlike any ever built before. Most of them were tested over desolate desert areas near Muroc, California. Daring young test pilots flew the X-series planes. However, this was a dangerous profession. Many pilots were killed or seriously injured while testing the X-series planes. The pilots who survived became the first men considered for the nation's astronaut program.

A COLD WAR IN SPACE BEGINS

The term *cold war* is used to describe U.S. relations with the Soviet Union from the end of World War II to 1991, when the Soviet Union collapsed. During this period, which is chiefly marked by a mutual mistrust and rivalry that led to a buildup of arms, both nations developed extensive nuclear weapons programs. Each thought the other was militarily aggressive, deceitful, and dangerous. Each feared the other wanted to take over the world. This paranoia was in full force when space exploration began.

The International Geophysical Year

In 1952 a group of American scientists proposed that the International Council of Scientific Unions (ICSU) should sponsor a worldwide research program to learn more about Earth's polar regions. Eventually, the project was expanded to include the entire planet and the space around it. The ICSU decided to hold the project between July 1957 and December 1958 and call it the International Geophysical Year (IGY). Geophysics is a branch of earth science that focuses on physical processes and phenomena in the earth and its vicinity.

The IGY time period was selected to coincide with an expected phase of heightened solar activity. Approximately every eleven years the Sun undergoes a one- to two-year period of extra radioactive and magnetic activity. This is called the solar maximum. The ICSU hoped that rocket technology would progress enough to put satellites in Earth orbit during the next solar maximum and collect data on this phenomenon.

Sixty-seven countries participated in various ways in the IGY project. The American delegation to the ICSU was led by the National Academy of Sciences, which consisted of a team of scientists from businesses, universities, and private and military research laboratories to conduct American activities during the IGY.

Ballistic Missiles

Following World War II both the United States and the Soviets began researching the feasibility of attaching warheads to long-range rockets that were capable of traveling halfway round the world. These weapons were eventually called intercontinental ballistic missiles (ICBMs). They could be equipped with conventional or nuclear warheads. The United States had introduced the

nuclear warfare age by dropping two atomic bombs on Japan to end World War II in August 1945.

By the early 1950s the U.S. Air Force was actively testing three different ICBMs under the Navaho, Snark, and Atlas programs. This work was highly classified as a matter of national security. The United States and the Soviet Union both engaged in massive spying campaigns throughout the cold war. In 1955 American spies brought word that the Soviets were close to completing ICBMs capable of reaching U.S. cities.

The Soviet rocket work was spearheaded by Sergei Korolev (1906–1966). He oversaw the development of the R-7, the world's first ICBM, and is considered the father of the Soviet space program.

Sputnik 1

Throughout the mid-1950s the United States worked to construct a successful science satellite for the IGY. This work proceeded separately from ICBM development. However, at the time only the military had the expertise and resources to build rockets capable of leaving Earth's atmosphere. The navy was charged with developing a rocket capable of carrying a package of scientific instruments into Earth orbit. In 1957 testing was still ongoing and proceeding poorly when the United States received shocking news.

On the evening of October 4, 1957, the Soviet Union news service announced that the nation had successfully launched the first-ever artificial satellite into Earth orbit. It was called *Sputnik*, which means "companion" in English. The word also translates as "satellite," because a satellite is Earth's companion in an astronomical sense. Launched atop an R-7 Semiorka rocket, the satellite weighed 184 pounds, was about the size of a basketball, and circled Earth every ninety-eight minutes.

A Secret Surprise

The launch announcement of *Sputnik 1* was both a disappointment and a surprise to American scientists. They knew their Soviet counterparts were working on a science satellite for the IGY but had no idea the Soviets had progressed so quickly. The American scientists had openly shared information about their research during ICSU meetings. By contrast, the Soviet government forbade its scientists from disclosing any details about their work. *Sputnik 1* had been developed and launched in near total secrecy. According to Hugh Sidey, in "Oct. 4, 1957: The Space Race Lifts Off" (*Time*, March 31, 2003), Lloyd Berkner, the president of the ICSU, learned about the launch while at a dinner party at the Soviet embassy in Washington, D.C., when a reporter from the *New York Times* whispered the news to him.

The American public was even more shocked by the announcement. Millions went outside in the darkness to look for the satellite in the night sky. Witnesses said it was a tiny twinkling pinpoint of light that moved steadily across the horizon. The satellite continuously broadcast radio signals that were picked up by ham radio operators all over the world. Ham radio is communication using short-wave radio signals on small amateur stations.

The *Sputnik 1* signals were another unpleasant surprise for American scientists. It had been universally agreed that IGY satellites would broadcast radio signals at a frequency of 108 megahertz. The United States had already built a satellite tracking system designed for this frequency. However, *Sputnik 1* transmitted at much lower frequencies, ensuring that U.S. scientists would not be able to pick up its data.

Sputnik 2—A Dog in Space

The success of *Sputnik 1* caught the United States off guard and unprepared. For the first time, the American public realized that the Soviets probably had the capability to launch long-range nuclear missiles against the United States. A month later there was even further dismay when the Soviets launched a second satellite.

Sputnik 2 was much larger than its predecessor and carried a live dog, a husky-mix named Laika, into orbit. The American press nicknamed her "Muttnick." It was a one-way trip for her as the Soviet scientists had not yet worked out how to bring the spacecraft safely back to Earth. At the time the Soviet news agency bragged that Laika survived for a week aboard the spacecraft. Decades later scientists admitted that Laika died only hours after launch when she panicked and overheated in her tiny cabin.

The United States Reacts

The American public was scared by the size of *Sputnik 2*, which weighed more than one thousand pounds. Furthermore, it was common knowledge that the United States did not have a rocket capable of carrying that much weight into space. There was an uproar in the media, and politicians demanded to know how the Soviet Union had gotten so far ahead of the United States in space technology. President Dwight D. Eisenhower (1890–1969) charged the U.S. military to do whatever it took to put a satellite in space.

The U.S. Navy's efforts to build a satellite had proved unsuccessful. The military turned to von Braun and his team of rocket scientists working for the U.S. Army. On January 31, 1958, the first American satellite soared into orbit. It was named *Explorer 1* and rode atop a Jupiter-C rocket developed by the von Braun team at Huntsville, Alabama. (See Figure 1.3.)

A few months later the Soviets answered with *Sputnik 3*, a miniature physics laboratory sent into orbit to collect scientific data.

In October 1958 the United States formed the National Aeronautics and Space Administration to oversee the nation's

FIGURE 1.3

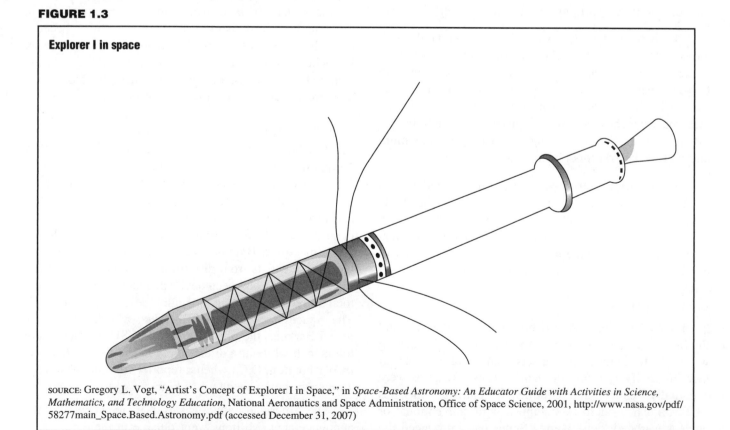

Explorer I in space

SOURCE: Gregory L. Vogt, "Artist's Concept of Explorer I in Space," in *Space-Based Astronomy: An Educator Guide with Activities in Science, Mathematics, and Technology Education,* National Aeronautics and Space Administration, Office of Space Science, 2001, http://www.nasa.gov/pdf/58277main_Space.Based.Astronomy.pdf (accessed December 31, 2007)

space endeavors. Even though it was a civilian agency charged with operating peaceful missions in space, NASA would rely heavily on military resources to achieve its goals.

FIRST HUMAN IN SPACE

On April 12, 1961, the cosmonaut (Russian astronaut) Yuri Gagarin (1934–1968) became the first human to travel beyond Earth's atmosphere, enter the frontier of space, and return safely to Earth. Gagarin was born in a village near Gzhatsk (now Gagarin) in central Russia. He grew up in a peasant family, dreaming of becoming a pilot. Before being recruited to be a cosmonaut, Gagarin was serving as a lieutenant in the Soviet air force.

The article "Gagarin: Son of a Peasant, Star of Space" (BBC News, April 1, 1998) reports that his flight took him roughly 300 kilometers (186 miles) above Earth and that he spent 1 hour and 48 minutes circling the planet, completing one entire orbit and part of another one. His cramped spacecraft was equipped with a radio for communicating with ground control. Looking down at the planet beneath him, he said, "The Earth is blue. How wonderful. It is amazing."

The weightlessness bestowed by space travel had always been a worry for scientists. There is a common misconception among the public that there is no gravity in space. This is not true. Actually, the force of gravity remains strong for great distances around Earth. Objects and people that leave Earth's atmosphere experience weightlessness, because they are in free fall toward Earth throughout their trip.

At the time of Gagarin's flight, scientists were not sure how the human body would react to weightlessness. His spacecraft included a computerized automatic pilot, in case Gagarin lost consciousness or was unable to move. This fear proved to be unfounded. The mission showed that humans can not only withstand weightlessness but can also function quite well in it.

Gagarin returned to Earth safely. He ejected from his spacecraft somewhere over Russia and parachuted to the ground. He became a national hero and an international sensation. His picture was on the front page of every major newspaper in the world.

The scientific teams in the United States were impressed with Gagarin's accomplishment but also envious of it. In "Yuri Gagarin: First Man in Space" (http://www.nasa.gov/mission_pages/shuttle/sts1/gagarin_anniversary.html, December 20, 2007), NASA notes that an agency spokesman congratulated the Soviets for their achievement and summed up the U.S. space program with these glum words: "So close, but yet so far." In Huntsville, Alabama, von Braun was more blunt, saying, "To catch up, the U.S.A. must run like hell."

RACE TO THE MOON

In "Alan B. Shepard, Jr." (February 04, 2005, http://history.nasa.gov/40thmerc7/shepard.htm), Tara Gray states that a month later the first American entered space. On May 5, 1961, Alan B. Shepard Jr. (1923–1998) soared to an altitude of 116 miles in the spaceship *Freedom 7*. He spent fifteen minutes and twenty-eight seconds in a suborbital flight. Suborbital means less than one orbit. In other words, a suborbital flight does not complete an entire circle around Earth. Shepard's flight was much shorter in distance and time than Gagarin's flight had been. A few months later Gherman Titov (1935–2000), the second cosmonaut in space, completed seventeen and a half orbits around Earth. NASA knew it would be a year or more before it could accomplish a similar feat.

The United States was tired of coming in second place. Because there was no way to beat the Soviets at the orbital space race, President John F. Kennedy (1917–1963) decided to start a new race. His advisers recommended that the United States put a manned spacecraft in orbit around the Moon or even land a man on the Moon. Either one would require the development of a huge new rocket to supply the lifting power needed to boost a spaceship out of Earth orbit. Neither the Soviets nor the Americans had such a rocket.

On May 25, 1961, President Kennedy revealed his decision to the world in the speech "Special Message to the Congress on Urgent National Needs" (http://www.jfklibrary.org/). His words ignited the biggest race in human history: "First, I believe that this nation should commit itself to achieving the goal, before this decade is out, of landing a man on the moon and returning him safely to the earth. No single space project in this period will be more impressive to mankind, or more important for the long-range exploration of space; and none will be so difficult or expensive to accomplish."

AIMING FOR DRY SEAS

Suddenly, all eyes were on the Moon. Earth's closest neighbor had been a subject of fascination since the first humans gazed up at the night sky.

Most of the features on the Moon were named during the 1600s by the Italian astronomer Giambattista Riccioli (1598–1671). Riccioli was a Jesuit priest, a member of the Roman Catholic order the Society of Jesus, which is devoted to missionary and educational work. At the request of the church, Riccioli devoted his life to astronomy and telescopic studies. At the time, the writings of Kepler and Copernicus were popular and controversial. In keeping with church doctrine, Riccioli disputed Copernicus's claim that Earth was not the center of the universe.

Despite this gross error, Riccioli's work proved useful to later scientists. He published a detailed lunar map that he developed with Francesco Maria Grimaldi (1618–1663), a fellow Jesuit and Italian physicist. This map featured Latin names for lunar features, elevations and depressions were named after famous astronomers and philosophers, and large dark flat areas that looked like bodies of water were named Oceans or Seas.

Four hundred years later, humans on opposite sides of Earth took aim at these features. During the early and mid-1960s NASA and the Soviets sent dozens of photographic probes to take pictures of the Moon. Some probes proved successful, and some did not. Four NASA probes crashed into the Moon, but they had beamed back valuable photographs before impacting the lunar surface. In February 1966 the Soviet probe *Luna 9* softly set down in the Ocean of Storms, the largest of the lunar "seas." Four months later, NASA's *Surveyor 1* probe landed nearby.

Both countries needed lunar data to support their efforts to send humans to the Moon. During this time Soviet officials did not even acknowledge that they had a manned lunar program. Those in the U.S. program suspected that they did but could not be sure. It was not until years later, when Sergei Leskov recounted the story in "How We Didn't Get to the Moon" (*Izvestiya*, August 18, 1989), that the United States learned how determined the Soviet Union was at trying to beat the Americans to the Moon.

HARD WORK

The U.S. effort to put men on the Moon was named the Apollo program. It actually included three phases:

- Mercury—suborbital and orbital missions of short duration

- Gemini—longer duration orbital missions including extravehicular activity (space walking) and docking of spacecraft in space

- Apollo—Manned lunar landings in which a module containing two astronauts softly lands on the Moon; a third astronaut remains in lunar orbit while the other two explore the Moon's surface

Shepard's historic 1961 flight was considered the first Mercury mission. Over the next two years five more successful Mercury flights were conducted. In 1965 a series of ten manned Gemini missions began. They were completed near the end of 1966.

Soon after it started, it became apparent that the Moon program was going to be expensive. On September 12, 1962, President Kennedy (http://er.jsc.nasa.gov/seh/ricetalk.htm) reinforced his commitment to the project during a speech at Rice University in Houston, Texas. Kennedy said, "We choose to go to the moon. We choose

to go to the moon in this decade and do the other things, not because they are easy, but because they are hard, because that goal will serve to organize and measure the best of our energies and skills, because that challenge is one that we are willing to accept, one we are unwilling to postpone, and one which we intend to win."

ROCKETS ARE KEY

One key goal in the United States and the Soviet Union was the development of a large and powerful rocket—a so-called superbooster. NASA called its superbooster a Saturn rocket, and the Soviets named their rocket the N-1.

Development of the Saturn rocket series began in 1961 under the direction of von Braun. He had actually been pitching the idea to the military for several years. Before the Apollo program NASA used relatively small rockets that were capable of lifting a few hundred to a few thousand pounds into Earth orbit.

The Scout rocket was used to launch small satellites and probes weighing up to three hundred pounds. It was devised by combining aspects of rockets used by the armed forces (the navy's Polaris and Vanguard rockets and the army's Sergeant rockets). The Thor, Atlas, and Titan series evolved from air force rockets first developed as ICBMs. During the mid-1960s the military replaced most of its Atlas rockets with Minuteman missiles. Modified Atlas rockets were used to launch satellites and for the Mercury program. The Titan II was used during the Gemini program.

The Saturn series evolved from von Braun's Jupiter rockets. Legend has it that the Saturn got its name because it was one step beyond the Jupiter rocket, just as Saturn is the next step beyond Jupiter in the solar system. The Saturn V, with a height of 364 feet, is the largest rocket ever built. (See Figure 1.4.) It had to be to push the one-hundred-ton *Apollo* spacecraft toward the Moon.

APOLLO: TRAGEDY AND TRIUMPH

The Soviet space program continued to flourish. In September 1968 an unmanned probe called *Zond 5* became the first spacecraft to travel around the Moon and return to Earth. The pressure was on NASA to speed up the Apollo program.

On January 27, 1967, three American astronauts—Virgil I. Grissom (1936–1967), Edward H. White (1930–1967), and Roger B. Chaffee (1935–1967)—were killed when a flash fire raced through their capsule during a routine practice drill. They were the first human casualties of the space program. To honor their memory, their tragic mission was named *Apollo 1*. The tragedy stunned

FIGURE 1.4

Saturn 5 rocket being transported to launch pad

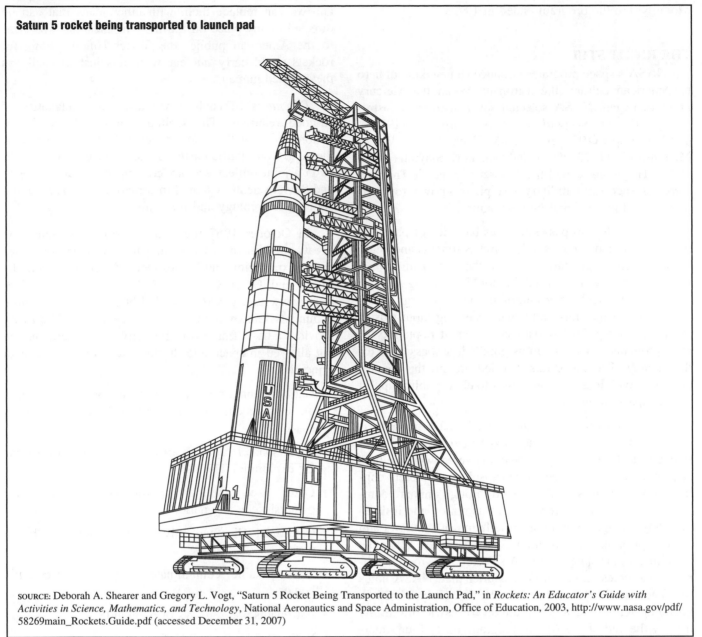

SOURCE: Deborah A. Shearer and Gregory L. Vogt, "Saturn 5 Rocket Being Transported to the Launch Pad," in *Rockets: An Educator's Guide with Activities in Science, Mathematics, and Technology*, National Aeronautics and Space Administration, Office of Education, 2003, http://www.nasa.gov/pdf/58269main_Rockets.Guide.pdf (accessed December 31, 2007)

the nation. Some politicians even called for the program to end, but Apollo continued.

The next manned Apollo mission was launched on October 11, 1968. *Apollo 7* successfully conducted a flight test and returned to Earth. It was followed in rapid succession by the more ambitious missions of *Apollo 8*, *Apollo 9*, and *Apollo 10*, each of which tested a lunar or command module in lunar or Earth orbit. The mission to set humans on the Moon was named *Apollo 11* and scheduled for July 1969.

By this time the Soviets had desperately tried to get their own manned lunar program going. However, the N-1 rocket kept failing its launch tests. The Soviets realized that it would not be ready before the *Apollo*

11 launch. Still hoping to steal some of the thunder from the Americans, the Soviets launched a robotic probe named *Luna 15* to the Moon. It was designed to gather samples from the lunar surface and return to Earth before the *Apollo 11* expedition. Launched on July 13, 1969, *Luna 15* completed fifty-two Moon orbits before it crashed into the lunar surface on July 21, 1969, and was lost.

Meanwhile, on July 20, 1969, *Apollo 11* set down safely on the Moon near the Sea of Tranquillity. Late that evening the astronaut Neil A. Armstrong (1930–) stepped out of the spacecraft to become the first human to stand on the Moon. Approximately half a billion people on Earth watched the historic event on television. Four days later the *Apollo 11* crew returned to Earth to a heroes' welcome. There were six more Apollo missions to the Moon before the program ended in 1972.

THE RIGHT STUFF

NASA's space program introduced a new kind of hero to American culture: the astronaut. When the Mercury program began, NASA selected seven men to be astronauts: Grissom, Shepard, M. Scott Carpenter (1925–), Gordon Cooper (1927–2004), John Glenn (1921–), Walter M. Schirra Jr. (1923–2007), and Donald K. Slayton (1924–1993). They were called the "Mercury Seven." The men were all successful military test pilots known for their bravery and professional piloting skills.

The men had to pass strenuous batteries of physical, mental, and medical tests to become astronauts and begin their training to go into space. To the American public, the Mercury Seven captured the bold and daring spirit of famous flyers such as Richthofen and Lindbergh. They were instant superstars and began receiving thousands of fan letters. Once NASA realized the great popularity of the astronauts, it used them as goodwill ambassadors for the agency. The astronauts traveled around the country speaking to civic groups and clubs to elicit public support for the space program.

NASA scientists originally envisioned astronauts as mere guinea pigs for space experiments. They were intended to be passive passengers covered with medical sensors and sealed inside space capsules completely controlled by operators on the ground through onboard computers. The astronauts rebelled at this notion and insisted on many changes, including installation of windows and manual piloting controls on the space capsules. When the Gemini program began, NASA selected nine more astronaut candidates and soon dozens after that. NASA notes in "The Apollo Program (1963–1972)" (July 24, 2007, http://nssdc.gsfc.nasa.gov/planetary/lunar/apollo.html) that by the end of the Apollo program, thirty-four American astronauts had traveled into space.

In 1979 the story of the original Mercury Seven was profiled in the book *The Right Stuff* by Tom Wolfe. In the book, Wolfe describes the tremendous pressures put on the first astronauts during the space program, their dedication to serving their country, and how they reacted to fame and glory. In 1983 the book was made into a popular movie of the same name.

DÉTENTE IN SPACE

During the early years of space flight, American relations with the Soviet Union were at their worst. John Pike et al. explain in "R-46" (July 29, 2000, http://www.fas.org/nuke/guide/russia/icbm/r-46.htm) that only months after the Soviets put their first cosmonauts in space the Soviet premier Nikita Khrushchev (1894–1971) made the veiled threat, "We placed Gagarin and Titov in space, and we can replace them with other loads that can be directed to any place on Earth." The meaning was clear to the American public: the Soviet Union's powerful rockets could carry nuclear warheads just as easily as they carried humans.

Détente is a French word that means a relaxation of strained relations. The United States and the Soviet Union occasionally enjoyed periods of détente during the cold war, particularly in their space activities. In 1965 a joint project was undertaken in which American and Soviet scientists shared information they had learned about space biology and medicine.

In October 1967 the two countries negotiated the Treaty on Principles Governing the Activities of States in the Exploration and Use of Outer Space, Including the Moon and Other Celestial Bodies (January 1, 2004, http://www.state.gov/t/ac/trt/5181.htm), which is more commonly known as the Outer Space Treaty. The treaty provides a basic framework for activities that are and are not allowed in space and during space travel. The main principles are:

- Nations cannot place nuclear weapons or other weapons of mass destruction in Earth orbit or elsewhere in space.
- Outer space is open to all humankind and all nations for exploration and use.
- Outer space cannot be appropriated or claimed for ownership by any nation.
- Celestial bodies can only be used for peaceful purposes.
- Nations cannot contaminate outer space or celestial bodies.
- Astronauts are "envoys of mankind."
- Nations are responsible for all their national space activities whether conducted by governmental agencies or nongovernmental organizations.
- Nations are liable for any damage caused by objects they put into space.

The Outer Space Treaty was signed on January 27, 1967, by the United States, the Soviet Union, and the United Kingdom. Over the next four decades it would be signed by more than one hundred nations.

In 1969 NASA proposed the development of American and Soviet spacecraft that could dock with each other in space for future missions of mutual interest. In July 1975 the docking procedure proved to be successful during the Apollo-Soyuz Test Project. The mission was largely symbolic, and many people considered it wasted money that could have been spent on space exploration.

Near the end of the Apollo program the two countries agreed to a number of cooperative projects including the sharing of lunar samples, weather satellite data, and space medical data.

PARKED IN LOW EARTH ORBIT

In the minds of most Americans, the space race was over the day *Apollo 11* set down on the Moon. Even though NASA carried out six more Apollo missions, public interest and political support for them faded quickly. Neither the U.S. nor the Soviet government was interested in racing to somewhere else in space. Both governments decided to concentrate on putting manned scientific space stations in low Earth orbit (LEO).

LEO is approximately 125 to 1,200 miles above Earth's surface. LEO is the orbit of choice for most satellites and for all crewed missions. Spacecraft in LEO travel at about seventeen thousand miles per hour and circle Earth once every ninety minutes or so. Below this altitude air drag from Earth's atmosphere is still dense enough to pull spacecraft downward quickly. Beyond LEO lies a thick region of radiation known as the inner Van Allen radiation belt. This region poses a hazard to human life and to sensitive electronic equipment.

Soviet Programs

Between 1971 and 1986 the Soviets put eight space stations into LEO or just below it. These included stations called *Salyut 1* through *Salyut 7* and the more ambitious space station *Mir*. Dozens of cosmonauts visited and inhabited the stations, often for many months. The Soviets repeatedly set and broke human space duration records at their stations. In 1995 the cosmonaut Valery Polyakov (1942–) completed a 437.7-day mission aboard *Mir*. Even in 2008 this stood as the longest period spent in space by any human. Eventually, all the Soviet stations fell out of orbit and were destroyed by reentry to Earth's atmosphere. Even though none were meant to be "permanent," the *Mir* station did stay in orbit for fifteen years.

U.S. Programs

In 1973 NASA launched its own space station called *Skylab*. It orbited within LEO of 268 to 270 miles above Earth. NASA wanted to build a large space station in which to conduct scientific investigations in LEO. Without political support the agency had to put this plan on hold. Instead, NASA concentrated on a new type of reusable space plane called the space shuttle. The space shuttle was to the be the workhorse of the U.S. space program, ferrying astronauts and supplies back and forth to the space station.

NASA received the funding it needed to develop the shuttle by promising to build a vehicle that could carry military, weather/science, and commercial satellites into LEO. Before the shuttle program, all satellites were launched aboard expendable rockets that could not be reused. The reusability of the shuttle was one of its best selling points. Also, each shuttle could carry a crew of five to seven people that could conduct scientific experiments in LEO and deploy and repair satellites as needed.

Despite a number of design challenges, the first space shuttle was ready for flight by 1981. On April 12, 1981, the first test mission was conducted. Before the end of the year a space shuttle carried an orbiting solar observatory into LEO. Two dozen more missions were carried out before disaster struck in 1986. By this time there were four space shuttles in NASA's fleet. Missions were rotated between the vehicles to perform needed maintenance and repairs.

On January 28, 1986, the space shuttle *Challenger* exploded seventy-three seconds after liftoff. All seven crewmembers aboard were killed. The shuttle fleet was grounded for more than two years, during which time NASA restructured the program and redesigned key elements of the spacecraft. In October 1988 space shuttle flights resumed once again.

By this time the Soviet Union was politically disintegrating. Within three years the United States' former archenemy had splintered into dozens of individual republics, and the cold war was officially over. The Russian Republic took over the space program begun by the Soviet Union. The Soviet space program came under the operation of the new Russian Space Agency in 1992. The agency was renamed the Russian Aviation and Space Agency (Rosaviakosmos) in 1999, when it was assigned additional responsibilities in aviation. In 2004 those responsibilities were removed and the agency was renamed the Russian Federal Space Agency (Roscosmos).

International Plans

During the 1990s the United States and Russia entered a new era of cooperative space ventures. American astronauts visited the *Mir* station and Russian cosmonauts traveled aboard U.S. space shuttle missions. In 1993 the United States invited Russia to join in building an *International Space Station* (*ISS*) to be put in LEO. The Russians agreed. The *ISS* program eventually included Canada, Japan, and eleven European nations as full partners and Brazil as a contributing partner.

ISS construction began in 1998. The station was designed for continuous human inhabitation and detailed scientific investigations. The Americans and Russians took turns adding components to the station and crewing it with astronauts and cosmonauts. All transport of heavy matériel was delegated to the U.S. space shuttle fleet because the Russians did not have a spacecraft capable of carrying heavy weight into LEO. Throughout 1999 and the next three years nearly all shuttle missions were devoted to *ISS* construction.

During the first mission of 2003 another space shuttle was lost in an accident. On February 1, 2003, the space shuttle *Columbia* disintegrated during reentry over the western United States. Again, seven crewmembers were killed. The shuttle fleet was grounded for more than two years, ceasing construction on the *ISS*. Russian spacecraft ferried supplies to the station and handled crew changes.

In July 2005 the Space Shuttle Program resumed operations with a successful return-to-flight test mission. *ISS* construction proceeded in 2006 and 2007 as six space shuttle missions were conducted. Additional missions are planned through 2010, when the Space Shuttle Program is scheduled to end.

A NEW VISION

The United States' dedication to the *ISS* changed dramatically in January 2004, when President George W. Bush (1946–) announced a new goal for the nation's space program: to return to the Moon and travel to Mars and beyond. The so-called Vision for Space Exploration (http://www.nasa.gov/missions/solarsystem/explore_main _old.html) requires the development of a new fleet of spacecraft capable of carrying astronauts beyond LEO into the solar system.

SPACE-AGE SCIENCE FICTION

The advent of the space age introduced a wealth of information to science-fiction authors. They were able to produce works that were more sophisticated than those of the past.

One of the most innovative of these authors was Gene Roddenberry (1921–1991). During the mid-1960s he created the television show *Star Trek*. This was a futuristic tale about a mixed crew of humans and aliens that explored the galaxy in the starship *Enterprise* during the twenty-third century. The television show was not popular during its original run but over the next few decades it developed a loyal fan base and spawned a number of movies.

In 1974 thousands of *Star Trek* fans wrote to the U.S. government requesting that one of the newly developed space shuttles be named *Enterprise*. NASA gave the name to the prototype shuttle model used for flight testing.

Another notable science-fiction work of the 1960s was the film *2001: A Space Odyssey* (1968), which was based on a story by Arthur C. Clarke (1917–2008). Astronauts exploring the Moon find a mysterious artifact. Believing that it came from Jupiter, they set off for that planet on an amazing spacecraft. The ship is equipped with a super-computer named HAL that malfunctions and turns against the human crew. The film features little dialogue,

but it became a hit for its very imaginative plot and spectacular views of futuristic space travel.

In 1977 the science-fiction film *Star Wars* debuted and became one of the most popular movies of all time. Set "a long time ago in a galaxy far, far away," the film tells the story of an adventurous young man who leaves his home world to join a band of rebels fighting against a tyrannical empire. The movie was renowned for its story, characters, adventure, and special effects. The *Star Wars* franchise went on to include five more highly successful films and a book series.

Hollywood movies featuring hostile space aliens invading Earth were a staple of 1950s pop culture. Such films captured the paranoia and fear that Americans felt about the communist threat from the Soviet Union. Beginning in the 1970s a gentler viewpoint of aliens emerged in movies such as *Close Encounters of the Third Kind* (1977), *ET: The Extraterrestrial* (1982), *Cocoon* (1985), and *Contact* (1997). However, horrific and murderous aliens remain a staple of science-fiction films, as evidenced in the popularity of *Alien* (1979) and its sequels, *Independence Day* (1996), and *War of the Worlds* (2005).

ROBOTIC SPACE EXPLORERS

Space programs that use human explorers are expensive. It is cheaper to build and send mechanized (robotic) spacecraft to do the exploring. During the 1960s the Apollo program dominated the spotlight, but it was not the only space exploration project in operation.

Beginning in 1962 NASA launched robotic probes that flew by Mercury, Venus, and Mars and beamed back photographs of them. During the 1970s more sophisticated robotic spacecraft landed on Mars or were sent to fly by the outer planets (Jupiter, Saturn, Uranus, Neptune, and Pluto). These missions were given heroic names, including Mariner, Viking, and Voyager.

In 1990 a robotic spacecraft called *Magellan* was put into orbit around Venus on a four-year mission to collect data about the planet. The spacecraft was named after Ferdinand Magellan (1480?–1521), the Portuguese explorer who led the first sailing expedition to circumnavigate the world. In 1995 a spacecraft named after Galileo Galilei began orbiting Jupiter.

Interplanetary exploration is tough, even for machines. During the 1990s NASA lost five out of the six robotic spacecraft that it sent to Mars. In 2001 NASA sent *Mars Odyssey*, which went into orbit around the planet. It was joined two years later by the European Space Agency (ESA) spacecraft *Mars Express Orbiter*. However, a lander from this mission was lost on its way to the surface. In 2004 NASA's Mars Exploration mission successfully put down two rovers on Mars: *Spirit* and *Opportunity*. The rovers were expected to last about three months, but as of

February 2008 they were still exploring the surface of Mars.

In June 2004 NASA's *Cassini* spacecraft went into orbit around Saturn after a seven-year journey from Earth. The orbiter released the ESA-provided *Huygens* probe, which provided the first-ever close-up photographs of Titan, Saturn's largest moon. Also in 2004 NASA launched the *Messenger* orbiter toward Mercury. That spacecraft is scheduled to arrive there in 2011. In 2006 two new robotic explorers—NASA's *Mars Reconnaissance Orbiter* and the ESA's *Venus Express Orbiter*—went into orbit around their respective target planets. In 2007 NASA launched the Phoenix Mars mission, which will send a lander to the planet in May 2008.

Not all space exploration requires long-distance travel. Advances in computers and telescopes have allowed scientists to do a lot of exploring with robotic spacecraft stationed nearby Earth. Dozens of these high-technology machines take photographs, measure radiation waves, and collect data on galactic and solar phenomena.

The latest generation of robotic explorers are designed to snatch samples in outer space and return them to Earth. The first such mission to return was conducted by the NASA spacecraft *Genesis*. In September 2004 it crash-landed in the Utah desert following an equipment malfunction during reentry. Regardless, some of its valuable cargo was saved—samples of the solar wind (charged particles emitted from the Sun) collected a million miles from Earth. Also in 2004 the NASA spacecraft *Stardust* sailed nearby the comet Wild 2 as it journeyed around the Sun. *Stardust* collected dust particles believed to be 4.5 billions years old and returned them safely to Earth in January 2006.

In November 2005 Japan's *Hayabusa* spacecraft landed on the asteroid Itokawa between Earth and Mars to collect dust samples. Equipment and communication problems have plagued the mission, and scientists are hopeful, but not certain, that the samples were collected and will return to Earth in 2010.

APPLICATION SATELLITES

Application satellites are spacecraft put into Earth orbit to serve as tools of earth science or for navigation, communication, or other commercial purposes. Even though they are not really space explorers, they would not be possible without the technology of the space age.

On April 1, 1960, NASA launched the first successful meteorological satellite *TIROS 1* (Television Infrared Observation Satellite). The spacecraft was equipped with television cameras to film cloud cover around Earth. This is an example of an active satellite (one that collects data or performs some other activity and transmits signals back to Earth).

Over the next few decades weather satellites grew increasingly more sophisticated in their capabilities. The primary satellites that followed *TIROS 1* were *Nimbus*, *TOS* (TIROS Operational Satellite), *ITOS* (Improved TOS), *SMS* (Synchronous Meteorological Satellite), *NOAA* (National Oceanic and Atmospheric Administration), and *GOES* (Geostationary Operational Environmental Satellite). Other application satellites perform various duties for earth scientists, such as mapping oceans and land masses or measuring the heat and moisture content of Earth's surface.

On August 12, 1960, NASA launched *ECHO 1*, its first communications satellite. It was a large metallic sphere that reflected radio signals. NASA maintains a whole series of communication satellites in Earth orbit that allow the agency to communicate with astronauts and relay data to robotic spacecraft during missions. They are called Tracking and Data Relay Satellites.

Many communications satellites are placed in Earth orbit 22,241 miles from the planet's surface. At this distance they are anchored in place by Earth's gravity and are in synch with its revolution rate. In other words, they move around Earth at the same speed that it revolves around its axis. This is called a geosynchronous orbit. Some satellites are placed in a geosynchronous orbit directly above Earth's equator and appear from Earth to hover in space at the exact same location all the time. They are in a geostationary orbit.

Navigation is the act of determining one's position relative to other locations. Before the invention of satellites, navigational signals were transmitted by land-based systems using antennas. (See Figure 1.5.) These antennas sent low-frequency radio signals that traveled along Earth's surface or reflected off the ionosphere to reach their target receptor. The ionosphere is a layer of atmosphere that begins about thirty miles above Earth's surface. Atmospheric gases undergo electrical and chemical changes within the ionosphere. This is what gives it reflective properties.

During the 1970s the U.S. military developed a space-based navigational system called the Global Positioning System (GPS). This system relies on satellites in Earth orbit to handle signal transmissions. (See Figure 1.6.) During the 1980s GPS was made available for international civil use. Over the next two decades it became one of the most popular navigational tools in the world.

SPACESHIPONE

SpaceShipOne was the first privately built and financed craft to fly a human into space. For more than three decades, the only way for humans to access space was through government-operated space programs. This

FIGURE 1.5

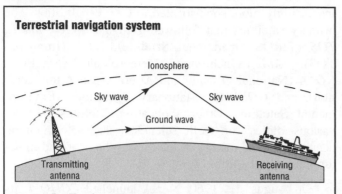

Terrestrial navigation system

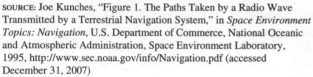

SOURCE: Joe Kunches, "Figure 1. The Paths Taken by a Radio Wave Transmitted by a Terrestrial Navigation System," in *Space Environment Topics: Navigation*, U.S. Department of Commerce, National Oceanic and Atmospheric Administration, Space Environment Laboratory, 1995, http://www.sec.noaa.gov/info/Navigation.pdf (accessed December 31, 2007)

FIGURE 1.6

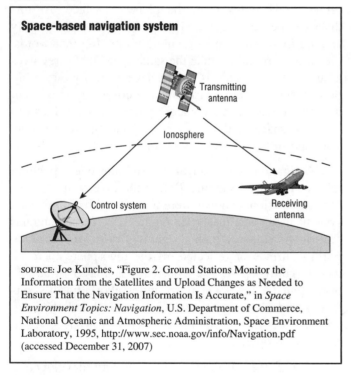

Space-based navigation system

SOURCE: Joe Kunches, "Figure 2. Ground Stations Monitor the Information from the Satellites and Upload Changes as Needed to Ensure That the Navigation Information Is Accurate," in *Space Environment Topics: Navigation*, U.S. Department of Commerce, National Oceanic and Atmospheric Administration, Space Environment Laboratory, 1995, http://www.sec.noaa.gov/info/Navigation.pdf (accessed December 31, 2007)

all changed on June 21, 2004, when *SpaceShipOne* carried Mike Melvill (1941–) to an altitude of sixty-two miles (one hundred kilometers), which is considered the boundary of space by the FAI.

SpaceShipOne was designed and built by Scaled Composites, a California-based firm. The funding was provided by the American billionaire Paul G. Allen (1953–), a cofounder of the Microsoft Corporation. Allen financed the project as a way to have some meaningful impact on space exploration. During the development of *SpaceShipOne*, Allen became aware of the Ansari X Prize (http://www.xprize.org/)—a $10 million prize

offered by private investors to the developers of the first nongovernmental reusable space plane. The Ansari X Prize was the brainchild of Peter H. Diamandis (1961–), an aerospace engineer and entrepreneur in space tourism. His inspiration was the Orteig Prize, which was won in 1927 by Lindbergh, when he flew nonstop across the Atlantic Ocean between New York and Paris. Lindbergh's flight incited interest and investment in aviation. Diamandis believed his prize would launch another new industry: private space travel.

In 1994 Diamandis started the X Prize Foundation to raise money for the prize. His first investors were businesspeople in St. Louis, Missouri, the same city that played a key role in Lindbergh's flight many years before. Over the next decade Diamandis received support from a number of backers, including Arthur C. Clarke, the astronaut Edwin E. (Buzz) Aldrin Jr. (1930–), and Erik Lindbergh (1965–), Lindbergh's grandson. However, the foundation still struggled to raise the funds it needed.

In 2004 the foundation received a financial boost. Space enthusiasts Anousheh Ansari (1966–) and her brother-in-law Amir Ansari (1970–) made a multimillion-dollar contribution to the prize fund. The Ansaris were born in Iran but had immigrated to the United States and formed a successful telecommunications business. The X Prize was renamed the Ansari X Prize in their honor.

By 2004 dozens of teams were developing rockets and spacecraft to compete for the prize. The rules required that the spacecraft carry three people (or at least one person plus the equivalent weight of two people) to an altitude of at least one hundred kilometers. The feat had to be accomplished twice within a two-week period using the same spacecraft.

Scaled Composites used a two-part flight sequence to boost *SpaceShipOne* into space. A manned twin-turbojet plane called *White Knight* lifted off from a runway carrying the smaller manned space plane attached to its belly. (See Figure 1.7.) After reaching an altitude of approximately forty-seven thousand feet, the space plane was released. Immediately, its rockets were fired to propel it vertically into space. It then turned and reentered the atmosphere and glided to a landing at the same air strip from which it took off.

On September 29, 2004, *SpaceShipOne* achieved an altitude of 63.9 miles (102.8 kilometers) with Melvill at the controls. The successful flight garnered international media coverage and increased interest in the competition. On October 4, 2004, a large crowd gathered at an airstrip in Mojave, California, to watch *SpaceShipOne* attempt to make history. They were not disappointed. Brian Binnie (1953–) took the space plane to an altitude of 69.6 miles

FIGURE 1.7

White Knight and SpaceShipOne in flight

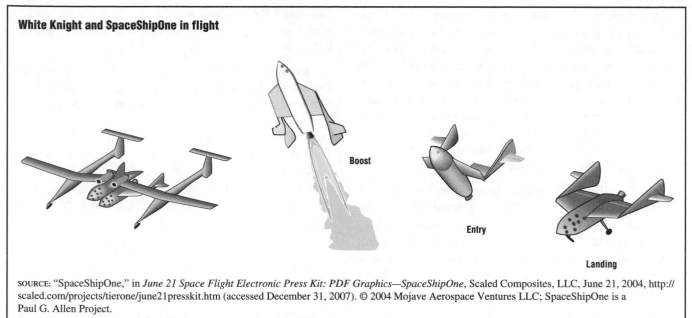

Boost

Entry

Landing

SOURCE: "SpaceShipOne," in *June 21 Space Flight Electronic Press Kit: PDF Graphics—SpaceShipOne*, Scaled Composites, LLC, June 21, 2004, http://scaled.com/projects/tierone/june21presskit.htm (accessed December 31, 2007). © 2004 Mojave Aerospace Ventures LLC; SpaceShipOne is a Paul G. Allen Project.

(112 kilometers) to win the Ansari X Prize. The news was broadcast around the world, and President Bush telephoned the team to offer his congratulations.

The people behind the Ansari X Prize and *SpaceShipOne* purposely used parallels to events in aeronautical history to build their legacy. The concept of the prize drew on the symbolism and romanticism attached to Lindbergh's heroic flight. Important announcements and flights were conducted on dates of significance to space enthusiasts. The first test flight of *SpaceShipOne* to break the sound barrier occurred on December 17, 2003—the one hundredth anniversary of the first powered flight of the Wright brothers. The Ansari's multimillion dollar contribution to the X Prize fund was announced on May 5, 2004, the forty-third anniversary of Shepard's flight into space. The date October 4 was chosen as the day for *SpaceShipOne*'s prize-winning flight attempt, because it was the date in 1957 when the Soviet Union launched *Sputnik 1*, the first artificial satellite to go into space.

According to Diamandis, the X in X Prize stood for the Roman numeral ten (as in the $10 million prize) and for the X in "experimental" (as in the famous X-series of experimental planes flown during the 1950s and 1960s). The X-series flights were extremely important to the development of space travel. The *White Knight* carrier plane was named after two test pilots (Robert White and William "Pete" Knight) who flew the X-15 aircraft in the early 1960s. *SpaceShipOne*'s prize-winning flight broke the altitude record set by an X-15 in 1963, a record that had stood for more than four decades.

However, the achievements of *SpaceShipOne* will likely be remembered for their effects on the future of aeronautics, not their ties to the past. The first nongovernmental manned space flight offers tantalizing prospects for private individuals to travel into space. It may represent the birth of a new industry and a means for many people to experience the adventure of space flight. (For further information on *SpaceShipOne*, see Chapter 3.)

SPACE COMMERCE

The space age introduced new areas of commerce for the world's entrepreneurs. Companies engaged in aviation, aeronautics, and aerospace activities have been the most direct beneficiaries. However, other industries have seized upon space-based opportunities, primarily the businesses of commercial satellite services and space tourism.

In 2004 President Bush directed NASA to pursue greater participation of private industry in space exploration. One result was the Commercial Orbital Transportation Services (COTS) Program. NASA reports in the press release "NASA Invests in Private Sector Space Flight with SpaceX, Rocketplane-Kistler" (August 18, 2006, http://www.nasa.gov/mission_pages/exploration/news/COTS_selection.html) that the COTS Program designated $500 million in seed money for commercial enterprises that can develop reliable and cost-effective space transportation systems. The final systems will not be turned over to the government, but remain in private hands. NASA plans to be a launch customer of the new services. In August 2006 the money was split between two companies: Space Exploration Technologies (SpaceX) of California and Rocketplane-Kistler of Oklahoma. They will use the money, along with privately raised funds, to develop new space vehicles and systems useful for crewed missions to the *ISS* and possibly beyond.

Commercial Satellite Services

In 1962 Congress passed the Communications Satellite Act, opening the door for commercial use of satellites in space. For decades these satellites could only be launched by national space agencies (such as NASA). In 1980 Arianespace (a subsidiary of the ESA) became the world's first commercial space transportation company. Arianespace began offering satellite launches using Ariane rockets at its spaceport in French Guiana (a small country along the northern coast of South America). Its first client was an American telecommunications company.

In 1984 the Commercial Space Launch Act was passed in the United States. The act granted power to the U.S. private sector to develop and provide satellite launching, reentry, and associated services and noted that this "would enable the United States to retain its competitive position internationally, contributing to the national interest and economic well-being of the United States."

The Boeing Corporation is a large U.S. aerospace company and a prime NASA contractor. In 1995 Boeing formed a satellite launching business with Russian, Norwegian, and Ukrainian partners. The Sea Launch Company (February 15, 2000, http://www.boeing.com/special/sea-launch/organization.htm) is headquartered in Long Beach, California, and operates a rocket launch platform on a modified oil-drilling platform in the South Pacific Ocean. Boeing owns a 40% share in the company. Its partners include RSC Energia of Russia (25% share); Aker ASA of Norway (20% share); and SDO Yuzhnoye/PO Yuzhmash of Ukraine (15% share). More than a dozen launches of commercial satellites have taken place from the Sea Launch facility since the first launch in 1999.

The Commercial Space Act of 1998 encouraged NASA to set policies to encourage and facilitate the participation of the private sector in the operation, use, and servicing of the *ISS*. This act received little attention until 2004, when President Bush announced his plan to retire the space shuttle fleet by 2010. The United States expects it will need commercial services to take over many of the tasks historically performed by the shuttle for the *ISS* program. This should open up many new opportunities in space for enterprising companies.

Space Tourism

Before the 2000s space tourism was limited to occasional space station visits taken by a handful of individuals for multimillion dollar fees. These trips were granted by the Russian Space Agency to raise badly needed funds. Private space tourism companies formed and accepted deposits for future spaceflights on not-yet-developed spacecraft, but these ventures sounded like science fiction to most people. This all changed in 2004 with the successful suborbital excursions of *SpaceShipOne*. Suddenly, space station visits by private individuals became a viable possibility. New space tourism businesses formed, and the U.S. government rushed to set regulations for private space transportation, an entirely new industry.

COMMERCIAL PASSENGERS ON RUSSIAN MISSIONS. During the late 1980s the Soviet space program was in dire need of money. The Soviet Union was splintering into individual nations, and funds for space travel were in short supply. In 1990 the agency received $28 million from a Japanese media company to take the journalist Tohiro Akiyama (1942–) aboard *Mir*. A year later a London bank paid an undisclosed amount of money to allow the British chemist Helen Sharman (1963–) to spend a "space vacation" aboard *Mir*.

In 2001 Rosaviakosmos charged Dennis Tito (1940–), an American businessman, $20 million for a "space vacation" aboard the *ISS*. Over the next five years, three more space tourists paid $20 million to be transported by the Russians to the *ISS*: the South African businessman Mark Shuttleworth (1973–) in 2002; the American scientist and businessman Greg Olsen (1945–) in 2005; and Anousheh Ansari in 2006. Charles Simonyi (1948–), a Hungarian-born businessman, paid $25 million in April 2007 to be the fifth space tourist. The sixth and most recent space tourist is Sheikh Muszaphar Shukor (1972–), a surgeon from Malaysia, who visited the *ISS* in October 2007. Unlike the other space tourists, he did not spend his own money for the trip; instead, it was paid for by Malaysia as part of a purchase of Russian fighter jets.

Russia's *ISS* partners (including NASA) have not shown any interest in space tourism. Initially, NASA refused to let tourists aboard the *ISS*, but it relented after heated negotiations with Rosaviakosmos. The Russian agency has stated publicly that it hopes to develop space tourism as a thriving business. It sells tourist packages that allow people to undergo simulated cosmonaut training at its facilities in Zvezdny Gorodok (Star City).

THE FUTURE OF PRIVATE SPACE TRAVEL. The first five tourist trips to the *ISS* were brokered by the American company Space Adventures (2008, http://72.29.31.40/index.cfm?fuseaction=orbital.Clients). The Virginia-based company was founded in 1998 by Diamandis. It also has plans to market suborbital flights aboard a new space plane being developed by a Russian contractor. The plane will take tourists to an altitude just over sixty-two miles above Earth.

Other companies known to be developing commercial spacelines include Virgin Galactic, SpaceX, Rocketplane-Kistler, and Armadillo Aerospace.

The Commercial Space Launch Amendments Act of 2004 instructed the Federal Aviation Administration (FAA) to begin formulating rules to govern the transport of passengers into space aboard commercial spacecraft.

TABLE 1.1

Number of successful space launches worldwide, 1998–2007

	1998	1999	2000	2001	2002	2003	2004	2005	2006	2007	Total	Percent of launches
India	0	1	0	2	1	2	1	1	1	3	12	2%
SEA	0	1	2	2	1	3	3	4	0	0	16	3%
Japan	1	0	0	1	3	2	0	2	6	2	17	3%
China	6	4	5	1	4	6	8	5	6	10	55	9%
ESA	11	10	11	7	11	4	3	5	5	6	73	11%
US	34	28	28	21	17	23	16	12	22	17	218	34%
Russia	24	26	35	23	23	21	22	23	23	26	246	39%
Total	**76**	**70**	**81**	**57**	**60**	**61**	**53**	**52**	**63**	**64**	**637**	

SEA = South East Asia.
ESA = European Space Agency.

SOURCE: Adapted from "World Space Launches," in *Office of Space Operations*, National Aeronautics and Space Administration, December 29, 2007, http://www.hq.nasa.gov/osf/relatedlinks.htm (accessed December 31, 2007)

In 2006 the FAA issued "Human Space Flight Requirements for Crew and Space Flight Participants; Final Rules" (*Federal Register*, vol. 71, no. 241, December 15, 2006). The FAA refers to space tourists as "space flight participants." The rules cover issues such as crew training, pilot certification, and requirements for informed consent about the risks of space flight.

Those who do not make it into space during their lifetime also have another option. Several companies around the world offer services to send the cremated ashes of a loved one into space. The service costs anywhere from $5,000 to $15,000.

Commercial Ventures on the Moon?

The U.S. Vision for Space Exploration unveiled in 2004 has spawned interest in possible commercial ventures on the Moon. The lunar surface contains a variety of substances that might be useful in spaceflight or energy applications. Moon soil is rich in oxygen (a spacecraft fuel) and helium-3, an element rare on Earth that could potentially be used in fusion reactions as an energy source.

In September 2007 the X Prize Foundation teamed up with the Internet company Google to offer the Google Lunar X Prize (http://www.googlelunarxprize.org/) for the first privately funded robotic Moon rover. The rover must land on the Moon, rove the surface for at least five hundred meters, and relay specific data and images back to Earth. The prize awards a total of $30 million, including a $20 million grand prize, $5 million for second place, and a $5 million bonus prize for a grand prize or second-place recipient that exceeds the mission requirements. SpaceX will supply the launch vehicle for the Moon rover.

SPACE LAUNCHES

NASA tracks the number of spacecraft launches conducted worldwide each year. Table 1.1 shows the figures for 1998 through 2007. The United States (34%) and Russia (39%) account for 73% of all launches. However, both countries launch satellites for other nations.

Only a handful of launches take place each year to support human spaceflight programs operated by the United States, Russia, and China. The vast majority of launches take place to put unmanned commercial, science, and military satellites into Earth orbit. The science missions are largely devoted to earth science, studying Earth's weather, climate patterns, atmospheric conditions, and so on. Military satellites perform reconnaissance (spying) from space or support the communication and navigation needs of armed forces around the world.

SPACE CASUALTIES

Exploration has always been dangerous. Many ancient explorers died during their journeys across deserts, seas, mountains, and jungles. Space exploration has its own casualties.

During the earliest days of space travel dozens of animals were sacrificed for the space program. The United States sent a variety of small animals and primates up in rockets to test the safety of space flight for humans. Few survived the flight or the examination afterward. Some of the so-called astro-monkeys and astro-chimps that lost their lives were named Able, Albert, Bonny, Goliath, Gordo, and Scatback. The Soviets preferred dogs to test their spacecraft. Dogs named Bars, Laika, Lisichka, Mushka, and Pchelka died as a result.

Space programs in both countries have suffered human losses throughout the years as well:

- January 27, 1967—*Apollo 1* crew died during a flash fire aboard a capsule on the launch pad undergoing routine testing. The casualties were Grissom, White, and Chaffee.

- April 24, 1967—*Soyuz 1* cosmonaut Vladimir Komarov (1927–1967) died during descent to Earth when his parachutes failed to function properly.

- June 30, 1971—*Soyuz 11* crew died during descent to Earth when their spacecraft lost its atmosphere due to a leaky valve. The casualties were Georgi Dobrovolsky (1928–1971), Vladislav Volkov (1935–1971), and Viktor Patsayev (1933–1971).

- January 28, 1986—The space shuttle *Challenger* crew died shortly after launch because of an explosion caused by leaking hot gases. The casualties were Francis R. Scobee (1939–1986), Michael J. Smith (1945–1986), Judith A. Resnik (1949–1986), Ron McNair (1950–1986), Ellison S. Onizuka (1946–1986), Gregory B. Jarvis (1944–1986), and Christa McAuliffe (1948–1986).

- February 1, 2003—The space shuttle *Columbia* crew died during Earth reentry when a damaged wing allowed hot gases to enter the spacecraft, tearing the shuttle apart. The casualties were Rick D. Husband (1957–2003), William C. McCool (1961–2003), David M. Brown (1956–2003), Kalpana Chawla (1962–2003), Michael P. Anderson (1959–2003), Laurel B. Clark (1961–2003), and Ilan Ramon (1954–2003).

In January 2004 the NASA administrator Sean O'Keefe (1956–) announced that the last Thursday in January will become a day of remembrance for lives lost in the U.S. space program. Each year on this day, NASA employees will observe a moment of silence, and flags will be flown at half-staff to honor the dead.

Like all journeys of discovery, space exploration is a bold and perilous undertaking. Major sacrifices have been made to move humankind closer to the stars. In September 13, 1962, President Kennedy (http://www.fordham.edu/ halsall/mod/ 1962JFK-space.html) aptly described the combination of fear, hope, and yearning that characterizes every journey into space: "As we set sail, we ask God's blessing on the most hazardous and dangerous and greatest adventure on which man has ever embarked."

CHAPTER 2
SPACE ORGANIZATIONS PART 1: THE NATIONAL AERONAUTICS AND SPACE ADMINISTRATION

It is the policy of the United States that activities in space should be devoted to peaceful purposes for the benefit of all mankind.

—National Aeronautics and Space Agency Act of 1958

Once it became obvious that space exploration was an achievable reality, it became a national priority for rich and powerful countries. Following World War II (1939–1945), there were only two superpowers in the world—the United States and the Soviet Union—and they considered each other enemies.

Both superpowers had military, scientific, and political reasons to pursue space travel. Outer space was a potential battlefield and provided an opportunity to spy on enemies on the other side of the world. Scientists, however, valued space travel for another reason. They wanted to gather data from space to help them unravel the mysteries of the universe. From a political standpoint, a successful space program was a source of national pride and a symbol of national superiority. This motivation above all others drove the earliest decades of space exploration.

The Soviet Union's space program was under the control of the military. In contrast, the United States split its space program into two parts. The U.S. military was given control over space projects related to national defense, and a new civilian agency called the National Aeronautics and Space Administration (NASA) was formed in 1958 to oversee peaceful space programs.

Throughout its history, NASA has been associated with spectacular feats and horrific disasters in space exploration. It has received great praise for its successes and harsh criticism for its failures. Space travel is an expensive enterprise. As a government agency, NASA is bound by federal budget constraints. This budget rises and falls according to the political climate. U.S. presidents set space goals, but Congress sets NASA's budget.

In 1961 President John F. Kennedy (1917–1963) charged NASA with the monumental task of putting a man on the Moon before the end of the decade. Congress allocated billions of dollars to NASA, and this goal was accomplished. Later presidents also set grand goals for the agency, but none of these were realized. Every major endeavor went over budget and fell behind schedule, the public seemed to lose interest in space travel, and Congress lacked the political motivation to increase NASA's funding. In 1965 NASA's budget comprised nearly 4% of the federal budget. By 1974 this percentage was less than 1%. It has remained near this level for more than thirty years. (See Figure 2.1.)

Since the 1980s NASA's reputation has suffered. Between 1986 and 2003 the agency experienced a string of failures. Four spacecraft sent to Mars were lost. A space telescope was launched into space with a faulty mirror. Worst of all, two catastrophic disasters killed fourteen astronauts. Critics complained that NASA had become overconfident, too bureaucratic, and had lost its technological edge.

In 2004 and 2005 NASA received a huge boost in prestige with the success of its robotic (unmanned) missions to Mars and Saturn. This was accompanied by a declaration from President George W. Bush (1946–) that NASA should set bold new goals to send crewed missions to the Moon and Mars. It remains to be seen whether Congress will fund these enterprises and whether NASA will be able to overcome the many obstacles in its path to space.

A NEW AGENCY IS BORN

NASA was founded on October 1, 1958, following enactment of the National Aeronautics and Space Act of 1958 (http://www.nasa.gov/offices/ogc/about/space_act1.html). The stated purpose of the act was "to provide for research

FIGURE 2.1

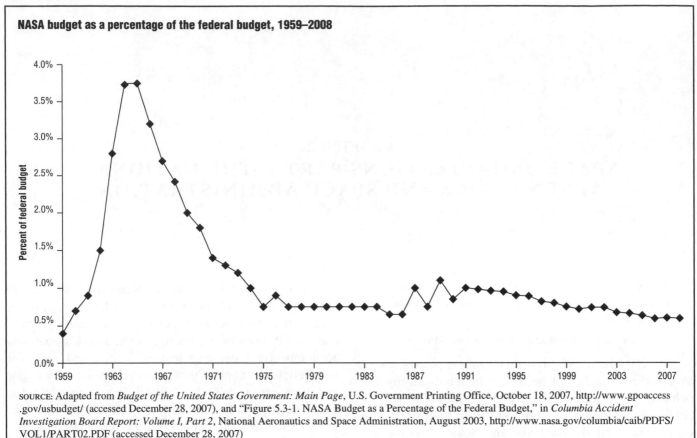

NASA budget as a percentage of the federal budget, 1959–2008

SOURCE: Adapted from *Budget of the United States Government: Main Page*, U.S. Government Printing Office, October 18, 2007, http://www.gpoaccess .gov/usbudget/ (accessed December 28, 2007), and "Figure 5.3-1. NASA Budget as a Percentage of the Federal Budget," in *Columbia Accident Investigation Board Report: Volume I, Part 2*, National Aeronautics and Space Administration, August 2003, http://www.nasa.gov/columbia/caib/PDFS/ VOL1/PART02.PDF (accessed December 28, 2007)

into problems of flight within and outside the earth's atmosphere, and for other purposes."

The act specifically mandated that NASA would be a civilian agency with control over all nonmilitary aeronautical and space activities within the United States. The research and development of weapons and national defense systems remained under the control of the U.S. Department of Defense (DOD). However, the act called for sharing of information between the two agencies. Cooperation by NASA in space ventures with other countries was allowed if the purpose was "peaceful application of the results."

The act outlined eight objectives for NASA:

- To expand human knowledge about atmospheric and space phenomena

- To improve all aspects of aeronautical and space vehicles

- To develop and operate vehicles capable of carrying supplies, equipment, scientific instruments, and living organisms into space

- To conduct long-range studies into the potential benefits, opportunities, and problems associated with astronautical and space activities

- To preserve the role of the United States as a leader in aeronautical and space science and technology and its application

- To share discoveries of military value with agencies involved in national defense

- To cooperate with other nations in peaceful ventures

- To cooperate with other U.S. agencies in utilizing national scientific and engineering resources in the most effective and efficient means possible

PEACEFUL VERSUS MILITARY PURPOSES

In "NACA—90 Years Later" (*X-Press*, vol. 47, no. 2, March 25, 2005), NASA notes that it consolidated the resources of several government organizations, chiefly the National Advisory Committee for Aeronautics (NACA). The NACA was originally named the Advisory Committee for Aeronautics when it was formed in 1915 "to supervise and direct the scientific study of the problems of flight, with a view to their practical solution." At the time, World War I (1914–1918) was raging in Europe. German zeppelins had dropped bombs on Britain earlier that year, ushering in a new means of waging war.

Even though the NACA's formation was driven by war, the agency also conducted aircraft research and set policy and regulations for commercial and civil aviation. In 1926 the Air Commerce Act was passed, which freed the NACA of regulatory responsibilities. The agency turned its full attention to aeronautical research and development at its Langley Aeronautical Laboratory in Virginia and later Ames Aeronautical Laboratory at Moffett Field, California, and a testing facility at Wallops Island, Virginia. NACA research and development benefited both military and civilian aviation.

On October 14, 1947, U.S. Air Force captain Charles (Chuck) Yeager (1923–) made the first supersonic flight in an X-1 aircraft, a rocket-powered research plane developed by the air force and the NACA. The NACA played an integral role in developing and testing the X-series of experimental aircraft. In 1952 the NACA began researching the challenges of space flight. Two years later the agency recommended that the U.S. Air Force develop a manned research vehicle to travel beyond Earth's atmosphere.

In October 1957 the Soviet Union launched *Sputnik 1*, the world's first artificial satellite. Jerry Woodfill of NASA explains in "Days of Air and Space" (January 24, 2001, http://er.jsc.nasa.gov/seh/daysJan1.html) that a few months later the American Rocket Society, a private space organization, and the Rocket and Satellite Research Panel, which monitored all U.S. outer space research, urged President Dwight D. Eisenhower (1890–1969) to establish a new agency to assume responsibility for all U.S. nonmilitary space projects. The agency was to pursue "broad cultural, scientific, and commercial objectives" and be independent of the DOD. The director of the NACA provided a counter-recommendation that the new agency operate under joint control of the NACA, the DOD, the National Academy of Sciences, and the National Science Foundation in support of military and nonmilitary projects.

Eugene M. Emme indicates in *Aeronautics and Astronautics: An American Chronology of Science and Technology in the Exploration of Space, 1915–1960* (1961) that in January 1958 President Eisenhower wrote Soviet premier Nikolay Bulganin (1885–1975) and proposed that the two countries "agree that outer space should be used only for peaceful purposes." Bulganin refused to agree to the proposal unless the United States ceased all nuclear weapons testing and disbanded all its military bases on foreign soil. These conditions were unacceptable to the United States.

In July 1958 President Eisenhower signed the National Aeronautics and Space Act, turning over all nonmilitary space projects to NASA. The new agency absorbed the personnel and facilities of the NACA, which ceased to exist.

According to Steven J. Dick and Steve Garber of NASA, in *Celebrating NASA's Fortieth Anniversary 1958–1998* (February 8, 2005, http://www.history.nasa.gov/40thann/40home.htm), NASA began with approximately eight thousand employees and an annual budget of $100 million. About half of the agency's first employees were civilian personnel working on space projects at the U.S. Army's Redstone Arsenal in Huntsville, Alabama. They included a rocketry team headed by Wernher von Braun (1912–1977). Von Braun was a German rocket scientist who moved to the United States following World War II, and he played a major role in building the U.S. rocket program at NASA.

T. Keith Glennan (1905–1995) served as the agency's first administrator. Under his direction NASA took control of the DOD's Jet Propulsion Laboratory in California and parts of the Naval Research Laboratory in Washington, D.C. NASA also took over several satellite and lunar probe programs being operated by the U.S. Air Force and the DOD's Advanced Research Projects Agency. The military retained control over reconnaissance satellites, ballistic missiles, and a handful of other DOD space projects that were then in the research stage.

John A. Pitts of NASA explains in *The Human Factor: Biomedicine in the Manned Space Program to 1980* (1985) that President Eisenhower believed the civilian space program should be "small in scale and limited in its objectives."

NASA SHOOTS FOR THE MOON

NASA did not stay small for long, because it had grand plans. In February 1960 NASA presented to Congress a ten-year plan for the nation's space program. It included an array of scientific satellites; robotic probes to the Moon, Mars, and Venus; development of new and powerful rockets; and manned spaceflights to orbit Earth and the Moon. NASA estimated the program would cost around $12 billion.

Congress was politically motivated to support the program. The Soviet Union had already landed a probe on the Moon as part of its Luna Project. At the time NASA was continuing the Pioneer Project begun by the NACA to obtain data from probes sent to the Moon. The first three Pioneer rockets had launched during 1958 but failed to escape Earth's gravity. In March 1959 *Pioneer 4* was the first U.S. spacecraft to escape Earth's gravity. It passed within 37,300 miles of the Moon. However, the Soviet's *Luna 1* probe had already passed much closer to the Moon. The United States was behind in the space race.

After Kennedy was elected president in November 1960, he charged Vice President Lyndon B. Johnson (1908–1973) with finding a way for the United States to

TABLE 2.1

Project Mercury manned flights

Date of launch	Mercury flight no.	Spacecraft name	Flight type	Highest altitude	Time in space	Astronaut
5/6/1961	3	Freedom 7	Sub orbital	116 miles	15 min 28 sec	Alan Shepard
7/21/1961	4	Liberty Bell 7	Sub orbital	118 miles	15 min 37 sec	Gus Grissom
2/20/1962	6	Friendship 7	3 orbits	162 miles	4 hr 55 min	John Glenn
5/24/1962	7	Aurora 7	3 orbits	167 miles	4 hr 56 min	Scott Carpenter
10/3/1962	8	Sigma 7	6 orbits	176 miles	9 hr 13 min	Walter Schirra
5/15/1963	9	Faith 7	22.5 orbits	166 miles	1 day 10 hr 19 min	Gordon Cooper

SOURCE: Created by Kim Masters Evans for Gale, Cengage Learning, 2008

beat the Soviets to a major space goal. NASA pushed for a manned lunar landing, and Johnson agreed. On May 25, 1961, in the speech "Special Message to the Congress on Urgent National Needs" (http://www.jfklibrary.org/), President Kennedy asked Congress to provide financial support to NASA to put a man on the Moon before the end of the decade.

Hugh L. Dryden (1898–1965), the deputy administrator of NASA, named the Moon effort the Apollo program. It was named after the mythical Greek god Apollo, who drove the chariot of the Sun across the sky.

Catching Up

NASA had a lot of work to do just to catch up with the Soviets in space. In April 1961 they had put the first human in Earth orbit. Cosmonaut Yuri Gagarin (1934–1968) circled Earth one time in a flight that lasted 1 hour and 49 minutes. It would be nearly a year before NASA could even come close to this achievement, with the flight of John Glenn (1921–) in *Friendship 7* on February 20, 1962.

When it was first created in 1958, NASA was concerned with finishing ongoing NACA projects. These included a weather satellite, a military spy satellite, and the Pioneer lunar space probes. These probes were intended to go into lunar orbit or impact the Moon's surface while sending back photographs and scientific data. *Pioneer 4* provided NASA with valuable new radiation data needed for the ongoing Mercury project.

The Mercury Project

The Mercury project actually began in 1958, only a week after NASA was created. The official announcement was made on December 17, 1958—the fifty-fifth anniversary of the Wright brothers' flight. The project was named after the mythical Roman god Mercury, the winged messenger.

The Mercury project had three specific objectives:

- Put a manned spacecraft into Earth orbit

- Investigate the effects of space travel on humans

- Recover the spacecraft and humans safely

On May 5, 1961, the astronaut Alan B. Shepard Jr. (1923–1998) became the first American in space when he took a fifteen-minute suborbital flight. Shepard's flight was far shorter than Gagarin's had been and included only five minutes of weightlessness. NASA desperately needed more data on the effects of weightlessness on humans. This was considered a key element to manned flights to the Moon. Between 1961 and 1963 six Mercury astronauts made six successful space flights and spent a total of 53.9 hours in space. (See Table 2.1.)

Is It Worth It?

The United States paid a high price for NASA's Moon program. It was conducted during one of the most turbulent times in U.S. history. The 1960s were characterized by social unrest, protest, and national tragedies.

On November 22, 1963, President Kennedy was assassinated in Dallas, Texas, and Vice President Johnson assumed the presidency. Johnson had always supported the space program and had been instrumental in passing the bill that created NASA. He assured NASA that the Apollo program would continue as planned. On November 29, 1963, Johnson announced that portions of the U.S. Air Force missile testing range on Merritt Island, Florida, would be designated the John F. Kennedy Space Center.

In 1964 the social scientist Amitai Etzioni (1929–) published *The Moon-Doggle*, a book that was extremely critical of NASA. The title was a play on the word *boondoggle*, which means a wasteful and impractical project. Etzioni criticized the agency for spending too much money on manned space flights when unmanned satellites could achieve more for less money. He also questioned the scientific value (and costs) of sending astronauts to the Moon. Etzioni was not alone in feeling this way. American society was increasingly concerned with pressing social and national issues, including the escalating war in Vietnam and civil rights. Arnold S. Levine of NASA indicates in *Managing NASA in the Apollo Era* (1982) that during this period NASA's budget increased from $964 million in 1961 to $3.7 billion in 1963. By 1964 it had risen to $5.1 billion and would remain at this level for two more years.

The Gemini Project

NASA scientists realized during the Mercury missions that they needed an intermediate step before the Apollo flights. They had to be sure that humans could survive and function in space for up to fourteen days. This was the amount of time estimated for a round trip to the Moon. The program that was designed to test human endurance in space was named the Gemini project, after the constellation represented by the twin stars Castor and Pollux. The name was chosen because the Gemini space capsule was designed to hold two astronauts, rather than one.

A major goal of the Gemini project was to successfully rendezvous orbiting vehicles into one unit and maneuver that unit with a propulsion system. This was a feat that would be necessary to achieve the Moon landings. The last Gemini goal was to perfect atmospheric reentry of the spacecraft and perform a ground landing, rather than a landing at sea. All the goals except a ground landing were achieved.

Between 1965 and 1966 NASA completed ten Gemini missions with seventeen astronauts, who spent a total of more than forty days in space. (See Table 2.2.) The *Gemini IV* mission featured the first extravehicular activity by an American. The astronaut Edward H. White (1930–1967) spent twenty-two minutes outside his spacecraft during a "space walk." The longest duration Gemini flight (*Gemini VII*) took place in December 1965, lasting fourteen days.

Moon Resources

By 1967 NASA scientists and engineers had been studying the details of a Moon landing for more than six years. According to Levine, NASA's budget at the time was $4.9 billion, with about 90% of that money going to outside contractors and university research programs. In 1967 more than 307,000 people at installations around the country worked in support of the Apollo program. NASA's employees numbered about 34,100.

Rangers and Surveyors

A series of nine Ranger probes had been launched between 1961 and 1965. They were designed to flight-test lunar spacecraft, take photographs of the Moon, and collect data on radiation, magnetic fields, and solar plasma (charged gases emitted from the Sun).

The first two probes in the series failed to escape Earth orbit. *Ranger 3* was supposed to impact the Moon, but missed it by twenty-three thousand miles. On April 26, 1962, *Ranger 4* crashed into the far side of the Moon. It was the first American object to reach another celestial body. However, its central computer had failed during the flight, so no data was transmitted. After two more failed attempts NASA finally achieved success. On July 31,

TABLE 2.2

Gemini program manned flights

Dates	Gemini flight no.	Astronauts	Achievements
March 23, 1965	III	Virgil I. Grissom John W. Young	3 orbits. Only Gemini spacecraft to be named (Molly Brown).
June 3–7, 1965	IV	James A. McDivitt Edward H. White	First American EVA—a 22 minute space walk by White
August 21–29, 1965	V	Gordon Cooper Charles Conrad Jr.	120 orbits. First use of fuel cells for electrical power.
December 4–18, 1965	VII	Frank Borman James A. Lovell Jr.	Longest mission at 14 days
December 15–16, 1965	VI-A	Walter M. Schirra Jr. Thomas Stafford	First space rendezvous (with Gemini VII)
March 16, 1966	VIII	Neil A. Armstrong David R. Scott	First space docking (with unmanned craft)
June 3–6, 1966	IX-A	Thomas Stafford Eugene A. Cernan	2 hours of EVA
July 18–21, 1966	X	John W. Young Michael Collins	Rendezvous with Gemini VIII
September 12–15, 1966	XI	Charles Conrad Jr. Richard F. Gordon Jr.	Record altitude (739.2 miles)
November 11–15, 1966	XII	James A. Lovell Jr. Edwin E. (Buzz) Aldrin Jr.	Record EVA by Aldrin (5 hours 30 minutes)

Note: EVA is extravehicular activity.

SOURCE: Created by Kim Masters Evans for Gale, Cengage Learning, 2008

1964, *Ranger 7* crashed into the Moon after transmitting the first close-up photographs of the lunar surface.

During 1965 *Ranger 8* and *Ranger 9* took hundreds of vital photographs before their impact. Nearly two hundred photographs taken by *Ranger 9* were broadcast live on television as the probe hurtled toward the lunar surface.

On June 2, 1966, NASA achieved another milestone when the *Surveyor 1* spacecraft made a controlled "soft landing" on the Moon in the Ocean of Storms. The ability to do a soft landing was considered crucial to putting a human safely on the Moon. *Surveyor 1* returned a host of high-quality photographs. However, NASA was still running behind the Soviet space program. The Soviet spacecraft *Luna 9* had soft-landed in the Ocean of Storms four months before *Surveyor 1* got there. *Luna 9* also provided the first television transmission from the lunar surface.

In all, NASA sent seven Surveyor spacecraft to the Moon between 1966 and 1968. Two lost control and crashed, whereas the remaining five achieved soft landings. In 1967 *Surveyor 6* was particularly successful. During its mission NASA controllers were able to lift the spacecraft about ten feet off the ground and set it softly back down again. NASA was ready to put humans aboard a lunar lander.

Apollo Spacecraft

The Apollo spacecraft had three parts:

- Command module containing the crew quarters and flight control section

- Service module for the propulsion and spacecraft support systems

- Lunar module to take two of the crew to and from the lunar surface

Figure 2.2 shows the three modules stacked atop a rocket for launch. The massive Saturn V rocket developed by von Braun was the launch vehicle selected for the Apollo spacecraft.

The astronauts rode in the command module during launch and reentry. Food, water, and fuel were carried in the service module. While together, the command module and service module were called the CSM. When the three modules reached lunar orbit, the lunar module was detached for the journey to and from the Moon's surface.

After the lunar module ascended from the lunar surface it docked with the CSM. Once the two astronauts had moved safely into the CSM, the lunar module was jettisoned away from the spacecraft. Only the CSM made the journey back toward Earth. The service module was jettisoned away just before reentry into Earth's atmosphere. The command module with all three astronauts aboard was designed to splash down into the sea.

A Tragic Setback

NASA lost its first astronauts during the Apollo program. In 1966 three unmanned Apollo spacecraft were launched to test the structural integrity of the spacecraft and the flight systems. These were called the Apollo-Saturn missions and were numbered *AS-201* through *AS-203*.

On January 27, 1967, NASA was preparing a spacecraft for mission *AS-204*, the first manned test flight. During a launch pad test of the spacecraft, a flash fire broke out and killed all three astronauts in the command module. NASA renamed the mission *Apollo 1* in their honor.

The tragedy temporarily devastated morale at NASA. The agency was not treated kindly by the media. Many newspapers questioned whether a manned lunar mission was worth the risk. Rumors even circulated that the astronauts had been murdered by NASA for criticizing the agency or for other sinister reasons.

The exact cause of the spark that started the fire was never discovered. An extensive investigation conducted by NASA found that a variety of factors contributed to the astronauts' deaths. Some were operational problems: a hatch that was difficult to open, the presence of 100% oxygen in the module, and the use of flammable materials inside the module. The investigation also revealed a number of management and contractor problems. NASA set about redesigning the Apollo modules and reorganized top management staff. The Moon landing that was scheduled for late 1968 was delayed until 1969 due to the *Apollo 1* tragedy.

FIGURE 2.2

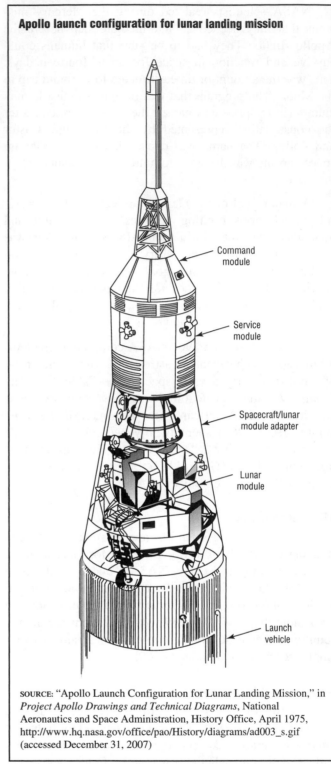

Apollo launch configuration for lunar landing mission

Command module

Service module

Spacecraft/lunar module adapter

Lunar module

Launch vehicle

SOURCE: "Apollo Launch Configuration for Lunar Landing Mission," in *Project Apollo Drawings and Technical Diagrams*, National Aeronautics and Space Administration, History Office, April 1975, http://www.hq.nasa.gov/office/pao/History/diagrams/ad003_s.gif (accessed December 31, 2007)

One Giant Leap

By late 1968 the Apollo program was making tremendous strides. The first manned flight, *Apollo 7*, was launched on October 11, 1968. *Apollo 7* included the first live television broadcast from a manned spacecraft. Watching the astronauts on television helped rekindle a feeling of excitement about the space program. The

American public grew more excited as one Apollo mission after another was successful. In May 1969 the *Apollo 10* mission featured the first live color television pictures broadcast from outer space.

Two months later *Apollo 11* was launched into space with three astronauts aboard. Their names were Neil A. Armstrong (1930–), Michael Collins (1930–), and Edwin E. (Buzz) Aldrin Jr. (1930–). On July 20, 1969, at 4:18 p.m. eastern daylight time (EDT), the lunar module softly landed near the Sea of Tranquillity. Armstrong reported, "Houston, Tranquillity Base here. The Eagle has landed."

At 10:56 p.m. EDT Armstrong opened the door of the lunar module and climbed down a short ladder. As he put his left foot onto the surface of the Moon, he said, "That's one small step for man, one giant leap for mankind." It was the first time in history that a human being had set foot on another celestial body.

The event was televised live to a worldwide audience estimated at 528 million people. They watched as Armstrong and Aldrin explored the lunar surface for two hours and thirty-one minutes. The astronauts planted an American flag in the dusty soil and collected forty-eight pounds of Moon rocks. They unveiled a plaque attached to the descent stage (the lower part) of the lunar module. The plaque read: "Here men from the planet Earth first set foot upon the Moon, July 1969 A.D. We came in peace for all mankind." The plaque bore the signatures of all three astronauts and President Richard M. Nixon (1913–1994).

The two astronauts climbed back into the lunar module. On July 21, 1969, the ascent portion of the module lifted off the lunar surface, leaving the descent stage behind. Armstrong and Aldrin had spent twenty-one hours and thirty-six minutes on the surface of the Moon. They then docked with the CSM piloted by Collins. Once reunited, the three astronauts headed for Earth, leaving the lunar module ascent stage in orbit around the Moon (it eventually crashed into the Moon, but the impact site is not known). On July 24, 1969, their command module safely splash-landed in the Pacific Ocean.

The Can-Do Culture

NASA had achieved something that many people thought could not be done. The agency found itself heaped with praise and congratulations. Putting a man on the Moon was considered an enormous milestone in technological progress. In addition, it had been done before the end of the decade, just as President Kennedy had requested. The achievement fostered a tremendous sense of pride and confidence among NASA personnel. The agency was left with an optimistic conviction that it could do anything, an attitude that came to be known as NASA's "can-do culture."

NASA's critics believe that the agency's can-do culture caused it to make many overly optimistic promises during the following decades. NASA continued to set bold goals for the nation's space program and promise Congress that it could achieve them, just like it had accomplished the Moon landing. The problem was that these goals did not receive nearly as much financial support as the Apollo program received. The Moon landing was possible because NASA was given the necessary resources. Putting a man on the Moon within a decade had taken the talents of hundreds of thousands of people and nearly $24 billion of taxpayers' money. Neither Congress nor the American people were ever inclined again to devote so many resources to a space venture.

Apollo Fizzles Out

NASA launched six more Apollo missions following *Apollo 11*. In November 1969 the *Apollo 12* crew landed near the Ocean of Storms and found the *Surveyor 3* lunar probe sent several years before.

Five months later *Apollo 13* was launched. Two days into the flight an oxygen tank suddenly ruptured aboard the service module. The pressure in the cabin dropped quickly. Fearing the crew would otherwise be lost, NASA devised a way for the astronauts to rely on the limited resources in the lunar module to limp back to Earth. The spacecraft splashed down safely on April 17, 1970.

Once again NASA had achieved a near-miracle. Even though on the surface *Apollo 13* appeared like a failure, NASA classified it as a success, because the agency learned so much about handling emergencies during space flight. The experience was later captured in the 1995 movie *Apollo 13*. The movie made famous a phrase uttered by the *Apollo 13* commander James A. Lovell Jr. (1928–) following the oxygen tank rupture. Lovell calmly said, "Houston, we have a problem."

The next Apollo launch was postponed, while NASA worked on problems brought to light by the *Apollo 13* incident. In February 1971 *Apollo 14* successfully reached the Moon for a lunar exploration mission at Fra Mauro. The astronauts took along a new cart that was specially designed to hold Moon rocks. Later that year the *Apollo 15* crew took a lunar rover—one of three that NASA had built at a cost of $40 million—that resembled a dune buggy. The astronauts zoomed around the Hadley-Apennine region at a top speed of eight miles per hour. They collected nearly 170 pounds of Moon rocks. The lunar rover was so effective it was used on all the remaining Apollo missions.

In April 1972 *Apollo 16* set down in the Descartes Highlands of the Moon. It was the first mission to explore the highlands and the southern-most landing site of all the Apollo missions. In December 1972 the *Apollo 17* crew explored the highlands and a valley in the Taurus-Littrow

TABLE 2.3

Apollo program manned missions

Name	Dates	Spacecraft call signs	Crew	Mission time	Note
Apollo 1	January 27,1967	Not used	Virgil I. Grissom (Commander), Edward H. White, Roger B. Chaffee		Spacecraft caught on fire on landing pad during practice drill. All astronauts killed.
Apollo 7	October 11–22 1968	Not used	Walter M. Schirra Jr. (commander), Donn F. Eisele (CM pilot), R. Walter Cunningham (LM pilot)	10 days, 20 hours	CSM piloted flight demonstration in Earth orbit. First live TV from manned spacecraft.
Apollo 8	December 21–27, 1968	Not used	Frank Borman (commander), James A. Lovell Jr. (CM pilot), William A. Anders (LM pilot)	6 days, 3 hours	First manned lunar orbital mission. Live TV broadcasts.
Apollo 9	March 03–13, 1969	CM: Gumdrop LM: Spider	James A. McDivitt (commander), David R. Scott (CM pilot), Russell L. Schweickart (LM pilot)	10 days, 1 hour	First manned flight of all lunar hardware in Earth orbit. Schweickart performed 37 minutes EVA. First manned flight of lunar module.
Apollo 10	May 18–26, 1969	CM: Charlie Brown LM:Snoopy	Thomas P. Stafford (commander), John W. Young (CM pilot), Eugene A. Cernan (LM pilot)	8 days, 3 minutes	Practice for Moon landing. First manned CSM/LM operations in cislunar and unar environment; First live color TV from space.
Apollo 11	July 16–24, 1969	CM: Columbia LM: Eagle	Neil A. Armstrong (commander), Michael Collins (CM pilot), Edwin E. (Buzz) Aldrin Jr. (LM pilot)	8 days, 3 hours, 18 minutes	First manned lunar landing mission and lunar surface EVA.
Apollo 12	November 14–24, 1969	CM: Yankee Clipper LM: Intrepid	Charles Conrad Jr. (commander), Richard F. Gordon Jr. (CM pilot), Alan L. Bean (LM pilot)	10 days, 4 hours, 36 minutes	Lunar landing and lunar exploration.
Apollo 13	April 11–17, 1970	CM: Odyssey LM: Aquarius	James A. Lovell Jr. (commander), John L. Swigert Jr. (CM pilot), Fred W. Haise Jr. (LM pilot)	5 days, 22.9 hours	Mission aborted before spacecraft reached Moon.
Apollo 14	January 31– February 09, 1971	CM: Kitty Hawk LM: Antares	Alan B. Shepard Jr. (commander), Stuart A. Roosa (CM pilot), Edgar D. Mitchell (LM pilot)	9 days	Lunar landing and lunar exploration.
Apollo 15	July 26– August 07, 1971	CM: Endeavor LM: Falcon	David R. Scott (commander), Alfred M. Worden (CM pilot), James B. Irwin (LM pilot)	12 days, 17 hours, 12 minutes	Lunar landing and lunar exploration.
Apollo 16	April 16–27, 1972	CM: Casper LM: Orion	John W. Young (commander), Thomas K. Mattingly II (CM pilot), Charles M. Duke Jr. (LM pilot)	11 days, 1 hour, 51 minutes	Lunar landing and lunar exploration.
Apollo 17	December 07–19, 1972	CM: America LM: Challenger	Eugene A. Cernan (commander), Ronald E. Evans (CM pilot), Harrison H. Schmitt (LM pilot)	12 days, 13 hours, 52 minutes	Last lunar landing mission.

Note: EVA is extravehicular activity. CM is command module. CSM is command and service module. LM is lunar module.

SOURCE: Created by Kim Masters Evans for Gale, Cengage Learning, 2008

area of the Moon. For the first time the mission crew included a scientist, the geologist Harrison H. Schmitt (1935–). The astronauts collected 243 pounds of Moon rocks, the most of any Apollo mission. On December 19, 1972, *Apollo 17* splashed down safely in the Pacific Ocean. With the successful completion of the *Apollo 17* mission, the Apollo program was over.

Table 2.3 summarizes information about all the Apollo missions. In all, NASA put twelve astronauts on the Moon: Armstrong, Aldrin, Charles Conrad Jr. (1930–1999), Alan L. Bean (1932–), Shepard, Edgar D. Mitchell (1930–), David R. Scott (1932–), James B. Irwin (1930–1991), John W. Young (1930–), Charles M. Duke Jr. (1935–), Eugene A. Cernan (1934–), and Schmitt. They collected 840 pounds of rocks, soil, and other geological samples from the Moon.

The missions that followed *Apollo 11* never captured the public's imagination the same way that the first Moon landing did. The feeling was that the United States had already achieved its goal of beating the Soviet Union to the Moon, and continued lunar exploration held little

appeal for many people. Furthermore, the country was engaged in a costly and demoralizing war in Vietnam. Levine indicates that in 1970 NASA's budget was cut to $3.7 billion, down from $5 billion in the mid-1960s. NASA had to cancel its planned remaining Apollo missions: *Apollo 18*, *Apollo 19*, and *Apollo 20*.

SPACE SCIENCE SUFFERS

Putting a man on the Moon was conducted mostly for political purposes. It bolstered national pride and prestige and was largely a symbolic endeavor. Many scientists thought the Apollo program achieved far less in scientific terms than unmanned probes could have accomplished. One reason the program was so expensive was that so many resources had to be devoted to keeping fragile humans alive and safe in the harsh environment of space. Critics said this money could have been invested in robotics research and development to produce a fleet of unmanned probes and sample collectors to explore the Moon and far beyond.

The debate over human exploration versus robotic exploration began in the 1950s and still goes on in the 2000s. NASA's Ranger and Surveyor probes of the early 1960s were originally designed to collect data to support many research goals within astronomy and space science. Once the Apollo program began, these probes were retooled to gather data important to the manned program. This was called human factors research and was a small part of the discipline called space biology. NASA's focus on human factors at the expense of broader research in space biology, space science, and astronomy brought harsh criticism from scientists.

In 1967 a committee appointed by President Johnson recommended that the nation establish a well-rounded space program following Apollo with more emphasis on science and less emphasis on human exploration. NASA did conduct unmanned space flights geared toward general space biology. In 1962 the Biosatellite program began with a series of three flights designed to test the rigors of space travel on subhuman beings. In 1969 *Biosatellite III* flew with a male pigtailed monkey named Bonnie aboard. The mission had to be ended early when Bonnie became sick. He died soon after returning to Earth.

During the early 1970s NASA wanted to build on its Apollo success with another ambitious manned space program. The agency angered many scientists when it lobbied Congress to allow it to transfer funds designated for the Biosatellite program to the manned program. Pitts notes that NASA pursued a plan of action that terminated "a relatively inexpensive, science-oriented project in favor of a relatively expensive, exploration-oriented manned program." This type of criticism was to plague NASA for decades to come.

NASA'S FIRST SPACE STATION

As early as the 1960s NASA made plans to put a manned space station in orbit around Earth. These plans took center stage at the agency when the Apollo program ended. For its next great project NASA envisioned an orbiting space station devoted to scientific research and a fleet of reusable space planes to carry humans to and from the station. In 1969 neither President Nixon nor Congress were interested in extending the Apollo program, let alone pursuing a new and costly endeavor. NASA found its budget cut year after year. Nevertheless, the agency devoted many of its resources to developing a new manned space program.

The first step was the temporary *Skylab* space station. This was a small scientific laboratory and solar observatory that could hold three crewmembers at a time. Three separate crews visited and lived in *Skylab* between May 1973 and February 1974. The first mission lasted twenty-eight days, the second fifty-nine days, and the third eighty-four days. *Skylab* saved money by using rockets and spacecraft components left over from the Apollo program. *Skylab* was considered key to gathering data on the effects of prolonged weightlessness and space flight on humans. As it had with its earlier space efforts, the United States lagged behind the Soviet Union in this area. *Salyut 1*, the first Soviet space station, was put into orbit two years before *Skylab*.

THE SHUTTLE PROGRAM

In 1972 development got under way at NASA on a reusable space plane called a shuttle. This program was supposed to produce a finished product within five years, but it eventually took twice that long. The first shuttle did not launch until 1981. By this time the Soviet space station *Mir* had been in orbit for several years. The Soviet space program had pursued—but failed to develop—a reusable space plane. Transportation to and from *Mir* was accomplished using expendable rocket boosters.

NASA relied on a series of space shuttles to conduct most Earth orbit operations. Throughout the early 1980s shuttles carried satellites for government, military, and commercial clients.

On January 28, 1986, the space shuttle *Challenger* exploded seventy-three seconds after liftoff, killing the seven astronauts aboard. The shuttle fleet was grounded for more than two years as a result. An investigation revealed that a faulty joint in a rocket booster had allowed hot gases to escape that ignited and destroyed the vehicle.

Government investigators also found fault with the entire shuttle program. They complained that NASA managers emphasized schedule over safety. Before the *Challenger* disaster, shuttles carried commercial and military satellites (called payloads) into space. To reduce the scheduling pressure, NASA decided to cease carrying commercial payloads. Military payloads were eventually phased out as well, leaving only scientific payloads. The shuttle's commercial and military clients were forced to use expendable rockets to launch their satellites into orbit.

The loss of the *Challenger* shuttle forced NASA to scale back shuttle operations. The tragedy brought harsh criticism of NASA from scientists and politicians alike. NASA's can-do culture was blamed for making the agency overconfident and overly optimistic about its abilities to safely operate a major space program on a limited budget.

Between 1994 and 1998 NASA shuttles played a major role in a cooperative space venture between the United States and Russia. (When the Soviet Union dissolved into several individual republics in 1991, Russia, the largest and most powerful, carried on the old Soviet space program under the new Russian Space Agency.) U.S. shuttles docked with the Russian *Mir* station for joint scientific missions of astronauts and cosmonauts. A decade before,

NASA had worked with its Soviet counterpart to develop mutual docking mechanisms on U.S. and Soviet spacecraft.

In October 1998 NASA achieved a public relations boost when Senator John Glenn flew into space aboard the shuttle *Discovery*. The seventy-seven-year-old Glenn was already a hero for his participation in the Mercury program of the early 1960s. In February 1962 Glenn had been the third American in space and the first to complete an Earth orbit during a five-hour trip aboard *Friendship 7*. In 1998 his space flight lasted nine days. He became the oldest person ever to travel into space. NASA scientists conducted extensive medical tests before, during, and after his flight to monitor his well-being. They were particularly eager to learn about the effects of weightlessness on an older person. Prolonged weightlessness in space is known to weaken human bones, a condition also seen on Earth in older people suffering from osteoporosis.

NASA's shuttle program continued into the twenty-first century, and was again touched by tragedy when the space shuttle *Columbia* broke apart on February 1, 2003, during reentry over the western United States. Seven crewmembers were killed. Investigators found that a piece of foam had fallen off the shuttle's external fuel tank during liftoff and smashed into *Columbia*'s wing. The resulting damage allowed super-hot gases to enter the shuttle during reentry and tear it apart.

This second shuttle tragedy shook NASA to the core. The agency had made many promises to Congress and the American public about better shuttle safety and reliability following the 1986 disaster. NASA's capability to operate a manned space program again came under attack. A government investigation blamed NASA for continuing to perpetuate the can-do culture in the face of serious operational and budget problems within the shuttle program. The shuttle fleet was grounded for more than two years.

In July 2005 a shuttle successfully carried out the first of two planned return-to-flight (RTF) missions. Even though the shuttle returned safely to Earth, video images revealed that foam had again shed from the external tank during liftoff. However, it fell harmlessly to the ground and did not damage shuttle components. NASA and the public faced the sobering realization that fixing the shuttle's safety problems had proved to be an elusive goal. The second RTF was postponed while engineers and scientists worked to ensure better safety in the shuttle program. The flight finally took place in July 2006. As of December 2007, five additional shuttle missions had been carried out.

THE *INTERNATIONAL SPACE STATION*

In 1988 the United States and fifteen other nations embarked on a new space venture called the *International Space Station* (*ISS*). The United States and Russia collaborated throughout the 1990s to lead construction of an orbiting space station designed for prolonged inhabitation by scientists engaged in space research. They invited other countries to participate by contributing parts, components, and scientific facilities or sending researchers to the station.

The Russian Space Agency was determined to play a major role in the *ISS*, but it had even less funding than NASA. Both agencies struggled to put U.S. and Russian modules into place and keep them operational. The station was scaled back in size and capability many times due to budget restrictions in both countries. The bulk of the heavy lifting required to put *ISS* modules into space was performed by space shuttles. The 2003 grounding of the fleet halted *ISS* construction. NASA continued to send astronauts to the *ISS*, but they had to travel aboard Russian spacecraft to get there until the space shuttle resumed operating.

NASA'S ROBOTIC SPACE PROGRAMS

Besides conducting several crewed missions, NASA has also sent a number of robotic spacecraft into outer space. These machines have achieved some incredible milestones in space exploration. Satellites have been put into Earth orbit since the earliest days of NASA's space program to collect weather data or serve military purposes. During the 1960s and 1970s lunar probes were sent to the Moon to support the Apollo program. At the same time, NASA began launching robotic explorers that traveled to other planets. These were followed by sophisticated observatories and other robotic spacecraft placed in orbit around Earth or the Sun or sent to intercept asteroids. These projects are considered crucial to enhancing human understanding of Earth, the surrounding solar system, and the universe at large. All these missions are examined in detail in subsequent chapters.

NASA'S ORGANIZATION AND FACILITIES

Agency-level management takes place at NASA headquarters in Washington, D.C. People at this level interact with national leaders and NASA customers regarding overall agency concerns, such as budget, strategy, policies, and long-term investments. The headquarters is considered the centralized point of accountability and communication between NASA and people outside the agency. In December 2007, 1,955 personnel were employed at the Washington site. (See Table 2.4.)

During 2004 and 2005 NASA made major changes to its organizational structure to streamline the agency. The reorganization was designed to eliminate the so-called stove-pipe effect, in which individual facilities and enterprises within the agency operated too independently and did not communicate well with one another or with

TABLE 2.4

NASA workforce, December 2007

NASA location	Full-time civil servants	Contractors	Other	Totals
Ames Research Center	1,225	1,156	87	2,468
Dryden Flight Research Center	515	509	0	1,024
Glenn Research Center	1,635	1,493	97	3,225
Goddard Space Flight Center	3,193	4,630	248	8,071
Johnson Space Center	3,265	12,809	32	16,106
Kennedy Space Center	2,100	11,287	0	13,387
Langley Research Center	1,920	1,521	44	3,485
Marshall Space Flight Center	2,581	4,087	137	6,805
Stennis Space Center	278	1,165	32	1,475
Jet Propulsion Laboratory	0	331	4,915	5,246
NASA Headquarters	1,268	637	50	1,955
Office of the Inspector General	213	12	0	225
NASA Shared Services Center	120	241	0	361
	18,313	39,878	5,642	63,833

SOURCE: Adapted from "All FAIR Inventory FTE by Center," in *Exploring the NASA Workforce*, National Aeronautics and Space Administration Shared Services Center, December 8, 2007, http://wicn.nssc.nasa.gov/ (accessed January 2, 2008)

NASA headquarters. Many critics had blamed NASA's management structure for contributing to the *Challenger* and *Columbia* disasters. According to NASA, in *FY 2005 Human Space Flight Transition Plan* (2004, http://www.nasa.gov/pdf/138907main_FY_2005_PAR-Part_1.pdf), the new system will ensure that "all parts of the Agency act as One NASA team to make decisions for the common good, collaborate across traditional boundaries, and leverage the Agency's many unique capabilities in support of a single focus: exploration."

NASA's organizational structure is shown in Figure 2.3. It includes four major divisions called mission directorates:

- Aeronautics Research—devoted to research and development of new aeronautical technologies and aviation systems

- Exploration Systems—responsible for biological research and technological development to support human and robotic exploration

- Science—charged with ensuring that missions are planned to reap scientific benefits, analyzing scientific data, and facilitating cross-transfer between earth and space science findings

- Space Operations—dedicated to directing launches and flight operations and related communications systems

NASA Facilities

Figure 2.4 shows the locations of NASA headquarters and various field facilities, including the ten major facilities called centers.

Even though each center supports multiple projects, it is assigned a particular area of expertise for which it is supposed to build and maintain human resources, facilities, and other capabilities. NASA calls these "centers of excellence."

AMES RESEARCH CENTER. The Ames Research Center (ARC) is located in Moffett Field, California. It was founded as an aeronautics research laboratory in 1939 next to a military base later named Moffett Field. The base was closed in 1994 and its facilities and runways were turned over to the ARC. The center conducts research in astrobiology (the origin, evolution, distribution, and destiny of life in the universe), air traffic management, supercomputing, artificial intelligence, nanotechnology, and other areas of importance to space exploration. It also performs wind tunnel testing and flight simulations. The ARC is a center of excellence for information technology. As of December 2007 it employed 2,468 people. (See Table 2.4.)

DRYDEN FLIGHT RESEARCH CENTER. The Dryden Flight Research Center (DFRC) is located at Edwards Air Force Base in Edwards, California. During the late 1940s the NACA conducted military testing of high-speed experimental aircraft at the base. In 1959 the high-speed flight station at the base was designated a NASA flight research center. The DFRC is NASA's primary installation for flight research. It also serves as a backup landing site for the space shuttle. The DFRC is a center of excellence for atmospheric flight operations. As of December 2007, 1,024 people were employed there. (See Table 2.4.)

GLENN RESEARCH CENTER. The Glenn Research Center (GRC) is located in Cleveland, Ohio, at Lewis Field next to Cleveland Hopkins International Airport. It began in 1941 as the NACA's Aircraft Engine Research Laboratory. The GRC researches and develops technologies in aeropropulsion, aerospace power, microgravity science, electric propulsion, and communications technologies for aeronautics and space applications. Its facilities include the nearby Plum Brook Station at which large-scale testing is conducted. The GRC is a center of excellence for turbomachinery (turbine-based machines). As of December 2007 it employed 3,225 people. (See Table 2.4.)

GODDARD SPACE FLIGHT CENTER. The Goddard Space Flight Center (GSFC) is located in Greenbelt, Maryland, a suburb of Washington, D.C. It was founded in 1959 as NASA's first space flight center. The GSFC is a major laboratory for developing robotic scientific spacecraft. The center also operates the Wallops Flight Facility near Chincoteague, Virginia, and the Independent Verification and Validation (IV&V) Facility in Fairmont, West Virginia. Wallops is NASA's principal installation for managing and implementing suborbital research programs. The IV&V facility was formed following the space shuttle

FIGURE 2.3

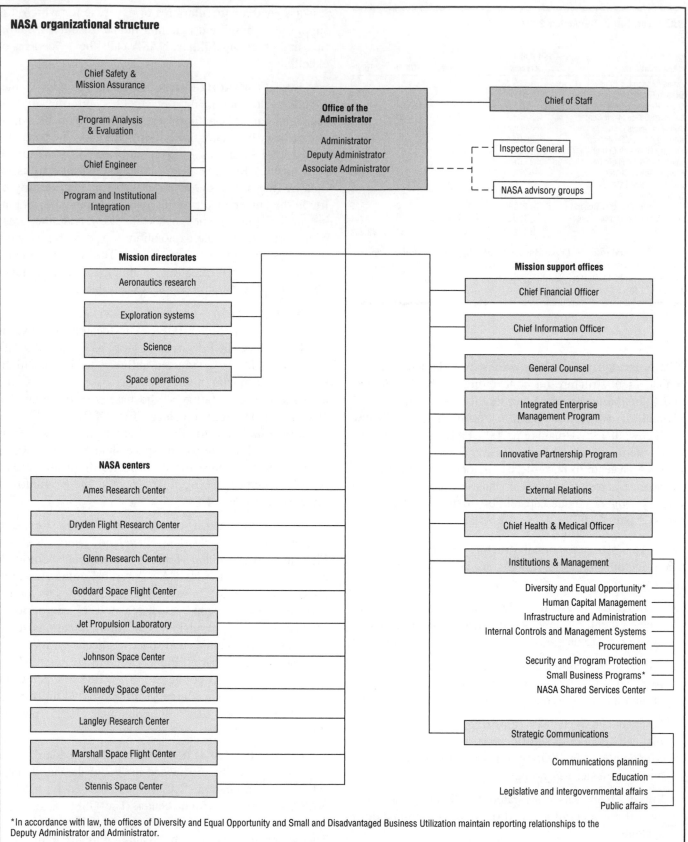

NASA organizational structure

Chief Safety & Mission Assurance

Program Analysis & Evaluation

Chief Engineer

Program and Institutional Integration

Office of the Administrator

Administrator
Deputy Administrator
Associate Administrator

Chief of Staff

Inspector General

NASA advisory groups

Mission directorates

Aeronautics research

Exploration systems

Science

Space operations

Mission support offices

Chief Financial Officer

Chief Information Officer

General Counsel

Integrated Enterprise Management Program

Innovative Partnership Program

External Relations

Chief Health & Medical Officer

Institutions & Management

Diversity and Equal Opportunity*
Human Capital Management
Infrastructure and Administration
Internal Controls and Management Systems
Procurement
Security and Program Protection
Small Business Programs*
NASA Shared Services Center

NASA centers

Ames Research Center

Dryden Flight Research Center

Glenn Research Center

Goddard Space Flight Center

Jet Propulsion Laboratory

Johnson Space Center

Kennedy Space Center

Langley Research Center

Marshall Space Flight Center

Stennis Space Center

Strategic Communications

Communications planning
Education
Legislative and intergovernmental affairs
Public affairs

*In accordance with law, the offices of Diversity and Equal Opportunity and Small and Disadvantaged Business Utilization maintain reporting relationships to the Deputy Administrator and Administrator.

SOURCE: "Organization Chart," in *NASA Organization Structure*, National Aeronautics and Space Administration, July 2007, http://www.nasa .gov/centers/hq/pdf/182318main_NASA_Org_Chart_July-2007.pdf (accessed October 3, 2007)

FIGURE 2.4

NASA sites

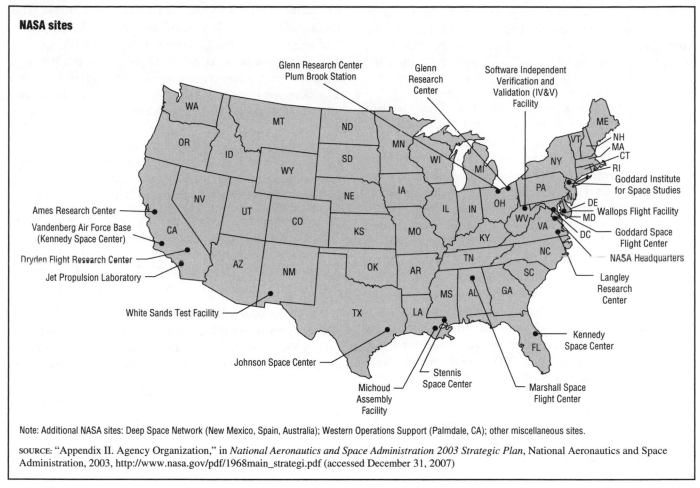

Note: Additional NASA sites: Deep Space Network (New Mexico, Spain, Australia); Western Operations Support (Palmdale, CA); other miscellaneous sites.

SOURCE: "Appendix II. Agency Organization," in *National Aeronautics and Space Administration 2003 Strategic Plan*, National Aeronautics and Space Administration, 2003, http://www.nasa.gov/pdf/1968main_strategi.pdf (accessed December 31, 2007)

Challenger accident to ensure that mission-critical software is safe and cost-effective.

In 1966 NASA established the National Space Science Data Center (NSSDC) at the GSFC. The NSSDC became the archive center for data from NASA's space science missions and continues to serve in this function. Space science data from NASA missions are made available to researchers and, in some cases, to the general public.

The GSFC is a center of excellence for earth science, physics, and astronomy. As of December 2007, 8,071 people were employed there. (See Table 2.4.)

JOHNSON SPACE CENTER. The Johnson Space Center (JSC) is located in Houston, Texas. It was established in 1961 to be the focus of the manned space flight program. At that time, it was known simply as the Manned Spacecraft Center. In 1973 the center was renamed the Lyndon B. Johnson Space Center in honor of the late president's support of NASA space programs during the 1950s and 1960s.

The JSC houses the program offices and mission control centers for the space shuttle and the *ISS*. JSC facilities are also used for astronaut training and spaceflight simu-

lations for both of these programs. Aircraft used to train astronauts and to support the Space Shuttle Program are stationed at nearby Ellington Field, a joint civilian and military airport operated by the city of Houston. The JSC is a center of excellence for human operations in space. As of December 2007 it employed 16,106 people. (See Table 2.4.)

KENNEDY SPACE CENTER. The Kennedy Space Center (KSC) is located on Merritt Island, Florida, next to the Cape Canaveral Air Force Station. The air force station was the site of the Mercury and Gemini launches of the early 1960s. The KSC was created specifically for the Apollo missions to the Moon. The center provides launch and landing facilities for the Space Shuttle Program and performs maintenance, assembly, and inspection services on the spacecraft. It is also responsible for packaging components of the laboratory experiments that are used on the space shuttle. The KSC is a center of excellence for launch and payload processing systems. As of December 2007, 13,387 people worked there. (See Table 2.4.)

LANGLEY RESEARCH CENTER. The Langley Research Center (LRC) is located in Hampton, Virginia. In 1917 it was established as the country's first civilian aeronautics laboratory. The LRC designs and develops military and civilian aircraft, conducts atmospheric flight research, and tests structures and materials in wind tunnels and other testing facilities. It is a center of excellence for structures and materials. As of December 2007 the LRC employed 3,485 people. (See Table 2.4.)

MARSHALL SPACE FLIGHT CENTER. The Marshall Space Flight Center (MSFC) is located near Huntsville, Alabama, on the Redstone Arsenal Site. During the 1950s a team of rocketry specialists led by von Braun worked at the arsenal site developing rockets for the U.S. military. In 1960 the site's space-related projects and personnel were transferred to the newly formed MSFC. The center developed the Saturn rockets used throughout the Apollo program. The MSFC manages the manufacturing contracts for the space shuttle's main engine, external tank, and reusable solid rocket motor. The center also conducts research in microgravity (an environment in which there is minimal gravitational force) and space optics and develops programs for space shuttle payloads. It is a center of excellence for space propulsion. As of December 2007, 6,805 people were employed there. (See Table 2.4.)

STENNIS SPACE CENTER. The Stennis Space Center (SSC) is located in Bay St. Louis, Mississippi. It was founded in 1961 as the static test facility for launch vehicles to be used in the Apollo program. The SSC is home to the largest rocket propulsion test complex in the United States. It is NASA's primary installation for testing and flight-certifying rocket propulsion systems for the space shuttle and other space vehicles. The center also works with government and commercial partners to develop remote sensing technology. The SSC is a center of excellence for rocket propulsion testing systems. As of December 2007 it employed 1,475 people. (See Table 2.4.)

Other NASA Facilities

There are many facilities and installations that provide support to the field centers and are either operated by NASA or under contract to NASA. Administrative functions, such as payroll, human resources, procurement, and information technology coordination, are performed at the NASA Shared Services Center (NSSC). The NSSC was launched in 2006 and is located at the SSC. It is a public-private venture between the agency, the states of Mississippi and Louisiana, and a private company. As of December 2007 it employed 361 people. NASA's Office of the Inspector General (OIG) is actually a collection of offices at various field facilities. The OIG conducts audits and investigations designed to prevent fraud, crime, waste, and mismanagement and to promote efficient use of resources within the agency. As of December 2007, 225 workers were employed at OIG offices. (See Table 2.4.)

JET PROPULSION LABORATORY. The Jet Propulsion Laboratory (JPL) is located in Pasadena, California. This facility is owned by NASA but operated under a contractual agreement by the California Institute of Technology. The JPL began informally during the 1930s as a group of student rocket enthusiasts under the direction of Professor Theodore von Kármán (1881–1963), the head of the university's Guggenheim Aeronautical Laboratory. These rocket scientists achieved funding for their projects from the U.S. Army, and by the 1940s they were investigating new technologies in aerodynamics and propellant chemistry under the name of the Jet Propulsion Laboratory. In 1958 the JPL was transferred from army jurisdiction to NASA.

Jet propulsion is no longer the primary focus at the JPL. The facility now serves as NASA's primary operator of robotic exploration missions. It also manages and operates NASA's Deep Space Network. As of December 2007 the JPL employed 5,246 people. (See Table 2.4.)

DEEP SPACE NETWORK. The Deep Space Network (DSN) is an international network of antennas that enables NASA mission teams to communicate with distant spacecraft. The DSN communications complexes are situated at three locations around the world (roughly 120 degrees apart): Goldstone, California; Robledo near Madrid, Spain; and Tidbinbilla near Canberra, Australia. (See Figure 2.5.) This placement allows the JPL operations control center to maintain constant contact with spacecraft as Earth rotates.

WHITE SANDS TEST FACILITY. The White Sands Test Facility (WSTF) is located in Las Cruces, New Mexico, a remote desert location. The WSTF provides services to military and government clients. It is NASA's primary facility for testing and evaluating rocket propulsion systems, spacecraft components, and hazardous materials used in space travel. The WSTF supports the space shuttle and *ISS* programs.

NASA'S WORKFORCE

People employed by federal agencies (excluding the military) are called civil servants. As of December 2007, NASA employed 18,313 full-time civil servants. (See Table 2.4.) Another 45,520 people supported NASA projects by working under contracts or grants handed out by the agency. The vast majority of these people work at or near NASA facilities.

The U.S. General Accounting Office (now the U.S. Government Accountability Office) explains in *NASA Personnel: Challenges to Achieving Workforce Reductions* (August 2, 1996, http://www.gao.gov/archive/1996/ns96176 .pdf) that at the height of Apollo development, the agency employed 35,900 civil servants in 1967. By the early 1990s this number had dropped to twenty-five thousand and continued to decrease over the next several years. NASA reduced

FIGURE 2.5

NASA Deep Space Network communications complexes

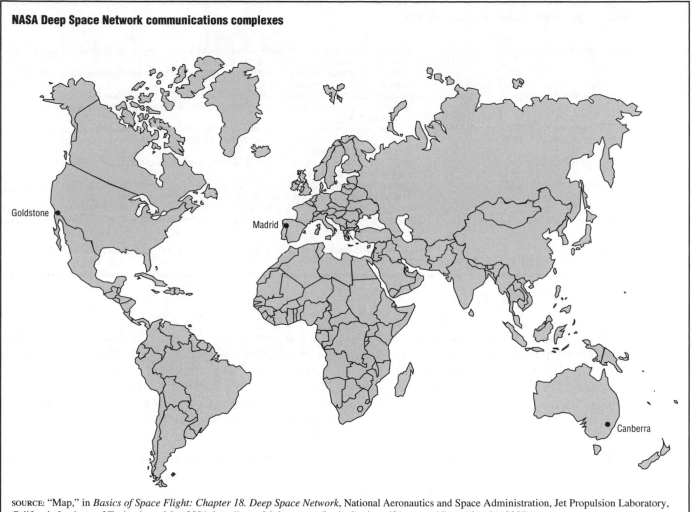

SOURCE: "Map," in *Basics of Space Flight: Chapter 18. Deep Space Network*, National Aeronautics and Space Administration, Jet Propulsion Laboratory, California Institute of Technology, May 2001, http://www2.jpl.nasa.gov/basics/basics.pdf (accessed December 31, 2007)

its workforce by offering employees cash bonuses to retire early and through normal attrition (not replacing workers who leave). During most of the 1990s the agency operated under a hiring freeze. One consequence of this was that few young people entered the NASA workforce during this period.

NASA divides its civil service workforce into four main categories:

• Scientists and engineers—highly educated professionals who conduct aerospace research and development or perform biological, life science, or medical research or services. This category includes space scientists, biologists, aerospace engineers, physicians, nurses, and psychologists.

• Technicians—technicians fall into two categories: some are specialists who provide services such as drafting or photographic development, whereas others are skilled at particular trades such as mechanics or electrical work.

• Professional administrators—these employees operate nontechnical functions such as management, legal affairs, public relations, and human resources.

• Clerical workers—this includes secretarial, administrative, and clerical positions.

According to the NSSC's Workforce Information Cubes for NASA (WICN; September 21, 2007, http://wicn.nssc.nasa.gov/), people engaged in technical work comprise approximately two-thirds of the agency's civil servant workforce.

The WICN notes that the vast majority of the agency's workforce is at least 40 years old, and the average NASA employee is 46.5 years old. Over two-thirds of the NASA employees are male. Most male employees work in science and engineering professions, whereas most of the female employees work in professional administrative positions. Approximately 75% of NASA employees are white.

TABLE 2.5

Innovative Partnerships Program network of participants

National Technology Transfer Center (NTTC)	Expedites the commercialization of federally funded research and development. Located on the campus of Wheeling Jesuit University, in Wheeling, West Virginia.
BizTech	A small business incubator, offering participating companies access to services at Marshall Space Flight Center laboratories in Huntsville, Alabama.
Florida/NASA Business Incubation Center (FNBIC)	A joint partnership of NASA's Kennedy Space Center, Brevard Community College, and the Technological Research and Development Authority. Offers support facilities and programs for developing ventures based on NASA technology.
Mississippi Enterprise for Technology (MsET)	Helps small businesses utilize the scientific knowledge and technical expertise at the Stennis Space Center.
NASA Small Business Innovation Research (SBIR) Program	Transfers technology developed by universities and federal laboratories to the marketplace through the entrepreneurship of a small business.
Federal Laboratory Consortium (FLC) for Technology Transfer	Promotes and facilitates the rapid movement of federal laboratory research results and technologies into the mainstream of the U.S. economy.
National Robotics Engineering Consortium (NREC)	Cooperative venture among NASA, the city of Pittsburgh, the state of Pennsylvania, and Carnegie Mellon's Robotics Institute. Its mission is to move NASA-funded robotics technology to industry.
Research Triangle Institute (RTI)	Provides a range of technology management services to NASA. Located in Research Triangle Park, North Carolina.
Montana State University TechLink Center	Provides ongoing support for adapting, integrating, and commercializing NASA technology. Located at Montana State University-Bozeman.

SOURCE: Adapted from "Innovative Partnerships Program Network" in *Spinoff 2006*, National Aeronautics and Space Administration, September 2006, http://www.sti.nasa.gov/tto/Spinoff2006/PDF/accessible.pdf (accessed December 31, 2007)

The WICN also indicates that most NASA workers have college degrees. Approximately a third of the workforce has advanced degrees beyond the bachelor level. The average salary for a NASA employee is about $98,000 per year. Scientists and engineers are the highest paid, whereas clerical employees are the lowest paid.

Contractors and Grantees

In December 2007, 45,520 people supported NASA services under contracts and grant arrangements. (See Table 2.4.) NASA's major contractors are manufacturing companies in the aerospace industry. The United Space Alliance (2008, http://www.unitedspacealliance.com/) is a joint venture between the Boeing and Lockheed Martin corporations. It performs the day-to-day operations of the Space Shuttle Program and employs over ten thousand people. Most of its employees work at the JSC and the KSC. The California Institute of Technology is another major contractor. It operates the JPL and employed 4,915 people as of December 2007. (See Table 2.4.)

NASA also funds research projects at private institutions, such as universities, and encourages commercial investment in space research. In 1985 Congress amended the National Aeronautics and Space Administration Act to direct NASA to "seek and encourage, to the maximum extent possible, the fullest commercial use of space." In response, NASA developed a Space Partnership Development (SPD) Office, an industry-university-government collaboration. Until the program was discontinued in 2006, the SPD managed twelve Research Partnership Centers at universities and nonprofit institutions engaged in space research and product development.

In 2004 President Bush urged NASA to expand its commercial partnerships to develop technology to sup-

port his new vision for the space agency for crewed missions to the Moon and Mars. NASA incorporated existing partnership arrangements into the Innovative Partnerships Program (IPP) under the direction of the Space Operations Mission Directorate. The IPP works with partners (called external agents) to develop technologies and products that will be useful to NASA and have commercial applications. Programs in the IPP network are described in Table 2.5.

Astronauts

Astronauts are the most famous NASA workers. In 1959 the first group of seven astronauts was chosen from five hundred candidates. All were military men with experience flying jets. At the time, spacecraft restrictions required that astronauts be less than five feet eleven inches tall. In the early days of the Apollo program, all astronauts were chosen from the military services. This soon changed, and NASA began including civilian pilots with extensive flight experience. During the mid-1960s NASA expanded the astronaut corps to include nonpilots with academic qualifications in science, engineering, or medicine.

In 1978 the first group of space shuttle astronauts was selected. For the first time the trainees included women and minorities. The unique environment aboard the space shuttle permitted even more opportunities for nonpilots to fly into space.

A typical shuttle crew includes a commander and a pilot. Both of these crewmembers are considered pilot astronauts. In addition, there can be three to five other crewmembers called mission specialists or payload specialists. Mission specialists are NASA astronauts (typically scientists) with specific onboard responsibilities during a mission. Payload specialists can be scientists, engineers, and ordinary citizens from the private or commercial sector or foreign astronauts invited by NASA to participate in a shuttle mission.

Space shuttle commanders, pilots, and mission specialists are career NASA astronauts, as are commanders and flight engineers who serve aboard the *ISS*.

The 1980s witnessed several firsts in NASA's astronaut corps. In June 1983 Sally Ride (1951–) became the first U.S. woman in space when she served as a mission specialist aboard the space shuttle *Challenger*. It was the shuttle's seventh mission. Two months later the mission specialist Guion Bluford (1942–) became the first African-American in space as part of the shuttle's next mission.

During the early 1980s NASA was enthusiastic about including private citizens on space shuttle flights. This was viewed as a way to better interest the public, and particularly children, in space travel. One of the most famous participants was Christa McAuliffe (1948–1986), the first schoolteacher selected to go into space. On January 28, 1986, she died along with her crewmates when the space shuttle *Challenger* exploded shortly after launch. This disaster ended NASA's policy of inviting private citizens on shuttle flights. Barbara Morgan (1951–), another teacher, trained with McAuliffe as her backup. Following the *Challenger* disaster, Jordan was named Teacher in Space Designee by NASA. She resumed her teaching career, but she also performed public relations duties for the agency. In 1998 Morgan was selected by NASA to be a mission specialist. She completed two years of astronaut training and flew aboard the space shuttle *Endeavour* in August 2007 on a mission to the *ISS*.

Astronaut Selection

NASA accepts applications from astronaut candidates on a regular basis. Civilian candidates submit their applications directly to NASA. Candidates in the armed forces are pre-screened by the military. Every two years NASA conducts a review process to select a new group of astronauts. This process begins in odd-numbered years and follows a specific format.

The latest selection process began in September 2007. (See Table 2.6.) The first day of July 2008 was the cutoff date for receipt of new applications. The applications are reviewed by the Astronaut Candidate Selection Rating Panel, which narrows the field to those applicants considered highly qualified and collects information about them. This information is used to select highly qualified applicants for extensive interviews and medical examinations. In early 2009 the selection process will be completed, and the names of the successful candidates will be released to the media. Those selected begin training soon afterward at the JSC. The training period lasts one to two years.

TABLE 2.6

Astronaut candidate selection process timeline, 2007–09

September 2007	Vacancy announcement opens in USA JOBS
July 1, 2008	Vacancy announcement closes
September–October 2008	Qualified applications reviewed to determine highly qualified applicants
October–November 2008	Highly qualified applications reviewed to determine interviewees
November 2008–January 2009	Interviewees brought to JSC for preliminary interview, medical evaluation, and orientation
February 2009	Finalists determined
February–March 2009	Finalists brought to JSC for additional interview and complete medical evaluation
May 2009	Astronaut candidate class of 2009 announced
August 2009	Astronaut candidate class of 2009 reports to the Johnson Space Center (JSC)

SOURCE: "Astronaut Candidate Selection Process Timeline," in *Astronaut Selection*, National Aeronautics and Space Administration, June 29, 2007, http://www.nasajobs.nasa.gov/astronauts/content/timeline.htm (accessed December 31, 2007)

Astronaut Pay Rates

In "Astronaut Selection" (June 29, 2007, http://www.nasajobs.nasa.gov/astronauts/content/faq.htm), NASA explains that civilian astronauts employed by the agency are civil servants. They are paid salaries based on the federal government's pay scale called the General Schedule (GS). There are fifteen GS pay levels ranging from the lowest (GS-1) to the highest (GS-15). NASA's mission specialists fall within grades GS-11 through GS-14, depending on their education, experience, and qualifications. In 2008 these grade scales covered a salary range between $59,493 and $130,257 per year.

Active-duty military personnel selected to be NASA astronauts remain on the military payroll during their assignment to the JSC.

NASA'S BUDGET

NASA is a federal government agency. For accounting purposes, the federal government operates on a fiscal year (FY) that begins in October and runs through the end of September. Thus, FY 2008 covered the time period October 1, 2007, through September 30, 2008. Each year by the first Monday in February the president must present a proposed budget to the U.S. House of Representatives. This is the amount of money that the president estimates will be required to operate the federal government during the next fiscal year.

It can take many months for the House to debate, negotiate, and approve a final budget. Then, the U.S. Senate also must approve the budget. This entire process can take longer than a year, which means that NASA can be well into a fiscal year (or even beyond it) before knowing the exact amount of money appropriated for that year.

TABLE 2.7

NASA budget request, fiscal year 2008

[In millions]

By appropriation account By mission directorate By theme	Fiscal year 2008
Science, aeronautics and exploration	**$10,483.1**
Science	5,516.1
Earth science	1,497.3
Heliophysics	1,057.2
Planetary science	1,395.8
Astrophysics	1,565.8
Exploration systems	3,923.8
Constellation systems	3,068.0
Advanced capabilities	855.8
Aeronautics research	554.0
Aeronautics technology	554.0
Cross-agency support programs	489.2
Education	153.7
Advanced business systems	103.1
Innovative partnerships program	198.1
Shared capability assets program	34.3
Exploration capabilities	6,791.7
Space operations	6,791.7
Space shuttle	4,007.5
International space station	2,238.6
Space and flight support	545.7
Inspector general	34.6
Total	**17,309.4**
Year to year change	3.1%

Note: Totals may not add due to rounding.

SOURCE: Adapted from "President's FY 2008 Budget Request," in *National Aeronautics and Space Administration: FY 2008 Budget Estimates*, National Aeronautics and Space Administration, February 5, 2007, http://www.nasa.gov/pdf/168653main_NASA_FY08_Budget_Summary.pdf (accessed October 3, 2007)

In February 2007 the NASA administrator Michael D. Griffin (1949–) outlined NASA's FY 2008 budget estimate at a news conference. The agency requested $17.3 billion, a 3.1% increase above the FY 2007 budget request. (See Table 2.7.)

Table 2.7 shows the FY 2008 budget request broken down by mission directorate and theme. The Space Shuttle Program was the single most expensive undertaking. It was estimated to cost approximately $4 billion to operate for the year. Together, the space shuttle and *ISS* programs accounted for $6.2 billion (or 36% of the entire budget) for FY 2008. They are overseen by the Space Operations Mission Directorate.

The Science Mission Directorate was the next most expensive category in the budget. NASA requested $5.5 billion to support robotic investigations of the solar system. More than $3.9 billion was devoted to the Exploration Systems Mission Directorate. This money supported research and development of new spacecraft and technologies to send human explorers to the Moon and Mars.

Table 2.8 shows NASA's expectations for future budgets through FY 2012. The long-term plan assumes that the Space Shuttle Program costs will decrease slowly until 2010 and disappear by 2012. The money saved by eliminating the shuttle program will give a funding boost to the new lunar and Martian exploration programs.

NASA'S GOALS FOR THE FUTURE

NASA's stated overall goal for the future is to improve life on Earth, while extending human life to outer space and searching for other life in the universe. NASA believes this goal will be achieved through three broad missions:

- Understanding and protecting Earth

- Exploring the universe and searching for life

- Inspiring young people to appreciate the importance of space exploration

In February 2004 NASA's goals for the twenty-first century were redefined in *The Vision for Space Exploration* (www.nasa.gov/pdf/55583main_vision_space_exploration2.pdf). In this document, President Bush articulates his goals for the nation's space program over the next few decades:

- Implementing an affordable space exploration program that includes robotic spacecraft and human explorers

- Putting astronauts on the Moon by 2020

- Developing new technologies and equipment needed to acquire data about potential destinations for human astronauts

- Promoting international and commercial participation in the exploration program

The president calls for the space shuttle fleet to be retired by 2010. NASA's participation in the *ISS* will end in 2016 with the completion of specific research objectives at the station.

NASA's plan for achieving the president's mandate includes ongoing missions, such as the Mars Exploration and Phoenix Mars missions, which will be used as stepping-stones to future exploration missions. NASA plans to use other robotic spacecraft to test new technologies and gather data about the Moon and Mars before sending humans to explore them.

Human travel to the Moon and Mars requires new launch and crew vehicles. A space shuttle cannot serve this purpose, because it was designed only for low Earth orbit. NASA no longer relies on the Saturn V rockets that lifted Apollo spacecraft into space. Under NASA's Constellation Program, new rockets called the Ares I and Ares V have been developed to propel crew and cargo

TABLE 2.8

NASA budget request, fiscal years 2009–12

[In millions]

By appropriation account By mission directorate By theme	FY 2009	FY 2010	FY 2011	FY 2012
Science, aeronautics and exploration	**$10,868.4**	**$11,364.2**	**$15,386.5**	**$15,888.6**
Science	5,555.3	5,600.6	6,656.9	5,002.7
Earth science	1,545.8	1,520.1	1,411.2	1,353.2
Heliophysics	1,028.4	1,091.3	1,241.2	1,307.5
Planetary science	1,676.9	1,720.3	1,738.3	1,748.2
Astrophysics	1,304.2	1,268.9	1,266.2	1,393.8
Exploration systems	4,312.8	4,757.8	8,725.2	9,076.8
Constellation systems	3,451.2	3,784.9	7,666.0	7,993.0
Advanced capabilities	861.6	973.0	1,059.1	1,083.9
Aeronautics research	546.7	545.3	549.8	554.7
Aeronautics technology	546.7	545.3	549.8	554.7
Cross-agency support programs	453.5	460.4	454.7	454.4
Education	152.8	152.7	149.8	149.6
Advanced business systems	69.4	71.6	67.6	67.5
Innovative partnerships program	197.2	199.8	200.0	200.0
Shared capability assets program	34.2	36.2	37.3	37.2
Exploration capabilities	**6,710.3**	**6,625.7**	**3,036.6**	**2,978.0**
Space operations	6,710.3	6,625.7	3,036.6	2,978.0
Space shuttle	3,650.9	3,634.4	116.2	0.0
International space station	2,515.1	2,609.2	2,547.5	2,600.8
Space and flight support	544.3	382.0	372.9	377.2
Inspector general	**35.5**	**36.4**	**37.3**	**38.3**
Total	17,614.2	18,026.3	18,460.4	18,905.0
Year to year change	1.8%	2.3%	2.4%	2.4%

Note: Totals may not add due to rounding.

SOURCE: Adapted from "President's FY 2008 Budget Request," in *National Aeronautics and Space Administration: FY 2008 Budget Estimates*, National Aeronautics and Space Administration, February 5, 2007, http://www.nasa.gov/pdf/168653main_NASA_FY08_Budget_Summary.pdf (accessed October 3, 2007)

into space. (See Figure 2.6.) Ares was the god of war in Greek mythology and was called Mars by the ancient Romans. NASA's new crew exploration vehicle is called Orion after the heroic hunter in Greek mythology (and a constellation of stars).

For Moon missions, NASA plans to launch both the Ares I and Ares V. The latter heavy-cargo vehicle will launch first into low Earth orbit. It will carry the earth departure stage and the lunar module needed by the astronauts to complete their journey. The crew will launch in the Orion atop the Ares I rocket. (See Figure 2.7.) Orion will be capable of docking with the *ISS*, as needed. The Orion design is based on the Apollo crew capsule, but will be roomier, with space for up to six astronauts. During Moon missions the Orion will dock with the lunar module in low Earth orbit and both will be propelled toward the Moon by the earth departure stage. When in lunar orbit, the Orion can remain untended while all the astronauts use the lunar lander to travel to the Moon's surface.

NASA expects the first manned Orion flight to the Moon to occur in 2020. This will be followed by the establishment of a lunar outpost and preparation for a crewed mission to Mars. NASA's ability to implement this long-range plan is dependent on congressional approval of projected budgets and on the successful implementation of new technologies.

FIGURE 2.6

Transition from the Space Shuttle to the Constellation spacecraft

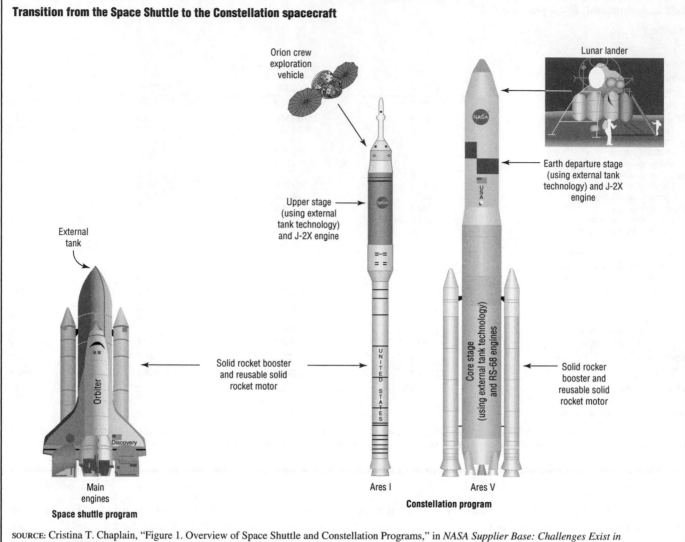

Orion crew
exploration
vehicle

Lunar lander

Upper stage
(using external
tank technology)
and J-2X engine

Earth departure stage
(using external tank
technology) and J-2X
engine

External
tank

Orbiter

Discovery

Solid rocket booster
and reusable solid
rocket motor

Core stage
(using external tank technology)
and RS-68 engines

Solid rocker
booster and
reusable solid
rocket motor

Main
engines

Ares I

Ares V

Space shuttle program

Constellation program

SOURCE: Cristina T. Chaplain, "Figure 1. Overview of Space Shuttle and Constellation Programs," in *NASA Supplier Base: Challenges Exist in Transitioning from the Space Shuttle Program to the Next Generation of Human Space Flight Systems*, U.S. Government Accountability Office, July 2007, http://www.gao.gov/new.items/d07940.pdf (accessed October 16, 2007)

FIGURE 2.7

Orion spacecraft and crew module

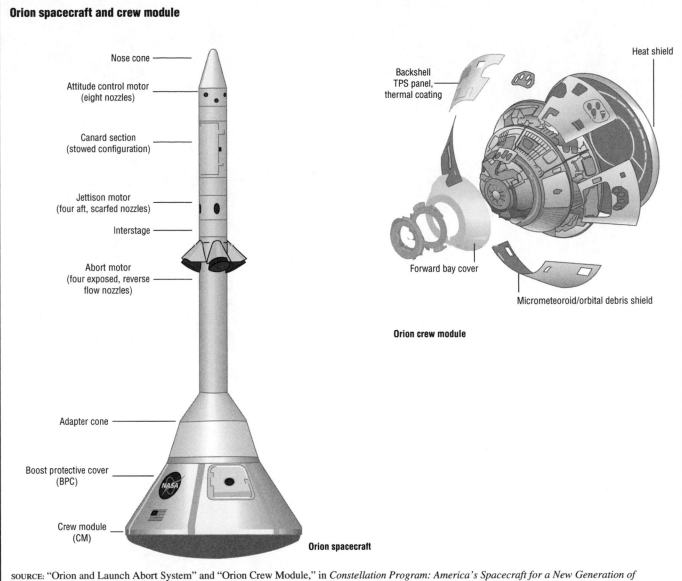

Nose cone

Attitude control motor
(eight nozzles)

Canard section
(stowed configuration)

Jettison motor
(four aft, scarfed nozzles)

Interstage

Abort motor
(four exposed, reverse
flow nozzles)

Adapter cone

Boost protective cover
(BPC)

Crew module
(CM)

NASA

Orion spacecraft

Backshell
TPS panel,
thermal coating

Heat shield

Forward bay cover

Micrometeoroid/orbital debris shield

Orion crew module

SOURCE: "Orion and Launch Abort System" and "Orion Crew Module," in *Constellation Program: America's Spacecraft for a New Generation of Explorers: The Orion Crew Exploration Vehicle*, National Aeronautics and Space Administration, 2006, http://www.nasa.gov/pdf/166914main_FS_Orion508c.pdf (accessed October 5, 2007)

CHAPTER 3
SPACE ORGANIZATIONS PART 2: U.S. MILITARY, FOREIGN, AND PRIVATE

Outer space, including the Moon and other celestial bodies, shall be free for exploration and use by all States.

—United Nations, Treaty on Principles Governing the Activities of States in the Exploration and Use of Outer Space, Including the Moon and Other Celestial Bodies (October 10, 1967)

Even though the National Aeronautics and Space Agency (NASA) is the best-known space organization in the world, it is not the only one. The U.S. military and many foreign governments also have active space programs. In fact, the U.S. military program existed even before NASA was formed. Most modern military space ventures center around ballistic missiles and data-gathering satellites. The United States officially holds the policy that it will not develop space weapons, only defensive systems. Some critics complain that the line between the two is growing vague.

Chief among the foreign governments with space programs is the Russian space program operated by the Russian Federal Space Agency (Roscosmos). The Russian agency continues the program begun by the Soviet Union decades ago. For about half of the twentieth century, the Soviet Union engaged in a bitter cold-war rivalry for space supremacy with the United States. The Soviets achieved many milestones in space ahead of the United States, including the first manned space flight in 1961.

In 1991 the Soviet Union splintered into individual nations (including Russia) that were friendlier with the United States. Civilian space agencies in the United States and Russia struggled to carry on ambitious space programs as their funding was cut. They began working together on many space ventures. Eventually, space programs were developed in Europe, China, Japan, and other countries. This presented opportunities for new alliances in space.

In the past private organizations contributed to space exploration indirectly by promoting space programs and gathering together individuals interested in rocket science, physics, astronomy, space travel, or space commerce. In 2004 the private sector opened a new era in space exploration when the first privately funded manned vehicle traveled into space and back. Private space ventures are expected to grow quickly during the twenty-first century.

U.S. MILITARY SPACE PROGRAMS

The United States must win and maintain the capability to control space in order to assure the progress and pre-eminence of the free nations.

—General Thomas White, U.S. Air Force Chief of Staff, 1959

The U.S. military had space aspirations long before spaceflight was possible. The three main branches of the military, the army, air force, and navy, began space programs following World War II (1939–1945). They sometimes collaborated, but more often they competed against each other to develop rockets, satellites, and manned space programs.

In 1958 President Dwight D. Eisenhower (1890–1969) limited the military's role in space when he created NASA as a civilian agency. NASA was given responsibility for the nation's manned space programs. The military was allowed to pursue space projects that benefited national defense. Despite the separation, the two programs still overlapped. Even in the twenty-first century NASA is dependent on military resources to carry out human space exploration projects.

The U.S. Department of Defense (DOD) operates a comprehensive space program including a missile defense system and communication, navigation, and spy satellites. Cristina T. Chaplain of the U.S. Government Accountability Office (GAO) reports in *Space Acquisitions: Actions Needed to Expand and Sustain Use of Best Practices* (April 19, 2007, http://www.gao.gov/new.items/d07730t.pdf) that the DOD budget for development and procurement of space systems in fiscal year (FY) 2008 was more than $22 billion. By comparison, NASA indicates in *National Aeronautics and Space Administration: FY 2008 Budget Estimates* (February 5, 2007, http://www.nasa.gov/pdf/168653main _NASA_FY08_Budget_Summary.pdf) that its budget request for FY 2008 was $17.3 billion.

World War II to 1955

The military space program began in earnest as World War II ended. In May 1945 a group of German rocket scientists led by Wernher von Braun (1912–1977) surrendered to U.S. forces. Under Operation Paperclip the U.S. Army signed a contract with von Braun's team and moved it to Fort Bliss, Texas, to work on the U.S. rocket program. The army also captured many German V-2 rocket parts. The von Braun team assembled the parts and launched rockets at the White Sands Proving Ground in New Mexico. On February 24, 1949, the team launched the first rocket from U.S. soil to travel beyond Earth's atmosphere and penetrate outer space. It was called *Bumper Round 5*.

Meanwhile, the U.S. Air Force had its own space program that included the development of guided missiles and robotic aircraft at the Holloman Air Force Base (AFB) near Alamogordo, New Mexico. As early as 1946 the air force was launching rockets into the upper atmosphere that carried fruit flies, fungus spores, and small mammals. An Aeromedical Field Laboratory was established at the base as part of the air force's Man in Space program. The laboratory researched the new field of space biology and conducted high-altitude balloon flights with animals and humans.

By the early 1950s the air force was launching rockets to test the effects of weightlessness and radiation on mice and monkeys. Some of the animals survived the flights, and some perished. According to John A. Pitts of NASA, in *The Human Factor: Biomedicine in the Manned Space Program to 1980* (1985), at least four rhesus monkeys died when parachutes failed to open during the descent of their spacecraft. In 1952 the air force ended its space biology program and turned toward ballistic missiles. However, by that time the air force had accumulated a wealth of knowledge and resources in the field of bioastronautics.

In 1950 the army moved von Braun's rocket team from New Mexico to the Redstone Arsenal in Huntsville, Alabama. Four years later von Braun proposed that the army launch an unmanned satellite into orbit using a Redstone missile as the main booster. The plan was eventually called Project Orbiter.

The navy also pursued rocket research following World War II using captured German rockets. The Naval Research Laboratory (NRL) in Washington, D.C., equipped V-2 rock-ets with atmospheric probes and other scientific instruments. The NRL had a long and distinguished history in scientific research. It had been established in the 1920s at the urging of the famous inventor Thomas Edison (1847–1931). The NRL invented the modern U.S. radar system and used V-2 rockets to obtain a far-ultraviolet spectrum of the Sun and to discover solar x-rays. As the supply of V-2 rockets began to run out, the NRL developed its own rockets called Vikings and Aerobees.

1955 to 1958

In 1955 the United States decided to launch an unmanned satellite as part of the International Geophysical Year (IGY) project. The IGY was to run from July 1957 to December 1958. Various government agencies submitted proposals to develop the satellite. These included proposals from all three military branches: the army's Project Orbiter, based on a Redstone rocket; an air force proposal, based on an Atlas rocket; and the navy's Project Vanguard, based on a Viking missile. Project Vanguard was selected, and the NRL was delegated responsibility for developing the satellite and including a scientific experiment on it.

The first test flights of Project Vanguard were conducted in December 1956 and May 1957. Even though both tests were successful, the project proceeded slowly. In October 1957 the Soviet Union successfully launched *Sputnik 1*, the world's first artificial satellite, into Earth orbit. The United States was stunned that the Soviets had achieved this great milestone. In response, the DOD pressured the navy to accelerate the Vanguard schedule. In early November 1957 the Soviets launched *Sputnik 2* with a dog named Laika aboard.

Meanwhile, von Braun's team at the Redstone Arsenal had developed the Jupiter ballistic missile. Throughout the mid-1950s the army had tried to convince the DOD that a Redstone or Jupiter rocket should be used to put a satellite into orbit. After *Sputnik 1* the DOD was ready to listen. In November 1957 the army was authorized to pursue Project Explorer as a backup to Project Vanguard. A month later the first full-scale Vanguard launch attempt failed when the rocket exploded two seconds after liftoff.

On January 31, 1958, the army successfully launched into space *Explorer 1*, the first U.S. satellite, using a Jupiter-C rocket. The satellite was eighty inches long and six and a quarter inches wide and weighed nearly thirty-one pounds. The scientific payload included temperature gauges and instruments to detect cosmic rays and the impacts of micrometeorites. The payload was developed under the direction of James Van Allen (1914–2006), a physics professor at the University of Iowa. Data from *Explorer 1* and the later *Explorer 3* satellite led to Van Allen's discovery of radiation belts around Earth. The existence of the belts was confirmed in 1958 by the Soviet satellite *Sputnik 3*. (See Figure 3.1.)

FIGURE 3.1

Sputnik 3

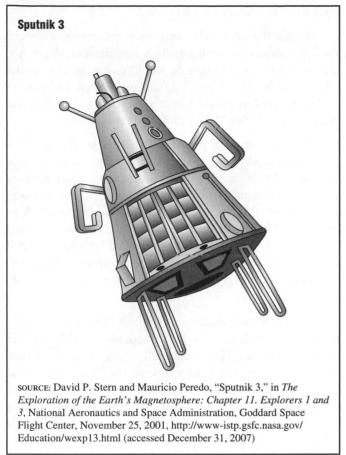

SOURCE: David P. Stern and Mauricio Peredo, "Sputnik 3," in *The Exploration of the Earth's Magnetosphere: Chapter 11. Explorers 1 and 3*, National Aeronautics and Space Administration, Goddard Space Flight Center, November 25, 2001, http://www.istp.gsfc.nasa.gov/Education/wexp13.html (accessed December 31, 2007)

On March 17, 1958, the navy finally got its *Vanguard* satellite into orbit. *Vanguard Test Vehicle 4* was launched at Cape Canaveral, Florida, and put the grapefruit-sized, three-pound satellite into Earth orbit. It was the first orbiting satellite to be powered by solar energy. Solar cells also powered its radio until the radio failed in 1964. As of March 2008, the silent *Vanguard* satellite continued to orbit Earth. It has remained in orbit longer than any human-made object in space.

The satellite successes of the 1950s encouraged the air force's space ambitions. It began planning a manned spaceflight program called Dyna-Soar (short for Dynamic Soaring). This was to be an aircraft based on the X-15 experimental plane that could be launched into orbit by a missile, but glide back to Earth and land on an airstrip. Another project was called Man in Space Soonest (MISS). MISS called for a manned satellite to be launched by 1960, a manned laboratory to be in Earth orbit by 1963, and a manned lunar landing to take place by 1965.

In June 1958 the air force announced a list of test pilots chosen to participate in the MISS project. (The list included only one pilot who eventually became an astronaut: Neil A. Armstrong [1930–].) These would have been the very first American astronauts. Four months later, NASA was formed and took responsibility for manned spaceflights. Dynasoar and MISS were canceled. Most of the would-be astronauts were given NASA assignments.

NASA Takes Over

Throughout the 1950s the air force had lobbied congressional leaders to be given control of the nation's space program. The air force had excellent launch capabilities and extensive research and development capabilities in space science and bioastronautics.

According to Homer E. Newell of NASA, in *Beyond the Atmosphere: Early Years of Space Science* (1980), President Eisenhower feared that militarizing the nation's space program would accelerate the nuclear arms race with the Soviet Union and locate too much political power within the U.S. military-industrial complex. Many scientists were also opposed to military control of the space program. They feared that weapon development and manned space flights would receive priority over scientific objectives. As a compromise, several prominent U.S. scientists urged Congress to divide the space program into two parts, with manned programs operated by the military and science programs operated by NASA. In 1958, when the agency was put into operation, President Eisenhower decided to allow NASA to run the nation's space program.

Over the next few years most of the military's space programs, assets, and resources were turned over to NASA. The new agency was dependent on military scientists with expertise in space science, particularly those of the air force. Even after NASA was created, air force officials continued to lobby political leaders for control of space programs. In January 1961 President-elect John F. Kennedy (1917–1963) received a report from his science adviser, Jerome B. Wiesner (1915–1994), that was very critical of NASA and its plans to develop manned space projects. Some observers interpreted the report as promoting military control of the nation's space program.

Courtney G. Brooks, James M. Grimwood, and Loyd S. Swenson Jr. of NASA explain in *Chariots for Apollo: A History of Manned Lunar Spacecraft* (1979) that at the time NASA was engaged in the Mercury project and was also planning the Apollo trips to the Moon. The air force's Space Systems Division (SSD) proposed its own post-Mercury project called Lunex that promised to put three men on the Moon by 1967. The SSD estimated the cost of the project at $7.5 billion.

The army's plan for a manned spaceflight was called Project Adam. It called for one astronaut to be sealed inside a capsule atop a ballistic missile for his ride into orbit. Even though the army had excellent launch capabilities and rocket technology, it lacked expertise in bioastronautics. Project Adam did not include any monitoring of the human during his spaceflight to gain medical knowledge. The army also advocated a military outpost on the Moon as part of Project Horizon. This ambitious plan included a dock and fueling station in orbit around Earth.

The navy had its own plan for a manned spaceflight project called the Manned Earth Reconnaissance Project. However, the navy's space reputation was hurt by the poor performance of the Vanguard program. Also, the navy was dependent on the air force for launch facilities and bioastronautics capabilities.

NASA had its share of influential supporters, including Overton Brooks (1897–1961), the chairman of the House Committee on Science and Astronautics, and Vice President Lyndon B. Johnson (1908–1973). Neither wanted the military to control the nation's space ventures. In March 1961 Brooks wrote the president a letter in which he pushed Kennedy to make clear his intentions on the matter. Kennedy responded that he did not intend to "subordinate" NASA under military control. He increased NASA's budget and gave the agency responsibility for a manned lunar spaceflight.

NASA received assistance from the air force regarding several aspects of the early space programs. During the 1950s the air force obtained infant chimpanzees and monkeys that were trained at the Holloman AFB for spaceflights. Many of the animals were not named. A rhesus monkey named Sam (after the air force School of Aviation Medicine) flew aboard a Mercury test flight in 1959.

Another chimp was named Ham (an acronym for Holloman Aero Medical). During 1961 NASA launched Ham and another "chimponaut" named Enos into outer space to orbit Earth. The air force continued to run a space chimp colony until 1997, when twenty-one chimps were turned over to Save the Chimps (2004, http://www.savethechimps.org/about.asp), a chimpanzee rescue group in Florida.

Military and Intelligence Satellites

Following the formation of NASA, the U.S. military focused most of its space resources on the development of ballistic missiles and satellites. Satellites were designed for a variety of purposes, including communications, navigation, weather surveillance, and reconnaissance (spying).

During the late 1950s the air force worked with the Central Intelligence Agency to develop a reconnaissance satellite capable of photographing Soviet installations on the ground from space. The project was code-named Corona. Publicly, the United States called the satellite *Discoverer* and claimed that it conducted scientific research. More than one hundred Corona missions were flown during the 1960s and early 1970s. The Soviet

Union orbited its own spy satellites and also claimed that they were for scientific purposes.

Before the 1980s all satellites were launched aboard rockets called expendable launch vehicles (ELVs). Once above Earth's atmosphere, a satellite separated from its ELV, and the ELV burned up during reentry. During the 1970s the air force used a number of ELVs including the Scout, Thor, Delta, Atlas, and Titan rockets.

The development of the space shuttle introduced a new era in satellite deployment. The shuttle was reusable and included a crew of astronauts that could release, retrieve, and repair satellites as needed. The military was excited about this prospect. During space shuttle development the DOD insisted that the vehicles be designed to carry heavy military satellites and be able to orbit Earth along a polar path. Both requirements added substantially to the cost of the shuttle program and slowed its development.

The air force was given responsibility for developing a shuttle launch site at the Vandenberg AFB on the California coast. This would allow the shuttle to take off in a southerly direction toward the South Pole. The air force also developed a rocket for the shuttle program called the Interim Upper Stage (IUS). IUS boosters were designed to thrust satellites from the shuttle's typical orbit into higher orbits.

The first shuttle flight did not take place until April 1981. In June 1982 a shuttle carried a military satellite into orbit for the first time. In "Shuttle Missions" (February 23, 2008, http://www.nasa.gov/mission_pages/shuttle/shuttlemissions/list_main.html), NASA notes that shuttles carried six subsequent DOD satellites into space between 1984 and 1985. Four of these satellites were SYNCOM communication satellites. The other two missions were classified.

When the shuttle was first proposed, NASA promised that it would fly frequently and routinely into Earth orbit and would meet the military's scheduling demands for satellite launches. It soon became apparent that this was not the case. The shuttle program was plagued by problems and flew only a few times each year. The DOD decided it could not rely completely on shuttles for the nation's military missions. In 1984 air force officials convinced Congress to fund development of a fleet of new ELVs for military missions. NASA protested strongly against this action, but was overruled.

The initiative turned out to be a good one. The explosion of the space shuttle *Challenger* shortly after liftoff in 1986 forced NASA to make drastic changes in the shuttle program. This had profound effects on the military's space ambitions. The *Challenger* explosion happened only months before the first planned launch of a space shuttle for air force purposes from the Vandenberg AFB. Because of the changes made to NASA's program, the base's shuttle launch facilities were dismantled and most of the related equipment was turned over to NASA. The DOD focused more resources on developing ELVs.

In September 1988 the space shuttle resumed flying. NASA indicates in "Shuttle Missions" that between 1988 and 1992 shuttles carried less than ten military payloads into space. These were satellites that could not be launched aboard ELVs for various reasons.

Star Wars

On March 23, 1983, President Ronald Reagan (1911–2004) announced a new military space venture for the United States: the Space Defense Initiative (SDI). Basically, the plan called for the placement of a satellite shield in space that would protect the United States from incoming Soviet nuclear missiles. Reagan said the SDI would make nuclear weapons "impotent and obsolete."

According to the public broadcasting series *American Experience* (2000, http://www.pbs.org/wgbh/amex/reagan/index.html), earlier that month Reagan had denounced the Soviet Union as the "focus of evil in the modern world." The Soviet news agency TASS responded that Reagan was full of "bellicose lunatic anti-communism." Reagan's SDI proposal heightened tensions between the two countries. The Soviets warned that it would set off a new and more dangerous arms race. Later that year the Soviet Union broke off nuclear arms negotiations in Geneva, Switzerland.

The media nicknamed the SDI proposal the "Star Wars" program. (*Star Wars* had been a hit 1977 movie featuring elaborate space weapons.) Many scientists publicly questioned whether the SDI was technically feasible given the technologies of the times, major newspapers openly ridiculed the idea, and politicians complained about the potential costs. Discovering whether the SDI was even possible was expected to be immensely expensive. Some high-ranking government officials feared that the SDI would start an arms race in space.

In March 1984 the DOD established the Strategic Defense Initiative Organization (SDIO). Later that year the army successfully tested an interceptor missile as part of SDIO operations. The missile was launched from the Kwajalein Missile Range in the Marshall Islands. It flew above the atmosphere and then located and tracked a reentry missile that had been launched from the Vandenberg AFB. The interceptor missile homed in on the target using onboard sensors and computer targeting. It crashed into the target and destroyed it.

Reagan met with Soviet premier Mikhail Gorbachev (1931–) for private talks during 1985 and 1986. Both times they argued about the SDI. In a 1986 meeting in Reykjavik, Iceland, Gorbachev offered to cut Soviet mis-

sile stocks if the United States would cease development of the SDI project. Reagan refused. By this time the military had developed a working concept for the space shield that included many small, computerized satellites. The concept was called Brilliant Pebbles.

In 1989 President George H. W. Bush (1924–) assumed office. He supported the SDI project, so research and development on it continued. Two years later, the United States entered the Persian Gulf War (1990–1991) against Iraq. By this time the Soviet Union had dissolved into a number of independent republics. In 1993, during the administration of President Bill Clinton (1946–), the SDIO was redesignated the Ballistic Defense Missile Organization (BDMO). The new threat was considered to be limited-range missiles in the hands of unfriendly dictators and terrorists.

In 2002 the United States withdrew from the Anti-Ballistic Missile Treaty of 1972. This treaty with the Soviet Union (and later Russia) had strictly limited each nation's deployment of antiballistic missiles. Soon afterward, President George W. Bush (1946–) converted the BDMO into the Missile Defense Agency (MDA).

The goal of the MDA (July 10, 2007, http://www.mda.mil/mdalink/html/basics.html) is to intercept and destroy ballistic missiles along their flight path. There are three flight phases for an intercontinental ballistic missile (ICBM): boost phase, midcourse phase, and terminal phase. The boost phase occurs during the first three to five minutes after an ICBM is launched, when it is being powered by its engines. During the boost phase an ICBM can reach an altitude of up to three hundred miles. The midcourse stage takes the ICBM on a trajectory above the atmosphere through space and can last up to twenty minutes. During this phase the missile can release countermeasures and decoys. Once the missile reenters Earth's atmosphere it is in the terminal phase of its flight. This can last from thirty seconds to one minute. Preferably, interception and destruction would be done outside of Earth's atmosphere so that nuclear or biological warheads would be destroyed during reentry.

Space-Based Missile Defense Systems

As of March 2008, the DOD continued the development and testing of components for the ballistic missile defense system (BMDS). These include ground- and sea-based interceptor missiles and space-based tracking systems. Things that were once considered science fiction are slowly becoming viable components in the DOD arsenal. This is because of technological advances and a large influx of money to the program. MDA funding increased from $1.3 billion in FY 1985 to $9.5 billion in FY 2007. (See Figure 3.2.)

Since the 1970s the United States has relied on a space-based early missile warning system called the

FIGURE 3.2

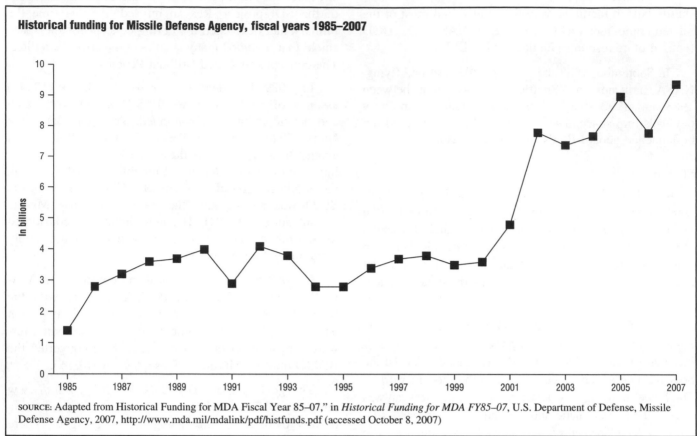

Historical funding for Missile Defense Agency, fiscal years 1985–2007

SOURCE: Adapted from Historical Funding for MDA Fiscal Year 85–07," in *Historical Funding for MDA FY85–07*, U.S. Department of Defense, Missile Defense Agency, 2007, http://www.mda.mil/mdalink/pdf/histfunds.pdf (accessed October 8, 2007)

Defense Support Program (DSP). The U.S. Air Force explains in the fact sheet "Defense Support Program Satellites" (January 2008, http://www.af.mil/factsheets/factsheet.asp?id=96) that the DSP consists of a series of satellites in geosynchronous orbit 22,300 miles from Earth's surface. The twenty-third (and reportedly last) launch of a DSP satellite took place in November 2007 at Cape Canaveral, Florida.

In 1996 the DOD began development of a replacement for the DSP called the Space Based Infrared System (SBIRS). The history and status of this system is described by the GAO in *Space Based Infrared System High Program and Its Alternative* (September 12, 2007, http://www.gao.gov/new.items/d071088r.pdf). According to the GAO, the initial program included satellites in high and low orbits around Earth. In 2001 the low-orbit program was renamed the Space Tracking and Surveillance System (STSS). Figure 3.3 compares the DSP, the SBIRS, and the STSS systems in terms of tracking capabilities. The new satellites are expected to be much more sensitive and accurate than existing DSP satellites. The GAO notes that the cost of the new systems has sky-rocketed from an original $4.2 billion estimate to $10.4 billion. The first new satellites were supposed to deploy in 2004; however, this schedule proved unfeasible. The GAO suggests that the "SBIRS has been burdened by

immature technologies, unclear requirements, unstable funding, underestimated software complexity, poor over-sight, and other problems that have resulted in billions of dollars in cost overruns and years in schedule delays."

In 2006 the DOD initiated the Alternative Infrared Satellite System (AIRSS) in case the SBIRS becomes unviable to complete. However, the GAO notes that the AIRSS suffers from technological and budget problems and will not likely produce an operational satellite by its proposed launch date of 2015.

Criticism

The nation's ballistic missile defense systems have evoked severe criticism from some in the scientific community. One of the most vocal critics is the Union of Concerned Scientists (USC), an organization of independent scientists who research and analyze policy issues, such as the environment and missile development. In 2004 the USC issued the report *Technical Realities: An Analysis of the 2004 Deployment of a U.S. National Missile Defense System* (http://www.ucsusa.org/global_security/missile_defense/technical-realities-national-missile-defense-deployment-in-2004.html) by Lisbeth Gronlund et al., who state, "The ballistic missile defense system that the United States will deploy later this year will have no demonstrated defensive capability and will be ineffective

FIGURE 3.3

Comparison of space based infrared systems

Capabilities

Legacy system: defense support program (DSP)
- Missile warning (with a classified probability of detection) for North America
- Detection and reporting of strategic and theater ballistic missiles and other infrared events of interest

In development: SBIRS high
- DSP successor
- Higher sensitivity—sees dimmer objects, more often
- Taskable sensor—can do many missions at once
- More accurate estimate of missile location—including launch point and impact point

In development: space tracking and surveillance system
- Space tracking and surveillance system formerly called SBIRS Low
- Critical element of the groundbased midcourse defense—managed by missile defense agency
- Tracks threat missiles through entire flight—from launch to intercept
- Sees extremely dim targets—can track and discriminate objects that are not burning
- Inherent capabilities also support other missions

Missions	DSP	SBIRS H	STSS
Missile warning	X	X	o
Missile defense		X	X
Technical intel		X	o
Battlespace characterization		X	o

X – Primary mission   o – Offers inherent capability

Note: SBIRS is space-based infrared system.

SOURCE: "Background: Space Based Infrared Systems," in *Space Based Infrared System High Program and Its Alternative*, U.S. Government Accountability Office, September 12, 2007, http://www.gao.gov/new. items/d071088r.pdf (accessed October 16, 2007)

against a real attack by long-range ballistic missiles. The administration's claims that the system will be reliable and highly effective are irresponsible exaggerations. There is no technical justification for deployment of the system, nor are there sound reasons to procure and deploy additional interceptors."

Gronlund et al. advocate new nonproliferation treaties with Russia and China to prevent an arms race in space between the three countries.

Space Weapons?

Historically, the United States has focused on developing defensive, rather than offensive, space-based assets. It is a party to the 1967 Treaty on Principles Governing the Activities of States in the Exploration and Use of Outer Space, Including the Moon and Other Celestial Bodies (January 1, 2004, http://www.state.gov/t/ac/trt/5181.htm), which states that nations may not "place in orbit around the Earth any objects carrying nuclear weapons or any other kinds of weapons of mass destruction, install such weapons on celestial bodies, or station such weapons in outer space

in any other manner." In addition, presidential space policy since the 1950s has focused on unarmed satellites to prevent a new arms race in space.

Tim Weiner reports in "Air Force Seeks Bush's Approval for Space Arms" (*New York Times*, May 18, 2005) that in 2005 the Bush administration was considering a change in space policy to allow the development of space weapons. Weiner claims that the air force wanted the capability to develop offensive and defensive space assets to protect the country. An air force spokesperson denied that the new policy would militarize space, but stated that it would ensure the United States has "free access in space." According to Weiner, the potential policy change drew objections from leaders in Canada, China, Russia, and the European Union. Critics fear that such a move would encourage countries such as China and Russia to build their own space weapons. Proponents argue that the United States must develop new space capabilities to protect vulnerable satellites on which the nation depends for communications, global positioning data, and military reconnaissance.

Weiner notes that a change in space policy would face many technical, financial, and diplomatic challenges. Critics argue that billions of dollars have been spent on missile defense systems that have not proven to be reliable. They fear that development of space weapons would be a wasteful expense and do little to combat the spread and very real threat of terrorist strikes.

Some critics complain that assets already being developed by the DOD are preludes to space weapons. In "Space Weapons Spending in the FY 2008 Defense Budget" (February 21, 2007, http://www.cdi.org/), Theresa Hitchens, Victoria Samson, and Sam Black suggest that "in the absence of a clear national consensus on military missions in space, the administration of George W. Bush is continuing to fund research that could result in the development and/or deployment of anti-satellite and space-based weapons." The researchers highlight five specific projects that they claim are included in the DOD's proposed budget for FY 2008:

- Space-Based Interceptor Test Bed—the DOD describes this as "a space-based defensive layer to complement the BMDS." The layer would be composed of defensive satellites capable of intercepting and killing enemy ballistic missiles.

- Near Field Infrared Experiment (NFIRE)—this satellite would carry infrared sensors capable of detecting and tracking ballistic missiles during their boost phase. The MDA's original proposal for NFIRE included a "kill vehicle" aboard the satellite that could be released to smash into a missile and destroy it in space. In 2004 the kill vehicle was canceled. Officially, the DOD cited technical reasons for the cancellation. However, critics believe that the agency backed down in the face of intense criticism for proposing an obvious space weapon. There is concern that that the satellite could still be used for destructive purposes.

- Experimental Spacecraft System (XSS)—this system consists of small, mobile satellites that can be maneuvered up to other orbiting objects and take pictures of them. The first microsatellite, *XSS-10*, was successfully tested in space in 2003 during a one-day trial. Even though the Pentagon denies that the XSS satellites are space weapons, critics claim it would be relatively easy to convert their photographic capabilities to firepower. Then they could seek out and destroy targets in orbit, such as the satellites of unfriendly countries. The development of antisatellite weapons is highly controversial. In 2005 the air force launched the much more sophisticated *XSS-11* into space. The satellite was about the size of a washing machine and weighed around two hundred pounds. Various news reports indicate that its tests were highly successful.

- Autonomous Nonsatellite Guardian for Evaluating Local Space (ANGELS)—ANGELS is the successor to the XSS program, but features satellites orbiting at a much higher altitude and with greater capabilities.

- Starfire Optical Range—these experiments are believed to involve advanced weapons systems including lasers that could be used against enemy satellites.

Other space weapons reportedly being considered by the DOD include the Common Aero Vehicle (CAV) and hypervelocity rods. The CAV would deliver high explosives from space with the capability to bomb targets thousands of miles from the United States. Hypervelocity rods are long metallic rods that would be delivered from space and—having built up tremendous speed during the long fall to Earth—smash into and destroy deep underground bunkers. They have been nicknamed "Rods from God" by the media.

U.S. Strategic Command

In 1985 the Reagan administration established the U.S. Space Command to oversee military space operations. Its commander was also in charge of the North American Aerospace Defense command, which protects the U.S. and Canadian air space. In 1992 President George H. W. Bush established the U.S. Strategic Command (StratCom) to oversee the nation's nuclear arsenal.

Following the terrorist attacks of September 11, 2001, President George W. Bush abolished the U.S. Space Command and assigned its responsibilities to StratCom, which is headquartered at the Offutt AFB in Nebraska. It is the command and control center for U.S. strategic forces, controls military space operations, and is responsible for early warning and defense against missile attacks.

StratCom has four space-related missions:

- Conduct satellite launches and operations including telemetry, tracking, and command. Satellite launches take place at Cape Canaveral, Florida, and the Vandenberg AFB in California.

- Support U.S. armed forces via use of communication, navigation, weather, missile warning, and intelligence satellites.

- Protect U.S. access to space and deny access to enemies.

- Research and develop space assets that can engage enemies from space. Such projects cannot at present be implemented due to long-standing U.S. policy against deploying orbiting weapons.

AIR FORCE SPACE COMMAND. Much of StratCom's space operations are carried out by the Air Force Space Command (AFSPC), which is headquartered at the Peterson AFB in Colorado. The AFSPC has facilities at three other Colorado locations (Cheyenne Mountain Air Station, Schriever AFB, and Buckley AFB) and in Alaska, California, Florida, North Dakota, Wyoming, Montana, New Hampshire, and Greenland.

The AFSPC operates the Global Positioning System and launches and operates satellites that provide weather, communications, intelligence, navigation, and missile warning capabilities. The command also provides services, facilities, and aerospace control for NASA operations. In 2004 the AFSPC established the National Security Space Institute to provide education and training in space-based topics.

The AFSPC's Space Control Center maintains a database of more than nine thousand objects known to be in Earth orbit. These include operating and inoperative satellites, pieces of rockets, and other objects. When a space shuttle mission is taking place, the center tracks the shuttle's path and establishes a twenty-five-mile-wide safety zone around the vehicle. (See Figure 3.4.) If the center determines that an object is on a collision path with the shuttle, the center notifies NASA so that evasive maneuvers can be performed.

The DOD Manned Space Flight Support Office

In 1958 the U.S. government established the DOD Manned Space Flight Support Office (DDMS) to support NASA's manned space flight programs. The DDMS provided medical support and communications, tracking, and data capabilities, and recovered astronauts and space capsules after splashdown for all manned programs from Mercury (1959–1963) through *Skylab* (1973–1974).

When the Space Shuttle Program began in the 1980s, the DDMS assumed responsibility for astronaut rescue and recovery, payload security, and a variety of contingency

FIGURE 3.4

Orbiter safety zone

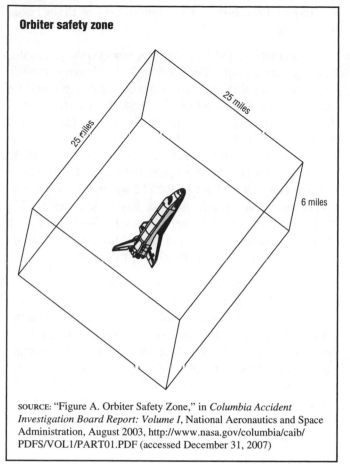

25 miles

25 miles

6 miles

SOURCE: "Figure A. Orbiter Safety Zone," in *Columbia Accident Investigation Board Report: Volume I*, National Aeronautics and Space Administration, August 2003, http://www.nasa.gov/columbia/caib/PDFS/VOL1/PART01.PDF (accessed December 31, 2007)

TABLE 3.1

International space agencies

Country	Name	Acronym
Argentina	Comisión Nacional de Investigaciones Espaciales	CONAE
Australia	Australian Space Office	ASO
Austria	Österreichische Gesellschaft für Weltraumfragen Ges.m.b.H (Austrian Space Agency)	ASA
Belgium	Belgium Federal Science Policy Office	SPO
Brazil	Agência Espacial Brasileira	AED
Bulgaria	Bulgarian Aerospace Agency	BASA
Canada	Canadian Space Agency	CSA
China	China National Space Administration	CNSA
Denmark	Dansk Rumforsknignsinstitut (Danish Space Research Institute)	DSRI
Finland	National Technology Agency of Finland	Tekes
France	Centre National d'Etudes Spatiales	CNES
Germany	Deutschen Zentrum für Luft- und Raumfahrt	DLR
Hungary	Magyar Ürkutatási Iroda (Hungarian Space Office)	HSO
India	Indian Space Research Organisation	ISRO
Indonesia	National Institute of Aeronautics & Space	I APAN
Israel	Israel Space Agency	ISA
Italy	Agenzia Spaziale Italiana	ASI
Japan	Japan Aerospace Exploration Agency	JAXA
Korea	Korea Aerospace Research Institute	KARI
Netherlands	Nationaal Lucht-en Ruimtevaartlaboratorium (National Aerospace Laboratory)	NAL
Norway	Norsk Romsenter (Norwegian Space Centre)	NSC
Poland	Space Research Centre	SRC
Portugal	Instituto Nacional de Engenharia e Tecnologia Industrial	INETI
Romania	Romanian Space Agency	ROSA
Russia	Russian Federal Space Agency	Roscosmos
Spain	Instituto Nacional de Técnica Aeroespacial	INTA
Sweden	Swedish National Space Board	SNSB
Ukraine	National Space Agency of Ukraine	NSAU
United Kingdom	British National Space Centre	BNSC

SOURCE: Created by Kim Masters Evans for Gale, Cengage Learning, 2008

services in the event of an emergency. Located near the Kennedy Space Center in Florida, the DDMS has at its disposal a number of air force and navy resources including helicopters, tanker aircraft, ships, air traffic control facilities, and medical and search-and-rescue personnel. The DDMS also supports potential emergency landing sites in Spain, Morocco, and Gambia.

SPACE AGENCIES AROUND THE WORLD

NASA and Roscosmos operate the two most active space programs in the world. Roscosmos evolved from the Soviet space agency. The Soviet space program achieved many important milestones in robotic and human spaceflight. Other nations with the resources to do so have ventured into space. Some have sent their astronauts aboard U.S., Soviet, or Russian spacecraft. Others have developed their own space vehicles and programs. This has created new opportunities for cooperation and competition among space-faring nations.

Table 3.1 lists the space agencies of various countries around the world. A few of the major programs are described in this chapter.

RUSSIA

The Russian Space Agency was officially created on February 25, 1992, by decree of the president of the Russian Federation. The agency inherited the technologies, programs, and facilities of the Soviet Union space program. In 1999 it was expanded to include the aviation industry, so its name was changed to the Russian Space and Aviation Agency (Rosaviakosmos). The aviation responsibilities were removed in 2004, so the agency was renamed the Russian Federal Space Agency (Roscosmos).

Sergei Korolëv

Sergei Korolëv (1906–1966) is considered the founder of the Soviet space program. Korolëv was born in Zhitomir, a town in what is now Ukraine. An engineer and aviator who began building rockets in the 1930s, he founded the rocket organization Gruppa Isutcheniya Reaktivnovo Dvisheniya (Group for Investigation of Reactive Motion). Following World War II the government appointed him to develop Soviet missile systems.

In August 1957 his team successfully tested the R-7, the world's first ICBM. The R-7 was powerful enough to carry a nuclear warhead to the United States or a satellite into outer space. In October 1957 an R-7 rocket carried

Sputnik 1 into orbit. The Soviet Union had beaten the United States into space.

VOSTOK. Korolëv's next challenge was to beat the United States to the Moon. In January 1959 the Soviet probe *Luna 1* flew past the Moon. In September 1959 *Luna 2* was deliberately crashed into the lunar surface, making it the first human-made object to reach the Moon. A month later *Luna 3* took the first photographs of the far side of the Moon. Korolëv was already working on a spacecraft for manned missions. It was a modified R-7 called Vostok. The Vostok included a sphere-shaped cosmonaut module that held one person. The module was too heavy for a parachute. Instead, it included an ejection seat so that the cosmonaut could eject from the module following reentry and parachute to Earth by himself.

Throughout 1960 and early 1961 the Vostok was tested unmanned, with dogs, small mammals, and a mannequin aboard. Vostok flying dogs included Strelka, Belka, Pchelka, Mushka, Chernushka, and Zvezdochka. Many of the dogs died during these tests. The mannequin was nicknamed Ivan Ivanovich, which is the Russian equivalent of "John Doe."

On April 12, 1961, the Soviets launched the first man into space aboard *Vostok 1*. His name was Yuri Gagarin (1934–1968). He was one of the twenty original cosmonauts selected by the Soviet Union in 1959 for manned spaceflights. In 1960 they began training at a sprawling new complex called Zvezdny Gorodok (Star City) in the Russian countryside. His flight made one orbit before he reentered the atmosphere and parachuted safely from the module, landing in a field. In total, his mission lasted one hour and forty-eight minutes. The following month, on May 5, 1961, the astronaut Alan B. Shepard Jr. (1923–1998) became the first American in space.

There were five more Vostok flights from 1961 through 1963. *Vostok 2* carried Gherman Titov (1935–2000) to seventeen orbits around Earth on August 6–7, 1961. *Vostok 3* and *Vostok 4* were launched only one day apart on August 11 and August 12, 1962, respectively. *Vostok 3* carried Andriyan Nikolayev (1929–2004), and *Vostok 4* carried Pavel Popovich (1930–). The two cosmonauts landed within minutes of each other on August 15, 1962. In June 1963 *Vostok 5* and *Vostok 6* also conducted a joint operation. *Vostok 5* launched on June 15 with Valery Bykovsky (1934–) aboard. It was followed one day later by *Vostok 6* with Valentina Tereshkova (1937–) aboard. Tereshkova was the first woman in space and had been personally selected for the task by Korolëv. The two cosmonauts returned to Earth on June 19, 1963.

The Vostok program and the U.S. Mercury project both took place between 1961 and 1963. The Soviet cosmonauts beat the U.S. astronauts into space and spent more time there. The longest Mercury flight lasted only one day and ten hours. The longest Vostok flight lasted nearly five days.

VOSKHOD. In 1964 the Soviets began testing a multipassenger spacecraft called Voskhod. The Voskhod module had a parachute descent system that eliminated the need for ejection seats. On October 12, 1964, *Voskhod 1* carried three men into space: Vladimir Komarov (1927–1967), the pilot; Boris Yegorov (1937–1994), a physician; and Konstantin Feoktistov (1926–), a scientist. Their flight lasted just over twenty-four hours and circled Earth sixteen times. A few months later *Voskhod 2* was put into orbit with two cosmonauts aboard: the pilot Pavel Belyayev (1925–1970) and the copilot Alexei Leonov (1934–). On March 18, 1965, Leonov conducted the first extravehicular activity (space walk) in history. It lasted twenty minutes.

Despite these successes, the *Voskhod 2* mission was plagued by life-threatening problems. Leonov's spacesuit and the vehicle's airlock and reentry rockets malfunctioned. The crew module spun out of control during reentry and landed in heavy woods far from its intended landing point. At the time, a number of crewed Voskhod missions were planned for the 1960s, including one with an allfemale crew. However, the problems of *Voskhod 2* and the death of Korolëv in January 1966 shook the Soviet space agency. All these planned missions were canceled.

N-1 ROCKET. During his lifetime, Korolëv was relatively unknown outside the Soviet Union. The Soviets were very secretive about national affairs and provided scant information to the foreign media. This was particularly true for the inner workings of the Soviet space program. It was only following Korolëv's death that the Western world learned about his many contributions to space travel. These included many rockets and launch vehicles, satellites and probes of different types, and manned spacecraft. His most famous spacecraft was the Soyuz. Modified versions of Soyuz rockets are still being used by Roscosmos in the twenty-first century.

Korolëv is also remembered for his one great failure: the N-1 rocket. This was supposed to be the superbooster that would launch a Soviet spacecraft called the L1 (or Zond) to the Moon. Korolëv's design team created the L1 from a modified Soyuz spacecraft. The N-1 superbooster was similar in scope to von Braun's Saturn V rocket. Korolëv worked on the N-1 project from 1962 until his death in 1966, but he never achieved an operational rocket. His successors continued the work after his death, but they, too, were unsuccessful.

On July 3, 1969, an unmanned N-1 rocket exploded only seconds before liftoff. The resulting fireball was so huge it destroyed the launch facilities. Thirteen days later a Saturn V rocket launched *Apollo 11* on its way to the Moon.

The Soviet space program was shrouded in secrecy. Successes were publicized, whereas failures and plans were not. Even though the Soviets had ambitions to land a man on the Moon, this goal was never announced publicly. It was only years later that the West learned about the failed Soviet Moon program in Sergei Leskov's article "How We Didn't Get to the Moon" (*Izvestiya*, August 18, 1989). Most observers in the United States assumed that the Soviet Union was aiming for the Moon, but this was not certain. In fact, as early as 1963 NASA critics in the United States asserted that the "Moon race" was a hoax advanced by the U.S. government to further its own aims. When the United States reached the Moon first, the Soviets insisted that they had never intended to go there. In "Yes, There Was a Moon Race" (*Air Force Magazine*, vol. 73, no. 4, April 1990), James E. Oberg states that "examination of newly disclosed evidence about one of the most intense phases of the superpower rivalry makes plain that US actions came in response to an authentic Soviet challenge."

Firsts in Space

Despite losing the Moon race, the Soviet space program achieved many firsts in space during the 1950s and 1960s:

- *Sputnik 1*—the first artificial satellite in orbit (October 4, 1957)

- *Sputnik 2*—the first space passenger, Laika the dog, spent eleven days in orbit (November 3, 1957)

- *Luna 2*—the first artificial object to reach a celestial body (September 14, 1959)

- *Vostok 1*—Gagarin is the first person to orbit Earth (April 12, 1961)

- *Vostok 2*—Titov is the first person to spend a full day in orbit (August 6–7, 1961)

- *Vostok 3* and *Vostok 4*—first spaceflight including two spacecraft in orbit at once (August 11–15, 1962)

- *Vostok 6*—Tereshkova is the first woman in space (June 16, 1963)

- *Voskhod 1*—first spaceflight including three people (October 12–13, 1964)

- *Voskhod 2*—Leonov is the first person to take a space walk (March 18, 1965)

The Soviet space program also experienced a tragic first in space. On April 23, 1967, the Soviet space agency launched *Soyuz 1* with Vladimir Komarov (1927–1967) aboard. A day later the flight ended in tragedy when the module's parachute failed during descent. Komarov died during the descent. He was the first human to die during a spaceflight. On June 30, 1971, three more cosmonauts— Georgi Dobrovolsky (1928–1971), Vladislav Volkov (1935–1971), and Viktor Patsayev (1933–1971)—died when their *Soyuz 11* spacecraft depressurized during descent after visiting the *Salyut 1* station. At the time, cosmonauts did not wear spacesuits during launch and reentry. This was later changed to provide them greater safety.

A New Focus

The Soviet's Moon program continued well into the 1970s. However, neither the N-1 nor a competing rocket called the Proton ever became dependable enough for manned launches. During the early 1970s the Soviets concentrated on perfecting their Soyuz rockets and building a space station. Like NASA, the Soviet space agency had always envisioned an orbiting space station as the next step after a lunar visit.

On April 19, 1971, the space station *Salyut 1* was launched into orbit. It was another first for the Soviet Union. The U.S. space station *Skylab* would not launch for another two years. Between 1971 and 1982 the Soviets put seven Salyut stations into orbit. These were designed to be temporary stations, with some of them falling out of orbit only months after being launched.

The last station, *Salyut 7*, stayed in orbit for nearly nine years, from April 1982 to February 1991. It hosted 10 crews of cosmonauts that spent a total of 861 days in space. The Soviet space program gained invaluable experience in long-duration exposure to weightlessness. The Salyut program was also notable in that cosmonauts and scientists from Cuba, India, and France were invited to visit the stations.

In 1972 the Soviet Union and the United States agreed to work together to achieve a common docking system for their respective spacecraft. This would permit docking in space of U.S. and Soviet spacecraft during future missions. On July 17, 1975, a Soviet Soyuz spacecraft carrying two cosmonauts docked with an Apollo spacecraft carrying three astronauts. (See Figure 3.5.)

The crewmembers conducted a variety of scientific experiments during the two-day docking period. Both spacecraft returned to Earth safely. The Apollo-Soyuz Rendezvous and Docking Test Project was the first union of spacecraft from two different countries.

By 1976 the Soviet space program was engrossed in another new project called Buran, a reusable space plane modeled after the U.S. space shuttle. The Buran program (like the U.S. shuttle program) was plagued by development, cost, and scheduling problems. Even though an unmanned Buran orbited Earth twice and landed successfully in November 1988, the program was halted soon afterward due to funding cuts.

The 1980s were a tense time in U.S.-Soviet relations. The Soviets were at war with Afghanistan and cracking down on dissidents in Poland. In 1983 the Soviet military

FIGURE 3.5

Apollo-Soyuz rendezvous and docking test project

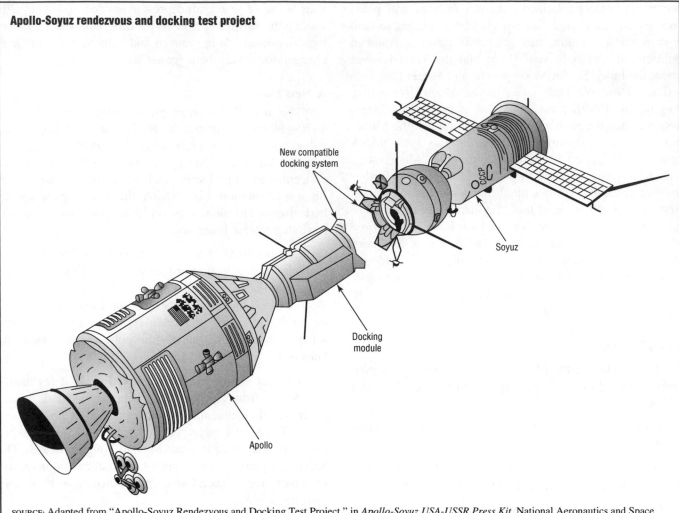

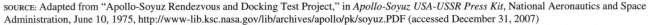

New compatible docking system

Soyuz

Docking module

Apollo

SOURCE: Adapted from "Apollo-Soyuz Rendezvous and Docking Test Project," in *Apollo-Soyuz USA-USSR Press Kit*, National Aeronautics and Space Administration, June 10, 1975, http://www-lib.ksc.nasa.gov/lib/archives/apollo/pk/soyuz.PDF (accessed December 31, 2007)

shot down a Korean jetliner that allegedly veered into Soviet air space. Sixty-two Americans were among the 269 passengers killed. The Soviet Union felt threatened by President Reagan's so-called Star Wars proposal to build a satellite shield. Furthermore, throughout the decade U.S.-Soviet arms talks repeatedly failed.

On February 19, 1986, the Soviet space agency launched the space station *Mir* into orbit. Unlike the temporary Salyut stations, *Mir* was designed to last for years and to be continuously inhabited. Dozens of cosmonauts, astronauts, and space tourists visited the station during its fifteen-year lifetime in space. On March 22, 1995, the cosmonaut Valery Polyakov (1942–) returned to Earth after spending 437.7 continuous days aboard *Mir*. It was a record for continuous space inhabitation that remained unbroken in March 2008.

The Russian Space Agency Takes Over

During the early 1990s the Soviet Union splintered into a number of individual republics. The largest of

these is Russia. In 1992 the new Russian government established the Russian Space Agency (RSA) to take over the space programs of the old Soviet Union. Russia and the United States began a new era of cooperation in space. In 1993 the two countries agreed to work together to build an *International Space Station* (*ISS*). Between 1994 and 1998 U.S. shuttles transported astronauts and cosmonauts to the *Mir* station. In 1998 *ISS* construction began when the Russians placed the first module (Zarya) into orbit. Construction is expected to take place at least through 2010. The *ISS* receives regular visits from Progress spacecraft. These are automated resupply vessels that bring consumables (food and water), spare parts, propellants, and other supplies to the station. The *ISS* has also relied heavily on the Russian Soyuz to ferry crewmembers to and from the station. It is likely that the Soyuz will be the only spacecraft capable of conducting *ISS* crew transports after the space shuttle ends operation in 2010 and until the next-generation U.S. spacecraft (the Ares) begins operating.

In 2006 Russian authorities announced a proposed successor to the Soyuz tentatively called the Advanced Crew Transportation System (ACTS). The ACTS will not only continue transports to the *ISS* in low Earth orbit but also be capable of achieving lunar orbits for any future Moon missions.

Roscosmos controls all the country's nonmilitary space flights. Military space ventures are controlled by Russia's Military Space Forces (VKS). The two agencies share control of the Baikonur Cosmodrome in Kazakhstan and the Gagarin Cosmonaut Training Center in Star City. The Plesetsk Cosmodrome launch facility in northern Russia is under the control of the VKS.

Russian Space Science

Even though the Soviet space program had an active space science program, budget constraints have severely restricted the scope of Roscosmos's endeavors in this area. In 1994 the agency cooperated with international partners to launch *CORONAS-I*, the first of three planned solar observatories. The second component, *CORONAS-F*, was launched in 2001. The third satellite, *CORONAS-Photon*, was scheduled for launch in 2008. Roscosmos has also launched several small Earth-observing satellites in recent years, including *Monitor-E* in 2005 and *Resurs-DK1* in 2006. The agency's Foton program features small satellites carrying recoverable experiment capsules. The payloads are put into Earth orbit for short periods of time (typically less than two weeks) and are recovered for scientific assessment after they return to Earth.

According to the article "Russia to Carry out up to 20 Space Projects by 2015" (Spacedaily.com, October 5, 2007), Russia's space plans through 2015 include more than twenty ambitious projects, including investigations of Earth's Moon and the Martian moon Phobos.

EUROPE

European countries can engage in space exploration through the European Space Agency (ESA), by collaborating with foreign space agencies (e.g., NASA), and/or through their own national space programs. European countries with national space programs include Austria, Belgium, Bulgaria, Denmark, Finland, France, Germany, Hungary, Italy, the Netherlands, Norway, Poland, Portugal, Romania, Spain, Sweden, and the United Kingdom. (See Table 3.1.) The French space program is one of the oldest and most active in Europe.

French Space Program

Following World War II, France engaged in rocket research and development with the help of German engineers and scientists who had developed the V series of rockets. This work largely took place in Vernon, France. In 1961 the French government founded the agency

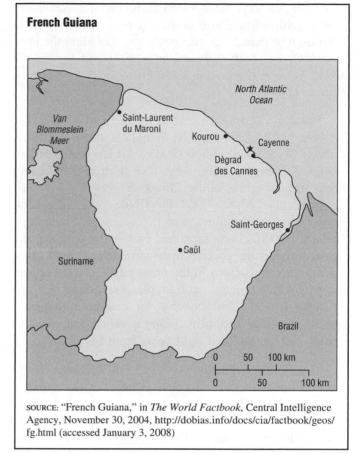

FIGURE 3.6

French Guiana

SOURCE: "French Guiana," in *The World Factbook*, Central Intelligence Agency, November 30, 2004, http://dobias.info/docs/cia/factbook/geos/fg.html (accessed January 3, 2008)

Centre National d'Etudes Spatiales (CNES) to lead the nation's space program. Three years later the French government established a space launch facility at Kourou in the French overseas territory of Guiana in northern South America. (See Figure 3.6.) Because of its nearness to the equator, Kourou is an ideal location from which to launch satellites into geostationary transfer orbit.

During the 1960s France developed the Diamant, Berenice, and Véronique launch systems. In 1965 a Diamant rocket was used to launch the first French satellite, *Astérix*, into orbit. By the end of the 1970s France had developed what would become the primary launch vehicle for European space craft: the Ariane rocket. Ariane is the French name for the Greek goddess Ariadne. In 1973 France joined with more than a dozen other European countries to form the ESA. The CNES continued to conduct national space ventures and collaborated with the ESA and other national space agencies.

On December 24, 1979, the first Ariane rocket launched into space from the Kourou spaceport. Since that time the Ariane design has undergone several modifications. The latest generation is the Ariane 5, a robust launch system capable of carrying two satellites at once into orbit. As of March 2008 more than 175 Ariane rockets had been launched into space. The vast majority of the flights have transported commercial communications satellites into Earth orbit. Ariane rockets have also been used to launch science payloads, including the joint NASA-CNES *TOPEX/Poseidon* (1992) and the ESA's *XMM Newton Observatory* (1999), *Spot 5* (2002), and *Rosetta* (2004).

Besides *TOPEX/Poseidon*, other joint ventures between NASA and the CNES include *Jason 1* (2001), *Calipso* (2006), and *Stereo* (2006). All are Earth observatories. The French agency has also contributed to many ESA missions, including *Mars Express* and *Venus Express*. As of March 2008, the CNES operated several Earth-observing satellites and the spaceborne telescope *COROT*. *COROT* was launched in December 2006 and began conducting precise measurements of light from distant stars. Pulsations in the measurements can indicate the passage of objects, such as planets, around stars. In May 2007 *COROT* discovered an exoplanet (a planet outside the solar system) orbiting a yellow star approximately fifteen hundred light years from Earth.

The CNES is headquartered in Paris, France, but it has additional facilities located throughout the country, including the Launcher Directorate in Evry and the Toulouse Space Centre. Launches take place at the Centre Spatial Guyanais (Guiana Space Centre) in French Guiana. In "Space Scientific Missions of the French National Space Agency" (February 15, 2008, http://smsc.cnes.fr/html-images/HomeGB.html), the CNES indicates that it has dozens of space missions in the study or development stage, such as the interplanetary mission *BEPICOLUMBO*, an orbital investigation of Mercury that is scheduled to be launched in 2013.

European Space Agency

The ESA was formed in 1973 from two existing organizations: the European Space Research Organisation and the European Launcher Development Organisation. As of February 2008, the ESA (http://www.esa.int/SPECIALS/About_ESA/SEMP936LARE_0.html) had seventeen member states:

- Austria
- Belgium
- Denmark
- Finland
- France
- Germany
- Greece
- Ireland
- Italy
- Luxembourg
- The Netherlands
- Norway
- Portugal
- Spain
- Sweden
- Switzerland
- United Kingdom

In addition, the ESA has agreements with Canada, the Czech Republic, Hungary, Romania, and Poland to participate in some projects. Even though the ESA is independent of the European Union (EU), it maintains close ties with the EU and the two organizations share a joint space strategy.

FACILITIES AND FUNDING. ESA headquarters are located in Paris, France. Other ESA facilities include the European Space Research and Technology Centre in Noordwijk, Netherlands; the European Space Operations Centre in Darmstadt, Germany; the European Astronauts Centre in Cologne, Germany; the European Space Research Institute in Frascati, Italy; and liaison offices in Belgium, Russia, and the United States. The ESA operates a launch base in French Guiana.

Each member state funds mandatory ESA activities based on that country's gross national product (the total value of goods and services produced by a country over a particular period of time). Mandatory activities include space science programs and the agency's general budget. In addition, the ESA operates optional projects in which countries may choose to participate and fund.

PAST AND CURRENT MISSIONS. On September 27, 2003, the ESA launched the first European mission to the Moon. *SMART-1* assumed orbit in November 2004 and began investigating the lunar surface. On September 3, 2006, the spacecraft was purposely crashed into the Moon at the Lake of Excellence. *SMART-1* gathered data on the morphology and mineralogical composition of the lunar surface.

In 2003 the ESA began participating in Double Star, the first Sino-European space mission. This joint effort with the China National Space Administration investigated physical processes occurring in Earth's magnetic environment. It included two satellites, *Double Star 1* and *Double Star 2*, which were launched aboard Chinese Long March 2C rockets in 2003 and 2004, respectively. Originally intended for a six-month mission, the spacecraft were viable for more than three years. Controllers lost contact with *Double Star 2* in August 2007, and the satellite was presumed lost. In October 2007 *Double Star 1* reentered Earth's atmosphere and was destroyed.

The ESA is a partner in the *ISS* program. The agency developed the data management system for the Russian segment launched in 2000. The ESA also constructed the Harmony connecting module. Harmony was delivered to the *ISS* aboard the U.S. space shuttle in October 2007. The ESA's Columbus research laboratory was scheduled to be delivered to the *ISS* in early 2008. In addition, new ESA-developed automated supply ships called automated transfer vehicles (ATVs) will begin delivering equipment, spare parts, food, water, and other consumables to the space station crew. The launch of the first ATV, dubbed "Jules Verne," was scheduled for early 2008. Future ESA components for the *ISS* include a robotic arm, a module containing life support equipment for the station's permanent crew, and a pressurized observation and work area.

The ESA also participates in Russia's Foton program. The most recent Foton mission, called *M3*, was launched in September 2007 and included a payload of more than forty ESA experiments. The *M3* capsule returned to Earth after twelve days and was successfully recovered.

As of January 2008, the ESA was directly operating ten space science missions and partnering with NASA in three others. (See Table 3.2.) The ESA's current projects include one comet investigation mission (*Rosetta*) and two interplanetary missions (*Venus Express* and *Mars Express*).

Rosetta left Earth in February 2004, for a rendezvous in May 2014 with the comet 67P/Churyumov-Gerasimenko. The comet orbits the Sun, completing one orbit approximately every six and a half years. *Rosetta* is designed to land on the nucleus of the comet and attach itself with a harpoon. It will collect images and conduct chemical analysis of the comet's surface.

The *Venus Express Orbiter* was launched in November 2005 and went into orbit around Venus in April 2006. As of March 2008, the ESA (http://sci.esa.int/science-e/www/area/index.cfm?fareaid=64) indicated that the orbiter was still performing sophisticated atmospheric studies and measuring surface temperatures.

The *Mars Express Orbiter* was launched in June 2003 and went into orbit around Mars in December 2003. The landing vehicle *Beagle 2* left the orbiter to land on the planet's surface. The ESA lost contact with the lander, which was declared lost. However, as of March 2008 the ESA (http://www.esa.int/esaMI/Mars_Express/index.html) reported that the orbiter continued to circle Mars and collect data with its scientific instruments.

The ESA was also responsible for the *Huygens* probe mission to Saturn. The probe was launched aboard the NASA spacecraft *Cassini* in October 1997. On December 25, 2004, *Cassini* released the probe for a three-week journey to the surface of Titan, Saturn's moon. It pene-

TABLE 3.2

European Space Agency (ESA) operational space science missions as of January 2008

Name	Launch date	Mission
Under direct ESA operation		
Venus Express	11/9/2005	Venus Orbiter
Rosetta	3/2/2004	Investigate comet 67P/Churyumov-Gerasimenko
Mars Express	6/2/2003	Mars Orbiter
Integral	10/17/2002	Space observatory
Envisat	3/1/2002	Observe & monitor Earth's environment
Proba	10/22/2001	Earth imager
Cluster-II	7/16/00 & 8/9/00	Four satellites investigating Earth's magnetosphere
XMM-Newton	12/10/1999	Space observatory
ERS-2	4/21/1995	Investigate Earth's land and oceans
In partnership with NASA		
SOHO	12/2/1995	Perform solar observations
Ulysses	10/6/1990	Investigate the Sun's polar regions
Hubble space telescope	4/24/1990	Space observatory

SOURCE: Created by Kim Masters Evans for Gale, Cengage Learning, 2008.

trated the thick cloud cover that hides the moon and touched down on January 14, 2005. The probe sampled Titan's atmosphere and provided the first photographs ever of its surface. The probe is named after Christiaan Huygens (1629–1695), the Dutch astronomer who discovered Saturn's rings and Titan. *Huygens* is the first probe to ever land on a celestial body in the outer solar system.

FUTURE MISSIONS. As of March 2008, the ESA (http://www.esa.int/SPECIALS/Operations/index.html) had a number of missions planned for the coming decades, including Earth and space observatories and interplanetary investigations. The Aurora Exploration Programme will use robotic missions to Mars to collect and return samples to Earth. The first mission in this program is tentatively titled ExoMars and is expected to launch in 2011.

CHINA

China's space program is overseen by the China National Space Administration and operated by the China Aerospace Science and Technology Corporation (CASC). The CASC is a state-run enterprise that develops and produces rockets, spacecraft, and related products. It has conducted satellite launches since 1970. CASC launch sites include Jiuquan in the Gobi desert, Taiyuan in northern China, and Xichang in southeastern China.

Tsien Hsue-shen

The Chinese space program began in the late 1950s under the direction of the rocket engineer Tsien Hsue-shen (1911–). Tsien was born in China, but immigrated to the United States during the 1930s, where he attended the Massachusetts Institute of Technology and the California

Institute of Technology (Cal Tech). He was a key member of the rocketry club at Cal Tech that evolved into NASA's Jet Propulsion Laboratory. He was also instrumental in the U.S. program to acquire and apply German rocket technology at the end of World War II. In 1950 Tsien was accused of being a communist spy and had his security clearance revoked. At the time, he was pursuing U.S. citizenship.

In 1955, after five years under virtual house arrest, Tsien was deported to China, where he was put in charge of the nation's budding space program. Under his leadership China developed successful satellite and missile systems. These included the antiship missile called Haiying by the Chinese and dubbed Silkworm by the Western media. During the cold war China sold Silkworms to a number of third-world countries considered unfriendly to the United States. Tsien also led development of the Chang Zheng (Long March) rockets that became the primary launch vehicle of the Chinese space program.

During the late 1960s Tsien fell out of favor with the Chinese leadership and was removed from his post. This disgrace resulted in Tsien receiving little credit within China for his accomplishments. However, the Western world considers him the father of the Chinese space program. In her 1995 biography of Tsien, *Thread of the Silkworm*, Iris Chang asserts that deporting the brilliant rocket scientist was "one of the most monumental blunders committed by the United States."

China Reaches Space

On April 24, 1970, *DFH 1*, the first Chinese satellite, was launched into Earth orbit. It was propelled into space by a Long March rocket. Since the 1970s China has conducted many satellite launches using Long March rockets. During the 1990s development began on capsules capable of carrying animals, and later humans, into space. In 1999 the first such spacecraft, *Shenzhou 1*, successfully completed fourteen orbits around Earth. Throughout the early 2000s the Shenzhou series was updated with newer and more powerful Long March rockets.

On October 15, 2003, China conducted its first human spaceflight. The taikonaut (Chinese astronaut) Yang Liwei (1965–) was launched aboard *Shenzhou 5*. Liwei spent twenty-one hours and twenty-three minutes in space and completed fourteen orbits. On October 12, 2005, *Shenzhou 6* carried two taikonauts into space: Junlong Fei (1965–) and Haisheng Nie (1964–). They spent just over four days orbiting Earth before touching down safely in Inner Mongolia.

On October 24, 2007, China used a Long March 3A rocket to launch a robotic Moon orbiter into space. The mission was called *Chang'e 1* in honor of the Chinese Moon goddess. The spacecraft entered lunar orbit several weeks later and was expected to conduct observations for up to a year. Future Chinese plans include Moon rovers capable of returning samples to Earth, interplanetary robotic probes, a space-based astronomical observatory, and a crewed lunar landing. The country has shown keen interest in participating in international space ventures and has agreements with Russia, Brazil, and the ESA. Marcia S. Smith of the Congressional Research Service estimates in *China's Space Program: An Overview* (October 18, 2005, http://www.unm.edu/~cstp/articles/RS21641.pdf) that China spends approximately $2 billion a year on its space program.

JAPAN

The Japan Aerospace Exploration Agency (JAXA) was created on October 1, 2003, by merging the Institute of Space and Astronautical Science, the National Space Development Agency of Japan, and the National Aerospace Laboratory of Japan. The JAXA is headquartered in Tokyo and has more than a dozen field facilities across Japan.

The first Japanese satellite, *Ohsumi*, was launched into space in February 1970 by a Lambda-4S rocket. *Ohsumi* remained in space for more than three decades and was destroyed in 2003 as it reentered Earth's atmosphere. It was the first of many satellites launched by the JAXA. Japanese launch vehicles for lightweight satellites are named after letters in the Greek alphabet. In 2001 a new heavy-lift rocket called the H-II became Japan's primary launch vehicle for heavier spacecraft. Two years later an H-II malfunctioned soon after liftoff and had to be destroyed, along with the two satellites it was carrying. A long safety review followed the incident. The H-II was not used again until February 2005, when it successfully launched a weather satellite into space.

As of 2008, JAXA (http://www.jaxa.jp/projects/index_e.html) operational missions included six Earth-observing satellites and three astronomical observatories. In addition, the agency was operating the solar orbiter *Nozomi*, the asteroid sampler *Hayabusa*, and the lunar orbiter *Kaguya*, and continuing development of the Kibo laboratory module for the *ISS*.

In September 2007 the JAXA launched the SELENE (Selenological and Engineering Explorer) toward the Moon for a one-year orbital mission. It includes three components. The primary satellite is called *Kaguya*, after a mythical Japanese Moon princess. Its two smaller satellites, *Okina* and *Ouna*, take different orbits around the Moon.

Nozomi was launched in July 1998 by an M-5 rocket and was to go into orbit around Mars in December 2003. An equipment failure prevented this from happening. Instead, JAXA was forced to put the spacecraft into a solar orbit.

Hayabusa was launched in May 2003 by an M-5 rocket to intercept the asteroid Itokawa. The asteroid orbits the Sun between Earth and Mars and is about twenty-three hundred feet by one thousand feet in size. It is named after Hideo Itokawa (1912–1999), who is considered the founder of Japan's space program. The robotic explorer was designed to land on the asteroid, take a surface sample, and return to Earth by 2007. In November 2005 the JAXA lost contact with the spaceship during the touchdown procedure. Even though contact was regained after a few days, it is not known for sure if *Hayabusa* was able to collect dust particles. In 2005 the JAXA announced that thruster problems were going to delay *Hayabusa*'s return to Earth until 2010. It is supposed to land in a desolate region of the Australian Outback.

The Kibo laboratory facility was originally supposed to be flown to the *ISS* in 2004 or 2005. It is a heavy component and must be transported by the space shuttle. Continuing problems with the space shuttle fleet have delayed the Kibo transport mission until 2008 or 2009.

The JAXA also participates in a number of scientific satellite projects with international partners. Future Japanese space projects include missions to the Moon, Venus, and Mercury. The Planet-C mission is planned for launch in May 2010 and will put an orbiter around Venus a year later. Mercury orbiters are under development for a mission in the early 2010s.

PRIVATE SPACE ORGANIZATIONS

Private space organizations have played a major role in advancing space exploration. As far back as the 1920s groups of scientists, hobbyists, and other enthusiasts were gathering together to share their passion for rocket science and space travel. Many of the early groups were absorbed by government and military space organizations or evolved into aerospace manufacturing businesses. Private groups continue to advance space flight by researching and developing new technologies, operating commercial space enterprises, promoting public interest in space, and influencing government decisions on the future of spaceflight.

During the 1990s new avenues arose for private parties to participate in space endeavors. The Russian government allowed high-paying space tourists to travel to the space station *Mir* for brief stays. The first nongovernmental launch facilities were developed for commercial satellites.

In 2004 a major milestone was achieved in space exploration: the first manned spacecraft developed and launched by a commercial enterprise traveled into space. This opens a whole new realm of space travel opportunities to private citizens.

Early European Organizations

One of the first private space organizations was the Verein für Raumschiffahrt (VfR; Society for Spaceship Travel). The VfR was formed in 1927 in Berlin by a group of scientists and authors interested in rocket research. In particular, they wanted to raise money to finance rocket experiments being conducted by Professor Hermann Oberth (1894–1989) at the University of Munich. During the early 1930s the group sponsored rocket research projects around Germany. The VfR included many famous members, including von Braun. The group disbanded in 1933 as the Nazi Party gained power in Germany.

The 1930s witnessed the formation of private space organizations throughout eastern and western Europe. In the Soviet Union there was the Gruppa Isutcheniya Reaktivnovo Dvisheniya. The British Interplanetary Society (BIS) was founded in 1933. This group of scientists and intellectuals is credited with advancing many important theories used in space flight, including a design for a lunar landing vehicle that was incorporated into Project Apollo. As of 2008 the BIS was active and published several influential journals.

American Institute of Aeronautics and Astronautics

In April 1930 a group of American scientists, engineers, and writers interested in space exploration formed the American Interplanetary Society. The founders included George Edward Pendray (1901–1987), inventor of the time capsule; David Lasser (1902–1996), an engineer and technical writer who advocated space travel; and Laurence Manning (1899–1972), a science-fiction writer. In 1934 the name of the group was changed to the American Rocket Society (ARS). By this time the members were predominantly rocket scientists who specialized in the research, design, and testing of liquid-fueled rockets. The ARS featured many prominent members including Robert Goddard (1892–1945), whose theories and experiments were instrumental in the development of rocket science during the early twentieth century.

During World War II several ARS members started the company Reaction Motors support the war effort. The company later developed rocket engines used in the famous X-series planes. Over the decades, the company evolved into ATK Thiokol Propulsion, the manufacturer of the space shuttle's rockets.

In 1932 a group of American aeronautical engineers and scientists formed the Institute of Aeronautical Sciences (IAS). Even though originally focused on Earth-bound aviation, the IAS grew increasingly interested in space flight. In 1963 the IAS merged with the ARS to become the American Institute of Aeronautics and Astronautics (AIAA).

As of 2008 the AIAA (http://www.aiaa.org/content .cfm?pageid=189) had more than thirty-one thousand members and was the largest professional society in the world devoted to aviation and spaceflight. Its stated purpose is "to advance the arts, sciences, and technology of aeronautics and astronautics, and to promote the professionalism of those engaged in these pursuits." The AIAA has published hundreds of books and hundreds of thousands of technical papers throughout its history.

The Planetary Society

The Planetary Society is a nonprofit space advocacy group based in Pasadena, California. It was founded in 1980 by the scientists Carl Sagan (1934–1996), Bruce C. Murray (1931–), and Louis Dill Friedman (1940–).

The society's (2008, http://www.planetary.org/pro grams/) stated purpose is: "The Planetary Society creates ways for the public to have active roles in space exploration. We develop innovative technologies, like the first solar sail spacecraft, we fund astronomers hunting for hazardous asteroids and planets orbiting other stars, we support radio and optical searches for extraterrestrial life, and we influence decision makers, ensuring the future of space exploration."

The society funds projects that support its goals and educate the public about space travel. It also encourages its members and the public to contact government leaders regarding space exploration projects. During the 1980s the society waged a campaign to encourage Congress to restore funding for NASA's Search for Extra-Terrestrial Intelligence (SETI) project. In the early 1990s the battle was over NASA's planned postponement of the Mars Observer mission. In late 2003 and early 2004 Planetary Society members sent thousands of postcards to congressional leaders to protest funding cuts for NASA's planned mission to Pluto. According to the Planetary Society, all three of these campaigns were successful in that government funding was restored to the projects.

In 1999 the society started the SETI@home project in which private citizens could allow their home computers to be used to analyze data recorded by a giant radio telescope as part of SETI. By the time the SETI@home project ended in December 2005, more than five million people had participated. The project was turned over to the University of California at Berkley Space Sciences Laboratory, which operates it under the Berkeley Online Infrastructure for Network Computing.

In the early 2000s the society launched the project Red Rover Goes to Mars to coincide with NASA's Mars Exploration missions. The project included an essay contest for students that resulted in the names used for the Mars rovers: *Spirit* and *Opportunity*. The contest was sponsored by the Planetary Society and the Lego toy company.

The two also funded the creation of DVDs that were mounted to the rovers for the missions. The DVDs were specially crafted out of silica glass (instead of plastic) and contain the names of nearly four million people who asked NASA to be listed. Each DVD surface features a drawing of an "astrobot" saying "Hello" to Mars. The spacecraft safely landed on Mars in January 2004. Photos transmitted to NASA by the rovers after landing showed that the DVDs survived the journey. The rovers are designed to remain on Mars and not return to Earth.

Other components of the Red Rover Goes to Mars project included a contest in which the winning students visited mission control during the Mars Exploration missions and a classroom project in which students built models of the Mars rover and the Martian landscape.

On June 21, 2005, the Planetary Society launched its first spacecraft, *Cosmos 1*, to test a solar sail in orbit around Earth. A solar sail is a novel technology that could power spaceflight in the future. It is composed of giant ultrathin silvery blades that unfurl after launch to reflect sunlight. The electromagnetic radiation of sunlight exerts force on the objects on which it shines. This force is fairly strong in outer space due to the absence of atmospheric friction, and it could potentially push a solar sail in much the same way that the wind pushes sailing ships on Earth's oceans.

Cosmos 1 was built in Russia with funding and technical support from the Planetary Society. Each blade of the solar sail was forty-seven feet long. The sail was to be launched by the Russian navy from a submarine. The mission was cosponsored by the media company Cosmos Studios through a contract with the RSA. It was the first space mission ever funded by a private space interest organization.

Cosmos 1 was lost soon after launch when its Russian-supplied Volna rocket failed to fire properly. The Planetary Society hopes to raise the money needed to fund a second solar sail.

Other programs being funded by the Planetary Society (http://www.planetary.org/explore/) as of 2008 include an exoplanet search and the Gene Shoemaker Near-Earth Object Grant Program. The society also provides grants to private observers around the world who help track small asteroids orbiting near Earth.

Space Entrepreneurs

Commercial enterprises have played an important role in space exploration through the decades. Government and military space programs would not have been possible without the contributions of labor and technology from companies in the aerospace business and related fields. Communication corporations were among the first to see the potential of satellites to grow and revolutionize their businesses. Demand for satellite launches from the commercial sector helped fund and drive many advances in rocket science and launch technology.

For decades satellites could only be launched at state-operated facilities. The 1990s witnessed the birth of commercial satellite launching organizations in several countries. One of the most unusual is the Sea Launch Company. The company formed in 1995 and included U.S., Russian, Ukrainian, and Norwegian companies engaged in the aerospace business. The consortium modified an ocean oil-drilling platform into a rocket launch platform and placed it in the middle of the Pacific Ocean along the equator. Since the first successful launch in 1999, more than a dozen commercial satellites have been put into orbit from the sea-based facility.

The 1990s also witnessed the first space tourists. The RSA allowed private citizens to visit the space station *Mir* and the *ISS* for fees ranging from $15 million to $30 million per tourist. Most of the trips were arranged through the private U.S. company Space Adventures. Formed in 1998 by the aerospace engineer Peter H. Diamandis (1961–), the company offers customers opportunities in space tourism and related entertainment areas, such as "zero gravity" experiences. The demand by private citizens for space travel is expected to grow substantially during the twenty-first century.

A New Way to Explore Space: Commercial Suborbital Flights

In 2004 a major milestone in space exploration was achieved when the first nongovernmental manned spacecraft traveled to space and back. The spacecraft was called *SpaceShipOne*, and it was funded by the private investor Paul G. Allen (1953–), the cofounder of the Microsoft Corporation. In 2001 Allen contracted the California design firm Scaled Composites to develop a reusable space vehicle capable of carrying at least one passenger to suborbital space. Aside from re-engaging the public's interest and passion in space exploration, Allen and *SpaceShipOne* set out to win the Ansari X Prize (http://www.xprize.org/). This prize was offered by a group of private investors called the X Prize Foundation, which was created by Diamandis. The Ansari family was the prime funder of the $10 million prize, which was available to any nongovernmental group that could achieve the following:

- Build a spaceship and fly three people (or at least one person plus the equivalent weight of two people) into space (defined as an altitude of 100 kilometers or 62.1 miles)

- Return safely to Earth

- Repeat the feat with the same spaceship within two weeks

On June 21, 2004, the test pilot Mike Melvill (1941–) of Scaled Composites became the first person to pilot a privately built plane into space when he took *SpaceShipOne* to an altitude of 62.2 miles during a test flight. On September 29, 2004, he achieved an altitude of 63.9 miles. Only five days later the pilot Brian Binnie (1953–) took the same plane to an altitude of 69.6 miles to win the Ansari X Prize.

The flights were conducted from an airstrip in Mojave, California. A carrier plane called *White Knight* transported *SpaceShipOne* to an altitude of approximately forty-seven thousand feet and released it. A rocket motor aboard the spaceship was fired to propel it vertically into space. The pilots experienced about three minutes of weightlessness at the height of their journeys. During reentry the wings of *SpaceShipOne* were maneuvered to provide maximum drag and slow its descent. The spacecraft glided back to the airstrip and landed like a plane. (See Figure 3.7.)

The *White Knight* was a manned twin-turbojet carrier aircraft designed to fly to high altitudes carrying a payload of up to eight thousand pounds. It was named after two U.S. Air Force pilots (Robert White and William "Pete" Knight) who earned their astronaut wings flying the experimental X-15 aircraft during the early 1960s.

SpaceShipOne used a unique hybrid rocket motor fueled by liquid nitrous oxide (laughing gas) and solid hydroxy-terminated polybutadiene (a major constituent of the rubber used in tires). The individual fuel components are nontoxic and are not hazardous to transport or store. They do not react when mixed together unless a flame is supplied. In *SpaceShipOne*, the nitrous oxide was gasified before combustion.

In July 2005 Burt Rutan (1943–), the president of Scaled Composites, and Richard Branson (1950–), the founder of the Virgin Group, announced the formation of a new aerospace production company: the Spaceship Company. Using original technology licensed from Allen, the company plans to build a small fleet of spacecraft based on the designs of the *White Knight* and *SpaceShipOne*. In 2004 Branson created Virgin Galactic, which bills itself as the world's first commercial spaceline. Virgin Galactic signed an agreement to become the first "launch customer" for the Spaceship Company aircraft.

On August 2, 2007, an explosion during a rocket ground test killed three workers at a Scaled Composites facility in the California desert. The explosion involved the firing of the nitrous-oxide delivery system. In January 2008 Virgin Galactic reported that work was proceeding on the development of the new *SpaceShipTwo* and *White-KnightTwo* spacecraft.

Virgin Galactic plans to sell suborbital space flights to tourists for approximately $200,000 per flight. In December 2005 the company announced its agreement with the state of New Mexico to build a spaceport near the White

FIGURE 3.7

Flight sequence for SpaceShipOne

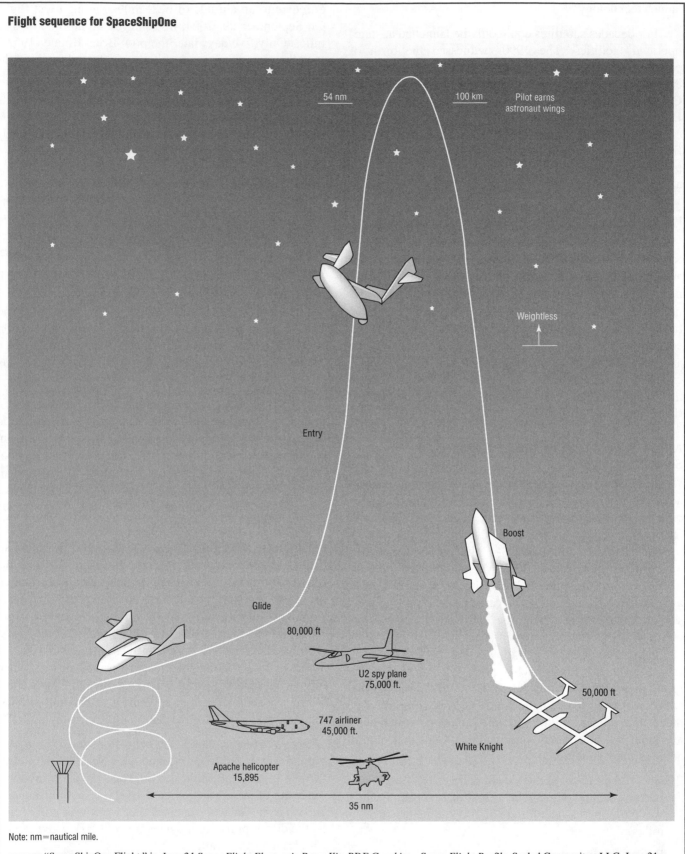

54 nm

100 km

Pilot earns
astronaut wings

Weightless

Entry

Boost

Glide

80,000 ft

U2 spy plane
75,000 ft.

50,000 ft

747 airliner
45,000 ft.

White Knight

Apache helicopter
15,895

35 nm

Note: nm=nautical mile.

SOURCE: "SpaceShipOne Flight," in *June 21 Space Flight Electronic Press Kit: PDF Graphics—Space Flight Profile*, Scaled Composites, LLC, June 21, 2004, http://scaled.com/projects/tierone/data_sheets/PDF/SS1_flight_profile.pdf (accessed December 31, 2007). 2004 Mojave Aerospace Ventures LLC; SpaceShipOne is a Paul G. Allen Project.

Sands Missile Range. The company intends to begin commercial space flights from an airstrip in a Mojave, California, in 2008 or 2009 and switch its operations to the New Mexico site when the spaceport is complete.

In "Accidents Won't Stop Private Space Industry's Push to Final Frontier" (Wired.com, August 2, 2007), Michael Belfiore reports that as of August 2007 other companies had announced plans to conduct commercial space flights, including the European corporation EADS AStrium, Blue Origin (a company started by the Amazon.com chief executive officer Jeffrey Bezos [1964–]), and Bigelow Aerospace, a Las Vegas–based company funded by the real estate developer Robert Bigelow.

CHAPTER 4
THE SPACE SHUTTLE PROGRAM

It will revolutionize transportation into near space, by routinizing it.

—President Richard M. Nixon, January 5, 1972

The U.S. space shuttle was supposed to make space travel a routine and frequent occurrence. Its conceivers envisioned shuttles regularly transporting humans and cargo back and forth between Earth and a fleet of orbiting space stations. The shuttle was expected to be much cheaper than previous spacecraft, because it would be reusable. This would mean low operational and maintenance costs and a quick turnaround time between flights. It was predicted to bring in lots of money by hauling satellites into space for paying customers. The shuttle was going to be part of a massive transportation system and open up space the way the railroad opened up the western frontier of the United States during the nineteenth century.

This vision never became a reality. Shuttle flights did not become routine, common, or frequent. In "Shuttle Missions" (February 23, 2008, http://www.nasa.gov/mission_pages/shuttle/shuttlemissions/list_main.html), the National Aeronautics and Space Administration (NASA) indicates that between 1981 and 2007 space shuttles flew only 120 times, averaging less than 5 flights per year. Two shuttles exploded, killing fourteen crewmembers. Besides the human cost, the program experienced high operational and maintenance costs. Long turnaround times prevented the shuttle from flying frequently. However, the flights that took place did achieve many accomplishments. They put probes and observatories into space and were essential for building the *International Space Station* (*ISS*).

Nevertheless, many people believe that the United States has wasted too much time and money on a shuttle program that does not deliver what it promised. In January 2004 President George W. Bush (1946–) announced his own vision for the nation's space program. It focuses on trips to the Moon and Mars and calls for ending the

Space Shuttle Program (SSP) by 2010. Regardless, the dream of routine access to space remains an elusive one.

THE POST-APOLLO VISION

In the early 1960s NASA planners envisioned a space station program as the next step after Apollo. It was assumed that the United States would establish large space stations in orbit around Earth and possibly outposts on the Moon. In fact, NASA hoped to put at least one twelve-person space station in Earth orbit by 1975. This would require a new type of reusable space plane to carry cargo and personnel to and from the station.

However, these grand plans did not mesh with the political, cultural, and technological realities of the times. By the late 1960s the nation was heavily engaged in the Vietnam War (1954–1975). Domestic unrest and social issues dominated the political agenda into the early 1970s. Richard M. Nixon (1913–1994) was president of the United States from 1969 to 1974. According to historians, Nixon was not interested in pursuing any large and expensive vision for space exploration. T. A. Heppenheimer notes in *The Space Shuttle Decision: NASA's Search for a Reusable Space Vehicle* (1999) that in a March 1970 statement on space policy, Nixon said, "We must build on the successes of the past, always reaching out for new achievements. But we must also recognize that many critical problems here on this planet make high priority demands on our attention and our resources." NASA's budget was severely cut, and plans for space stations were put on hold.

Regardless, NASA did not give up on the shuttle program. It began promoting the project as a transport business, rather than as an exploratory adventure. NASA officials argued that a shuttle could haul government and commercial satellites into space in a cost-effective manner because it would be reusable. Furthermore, the shuttle astronauts could service and repair these satellites as needed. The shuttle was touted as an investment because it would make money from commercial customers and save the government money on launching satellites for weather, science, and military purposes.

This argument was successful. In *CAIB Report: Volume 1* (August 2003, http://caib.nasa.gov/news/report/pdf/vol1/full/caib_report_volume1.pdf), the *Columbia* Accident Investigation Board explains that in 1971 NASA was given a $5 billion budget over a five-year-period for the development of a shuttle program. This was later increased to $5.5 billion. NASA assured the White House that each shuttle would be good for one hundred flights and that each flight would have an average cost of $7.7 million. The planners agreed that the shuttle program would have to operate about fifty missions a year to satisfy demand for satellite launches. It was expected that the shuttle program would be operational by the end of the decade.

Heppenheimer suggests that President Nixon had strong political motives to approve the shuttle program. A presidential election was coming up in 1972, and he wanted to gain favor in states such as Florida and Texas that would benefit from new NASA projects. Also, the Soviet Union had already put the space station *Salyut 1* into orbit during 1971. The last Apollo mission was scheduled for 1972. On January 5, 1972, President Nixon announced to the nation that NASA would build a new Space Transportation System based on a new vehicle called a space shuttle.

SPACE SHUTTLE DESIGN AND DEVELOPMENT

Various space shuttle designs had been evolving since the 1950s. The U.S. Air Force had examined several options based on a reusable manned space plane that could be maneuvered in flight and glided to a landing. The best-known program was called Dyna-Soar (short for Dynamic Soaring). The Dyna-Soar concept included an expendable launch vehicle to carry a space plane out of Earth's atmosphere.

NASA engineers began designing a spacecraft much different from those used during the Apollo program. Apollo capsules and command modules were launched inside long cylindrical rockets. The thrust needed to get these vehicles off the ground was through the center of gravity of each rocket. The rockets were fueled by kerosene and liquid hydrogen-oxygen.

The shuttle design was completely different. At first, engineers hoped to develop a fully reusable vehicle. Budget constraints soon made it obvious that this was not going to be possible. Instead, NASA designed a three-part vehicle for the shuttle:

- A reusable space plane called an orbiter

- An expendable external liquid fuel tank for the orbiter's three main engines

- A reusable pair of external rocket boosters containing a powdered fuel

FIGURE 4.1

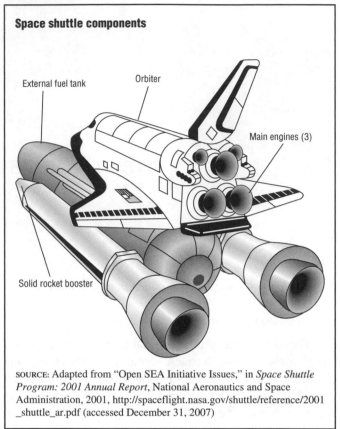

Space shuttle components

SOURCE: Adapted from "Open SEA Initiative Issues," in *Space Shuttle Program: 2001 Annual Report*, National Aeronautics and Space Administration, 2001, http://spaceflight.nasa.gov/shuttle/reference/2001_shuttle_ar.pdf (accessed December 31, 2007)

Figure 4.1 shows the major components of the space shuttle design. The launch sequence called for the fuel tank and the rocket boosters to be jettisoned away from the orbiter during the ascent phase. The rocket boosters were designed to be recovered and refilled with fuel for the next launch. The external tank was to be jettisoned above Earth's atmosphere and burn up during reentry.

The orbiter holds the crew compartment and payload bay. (For a typical orbiter layout, see Figure 4.2.) The payload bay measures sixty feet by fifteen feet. The shuttle was designed to transport the orbiter into space 115 to 690 miles above Earth's surface. This is considered low Earth orbit (LEO).

The orbiter had to be capable of maneuvering while in space and during landing. The early designs were based on the air force's X-series of high-performance aircraft. Unlike the Apollo capsules, the orbiter was intended to be reusable. It had to land on the ground, rather than splashdown in the ocean. At first, engineers included jet engines on the orbiter for use within Earth's atmosphere. These proved to be too expensive and too heavy for the structure and were eliminated. Instead, the orbiter was designed to glide through the air to its landing site.

The orbiter was built to carry a crew of seven under normal circumstances, for a typical mission time of seven

FIGURE 4.2

Orbiter

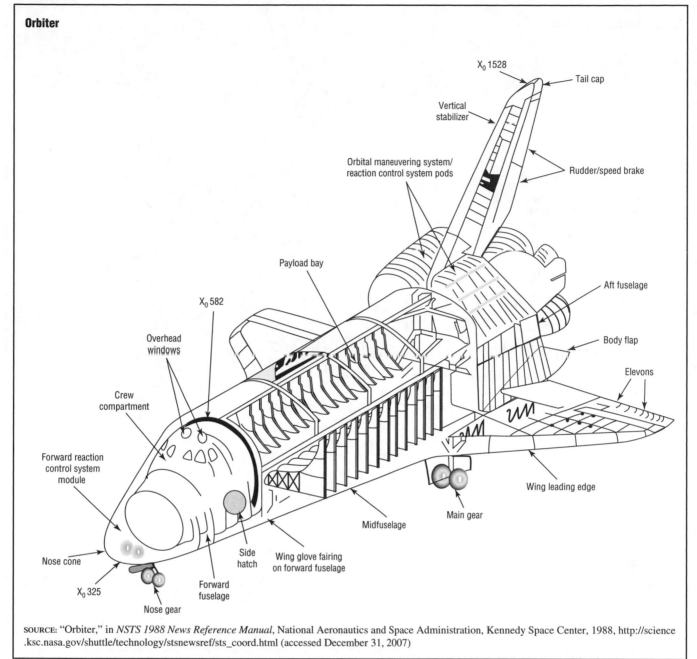

SOURCE: "Orbiter," in *NSTS 1988 News Reference Manual*, National Aeronautics and Space Administration, Kennedy Space Center, 1988, http://science .ksc.nasa.gov/shuttle/technology/stsnewsref/sts_coord.html (accessed December 31, 2007)

days in space. The maximum mission time for this crew number is thirty days (assuming that adequate supplies have been packed). The orbiter was designed to hold up to ten people in an emergency.

One of the most difficult design problems for the orbiter was a thermal protection system that could be reused. Previous spacecraft had been well protected from the intense heat of reentry, but their thermal protection materials were rendered unusable after one reentry. At first, designers hoped to cloak the orbiter in metal plates that could withstand high temperatures. This proved to be too heavy. So the orbiter was built out of light-weight aluminum, and its underside was covered with high-tech

thermal blankets and tiles. More than twenty-four thousand individual tiles had to be applied by hand. These light-weight tiles are made of sand silicate fibers mixed with a ceramic material.

The new spacecraft had to be light enough to get off the ground, but large enough to carry military payloads that weighed substantially more than what shuttle engineers had expected. The U.S. Department of Defense (DOD) also wanted the shuttle to be able to fly polar orbits (i.e., orbits crossing over the North and South Poles). This meant that a launching facility on the West Coast was required, so that the shuttle could launch in a southerly direction toward the South Pole. In April 1972

FIGURE 4.3

Space shuttle launch sites

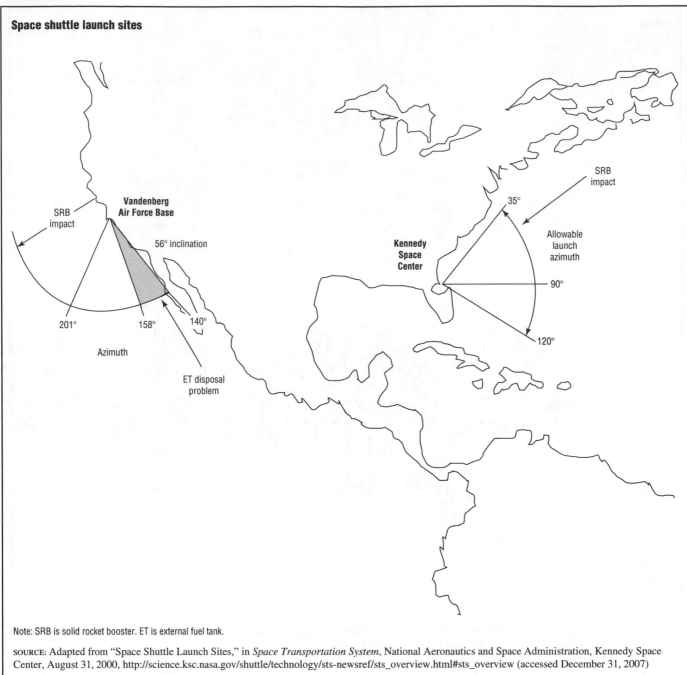

Note: SRB is solid rocket booster. ET is external fuel tank.

SOURCE: Adapted from "Space Shuttle Launch Sites," in *Space Transportation System*, National Aeronautics and Space Administration, Kennedy Space Center, August 31, 2000, http://science.ksc.nasa.gov/shuttle/technology/sts-newsref/sts_overview.html#sts_overview (accessed December 31, 2007)

it was decided that the air force would build this facility at the Vandenberg Air Force Base (AFB) in California.

The primary launch facility was authorized at the Kennedy Space Center (KSC) in Florida. The KSC location allowed the shuttle to launch in an easterly direction over the Atlantic Ocean and assume an equatorial orbit (an orbit along lines of latitude near or at the equator).

Figure 4.3 shows the original launch azimuths (angles) planned for the Vandenberg AFB and the KSC. The azimuths were chosen so that launch trajectories did not cross over heavily populated areas or foreign soil.

They also ensured that any parts jettisoned from the shuttle during ascent would fall harmlessly into the ocean. It was assumed that the shuttle would land at the Vandenberg AFB, the KSC, or the air force's White Sands Testing Facility in New Mexico.

The DOD insisted that the shuttle be designed to return to the Vandenberg AFB after only one polar orbit. This was a technological challenge because it meant that the shuttle had to fly more than one thousand miles to the east during reentry. Engineers call this the "cross-range requirement." To meet this requirement, the shuttle was given delta wings (symmetrical triangular wings designed

TABLE 4.1

Space shuttle statistics

	Overall shuttle	Orbiter
Length	184.2 feet	122.17 feet
Height	76.6 feet	56.67 feet
Wingspan	—	78.06 feet
Approximate weight		
Gross lift-off, which will vary depending on payload weight and onboard consumables	4.5 million pounds	—
Nominal end of mission landing with payload, which will vary depending on payload return weight	—	230,000 pounds
Thrust (sea level)	—	—
Solid rocket boosters	3,300,000 pounds of thrust each in vacuum	—
Orbiter main engines	—	393,800 pounds of thrust each at sea level at 104 percent
Cargo bay		
Length	—	60 feet
Diameter	—	15 feet

SOURCE: "Table," in *Space Transportation System*, National Aeronautics and Space Administration, Kennedy Space Center, August 31, 2000, http://science.ksc.nasa.gov/shuttle/technology/sts-newsref/sts_overview.html#sts_overview (accessed December 31, 2007)

for subsonic and supersonic flight) and an enhanced thermal protection system.

NASA had to meet the design demands of the military to keep the project moving forward. However, this added substantially to the development costs for the spacecraft. Most of the design work took place during the mid-1970s, which was a time of high inflation for the U.S. economy. High inflation means that the purchasing power of the dollar goes down. NASA would be designated funds in one year, but by the time those funds were received in the next year, their practical value had decreased.

The original date for the first space shuttle launch was to be March 1978. This date was postponed several times due to budget and equipment problems. The shuttle's main engines and thermal protection tiles proved to be particularly troublesome. In 1979 President Jimmy Carter (1924–) reassessed the need for the SSP and considered canceling it. According to the *Columbia* Accident Investigation Board, in *CAIB Report: Volume 1,* he decided to continue shuttle development because the United States wanted to launch intelligence satellites to monitor the Soviet Union's nuclear missile program. As a result, the White House and Congress put their support behind the space shuttle. In early 1981 NASA declared that development was complete. The shuttle was "finished" and was only 15% over its original budget.

Table 4.1 lists the major design parameters of the shuttle and the orbiter. Figure 4.4 shows various views of the space shuttle orbiter.

SPACE SHUTTLE FLIGHT PROFILE

The ten panels of Figure 4.5 illustrate the major steps in a space shuttle flight from launch to landing.

Launch

The countdown to launch begins approximately four days before liftoff. During this time many systems checks are conducted on the spacecraft and its components. The flight crew is taken to the orbiter approximately two and a half hours before liftoff and strapped into their seats.

The shuttle is launched in a vertical position, with its nose pointing up. At 6.6 seconds before launch, the three main engines at the rear of the orbiter are ignited. These engines burn fuel contained in the external fuel tank. The external fuel tank includes two separate compartments. Liquid hydrogen is kept in one compartment, and liquid oxygen in the other.

When the countdown reaches zero, the solid rocket boosters (SRBs) are ignited. The SRBs are metal housings filled with solid fuel (aluminum powder and other dry chemicals). Ignition of the SRBs provides the powerful push needed to lift the spacecraft off the ground and overcome the effects of Earth's gravity during ascent. The ride for the crew is very rough and bumpy while the SRBs are firing. However, the acceleration load on the humans is designed to stay below three Gs. In other words, the force of gravity "pushing" against the crew members as the shuttle accelerates is only three times the force of gravity on Earth.

Approximately two minutes after liftoff, the shuttle reaches a vertical distance of twenty-eight miles and travels at about three thousand miles per hour. At this point, the SRBs are jettisoned away from the vehicle because their fuel has been consumed. The SRBs are equipped with parachutes that open after the boosters have fallen a specified distance. The SRBs splash into the ocean and are retrieved for reuse.

The ride becomes smoother for the shuttle crew after the SRBs are jettisoned. The shuttle's main engines continue to fire until they have used up all the fuel in the external tank. This occurs at 8.5 minutes after liftoff. At this point, the shuttle is above Earth's atmosphere and traveling at a speed of five miles per second. The main engines are shut down and, seconds later, the external fuel tank is jettisoned away from the vehicle. The tank burns up during atmospheric reentry. Only the orbiter is left to continue the journey.

Orbit

The shuttle assumes an LEO, typically 150 to 250 miles above sea level, where it travels at about 17,600

FIGURE 4.4

Space shuttle orbiter

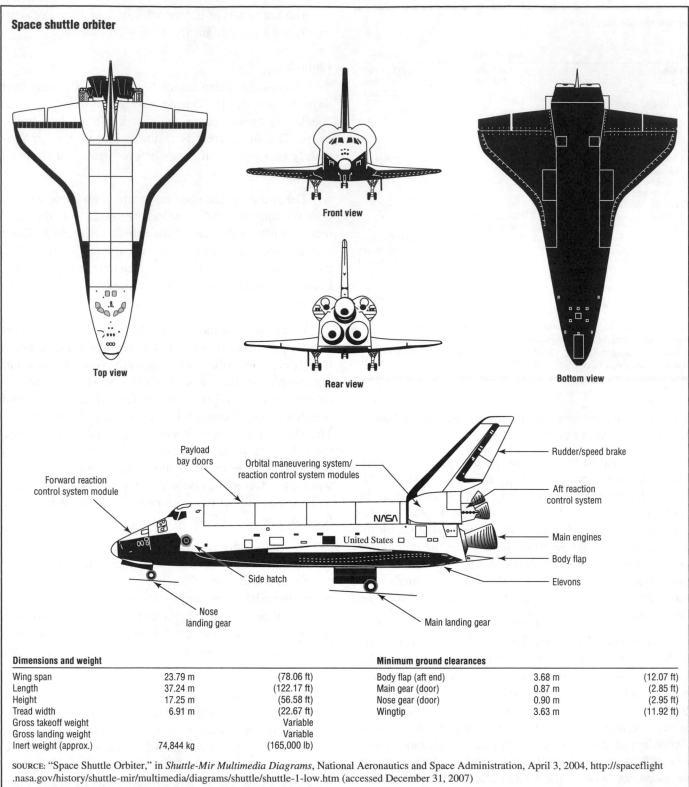

Front view

Top view

Rear view

Bottom view

Dimensions and weight			Minimum ground clearances		
Wing span	23.79 m	(78.06 ft)	Body flap (aft end)	3.68 m	(12.07 ft)
Length	37.24 m	(122.17 ft)	Main gear (door)	0.87 m	(2.85 ft)
Height	17.25 m	(56.58 ft)	Nose gear (door)	0.90 m	(2.95 ft)
Tread width	6.91 m	(22.67 ft)	Wingtip	3.63 m	(11.92 ft)
Gross takeoff weight		Variable			
Gross landing weight		Variable			
Inert weight (approx.)	74,844 kg	(165,000 lb)			

SOURCE: "Space Shuttle Orbiter," in *Shuttle-Mir Multimedia Diagrams*, National Aeronautics and Space Administration, April 3, 2004, http://spaceflight .nasa.gov/history/shuttle-mir/multimedia/diagrams/shuttle/shuttle-1-low.htm (accessed December 31, 2007)

miles per hour. It takes the craft approximately forty-five minutes after liftoff to reach its orbit.

The orbiter includes a series of small engines that allow the flight crew to maneuver while in space. These engines comprise the orbital maneuvering system (OMS) and the reaction control system (RCS).

The OMS engines are mounted on both sides of the upper aft fuselage. They provide the thrust needed to make major orbital maneuvers, for example, to move the shuttle into orbit, change orbits, and rendezvous with other spacecraft in orbit. Such instances are called orbit maneuver burns, because the engines are temporarily

FIGURE 4.5

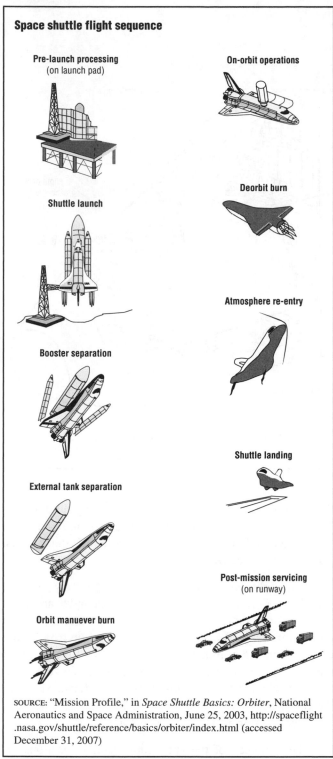

Space shuttle flight sequence

Pre-launch processing
(on launch pad)

Shuttle launch

Booster separation

External tank separation

Orbit manuever burn

On-orbit operations

Deorbit burn

Atmosphere re-entry

Shuttle landing

Post-mission servicing
(on runway)

SOURCE: "Mission Profile," in *Space Shuttle Basics: Orbiter*, National Aeronautics and Space Administration, June 25, 2003, http://spaceflight .nasa.gov/shuttle/reference/basics/orbiter/index.html (accessed December 31, 2007)

FIGURE 4.6

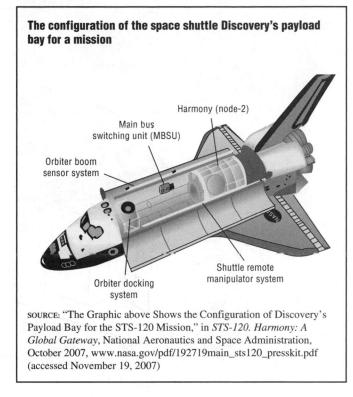

The configuration of the space shuttle Discovery's payload bay for a mission

Harmony (node-2)

Main bus switching unit (MBSU)

Orbiter boom sensor system

Shuttle remote manipulator system

Orbiter docking system

SOURCE: "The Graphic above Shows the Configuration of Discovery's Payload Bay for the STS-120 Mission," in *STS-120. Harmony: A Global Gateway*, National Aeronautics and Space Administration, October 2007, www.nasa.gov/pdf/192719main_sts120_presskit.pdf (accessed November 19, 2007)

The shuttle can carry satellites or heavy equipment needed for space station construction in its large payload bay. Some satellites are intended for LEO, whereas others orbit at much higher distances. Shuttle crews can deploy, retrieve, and service LEO satellites from their spacecraft. Satellites that require higher orbits can also be deployed from the shuttle. These satellites have built-in propulsion systems that boost them into their orbits once they are a safe distance away from the shuttle.

The payload bay is equipped with a fifty-foot-long robotic arm called the remote manipulator system (RMS). The RMS is also called the Canadarm, because it was developed by Canadian companies. A crewmember operates the RMS from the orbiter flight deck. The RMS is used to move things in and out of the cargo bay and on and off the *ISS* and to grab and position satellites. In 2005 a fifty-foot-long extension to the RMS was added to the shuttle. The orbiter boom sensor system (OBSS) is equipped with sensors and imaging systems and allows the crew to scan most of the outside of the orbiter for any damage.

The shuttle is equipped with specialized laboratories in which crewmembers can conduct experiments related to astronomy, earth sciences, medicine, and other fields. Most of these experiments take place in pressurized modules specifically designed for shuttle flights. Similar containers called multipurpose logistics modules (MPLMs) are used as cargo vessels to transport equipment and supplies to and from the *ISS*. Figure 4.6 shows how payloads were configured in the payload bay for a shuttle flight in 2007.

ignited to achieve them. The RCS engines are located along either side of the orbiter's tail and on its nose. They provide small amounts of thrust for delicate and exacting maneuvers.

During orbit the space shuttle crew performs a variety of tasks depending on the mission requirements. The shuttle was designed to carry payloads into space and to serve as a short-term laboratory for science experiments.

FIGURE 4.7

Shuttle crew module layout

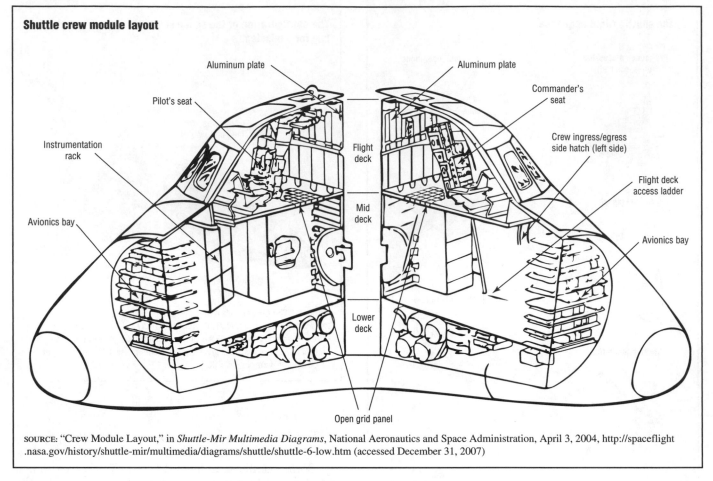

SOURCE: "Crew Module Layout," in *Shuttle-Mir Multimedia Diagrams*, National Aeronautics and Space Administration, April 3, 2004, http://spaceflight .nasa.gov/history/shuttle-mir/multimedia/diagrams/shuttle/shuttle-6-low.htm (accessed December 31, 2007)

A space shuttle crew normally consists of five members: a commander, a pilot, and three mission specialists. These are all NASA personnel. The commander has onboard responsibility for the mission, the crew, and the vehicle. The pilot assists the commander in operating and controlling the shuttle and may help deploy and retrieve satellites using the RMS. Mission specialists work with the commander and pilot and have specific responsibilities relating to shuttle systems, crew activities, consumables (food and water), scientific experiments, and/or payloads. Mission specialists are trained to perform extravehicular activities (EVAs; space walks) and to operate the RMS.

Besides the commander, pilot, and mission specialists, there may be one or two "guest" crewmembers called payload specialists. Payload specialists are not considered NASA astronauts. They perform specialized functions related to payloads and may be nominated by private companies, universities, foreign payload sponsors, or NASA. Payload specialists can also be foreign astronauts recommended by foreign space agencies.

The crew spends time in the crew module. This 2,325-cubic-foot module is pressurized and maintained at a comfortable temperature to provide what is called a "shirt-sleeve environment." The crew module includes

the flight deck, the mid-deck/equipment bay, and an airlock. The airlock contains two spacesuits and space for two crewmembers to put on and take off these suits. Spacesuits are required during EVAs.

The flight deck is the top level of the crew module. (See Figure 4.7.) This is where the commander and pilot spend most of their time during a mission. During launch and reentry they sit in the two seats facing the front of the orbiter with the commander on the left and the pilot on the right. The orbiter can be piloted from either seat. Two other crewmembers sit behind these seats further back in the flight deck. Any other crew members sit in the mid-deck section during launch and reentry.

The mid-deck of the crew cabin includes stations for meals, personal hygiene, and sleeping. This area includes the waste management system, a table, and stowage space for gear. In an emergency three additional seats can be placed in the mid-deck crew cabin for reentry. This allows the shuttle to carry ten crewmembers back to Earth. Such a contingency might be needed to rescue astronauts from the *ISS*.

Reentry and Landing

To reenter Earth's atmosphere, the shuttle has to decrease its speed by a substantial amount. This is performed via a deorbit burn in which the shuttle is turned upside down with its tail toward the direction it wants to go. The firing of the OMS engines slows the spacecraft down. It then flips over and reenters the atmosphere with the nose pointed up at an angle. (See Figure 4.5.) This ensures that the well-protected underside of the orbiter takes the brunt of reentry heat.

Reentry is a dangerous time for the shuttle. Any failure of the thermal protection system could allow super-hot gases to enter the orbiter. Reentry begins about seventy-six miles above Earth's surface. Following reentry, the shuttle glides through the air to its landing site.

Emergency Flight Options

The SSP includes a variety of flight options in the event of an emergency. If there is a problem with the main engines up to four minutes after liftoff, the shuttle can undergo a procedure called Return to Launch Site (RTLS) abort. The SRBs and external tank are jettisoned and the orbiter is maneuvered into position to glide back to the launch site. If an RTLS abort is not possible, there is also the option to land the orbiter at an overseas location. This is called a Transatlantic Abort Landing (TAL). There are three TAL landing locations along the western coast of Europe and Africa: Moron, Spain; Ben Guerur, Morocco, and Dakar, Senegal.

If the orbiter launches successfully but cannot reach its intended orbit, then an Abort-to-Orbit procedure is followed. This means that the spacecraft assumes a lower orbit than planned. If the orbiter cannot maintain any orbit, it returns to Earth for reentry and landing. It may travel once around Earth before it does so. This option is called the Abort Once Around.

The final emergency flight option is called the contingency abort. This procedure is undertaken if the orbiter cannot land on a landing strip for some reason. It calls for the orbiter to be put into a glide and the crew to use the in-flight escape system. This includes a pole that is extended out the side hatch door. The crewmembers can then slide along the pole to the end and parachute to the ground.

SSP ORGANIZATION

The SSP is administered and operated by NASA, with the help of thousands of contract employees. Figure 4.8 shows the locations of key NASA and contractor facilities involved in the SSP. Strategic management of the program is handled at NASA's headquarters in Washington, D.C. This is where major decisions are made about future missions.

The Johnson Space Center (JSC) in Houston, Texas, is home to the operational offices of the program. This office administers the Space Flight Operations Contract, a contract originally signed in 1996 between NASA and the United Space Alliance (a joint venture between the Boeing and Lockheed Martin corporations). The United Space Alliance (2008, http://www.unitedspacealliance .com/) performs the day-to-day operations of the SSP. The original contract included two two-year extension options, both of which were exercised by NASA. The contract expired at the end of September 2006; however, a new contract (Space Programs Operations Contract) was signed and is good through 2010—the expected end date of the SSP. As of 2008 the United Space Alliance employed more than ten thousand people. Most of these people work at the JSC, the KSC, and the Marshall Space Flight Center (MSFC) in Huntsville, Alabama.

The JSC also hosts the mission control center, astronaut training, and shuttle simulation facilities. The KSC supplies the shuttle launch and landing facilities; maintains and overhauls the orbiters; packages components for the orbiter laboratories; and assembles, tests, and refurbishes motors for the SRBs.

The manufacturing contracts for the SSP are overseen by NASA at the MSFC. Major contractors include Boeing, the United Technologies Corporation's Pratt & Whitney Rocketdyne, Lockheed Martin, and ATK Thiokol Propulsion. These companies manufacture the space shuttle main engines and turbopumps, the external tank, the solid rocket motors, and the reinforced carbon-carbon panels for the thermal protection system. The MSFC is also involved in the research and development of payloads that fly on the shuttles.

The shuttles' main engines and external tanks are tested at NASA's Stennis Space Center in Bay St. Louis, Mississippi. The Dryden Flight Research Center is located at the Edwards AFB in California. This is the backup landing site for the shuttle.

Other NASA centers assist the SSP by developing or testing shuttle components or fuels at their facilities. The shuttle thermal protection system is developed at the Ames Research Center in Moffett Field, California. The highly toxic fuels called hypergols that are used to run the orbiter's OMS and RCS engines are tested at the White Sands Test Facility in New Mexico. The orbiter structure is tested in wind tunnels at the Langley Research Center in Hampton, Virginia.

SPACE SHUTTLE MISSIONS

On April 12, 1981, *Columbia* became the first shuttle to fly into space. The flight's purpose was to test the shuttle's systems, and the mission lasted only two days. It was considered a huge success. Three more test flights were conducted during 1981 and 1982, all with the orbiter *Columbia*. On July 4, 1982, President Ronald Reagan (1911–2004) announced that shuttle testing was completed. The next flight of the shuttle was to begin its operational phase.

FIGURE 4.8

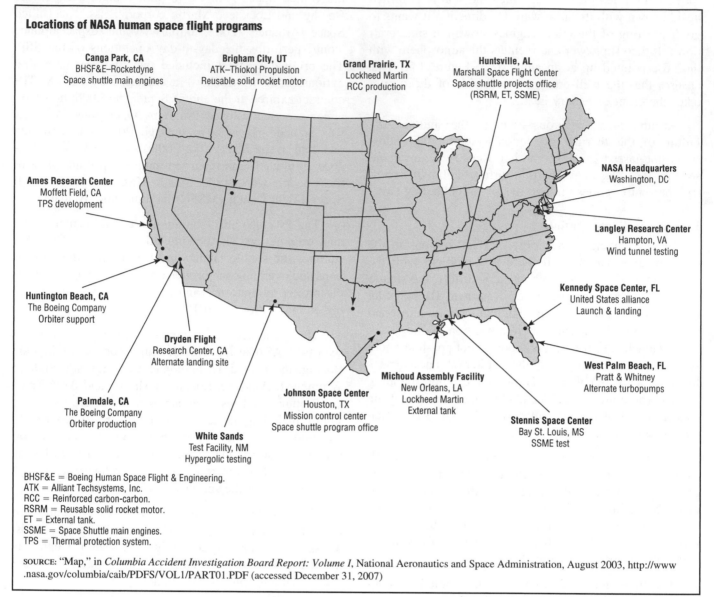

Locations of NASA human space flight programs

Canga Park, CA
BHSF&E–Rocketdyne
Space shuttle main engines

Brigham City, UT
ATK–Thiokol Propulsion
Reusable solid rocket motor

Grand Prairie, TX
Lockheed Martin
RCC production

Huntsville, AL
Marshall Space Flight Center
Space shuttle projects office
(RSRM, ET, SSME)

NASA Headquarters
Washington, DC

Ames Research Center
Moffett Field, CA
TPS development

Langley Research Center
Hampton, VA
Wind tunnel testing

Huntington Beach, CA
The Boeing Company
Orbiter support

Kennedy Space Center, FL
United States alliance
Launch & landing

Dryden Flight
Research Center, CA
Alternate landing site

West Palm Beach, FL
Pratt & Whitney
Alternate turbopumps

Palmdale, CA
The Boeing Company
Orbiter production

Johnson Space Center
Houston, TX
Mission control center
Space shuttle program office

Michoud Assembly Facility
New Orleans, LA
Lockheed Martin
External tank

White Sands
Test Facility, NM
Hypergolic testing

Stennis Space Center
Bay St. Louis, MS
SSME test

BHSF&E = Boeing Human Space Flight & Engineering.
ATK = Alliant Techsystems, Inc.
RCC = Reinforced carbon-carbon.
RSRM = Reusable solid rocket motor.
ET = External tank.
SSME = Space Shuttle main engines.
TPS = Thermal protection system.

SOURCE: "Map," in *Columbia Accident Investigation Board Report: Volume I*, National Aeronautics and Space Administration, August 2003, http://www
.nasa.gov/columbia/caib/PDFS/VOL1/PART01.PDF (accessed December 31, 2007)

Space shuttle flights including the orbiters *Columbia*, *Challenger*, *Discovery*, and *Atlantis* carried out twenty-four missions before disaster struck.

On January 28, 1986, *Challenger* broke apart only seventy-three seconds after liftoff. The seven crewmembers who were killed in the accident were Francis R. Scobee (1939–1986), Michael J. Smith (1945–1986), Judith A. Resnik (1949–1986), Ron McNair (1950–1986), Ellison S. Onizuka (1946–1986), Gregory B. Jarvis (1944–1986), and Christa McAuliffe (1948–1986). McAuliffe was a teacher who had been selected for the mission by NASA to capture the imagination of U.S. schoolchildren.

An investigation of the accident revealed that a faulty joint and seal in a solid rocket booster allowed hot gases to escape from the booster and ignite the hydrogen fuel. The resulting explosion tore the shuttle apart. The trag-edy brought intense scrutiny and criticism of the SSP from government investigators.

President Reagan appointed a panel called the Rogers Commission to investigate the accident. The commission issued its findings in *Report of the Presidential Commission on the Space Shuttle Challenger Accident* (February 3, 1986, http://science.ksc.nasa.gov/shuttle/missions/51-l/docs/rogers-commission/table-of-contents.html). The commission complained that the decision to launch *Challenger* was flawed because of poor communication. The managers making the launch decision did not have access to all the information. For example, they were not aware that some contractor engineers were concerned about the cold weather forecast for the morning of the launch. They feared that cold temperatures might compromise the integrity of the SRB seals. These fears were downplayed by NASA officials and not passed on to those making the launch decision.

TABLE 4.2

Orbiter vehicles

Orbiter name	NASA code number	Date completed	Date of first launch	Named after	Note
Enterprise	OV-101	September 1976	Not applicable	The starship Enterprise in the television series "Star Trek"	Used for testing only during the 1970s, never launched into space
Columbia	OV-102	March 1979	April 12, 1981	A ship captained by American explorer Robert Gray during the 1790s	Destroyed during reentry, February 1, 2003
Challenger	OV-99	July 1982	April 4, 1983	A British naval research vessel that sailed during the 1870s	Destroyed shortly after launch, January 28, 1986
Discovery	OV-103	November 1983	August 30, 1984	A ship captained by British explorer James Cook during the 1770s	First shuttle to dock with the International Space Station (1999)
Atlantis	OV-104	April 1985	October 3, 1985	A research vessel used by the Woods Hole Oceanographic Institute in Massachusetts from 1930 to 1966	First shuttle to dock with the Russian spacecraft Mir (1995)
Endeavour	OV-105	May 1991	September 12, 1992	A ship captained by British explorer James Cook during the 1760s	Built to replace Challenger. Endeavour was the first shuttle to fly to the International Space Station (1998)

SOURCE: Adapted from *Orbiter Vehicles*, National Aeronautics and Space Administration, February 1, 2003, http://science.ksc.nasa.gov/shuttle/resources/orbiters/orbiters.html (accessed December 31, 2007)

Besides problems specific to the *Challenger* accident, the commission blamed NASA for fostering an overall culture that put schedule ahead of safety concerns. To reduce the scheduling pressure, it was decided that the shuttle would cease carrying commercial satellites and phase out military missions as soon as possible. The air force had hoped to stage the first shuttle launch ever from the Vandenberg AFB in 1986. The *Challenger* accident and the resulting decision to cease carrying military payloads put an end to these plans. The launch facilities at Vandenberg were dismantled and abandoned, and most of the equipment was transferred to NASA facilities.

NASA explains in *Shuttle Triumphs and Tragedies* (October 25, 2006, http://aerospacescholars.jsc.nasa.gov/HAS/cirr/ss/2/6.cfm) that a number of organizational changes were made within NASA in response to the *Challenger* accident. Shuttle management was moved from the JSC to NASA headquarters in Washington, D.C. In addition, NASA created a new office in charge of safety, reliability, and quality assurance. The entire orbiter fleet was grounded and upgraded with new equipment and systems. A new orbiter named *Endeavour* was built to replace *Challenger*. A White House committee later estimated that the shuttle disaster cost the nation approximately $12 billion. This included the cost of building a new orbiter.

Table 4.2 provides general information about each orbiter in the shuttle fleet.

The shuttle flew again on September 29, 1988, with the successful launch of *Discovery* thirty-two months after the *Challenger* accident. Space shuttles flew eighty-seven successful missions between 1988 and 2002. Then, tragedy struck again. On February 1, 2003, *Columbia* broke apart during reentry over the western United States. Seven crewmembers were killed: Rick D. Husband (1957–2003), William C. McCool (1961–2003), David M. Brown (1956–2003), Kalpana Chawla (1962–2003), Michael P. Anderson (1959–2003), Laurel B. Clark (1961–2003), and Ilan Ramon (1954–2003). Ramon was a colonel from the Israeli air force who traveled on the shuttle as a guest payload specialist. Following the accident, the shuttle fleet was grounded for more than two years.

THE *COLUMBIA* ACCIDENT

Immediately after the *Columbia* disaster, President Bush appointed a panel to investigate what happened. The panel was called the *Columbia* Accident Investigation Board (CAIB). In August 2003 the CAIB released its report, *CAIB Report: Volume 1*, which concluded that the most likely cause of the accident was a damaged thermal protection tile on the orbiter's left wing. Video clips of the launch showed a large piece of foam falling off the external tank and striking the left wing eighty-two seconds after liftoff. This piece of foam fell a distance of only fifty-eight feet. However, the space shuttle was traveling very fast when this occurred, so the foam struck with extreme force.

NASA engineers knew about the foam strike, but were unsure whether it had caused any damage. Even though *Columbia* was in orbit, some engineers suggested that high-resolution photographs be taken of the orbiter using DOD satellites or NASA's ground-based telescopes. This suggestion was overruled by NASA officials, who believed that the foam strike did not endanger mission safety.

During reentry to Earth's atmosphere, one or more damaged thermal tiles along the left wing likely allowed hot gases to breach the shuttle structure. Aerodynamic stresses then tore it apart. Debris from the shuttle was found spread along a corridor across southeastern Texas and into Louisiana.

The CAIB was extremely critical of the entire SSP and complained that NASA shuttle managers had once again become preoccupied with schedule, rather than safety. Beginning in 1998 the SSP was under tremendous pressure to meet construction deadlines for the *ISS*. Nearly every shuttle flight undertaken between 1999 and 2003 was in support of the *ISS*.

The CAIB recommended a number of major changes within the SSP and within NASA management. One of the recommendations was that NASA develop a means for the shuttle crew to inspect the orbiter while docked at the *ISS* and repair any damage discovered. Such a procedure might have saved the *Columbia* crew. Implementation of the so-called Safe Haven program was recommended before any future shuttle flight.

THE RETURN TO FLIGHT

Soon after publication of the CAIB report, the NASA administration appointed a Return to Flight (RTF) Task Group to assess the agency's progress of implementing CAIB recommendations before shuttle flights were resumed. The task group was an independent advisory group consisting of more than two dozen non-NASA employees with expertise in engineering, science, planning, budget, safety, and risk management. Its members were granted access to NASA facilities and meetings as the agency regrouped and developed new safety strategies.

The most critical technical issue was debris shedding from the external tank during ascent and subsequent damage to the orbiter's thermal protection system. The primary focus was on eliminating external tank debris and using devices to detect debris impacts. The procedures were changed for applying foam insulation to the external tank, and quality control and inspection programs were expanded. Equipment changes were implemented to provide a smoother surface for foam application and to impede ice formation.

NASA decided that the first two shuttle flights after the *Columbia* disaster would be "test" flights to assess the effectiveness of new safety changes. *Discovery* was selected for the first RTF mission. More than one hundred cameras were installed on exterior spacecraft surfaces and at ground locations to provide an array of observation angles during ascent. The fifty-foot-long OBSS was installed on the end of the shuttle remote manipulator system to allow visual inspection of the wing tips and most of the orbiter underbelly while in flight. (See Figure 4.9.)

FIGURE 4.9

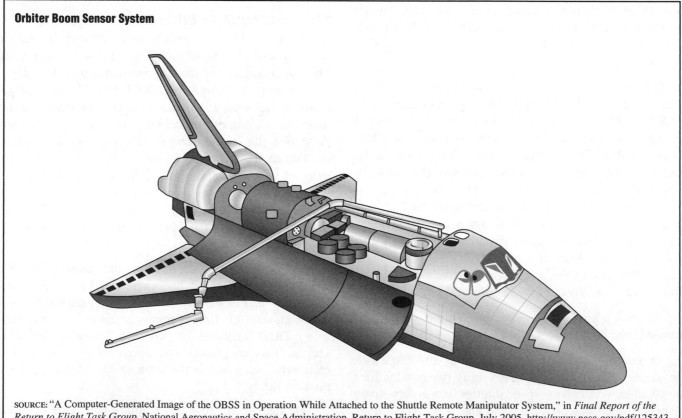

Orbiter Boom Sensor System

SOURCE: "A Computer-Generated Image of the OBSS in Operation While Attached to the Shuttle Remote Manipulator System," in *Final Report of the Return to Flight Task Group*, National Aeronautics and Space Administration, Return to Flight Task Group, July 2005, http://www.nasa.gov/pdf/125343 main_RTFTF_final_081705.pdf (accessed December 31, 2007)

TABLE 4.3

Status of Columbia Accident Investigation Board (CAIB) recommendations, 2005

CAIB number	CAIB recommendation	Return to flight status
3.2–1	External tank debris shedding	Not met
3.3–1	Reinforced carbon-carbon non-destructive inspection	Met
3.3–2	Orbiter hardening	Not met
3.4–1	Ground-based imagery	Met
3.4–2	High-resolution images of external tank	Met
3.4–3	High-resolution images of Orbiter	Met
4.2–1	Solid rocket booster bolt catcher	Met
4.2–3	Two person close-out inspection	Met
4.2–5	Kennedy Space Center foreign object debris definition	Met
6.2–1	Consistency with resources (schedule pressures)	Met
6.3–1	Mission management team improvements	Met
6.3–2	National Imagery and Mapping Agency agreement	Met
6.4–1	Thermal protection system inspection and repair	Not met
9.1–1	Detailed plan for organizational change	Met
10.3–1	Digitize closeout photos	Met

SOURCE: Adapted from "The Following Table Summarizes the Task Group's Assessment of the CAIB Return-to-Flight Recommendations," in *Final Report of the Return to Flight Task Group*, National Aeronautics and Space Administration, Return to Flight Task Group, July 2005, http://www.nasa.gov/pdf/125343main_RTFTF_final_081705.pdf (accessed December 31, 2007)

A team of image analysts was assembled at the JSC to inspect the images for any signs of damage. Dozens of sensors were installed on the wing edges of *Discovery* to take temperature readings and record the time and location of any debris impacts.

On July 26, 2005, *Discovery* launched from the KSC for a fourteen-day mission. The orbiter, with a seven-member crew onboard, docked with the *ISS* and unloaded equipment there. Three space walks were conducted including one in which astronauts tested new repair techniques for the thermal protection system. The shuttle landed safely at the Edwards AFB on August 9, 2005. NASA proclaimed the first RTF a success. However, camera footage showed that foam debris had shed from the external tank during shuttle ascent. Luckily, the debris did not hit the orbiter. NASA and the public realized that the hazard that had doomed *Columbia* had not been eliminated, but merely avoided by chance this time.

The *Final Report of the Return to Flight Task Group* (July 2005, http://www.nasa.gov/pdf/125343main_RTFTF_final_081705.pdf) was released to the public after the landing of *Discovery*. However, the task force's findings were communicated to NASA directors before launch. The task force reported that NASA had "met the intent" of twelve of the fifteen most critical recommendations made by the CAIB. (See Table 4.3.) The other three recommendations were considered "so challenging" that NASA was unable to comply with them before the RTF. The three problem areas were:

- External tank debris shedding
- Orbiter hardening
- Thermal protection system inspection and repair

The task force noted that "it has proven impossible to completely eliminate debris shedding from the External Tank. The hard fact of the matter is that the External Tank will always shed debris, perhaps even pieces large enough to do critical damage to the Orbiter." Technical and time limitations also prevented NASA from successfully hardening orbiter surfaces to prevent damage from debris impacts and from proving that a damaged thermal protection system could be repaired while a shuttle was in orbit.

On July 4, 2006, the second RTF mission began with the launch of *Discovery* on a thirteen-day mission. *Discovery* carried the Leonardo MPLM to the space station. The mission also involved crucial tests of the orbiter's thermal protection system and testing of techniques for inspecting and protecting the system. Over one hundred high-definition cameras recorded the launch and ascent phases so the images could be scoured for signs of damage to the orbiter. In addition, the shuttle crew used the OBSS to carefully inspect the craft while it was docked at the *ISS*. Fortunately, no significant damage was detected. *Discovery* landed safely on July 17, 2006.

MISSIONS SINCE THE RETURN TO FLIGHT

As of December 2007, the space shuttle had undertaken five successful missions since the second RTF flight. All the missions were dedicated to *ISS* assembly. Extensive imaging and visual inspections were conducted during each shuttle flight to identify any damage to the thermal protection system due to foam debris impacts during launch. In all cases the orbiters were deemed structurally sound for reentry. A freak hail storm in February 2007 damaged *Atlantis* as it sat on the launch pad for an expected launch of STS-117 in March 2007. That mission had to be delayed for nearly three months, seriously affecting the shuttle's future launch schedule. Prelaunch sensor problems postponed the scheduled launch of *Discovery* in December 2007. That mission was not expected to take place until February 2008, at the earliest.

ACCOMPLISHMENTS OF THE SSP

A historical summary of all the space shuttle missions conducted as of December 2007 is presented in Table 4.4.

NASA refers to each shuttle flight using a Space Transportation System (STS) number. Thus, STS-1 was the first shuttle flight into space. NASA assigns numbers to space shuttle flights in the order in which they are planned (or manifested). There is typically a period of several years between the time a mission is planned and the time of its scheduled launch. During this period

TABLE 4.4

Space shuttle missions, 1981–2007

Flight order	STS number	Orbiter name	Primary payload	Launch date	Landing date
1	STS-1	Columbia	Shuttle systems test	4/12/1981	4/14/1981
2	STS-2	Columbia	OSTA-1	11/12/1981	11/14/1981
3	STS-3	Columbia	Office of Space Science-1 (OSS-1)	3/22/1982	3/30/1982
4	STS-4	Columbia	DOD and Continuous flow electrophoresis system (CFES)	6/27/1982	7/4/1982
5	STS-5	Columbia	Canadian satellite ANIK C-3; SBS-C	11/11/1982	11/16/1982
6	STS-6	Challenger	TDRS-1	4/4/1983	4/9/1983
7	STS-7	Challenger	Canadian satellite ANIK C-2; PALAPA B1	6/18/1983	6/24/1983
8	STS-8	Challenger	India satellite INSAT-1B	8/30/1983	9/5/1983
9	STS-9	Columbia	Spacelab-1	11/28/1983	12/8/1983
10	STS-41-B	Challenger	WESTAR-VI; PALAPA-B2	2/3/1984	2/11/1984
11	STS-41-C	Challenger	LDEF deploy	4/6/1984	4/13/1984
12	STS-41-D	Discovery	SBS-D; SYNCOM IV-2; TELSTAR	8/30/1984	9/5/1984
13	STS-41-G	Challenger	Earth radiation budget satellite (ERBS); OSTA-3	10/5/1984	10/13/1984
14	STS-51-A	Discovery	Canadian communications satellite TELESAT-H; SYNCOM IV-1	11/8/1984	11/16/1984
15	STS-51-C	Discovery	DOD	1/24/1985	1/27/1985
16	STS-51-D	Discovery	Canadian satellite TELESAT-I; SYNCOM IV-3	4/12/1985	4/19/1985
17	STS-51-B	Challenger	Spacelab-3	4/29/1985	5/6/1985
18	STS-51-G	Discovery	MORELOS-A; Arab satellite ARABSAT-A; AT&T satellite TELSTAR-3D	6/17/1985	6/24/1985
19	STS-51-F	Challenger	Spacelab-2	7/29/1985	8/6/1985
20	STS-51-I	Discovery	American satellite ASC-1; AUSSAT-1; SYNCOM IV-4	8/27/1985	9/3/1985
21	STS-51-J	Atlantis	DOD	10/3/1985	10/7/1985
22	STS-61-A	Challenger	D-1 Spacelab mission (first German-dedicated Spacelab)	10/30/1985	11/6/1985
23	STS-61-B	Atlantis	MORELOS-B; AUSSAT-2; RCA Americom satellite SATCOM KU-2	11/26/1985	12/3/1985
24	STS-61-C	Columbia	RCA Americom satellite SATCOM KU-1	1/12/1986	1/18/1986
25	STS-51-L	Challenger	TDRS-B; SPARTAN-203	1/28/1986	Vehicle broke apart 73 seconds after liftoff
26	STS-26	Discovery	TDRS-C	9/29/1988	10/3/1988
27	STS-27	Atlantis	DOD	12/2/1988	12/6/1988
28	STS-29	Discovery	TDRS-D	3/13/1989	3/18/1989
29	STS-30	Atlantis	Magellan	5/4/1989	5/8/1989
30	STS-28	Columbia	DOD	8/8/1989	8/13/1989
31	STS-34	Atlantis	Galileo; SSBUV	10/18/1989	10/23/1989
32	STS-33	Discovery	DOD	11/22/1989	11/27/1989
33	STS-32	Columbia	SYNCOM IV-F5; LDEF retrieval	1/9/1990	1/20/1990
34	STS-36	Atlantis	DOD	2/28/1990	3/4/1990
35	STS-31	Discovery	HST deploy	4/24/1990	4/29/1990
36	STS-41	Discovery	Ulysses; SSBUV; INTELSAT solar array coupon (ISAC)	10/6/1990	10/10/1990
37	STS-38	Atlantis	DOD	11/15/1990	11/20/1990
38	STS-35	Columbia	ASTRO-1	12/2/1990	12/10/1990
39	STS-37	Atlantis	Gamma Ray Observatory (GRO)	4/5/1991	4/11/1991
40	STS-39	Discovery	DOD; Air Force Program-675 (AFP675); infrared background signature survey (IBSS); shuttle pallet satellite-II (SPAS-II)	4/28/1991	5/6/1991
41	STS-40	Columbia	Spacelab Life Sciences-1 (SLS-1)	6/5/1991	6/14/1991
42	STS-43	Atlantis	TDRS-E; SSBUV	8/2/1991	8/11/1991
43	STS-48	Discovery	Upper atmosphere research satellite (UARS)	9/12/1991	9/18/1991
44	STS-44	Atlantis	DOD; Defense Support Program (DSP)	11/24/1991	12/1/1991
45	STS-42	Discovery	IML-1	1/22/1992	1/30/1992
46	STS-45	Atlantis	ATLAS-1	3/24/1992	4/2/1992
47	STS-49	Endeavour	Intelsat VI repair	5/7/1992	5/16/1992
48	STS-50	Columbia	USML-1	6/25/1992	7/9/1992
49	STS-46	Atlantis	TSS-1; EURECA deploy	7/31/1992	8/8/1992
50	STS-47	Endeavour	Spacelab-J	9/12/1992	9/20/1992
51	STS-52	Columbia	USMP-1; laser geodynamic satellite-II (LAGEOS-II)	10/22/1992	11/1/1992
52	STS-53	Discovery	DOD; Orbital Debris Radar Calibration Spheres (ODERACS)	12/2/1992	12/9/1992
53	STS-54	Endeavour	TDRS-F; Diffuse X-ray Spectrometer (DXS)	1/13/1993	1/19/1993
54	STS-56	Discovery	ATLAS-2; SPARTAN-201	4/8/1993	4/17/1993
55	STS-55	Columbia	D-2 Spacelab mission (second German-dedicated Spacelab)	4/26/1993	5/6/1993
56	STS-57	Endeavour	SPACEHAB-1; EURECA retrieval	6/21/1993	7/1/1993

TABLE 4.4

Space shuttle missions, 1981–2007 [CONTINUED]

Flight order	STS number	Orbiter name	Primary payload	Launch date	Landing date
57	STS-51	Discovery	Advanced Communications Technology Satellite (ACTS)/Transfer Orbit Stage (TOS)	9/12/1993	9/22/1993
58	STS-58	Columbia	Spacelab SLS-2	10/18/1993	11/1/1993
59	STS-61	Endeavour	1st HST servicing	12/2/1993	12/13/1993
60	STS-60	Discovery	WSF; SPACEHAB-2	2/3/1994	2/11/1994
61	STS-62	Columbia	USMP-2; Office of Aeronautics and Space Technology-2 (OAST-2)	3/4/1994	3/18/1994
62	STS-59	Endeavour	SRL-1	4/9/1994	4/20/1994
63	STS-65	Columbia	IML-2	7/8/1994	7/23/1994
64	STS-64	Discovery	LIDAR In-Space Technology Experiment (LITE); SPARTAN-201	9/9/1994	9/20/1994
65	STS-68	Endeavour	SRL-2	9/30/1994	10/11/1994
66	STS-66	Atlantis	ATLAS-03	11/3/1994	11/14/1994
67	STS-63	Discovery	SPACEHAB-3; Mir rendezvous	2/3/1995	2/11/1995
68	STS-67	Endeavour	ASTRO-2	3/2/1995	3/18/1995
69	STS-71	Atlantis	First Shuttle-Mir docking	6/27/1995	7/7/1995
70	STS-70	Discovery	TDRS-G	7/13/1995	7/22/1995
71	STS-69	Endeavour	SPARTAN 201–03; WSF-2	9/7/1995	9/18/1995
72	STS-73	Columbia	USML-2	10/20/1995	11/5/1995
73	STS-74	Atlantis	Second Shuttle-Mir docking	11/12/1995	11/20/1995
74	STS-72	Endeavour	Space Flyer Unit (SFU); Office of Aeronautics and Space Technology Flyer (OAST-Flyer)	1/11/1996	1/20/1996
75	STS-75	Columbia	TSS-1 Reflight; USMP-3	2/22/1996	3/9/1996
76	STS-76	Atlantis	Third Shuttle-Mir docking; SPACEHAB	3/22/1996	3/31/1996
77	STS-77	Endeavour	SPACEHAB; SPARTAN (Inflatable Antenna Experiment)	5/19/1996	5/29/1996
78	STS-78	Columbia	Life and Microgravity Spacelab (LMS)	6/20/1996	7/7/1996
79	STS-79	Atlantis	Fourth Shuttle-Mir docking	9/16/1996	9/26/1996
80	STS-80	Columbia	Orbiting and Retrievable Far and Extreme Ultraviolet Spectrograph-Shuttle Pallet Satellite II (ORFEUS-SPAS II)	11/19/1996	12/7/1996
81	STS-81	Atlantis	Fifth Shuttle-Mir docking	1/12/1997	1/22/1997
82	STS-82	Discovery	Second HST servicing	2/11/1997	2/21/1997
83	STS-83	Columbia	MSL-1	4/4/1997	4/8/1997
84	STS-84	Atlantis	Sixth Shuttle-Mir docking	5/15/1997	5/24/1997
85	STS-94	Columbia	MSL-1 Reflight	7/1/1997	7/17/1997
86	STS-85	Discovery	Cryogenic Infrared Spectrometers and Telescopes for the Atmosphere-Shuttle Pallet Satellite-2 (CRISTA-SPAS-2)	8/7/1997	8/19/1997
87	STS-86	Atlantis	Seventh Shuttle-Mir docking	9/25/1997	10/6/1997
88	STS-87	Columbia	USMP-4, Spartan-201 rescue	11/19/1997	12/5/1997
89	STS-89	Endeavour	Eighth Shuttle-Mir docking	1/22/1998	1/31/1998
90	STS-90	Columbia	Final Spacelab mission	4/17/1998	5/3/1998
91	STS-91	Discovery	Ninth and final Shuttle-Mir docking	6/2/1998	6/12/1998
92	STS-95	Discovery	John Glenn's Flight; SPACEHAB	10/29/1998	11/7/1998
93	STS-88	Endeavour	First ISS Flight	12/4/1998	12/15/1998
94	STS-96	Discovery	1st ISS docking	5/27/1999	6/6/1999
95	STS-93	Columbia	Chandra X-Ray Observatory	7/22/1999	7/27/1999
96	STS-103	Discovery	HST repair - 3A	12/19/1999	12/27/1999
97	STS-99	Endeavour	Shuttle Radar Topography Mission (SRTM)	2/11/2000	2/22/2000
98	STS-101	Atlantis	ISS Assembly Flight 2A.2a	5/19/2000	5/29/2000
99	STS-106	Atlantis	ISS Assembly Flight 2A.2b	9/8/2000	9/20/2000
100	STS-92	Discovery	ISS Assembly Flight 3A, Z1 Truss and PMA 3	10/11/2000	10/24/2000
101	STS-97	Endeavour	ISS Assembly Flight 4A, P6 Truss	11/30/2000	12/11/2000
102	STS-98	Atlantis	ISS Assembly Flight 5A, U.S. Destiny Laboratory	2/7/2001	2/20/2001
103	STS-102	Discovery	ISS Assembly Flight 5A.1, Crew Exchange, Leonardo Multi-Purpose Logistics Module	3/8/2001	3/21/2001
104	STS-100	Endeavour	ISS Assembly Flight 6A, Canadarm2, Raffaello Multi-Purpose Logistics Module	4/19/2001	5/1/2001
105	STS-104	Atlantis	ISS Assembly Flight 7A, Quest Airlock, High Pressure Gas Assembly	7/12/2001	7/24/2001
106	STS-105	Discovery	ISS Assembly Flight 7A.1, Crew Exchange, Leonardo Multi-Purpose Logistics Module	8/10/2001	8/22/2001
107	STS-108	Endeavour	ISS Flight UF-1, Crew Exchange, Raffaello Multi-Purpose Logistics Module, STARSHINE 2	12/5/2001	12/17/2001
108	STS-109	Columbia	HST Servicing Mission 3B	3/1/2002	3/12/2002
109	STS-110	Atlantis	ISS Flight 8A, S0 (S-Zero) Truss, Mobile Transporter	4/8/2002	4/19/2002
110	STS-111	Endeavour	ISS Flight UF-2, Crew Exchange, Mobile Base System	6/5/2002	6/19/2002
111	STS-112	Atlantis	ISS Flight 9A, S1 (S-One) Truss	10/7/2002	10/16/2002
112	STS-113	Endeavour	ISS Flight 11A, P1 (P-One) Truss	11/23/2002	12/7/2002

priorities can change, and missions are often reshuffled or canceled. This explains why the STS numbers in Table 4.4 do not always match the flight order number. For example, *Columbia*'s flight in 2003 was called STS-107, yet it was actually the 113th flight of a space shuttle. The missions numbered STS-108 through STS-113 wound up

TABLE 4.4

Flight order	STS number	Orbiter name	Primary payload	Launch date	Landing date
113	STS-107	Columbia	SpaceHab-DM Research Mission, Freestar module	1/16/2003	Vehicle broke up during reentry 2/1/03
114	STS-114	Discovery	ISS Assembly Flight LF1, External Stowage Platform-2, Raffaello Multi-Purpose Logistics Module	7/26/2005	8/9/2005
115	STS-121	Discovery	ISS Flight ULF-1, Leonardo Multi-Purpose Logistics Module; One ISS Crew member	7/4/2006	7/17/2006
116	STS-115	Atlantis	ISS Flight 12A, P3/P4 trusses w/solar arrays, Photovoltaic radiator	9/9/2006	9/21/2006
117	STS-116	Discovery	ISS Flight 12A.1, P5 spacer truss, SpaceHab cargo module, resupply	12/9/2006	12/22/2006
118	STS-117	Atlantis	ISS Flight 13A, S3/S4 trusses w/solar arrays, Photovoltaic radiator, Crew Exchange	6/8/2007	6/22/2007
119	STS-118	Endeavour	ISS Flight 13A.1, S5 truss, resupply, SpaceHab cargo module	8/8/2007	8/21/2007
120	STS-120	Discovery	ISS Flight 10A, Harmony node, Crew Exchange	10/23/2007	11/7/2007

Notes:
ATLAS   Atmospheric Laboratory for Applications and Science
AUSSAT   Australian satellite
DOD   Department of Defense
EURECA   European retrievable carrier
HST   Hubble space telescope
IML   International Microgravity Laboratory
ISS   International Space Station
LDEF   Long duration exposure facility
MORELOS Mexican satellite
MSL   Microgravity Science Laboratory
OSTA   Office of Space and Terrestrial Applications
PALAPA   Indonesian satellite
SBS   Satellite business systems
SRL   Space Radar Laboratory
SSBUV   Shuttle solar backscatter ultraviolet
SYNCOM   Synchronous communication satellite
TDRS   Tracking and data relay satellite
TSS   Tethered satellite system
USML   United States Microgravity Laboratory
USMP   U.S. microgravity payload
WSF   Wake shield facility

SOURCE: Adapted from "Shuttle Missions," in *Mission Archives*, National Aeronautics and Space Administration, 2007, http://spaceflight.NASA.gov/shuttle/archives (accessed December 31, 2007)

launching before STS-107 because they moved up in priority as launch time approached.

Shuttle flights have deployed more than fifty satellites for military, governmental, and commercial clients. In addition, three interplanetary craft were launched from shuttles: the *Magellan* spacecraft that traveled to Venus, the *Galileo* spacecraft that traveled to Jupiter, and the *Ulysses* spacecraft that traveled to the Sun. Shuttles have also deployed important observatories into space, including the *Hubble Space Telescope* (*HST*), the *Compton Gamma Ray Observatory*, the *Diffuse X-Ray Spectrometer*, and the *Chandra X-Ray Observatory*.

The shuttle has carried more than three million pounds of cargo and over six hundred crewmembers into space. Hundreds of scientific experiments have been conducted in orbit. Shuttle crews have also serviced and repaired satellites as needed, particularly the *HST*. Between 1995 and 1998 shuttles docked nine times with the Russian space station *Mir*. Flights to construct the *ISS* began in 1998. Shuttles carried major pieces of the *ISS* into space and traveled to the station twenty-three times through the end of 2007.

Despite these accomplishments, the shuttle has not met many of the original goals that NASA set for the program. NASA planners had promised that the shuttle would fly dozens of times per year. As shown in Figure 4.10, the most shuttle flights ever accomplished in one year was nine flights in 1985. For the twenty-seven-year period from 1981 through 2007, the shuttle averaged fewer than five flights per year.

NASA also promised that each shuttle orbiter would be good for one hundred flights. Figure 4.11 shows the number of flights achieved by each orbiter in the shuttle fleet as of December 2007. *Discovery* has made thirty-four flights, the most of any orbiter. *Challenger* made only ten flights before it was lost. *Columbia* made twenty-eight flights during its lifetime.

FIGURE 4.10

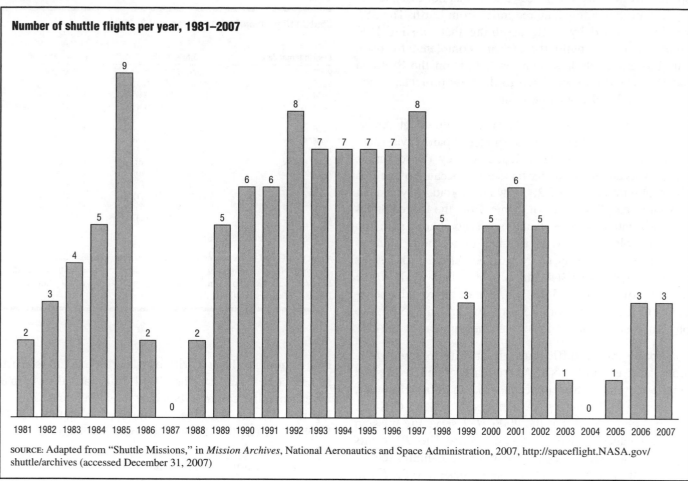

Number of shuttle flights per year, 1981–2007

SOURCE: Adapted from "Shuttle Missions," in *Mission Archives*, National Aeronautics and Space Administration, 2007, http://spaceflight.NASA.gov/ shuttle/archives (accessed December 31, 2007)

FIGURE 4.11

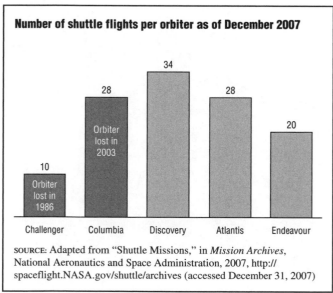

Number of shuttle flights per orbiter as of December 2007

SOURCE: Adapted from "Shuttle Missions," in *Mission Archives*, National Aeronautics and Space Administration, 2007, http:// spaceflight.NASA.gov/shuttle/archives (accessed December 31, 2007)

There are only three orbiters left in the fleet: *Discovery, Atlantis,* and *Endeavour.* As of 2008 *Discovery* was seventeen years old, and the other two were not much younger. Most of the original facilities and infrastructure built on the ground for the SSP are more than three decades old. To make matters worse, Hurricane Katrina inflicted severe damage to two crucial SSP facilities during the summer of 2005: the Michoud Assembly Facility in New Orleans, Louisiana, and the Stennis Space Center in Bay St. Louis, Mississippi.

The CAIB report was extremely critical of the SSP overall. Even though the panel acknowledged the shuttle as an "engineering marvel" with a wide range of abilities in Earth orbit, it nevertheless concluded that "the Shuttle has few of the mission capabilities that NASA originally promised. It cannot be launched on demand, does not recoup its costs, no longer carries national security payloads, and is not cost-effective enough, nor allowed by law, to carry commercial satellites. Despite efforts to improve its safety, the Shuttle remains a complex and risky system."

THE FUTURE OF THE SSP

In January 2004 President Bush announced a new vision for the future of the U.S. space program. It calls for NASA to send astronauts to the Moon by 2020 and to Mars after that. This would require a completely new spacecraft because the space shuttle was not designed to fly farther than a few hundred miles from Earth. The SSP would be ended by 2010, assuming that existing U.S. commitments to build the *ISS* are completed by then. The billions of dollars spent each year on the SSP and the *ISS* would be transferred to the new projects, which would also be allocated new funds.

During the grounding of the space shuttle fleet, American *ISS* crewmembers were transported aboard Soyuz rockets by the Russian Federal Space Agency (Roscosmos). NASA was unable to pay for this service because of the Iran Nonproliferation Act of 2000, which forbids payment of "extraordinary" amounts of money from the United States to Russia until it is proven that Russia is not sharing with Iran any technology related to missiles or weapons of mass destruction. To raise badly needed funds, Roscosmos charged "space tourists" millions of dollars to fly to the *ISS*. In November 2005 the U.S. Senate approved amendments to the Iran Nonproliferation Act allowing NASA to pay Roscosmos until 2012 for launches supporting the *ISS*.

Space shuttle difficulties affect other ongoing missions. For example, NASA originally planned to send shuttle astronauts to service the *HST* in 2006. However, in January 2004 the NASA administrator Sean O'Keefe (1956–) announced that the 2006 *HST* servicing mission had been canceled due to safety concerns. The *HST* orbits far from the *ISS*, and NASA feared that a shuttle sent to service the *HST* would not be able to make it to the *ISS* in case an emergency developed.

Cancellation of the shuttle servicing mission virtually ensured that the *HST* would malfunction to the point of

TABLE 4.5

Shuttle flight manifest as of January 3, 2008

Launch target date	Orbiter/flight	Mission
2008	Atlantis (STS-122)	ISS assembly
2008	Endeavour (STS-123)	ISS assembly
2008	Discovery (STS-124)	ISS assembly
2008	Atlantis (STS-125)	Hubble space telescope servicing mission 4
2008	Endeavour (STS-126)	ISS assembly
Under review	Discovery (STS-119)	ISS assembly
Under review	Endeavour (STS-127)	ISS assembly
Under review	Discovery (STS-128)	ISS assembly
Under review	Endeavour (STS-129)	ISS assembly
Under review	Discovery (STS-130)	ISS assembly
Under review	Endeavour (STS-131)	ISS assembly
Under review	Discovery (STS-132)	ISS assembly
Under review	Endeavour (STS-133)	ISS assembly

Note: ISS is International Space Station.

SOURCE: Adapted from "Launch Schedule," in *Consolidated Launch Manifest*, National Aeronautics and Space Administration, January 3, 2008, http://www.nasa.gov/mission_pages/station/structure/iss_manifest.html (accessed January 5, 2008)

being unusable. Then it will lose its orbit and fall to Earth sometime between 2011 and 2014. This caused an uproar in the scientific community and resulted in intense lobbying to NASA to reinstate the mission. In October 2006 Michael D. Griffin (1949–), the new NASA administrator, announced that the agency was reinstating the *HST* servicing mission. As of January 2008, this mission had not taken place, but it was listed on the proposed shuttle flight manifest. (See Table 4.5.) NASA plans to accomplish thirteen shuttle flights before the program ends in 2010.

CHAPTER 5
THE *INTERNATIONAL SPACE STATION*

I am directing NASA to develop a permanently manned space station and to do it within a decade.

—President Ronald Reagan, State of the Union Address, January 25, 1984

A space station is an orbiting structure designed to accommodate visiting crewmembers for an extended period. In 1984 the U.S. government envisioned building a continuously manned space station in which scientists would conduct long-term research in a microgravity (near weightlessness, almost zero gravity) environment. The station was to be large and spacious, with room for up to ten crewmembers at a time. The U.S. space shuttle was going to be the workhorse that carried cargo and astronauts to the station and back on a routine basis.

To save money on this expensive undertaking, the United States invited other countries to participate. Eventually, fifteen countries did so, including Russia, which assumed a major role in the project. The space station became an international venture. It also became extremely expensive. The design was changed several times to bring costs down. The development phase alone dragged on for more than a decade. In 1998 construction finally began on the *International Space Station* (*ISS*). After five years a small portion of the *ISS* was in orbit around Earth. Then the space shuttle *Columbia* exploded. The entire shuttle fleet was grounded while the National Aeronautics and Space Administration (NASA) investigated what went wrong. *ISS* construction was halted as well because only shuttles are powerful enough to haul heavy pieces of the *ISS* into space. This was a serious setback for the project.

In January 2004 President George W. Bush (1946–) set forth a new space agenda for the United States: sending astronauts to the Moon and Mars. The plan calls for aborting the shuttle program and ceasing *ISS* construction as soon as possible. That would mean a space station much smaller than expected, with limited research capabilities. Such a prospect is disappointing to many scientists around the world. However, others believe that even a downsized *ISS* is a major step on humanity's journey into outer space.

EARLY VISIONS OF A SPACE STATION

The first serious proposal for a space station was made in 1923 by Hermann Oberth (1894–1989). Oberth is considered one of the fathers of rocket science. His doctoral dissertation was "Die Rakete zu den Planetenräumen" ("The Rocket into Interplanetary Space").

Oberth proposed building an orbiting structure called a *weltraumstation* (space station) that would serve as a launching and refueling station for spacecraft engaged in deep space travel. Six years later he expanded on his ideas in *Wege zur Raumschiffart* (1929; *Methods of Achieving Space Flight*). Oberth's writings had a profound effect on the young Wernher von Braun (1912–1977), who later became a key developer of rocket science in the United States.

In 1929 Hermann Potocnik (1892–1929; also known as Herman Noordung) published his idea for an orbiting space station. Potocnik's spacecraft was wheel-shaped and primarily designed to be an observatory and scientific laboratory.

In 1952 von Braun published a drawing of his vision of a space station. It was a wheel-shaped structure that would orbit 1,075 miles above Earth and serve a variety of purposes. Von Braun envisioned the station aiding in navigation and weather forecasting on Earth and serving as a military outpost, spaceport, and launching platform for ventures into deep space.

According to NASA historians, the von Braun team encouraged NASA to build a space station before sending a man to the Moon. President John F. Kennedy (1917–1963) decided that the Apollo program should receive priority. However, a space station was always considered the next step after Apollo.

The U.S. Air Force pursued its own version of a space station during the 1960s. The Manned Orbiting Laboratory (MOL) included a large laboratory module that was reached by a Gemini-type spacecraft launched aboard a Titan rocket. The military hoped to use the MOL for reconnaissance missions and for weather observation. The U.S. government spent more than $1 billion researching and developing the MOL. The project suffered constant budget overruns and schedule delays and was finally canceled in 1969. By that time, unmanned reconnaissance satellites were available that could do much of what the MOL was to accomplish. Military astronauts who had been training in the MOL program were transferred to NASA.

THE AMERICAN *SKYLAB*

Long before an Apollo spacecraft landed on the Moon, NASA planners were looking ahead to their next great project. The Apollo Applications Program (AAP) began in 1963 with a plan to use leftover Apollo hardware in some kind of orbiting station including a laboratory, workshop, and space telescope. When the *Apollo 20* mission was canceled in 1970, the AAP inherited a Saturn V rocket. It used the rocket as the launch vehicle for a newly developed station called *Skylab*.

The *Skylab* program had two primary goals:

- Prove that humans could live and work in space for extended periods of time

- Expand knowledge of solar astronomy using a space-based telescope

The program was composed of four flights, as shown in Table 5.1.

The station was designed with two solar panels that were folded flat against the rocket during launch. Once in orbit, they were to open up like wings and harness the Sun's energy to provide electricity for the station. On May 14, 1973, the unmanned *Skylab* station was launched into orbit. It was damaged during liftoff when a protective shield came loose and smashed against the solar panels, ripping one of them off and damaging the other.

A team of three *Skylab* astronauts was scheduled to launch the next day. However, their flight was delayed for ten days as engineers assessed the damage to the station. The astronauts, called the *Skylab 2* crew, finally launched on May 25, 1973. They successfully docked with the station and began repairing its damaged components. Crewmembers deployed a temporary sail-like shield to replace the torn-off solar panel. Their mission lasted just over twenty-eight days, a new record for Americans in space. This record was bested by the astronauts of *Skylab 3* and *Skylab 4*.

The *Skylab* station weighed nearly one hundred tons and was about the size of a small three-bedroom house. It included a two-level workshop.

The *Skylab 3* mission included two spiders named Anita and Arabella. The spiders were part of an experiment suggested by Judith Miles, a high school student from Lexington, Massachusetts. She wondered if spiders would be able to spin their webs in microgravity. NASA scientists seized on the idea and sent the spiders into space in cages equipped with still cameras and television cameras. The public became enthralled in hearing about the two spiders.

Neither spider adjusted well to the new environment. Arabella's initial webs were sloppy and lopsided. However, after a few days the spider began spinning web patterns like it would on Earth. Both spiders died during the mission, apparently of dehydration. Their bodies were turned over to the Smithsonian Institution and were still kept there in 2008.

TABLE 5.1

Skylab statistics

	Skylab 1	Skylab 2	Skylab 3	Skylab 4
Launch date	5/14/1973	5/25/1973	7/28/1973	11/16/1973
Launch vehicles	Saturn V	Saturn 1B	Saturn 1B	Saturn 1B
Orbital parameters	268.1 × 269.5 miles	268.1 × 269.5 miles	268.1 × 269.5 miles	268.1 × 69.5 miles
Orbital inclination	50 degrees	50 degrees	50 degrees	50 degrees
Orbital period (approximate)	93 minutes	93 minutes	93 minutes	93 minutes
Distance orbit	26,575 miles	26,575 miles	26,575 miles	26,575 miles
Crew's mission distance		11.5 million miles	24.5 million miles	34.5 million miles
Crew's number of revolutions		404	585	1,214
Crew's mission duration		28 days 49 min	59 days 11 hrs 9 min	84 days 1 hr 16 min
Crew's experiment time		392 hr	1,081 hr	1,563 hr
Crew's EVA time		6 hr 20 min	13 hr 43 min	22 hr 13 min

Note: EVA is extravehicular activity.

SOURCE: Adapted from "Skylab Statistics," in *Skylab Program Overview*, National Aeronautics and Space Administration, Kennedy Space Center, December 12, 2000, http://www-pao.ksc.nasa.gov/kscpao/history/skylab/skylab-stats.htm (accessed December 31, 2007)

The *Skylab* was not designed for long-term use. It had no method of independent reboost to keep it from falling out of orbit. As a result, on July 11, 1979, the station reentered Earth's atmosphere and broke apart over the Pacific Ocean.

Despite its early mechanical problems, *Skylab* was considered a great success. The total number of hours spent in space by *Skylab* astronauts was greater than the combined totals of all space flights made up to that time. NASA gained valuable knowledge about human performance under microgravity conditions.

SOVIET AND RUSSIAN SPACE STATIONS

When the Soviets realized that they could not beat the Americans to the Moon during the 1960s, they turned their attention to other space goals. In 1971 they put the first of many Soviet space stations into orbit around Earth. Soviet and Russian cosmonauts spent the next three decades gaining valuable experience in long-duration space flight.

The Salyut Series

On April 19, 1971, the Soviet space station *Salyut 1* was launched from the Baikonur Cosmodrome in what is now Kazakhstan. The station was cylindrically shaped and approximately twelve meters long (about thirty-nine feet) and four meters (thirteen feet) wide at its widest point. It was placed into orbit approximately 200 kilometers (124 miles) above Earth.

The station was built so that Soviet scientists could study the long-term effects on humans living in space. A crew of three cosmonauts flew aboard *Soyuz 10* to the station a few days after the station was placed in orbit. However, they were unable to dock with it, so they were forced to end their mission early and return to Earth. In June 1971 the Soviet spacecraft *Soyuz 11* successfully docked with the station, and three cosmonauts inhabited it for twenty-four days. They were killed as they returned to Earth, when a valve opened on their spacecraft and allowed it to depressurize. At that time, cosmonauts did not wear pressurized space suits during launch or reentry.

The Soviet space agency canceled future flights to the station and began an extensive redesign of the Soyuz spacecraft. In October 1971 *Salyut 1* fell into Earth's atmosphere and was destroyed. In total, the Soviets put seven Salyuts into orbit. (See Table 5.2.) These stations were visited by cosmonauts and scientists from a number of countries, including France, India, and Cuba. In 1984 three Soviet cosmonauts spent 237 days aboard *Salyut 7*. This was a new record for human duration in space. *Salyut 7* was deorbited in February 1991.

Mir

In February 1986 the Soviet Union launched the new space station *Mir* into orbit. *Mir* was to be Russia's first continuously occupied space station. Even though originally planned to stay in orbit for five years, *Mir* survived for fifteen years. It finally tumbled to Earth in 2001.

Russian cosmonauts repeatedly set and broke space duration records aboard the *Mir* station. Vladimir Titov (1947–) and Musa Manarov (1951–) reached the one-year milestone when they completed 366 days in space in 1988. By 1995 the record was 437.7 days, set by Valery Polyakov (1942–). As of 2008, this was still the record.

The *Mir* is also famous for its nongovernmental inhabitants. Beginning in the 1980s the Soviet space program suffered financial difficulties. To raise funds, the space agency sold seats on *Mir* to a variety of foreign astronauts and adventurers. In 1990 the Japanese journalist Tohiro Akiyama (1942–) became the first citizen of Japan to fly in space and the first private citizen to pay for a space flight. Akiyama's television network paid $28 million to send him on a seven-day mission to *Mir*. In 1991 the British chemist Helen Sharman (1963–) spent eight days in space after winning a contest sponsored by a London bank.

Shuttle-*Mir* Missions

As early as 1978 NASA proposed a joint U.S.-Soviet mission to a Salyut station. NASA engineers discussed possible ways to dock a U.S. space shuttle with the station and hoped to put a scientific payload on board the station.

TABLE 5.2

The Salyut series of Soviet space stations

Name	Launch date	Deorbit date	Total crew occupancy time	Note
Salyut 1	April 1971	October 1971	24 days	Three cosmonauts died on their return to Earth.
Salyut 2	April 1973	April 1973	0 days	Unmanned. Station fell apart soon after reaching orbit.
Salyut 3	June 1974	January 1975	15 days	Hosted 1 crew. One unsuccessful docking.
Salyut 4	December 1974	February 1977	92 days	Hosted 2 crews and 1 unmanned craft. One abort.
Salyut 5	June 1976	August 1977	67 days	Hosted 2 crews. One unsuccessful docking.
Salyut 6	September 1977	July 1982	676 days	Hosted 16 crews and 1 unmanned craft.
Salyut 7	April 1982	February 1991	861 days	Hosted 10 crews

SOURCE: Created by Kim Masters Evans for Gale, Cengage Learning, 2008

Scientific hopes were overshadowed by international politics. In 1979 the Soviet Union began a war in Afghanistan. Two years later the Soviet government imposed martial law in Poland to suppress dissenters. The U.S. response to both incidents was a sharp reduction in cooperative efforts between the two countries. The Soviet empire began to dissolve during the late 1980s and was officially ended in 1991, when it separated into many independent countries. The largest of these was Russia, which inherited most of the Soviet space program.

In June 1992 U.S. president George H. W. Bush (1924–) and Russian president Boris Yeltsin (1931–2007) signed the Agreement between the United States of America and the Russian Federation Concerning Cooperation in the Exploration and Use of Outer Space for Peaceful Purposes. NASA and the Russian Space Agency (which had been recently created) worked out a plan for joint shuttle-*Mir* missions. Both agencies considered this a prelude to a joint U.S.-Russian space station. In fact, the shuttle-*Mir* program was officially called "Phase 1" at NASA. Phase 2 was to be the assembly of a space station. Phase 3 was to be the operation of a space station with the gradual addition of scientific and operational capabilities.

NASA set four goals for Phase 1:

- Learn to work with international partners
- Reduce the risks associated with developing and building a space station
- Gain American experience in long-duration missions
- Perform research in life sciences, microgravity, and environmental programs

In 1993 President Bill Clinton (1946–) met with Yeltsin and agreed to continue cooperative efforts in space exploration. On February 3, 1994, the space shuttle *Discovery* launched for the first time ever with a cosmonaut aboard. Exactly a year later the shuttle was launched again. This time the shuttle flew near *Mir*. In June 1995 the shuttle *Atlantis* docked with *Mir*. The shuttle was carrying four cosmonauts besides its American crew.

Between 1994 and 1998 space shuttles docked ten times with *Mir*. Figure 5.1 depicts a shuttle docked to the *Mir* space station. American astronauts logged nearly one thousand days of orbit time during Phase 1. One of them, Shannon Lucid (1943–), set the women's record for space flight duration: 188 days. A summary of all Phase 1 accomplishments is given in Table 5.3.

Mir Mishaps

When the first Americans arrived at *Mir* in 1995, the station had already been in orbit for nine years. They found a cramped and crowded spacecraft bulging with hoses, cables, and scientific equipment. Every closet and storage space was crammed full. Some gear and tools floated around, because there was no space left to stow or fasten them. Over the years, water droplets had escaped from environmental control systems and now clung to delicate electronics. *Mir*'s systems were plagued by computer crashes and battery problems. The cosmonauts spent the vast majority of their time doing repair and maintenance tasks.

On February 23, 1997, a fire broke out aboard *Mir* when a cosmonaut lit a lithium perchlorate candle. Flames one-foot long shot out of the unit and ignited the canister. At the time, there were six men aboard the station: four Russians, a German, and an American. The fire quickly filled the spacecraft with smoke. The Russians ordered everyone to evacuate the station. However, the fire blocked access to one of the two Soyuz capsules that served as their lifeboat. Only three men would be able to escape if the hull was breached.

The men fought the flames with towels and a few working fire extinguishers. Many of the ship's fire extinguishers malfunctioned or were bolted down and could not be released. After fifteen minutes the fire died, apparently snuffed out by lack of oxygen in its immediate area. The crew had donned respirators and floated quietly, barely moving for hours as they waited for the ship's ventilation system to remove the smoke.

Russian mission control downplayed the fire to the public and American officials, telling them it was a minor and isolated event. In truth, there had been a similar occurrence several years before in which a candle had burst into flames. Neither the most recent crew nor the public had been informed of that incident. Secrecy had always been a hallmark of the Soviet space program, and this culture persisted in the Russian space program of the 1990s.

The fire in February 1997 was followed by even more problems aboard *Mir*. Only a week later, a camera failed during a docking exercise and the station was nearly rammed by a supply ship. In late March the cooling system failed. The temperature rose to 95 degrees Fahrenheit on the station, and it was permeated by an odor of antifreeze. High carbon dioxide levels forced the crew to limit their physical activity.

Throughout the spring the crew struggled to repair the ailing ship. Another calamity struck on June 27, 1997, when the crew was conducting a docking test using a Progress supply ship. The cosmonauts did not trust the station's television images of the maneuver, so they tried to guess the distance by eyesight. The freighter slammed into the station and cracked its hull. Robert Zimmerman describes this incident in detail in *Leaving Earth: Space Stations, Rival Superpowers, and the Quest for Interplanetary Travel* (2003).

According to Zimmerman, the *Mir* crew felt their ears pop as the station began to lose pressure, and they could hear oxygen hissing out into outer space. The crash had breached the hull of the module called Spektr. Mission

FIGURE 5.1

Shuttle-Mir mated configuration

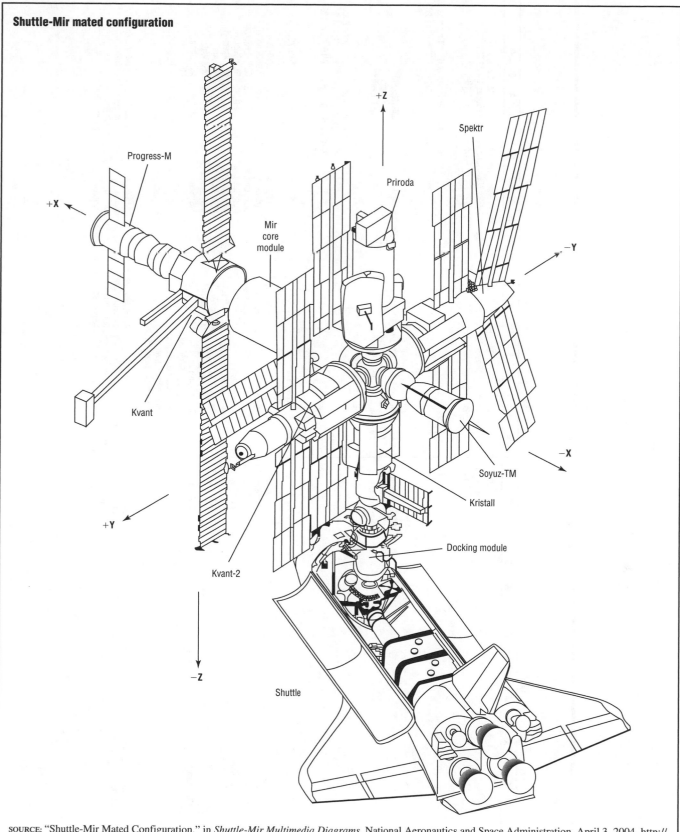

+Z

Spektr

Progress-M

Priroda

+X

Mir
core
module

−Y

Kvant

Soyuz-TM

−X

Kristall

Docking module

Kvant-2

+Y

−Z

Shuttle

SOURCE: "Shuttle-Mir Mated Configuration," in *Shuttle-Mir Multimedia Diagrams*, National Aeronautics and Space Administration, April 3, 2004, http:// spaceflight.nasa.gov/history/shuttle-mir/multimedia/diagrams/shutmir-low.htm (accessed December 31, 2007)

TABLE 5.3

Shuttle-Mir timeline, 1994–98

Year	1994	1995	1996
Month	J F M A M J J A S O N D	J F M A M J J A S O N D	J F M A M J J A S O N D
Russian flights/ progress resupply		Mir 18/19 (Soyuz TM 21 70) 3/14–9/11; Progress TM-27 4/9; Spektr launched 5/20; Mir 20 (Soyuz TM 22 71) 9/3–2/29	Mir 21 (Soyuz TM 23 72) 2/21–9/2; Priroda launched 4/23; Progress M31 5/6; Progress M32 7/26; Mir 22 (Soyuz TM 24 73) 8/18–3/2; Progress M33 11/20
Mir crews		CDR: Dezhurov ENG: Strekalov Astronaut: Thagard (Mir 19); CDR: Solovyev ENG: Budarin; CDR: Ghidzhenko ENG: Avdyev ESA: Reiter	CDR: Onufrienko ENG: Usachev; CDR: Korzun ENG: Kalen CNES: Deshays
Mir astronauts		Norman Thagard NASA 1 3/14–7/7 (115 days)	Shannon Lucid NASA 2 3/22–9/26 (188days); John Blaha NASA 3 9/16–1/22 (128days)
U.S. flights & shuttle crews	STS-60 Discovery 2/3–2/11 — CDR: Bolden PLT: Reightler MS: Chang-Diaz MS: J.Davis MS: Sega MS: Krikalev	STS-63 Discovery 2/3–2/11 (near Mir) CDR: Wetherbee PLT: Collins MS: Voss MS: Harris MS: Foale MS: Titov; STS-71 Atlantis 6/27–7/17 (docking 1) CDR: Gibson PLT: Precourt MS: E.Baker MS: Harbaugh MS: Dunbar MS: Thagard, Cosmonaut: Solovyev, Cosmonaut: Budarin, Cosmonaut: Dezhurov, Cosmonaut: Strekalov; STS-74 Atlantis 11/12–11/20 (docking 2) CDR: Cameron PLT: Halsell MS: J. Ross MS: McArthur MS: Hadfield	STS-76 Atlantis 3/22–3/31 (docking 3) CDR: Chilton PLT: Searfoss MS: Clifford MS: Godwin MS: Lucid MS: Sega; STS-79 Atlantis 9/16–9/26 (docking 4) CDR: Readdy PLT:Wilcutt MS: Akers MS: Apt MS: Walz MS: Blaha MS: Lucid
Events	Krikalev is 1st cosmonaut on shuttle	Shuttle approaches Mir; 1st U.S. Astronaut to launch on Soyuz 1st U.S. Astronaut on Mir; 1st Shuttle-Mir docking; Docking Module and cooperative solar array delivered	1st EVA during docked misson; Lucid sets record for women's longest time in space; 1st double Spacehab Module

TABLE 5.3

Shuttle-Mir timeline, 1994–98 [CONTINUED]

Year	1997												1998											
Month	J	F	M	A	M	J	J	A	S	O	N	D	J	F	M	A	M	J	J	A	S	O	N	D

Russian flights/progress resupply

1997: Mir 23 (Soyuz TM 25 74) 2/10–8/14 · Progress M34 4/6 · Progress 235 7/5 · Mir 24 (Soyuz TM 26 75) 8/5–2/19 · Progress 237 10/5

1998: Mir 25 (Soyuz TM 26 75) 1/29–8/25 · Progress 236 12/20 · Progress 240 3/15 · Progress 238 5/15

Mir crews

1997: CDR: Tsibliev / ENG: Lazutkin / DARA: Ewald · CDR: Solovyev / ENG: Vinogradov

1998: CDR: Musabayev / ENG: Budarin / CNES: Eyherts

Mir astronauts

1997: Jerry Linenger NASA 4 1/12–5/24 (132 days) · Micheal Foale NASA 5 5/15–10/7 (144 days) · David Wolf NASA 6 9/26–1/31 (128 days)

1998: Andrew Thomas NASA 7 1/22–6/12 (140 days)

U.S. flights & shuttle crews

1997:
STS-81 Atlantis 1/12–1/22 (docking 5) CDR: M.Baker / PLT: Jett / MS: Grunsfeld / MS: Ivins / MS: Wisoff / MS: Linenger / MS: Blaha ➝

STS-84 Atlantis 5/15–5/24 (docking 6) CDR: Precourt / PLT: Collins / MS: Noriega / MS: Lu / MS: Foale ▴ / MS: Linenger ➝ / MS: Kondakova / ESA: Clervoy

STS-86 Atlantis 9/25–10/6 (docking 7) CDR: Wetherbee / PLT: Bloomfield / MS: Lawrence / MS: Parazynski / MS: Foale ➝ / MS: Wolf ▴ / Cosmonaut: Titov / CNES: Chretien

1998:
STS-89 Endeavour 1/22–1/31 (docking 8) CDR: Wilcutt / PLT: Edwards / MS: Dunbar / MS: Anderson / MS: Reilly / MS: Wolf ▴ / MS: Thomas ➝ / Cosmonaut: Sharipov

STS-91 Discovery 6/2–6/12 (docking 9) CDR: Precourt / PLT: Gorie / MS: Lawrence / MS: Chang-Diaz / MS: Kavandi / MS: Thomas ➝ / Cosmonaut: Ryumin

Events

1997: Fire aboard Mir 1st Astronaut to perform EVA on Mir wearing Russian space suit. · Spektr collison Foale/ Solovyev EVA. · Titov 1st cosmonaut to perform EVA in U.S. space suit

1998: Wolf Solovyev EVA · Phase 1 ends

CDR = Commander.
CNES = Centre National d'Etudes Spatiales (French Space Agency).
DARA = Deutsche Agentur fur Raumfahrtangelegenheiten (Germany Space Agency).
ENG = Engineer.
ESA = European Space Agency.
EVA = Extravehicular activity.
PLT = Pilot.
MS = Mission specialist.
▴ = Crewmember launched to Mir on this flight, and returned on another flight.
➝ = Crewmember returned from Mir on this flight.

SOURCE: "Graphic Timeline," in *Timeline of Shuttle-Mir*, National Aeronautics and Space Administration, April 3, 2004, http://spaceflight.nasa.gov/history/shuttle-mir/images/timeline.pdf (accessed December 31, 2007)

control ordered the crew to close the hatch to that module to seal off the breach. This was impossible because previous crews had run electrical cables and wires through the doorway, so the hatch could not be closed all the way. The crew frantically began cutting and unhooking the wiring. Finally, they closed the door, isolating themselves in the base unit away from the leak.

The impact with the freighter knocked the station into an uncontrollable spin. Furthermore, disconnection from Spektr had cut power to vital systems. The crew floated in darkness for nearly thirty hours. Finally, they used the rockets on the Soyuz lifeboats to nudge the station out of its spin and into proper position.

The mishaps aboard *Mir* could not be downplayed anymore. Politicians and the press in the United States called for NASA to stop sending American astronauts to the trouble-prone station. Despite the pressure, NASA and the White House felt it was important to complete Phase 1. Shuttle flights continued to *Mir* throughout 1997 and into 1998.

AN INTERNATIONAL EFFORT

In his State of the Union Address (January 25, 1984, http://reagan2020.us/speeches/state_of_the_union_1984.asp), President Ronald Reagan (1911–2004) directed NASA to develop a space station before the end of the decade. The project was expected to cost the United States only around $8 billion because of the participation of foreign governments. By 1988 Canada, Japan, and nine European countries had signed formal agreements with the United States to participate in the project. Reagan named the new space station *Freedom*.

Freedom

Freedom was to include three separate components: a pressurized base unit in which the crew would live and work and two automated platforms that would support scientific experiments and observations of Earth's climate. At that time, designers envisioned a station that could accommodate a crew of up to ten people.

The project was plagued immediately by financial and technological problems that continued to get worse. Development costs increased even as NASA's budget shrank. Congress demanded several redesigns to save money. NASA eliminated the two automated platforms and scaled back the base unit. Each redesign resulted in a smaller station with less usable space and less electrical power available to scientists. NASA's foreign partners became increasingly annoyed about the design changes.

Meanwhile, the Space Shuttle Program was enmeshed in its own difficulties. The space shuttle was crucial to the station program, because it was to be the only means by which American flight crews could reach the station. The catastrophic breakup of the space shuttle *Challenger* in 1986 grounded the entire shuttle fleet for more than two years. It also raised questions about the safety and quality of NASA's operations.

Even as the space station shrank in volume, its weight increased. This required shuttle design changes to accommodate the extra weight. It was also decided to include some kind of lifeboat capability in the station in case its crew had to leave in an emergency. By December 1990 the cost of *Freedom* was estimated at $38 billion. This included the cost of shuttle launches required to build the station.

In 1991 a congressional committee recommended that NASA cancel the development of *Freedom*. A vote was held by the U.S. House of Representatives to determine its fate, and an amendment was passed to continue the program. This was the first of nearly two dozen votes that would take place over the next decade in the House and U.S. Senate on the fate of the space station. Each time the program was allowed to continue; however, some of the votes were extremely close. For example, in a June 1993 vote the station survived by a one-vote margin.

Station Alpha

When President Clinton took office in 1993, he ordered a sweeping revision to cut costs in the space station program. By that time, NASA had already spent more than $11 billion on design costs alone. However, not one piece of hardware had been launched into space. NASA designers presented the president with several different options for station components and functions, and he selected the plan Design Alpha. The new station was unofficially named Station Alpha.

By this time, the Soviet Union had collapsed. The Clinton administration began talks with the new Russian government and welcomed Russia's eagerness to participate in the space station project. According to Marcia S. Smith of the Congressional Research Service, in *NASA's Space Station Program: Evolution and Current Status* (April 4, 2001, http://www.hq.nasa.gov/office/pao/History/smith.htm), President Clinton saw Russian participation as a way to improve foreign relations and put pressure on the Russians to abide by newly signed ballistic missile agreements. He also wanted to provide Russian scientists with jobs to keep them from selling valuable information to the United States' enemies. NASA estimated that Russian participation would cut $2 billion off the $19 billion cost of completing Station Alpha and speed up its development by a year.

On September 2, 1993, the two countries signed the Joint Declaration on Cooperation in Space. By the end of the year, NASA and the Russian Space Agency had ironed out a detailed work plan for what was now called the *International Space Station*.

The *ISS* Plan

It was decided that the *ISS* would comprise individual segments called modules that would dock together to form the station. Each module was to be constructed on the ground and then launched into space. The space shuttle was expected to carry the heaviest loads to the station. Russia agreed to transport supplies and propellants to the *ISS* aboard its unmanned Progress spacecraft. In addition, Russian Soyuz spacecraft were offered as the station's lifeboats.

A rotating schedule for the first four modules was developed in which Russia would build the first and third modules and the United States would build the second and fourth modules. NASA agreed to pay for one of the Russian modules.

The collaboration with Russia raised some concerns among U.S. politicians and scientists. They publicly expressed fears that the cash-strapped Russian government would not be able to fulfill its obligations to the program. NASA had given the Russian Space Agency responsibility for two of the most important modules in the station. Failure to deliver them would cripple the entire project. U.S. fears grew even greater during the late 1990s as problems surfaced on the Russian space station *Mir*.

On January 29, 1998, the U.S. government signed the Agreement among the Government of Canada, Governments of Member States of the European Space Agency, the Government of Japan, the Government of the Russian Federation, and the Government of the United States of America Concerning Cooperation on the Civil International Space Station (http://www.canlii.org/ca/as/1999/c35/). This document outlined the agreement among the partners for design, development, operation, and utilization of the *ISS*. The previous year the United States had signed a separate agreement with Brazil giving it utilization rights in exchange for supplying *ISS* parts. Table 5.4 lists the nations that are *ISS* partners.

TABLE 5.4

International Space Station partner nations

United States
Russia
Canada
Japan

Belgium*
Denmark*
France*
Germany*
Italy*
Norway*
Spain*
Sweden*
Switzerland*
The Netherlands*

Brazil (utilization rights)

*Members of the European Space Agency.

SOURCE: Created by Kim Masters Evans for Gale, Cengage Learning, 2008

In early 1998 it was expected that at least forty spacecraft launches spread over five to seven years would be required to assemble more than one hundred components into the *ISS*. At that time, the station was designed for a crew of seven people. The space station was expected to be completed by 2005 or 2006 and cost the United States $26 billion to complete.

ISS Assembly Begins

On November 20, 1998, a Russian Proton K rocket was launched, carrying Zarya, the first module of the *ISS*. The Russians built Zarya, but the Americans paid for it. It was to be a U.S. component of the station. The module provides control and cargo capabilities. Zarya was self-propelled and was designed to keep the station in orbit until the service module arrived. After that it would serve as a passageway, storage facility, docking port, and fuel tank. Zarya weighed forty-four thousand pounds at launch.

Two weeks later, the shuttle *Endeavour* carried the module Unity to the station. Figure 5.2 shows the two modules docked together. Zarya is on the left and Unity is on the right. Unity is an American-built module with six docking ports for attachment to other modules. It provides a node (link) between modules. It is basically a passageway with some internal storage space. Unity is eighteen feet long and fifteen feet in diameter and weighed over twenty-five thousand pounds at launch.

Two more shuttle crews visited the *ISS* in 1999 and 2000 to outfit the modules with logistical equipment and supplies. On July 12, 2000, the Russians launched the service module Zvezda into space aboard a Proton K rocket. This module was built and funded by the Russians and was to be the core of their segment.

It included functions for station control, navigation, communications, and life support systems (including the crew quarters). At that time, it was expected that many of

FIGURE 5.2

Zarya/Unity modules

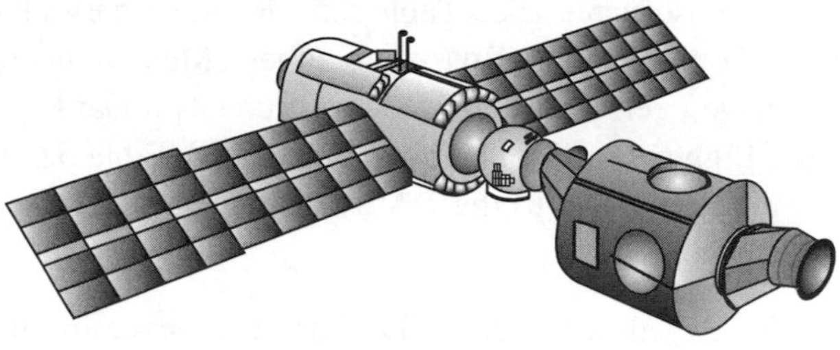

SOURCE: "Zarya/Unity," in *International Space Station Overview: Early Assembly Flight Summaries*, National Aeronautics and Space Administration, June 26, 2000, http://www.shuttlepresskit.com/ISS_OVR/early_assembly.htm (accessed December 31, 2007)

FIGURE 5.3

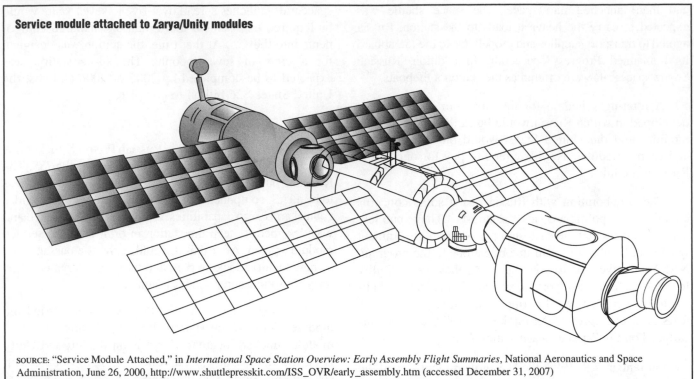

SOURCE: "Service Module Attached," in *International Space Station Overview: Early Assembly Flight Summaries*, National Aeronautics and Space Administration, June 26, 2000, http://www.shuttlepresskit.com/ISS_OVR/early_assembly.htm (accessed December 31, 2007)

these functions would be taken over by an American module to be added later. Zvezda's design was based on the core module of the *Mir* space station. Zvezda is forty-three feet long with a wingspan of ninety-eight feet and weighed forty-two thousand pounds at launch. It includes docking ports for Russian Soyuz and Progress spacecraft. Figure 5.3 shows the three modules hooked together. Zvezda is on the far left.

Throughout the summer of 2000 visiting Russian and American crews continued outfitting the modules and assembling the station. The station was also visited by an unmanned Russian Progress spacecraft carrying consumables (food and water), spare parts, and propellants.

On November 2, 2000, the first crew to actually inhabit the *ISS* arrived aboard a Soyuz spacecraft. It was called *ISS* Expedition 1. It included two Russian cosmonauts and one American astronaut. (See Table 5.5.) Resident crews have included only U.S. and Russian members. Many temporary visits have been made by NASA astronauts aboard space shuttle flights. (See Table 4.4 in Chapter 4.) Table 5.6 lists the temporary visits to the *ISS* by astronauts from foreign space agencies.

The Expedition 1 crew lived aboard the station until March 2001. They were visited by two shuttles, one of which brought the American lab module Destiny. This module was to be the primary research laboratory for U.S. payloads. It included many racks that could support

a variety of electrical and fluid systems during the performance of experiments. It also contains the control center for the *ISS* robotic arm.

In March 2001 the Expedition 2 crew arrived at the station aboard shuttle *Discovery*. The Expedition 1 crew returned to Earth aboard the space shuttle, leaving their Soyuz spacecraft at the station to serve as a lifeboat. The Expedition 2 crew included two American astronauts and one Russian cosmonaut. It had been decided to swap out the Expedition crews every four to six months and to rotate back and forth between crews that were predominantly Russian and crews that were predominantly American.

The Expedition 2 crew brought the Leonardo multi-purpose logistics module (MPLM). MPLMs are reusable pressurized shipping containers designed to be temporarily attached to the *ISS* for unloading. They are transported back and forth on space shuttles and carry a variety of cargo, equipment, and experiment racks. The Leonardo module was named by the Italian company that built it. It was loaded with garbage (expired batteries, used filters, etc.) for its return trip to Earth.

The Expedition 2 crew also attached the station's remote manipulator system. This is a robotic arm that was nicknamed Canadarm2, because it was built by Canadian companies. The space shuttle fleet utilizes another robotic arm called Canadarm1.

TABLE 5.5

International Space Station expedition crews as of December 2007

	Launch Date	Landing Date	Time in orbit	Crew members	Agency	Crew titles
Expedition 1	10/31/00	3/21/2001	140 days, 23 hr, 38 min	William Shepherd	NASA	Commander
				Yuri Gidzenko	Roscosmos	Soyuz commander
				Sergei Krikalev	Roscosmos	Flight engineer
Expedition 2	03/08/01	8/22/2001	167 days, 6 hr, 41 min	Yury Usachev	Roscosmos	Commander
				Susan Helms	NASA	Flight engineer
				James Voss	NASA	Flight engineer
Expedition 3	08/10/01	12/17/2001	128 days, 20 hr, 45 min	Frank Culbertson	NASA	Commander
				Vladimir Dezhurov	Roscosmos	Soyuz commander
				Mikhail Tyurin	Roscosmos	Flight engineer
Expedition 4	12/05/01	6/19/2002	195 days, 19 hr, 39 min	Yury Onufrienko	Roscosmos	Commander
				Dan Bursch	NASA	Flight engineer
				Carl Walz	NASA	Flight engineer
Expedition 5	06/05/02	12/7/2002	184 days, 22 hr, 14 min	Valery Korzun	Roscosmos	Commander
				Peggy Whitson	NASA	Science officer
				Sergei Treschev	Roscosmos	Flight engineer
Expedition 6	11/23/02	5/3/2003	161 days, 1 hr, 17 min	Ken Bowersox	NASA	Commander
				Nikolai Budarin	Roscosmos	Flight engineer
				Don Pettit	NASA	Science officer
Expedition 7	04/25/03	10/27/2003	184 days, 21 hr, 47 min	Yuri Malenchenko	Roscosmos	Commander
				Ed Lu	NASA	Science officer
Expedition 8	10/18/03	4/29/2004	194 days, 18 hr, 35 min	Michael Foale	NASA	Commander/science officer
				Alexander Kaleri	Roscosmos	Flight engineer
Expedition 9	04/18/04	10/19/2004	187 days, 21 hr, 17 min	Gennady Padalka	Roscosmos	Commander
				Mike Fincke	NASA	Flight engineer/science officer
Expedition 10	10/13/04	4/24/2005	192 days, 19 hr, 2 min	Leroy Chiao	NASA	Commander/science officer
				Salizhan Sharipov	Roscosmos	Soyuz commander/flight engineer
Expedition 11	04/14/05	10/10/2005	179 days, 23 min	Sergei Krikalev	Roscosmos	Commander
				John Phillips	NASA	Flight engineer/science officer
Expedition 12	09/30/05	04/08/06	189 days, 19 hr, 53 min	William McArthur	NASA	Commander/science officer
				Valery Tokarev	Roscosmos	Flight engineer
Expedition 13	03/29/06	09/28/06	182 days, 23 hr, 44 min	Pavel Vinogradov	Roscosmos	Commander
				Jeffrey Williams	NASA	Flight engineer
Expedition 14	09/18/06	04/21/07	215 days, 8 hr, 23 min	Micahael Lopez-Alegria	NASA	Commander
				Mikhail Tyurin	Roscosmos	Flight engineer
				Sunita Williams	NASA	Flight engineer (arrived 12/9/06)
Expedition 15	04/07/07	10/21/07	197 days, 1 hr, 39 min	Fyodor Yurchikhin	Roscosmos	Commander
				Oleg Kotov	Roscosmos	Flight engineer
				Clayton Anderson	NASA	Flight engineer (arrived 6/8/07)
				Sunita Williams	NASA	Flight engineer (departed 6/22/07)
Expedition 16	10/10/07	Ongoing	Ongoing	Peggy Whitson	NASA	Commander
				Yuri Malenchenko	Roscosmos	Flight engineer and Soyuz commander
				Daniel Tani	NASA	Flight engineer (arrived 10/23/07)
				Clayton Anderson	NASA	Flight engineer (departed 11/7/07)

SOURCE: Adapted from "Mission Archives," in *International Space Station Expeditions*, National Aeronautics and Space Administration, December 19, 2007, http://www.nasa.gov/mission_pages/station/expeditions/index.html (accessed January 1, 2008)

When the space shuttle *Endeavour* visited the *ISS* in April 2001, the crew included the European Space Agency (ESA) astronaut Umberto Guidoni (1954–). He was the first European to board the space station.

Tito Comes Aboard

Also in April 2001 the Russians sent the first taxi to the station to replace the Soyuz lifeboat left by the Expedition 1 crew. The taxi crew included the U.S. millionaire Dennis Tito (1940–). A year earlier, Tito had paid $20 million for a visit to the *Mir* space station. When the Russians decided to deorbit *Mir*, they rescheduled Tito for a trip to the *ISS*. They hoped he would be the first of many space tourists to pay to fly on *ISS* taxis. The Russian Space and Aviation Agency (Rosaviakosmos) desperately needed the money.

NASA and the European partners in the *ISS* were not happy with the decision. When Tito and the two cosmonauts showed up at the Johnson Space Center for training, NASA would not let Tito entry the facility. The cosmonauts responded by refusing to undergo training. The standoff resulted in a flurry of negotiations between NASA and Rosaviakosmos. The Americans finally agreed to allow Tito to train in the United States, but they continued to argue that he posed a safety risk to the station and banned him from the American segments of the *ISS*. NASA repeatedly asked Rosaviakosmos to postpone Tito's flight, but the Russians would not agree.

On April 28, 2001, a Soyuz blasted off with Tito and the two cosmonauts aboard. Two days later it docked with the *ISS*. Tito spent his time aboard *ISS* in the Russian segment taking pictures of Earth and listening to opera. The crew stayed at the station for four days before returning to Earth aboard the old Soyuz lifeboat.

TABLE 5.6

Foreign astronauts that have visited the International Space Station as non-resident crewmembers

Start date	End date	Mission	Crewmember	Agency	Home country
4/19/2001	5/1/2001	STS-100	Umberto Guidoni	ESA	Italy
10/21/2001	10/31/2001	Andromède	Claudie Haigneré	ESA	France
			Victor Afanassiev	Roscosmos	Russia
			Konstantin Kozeev	Roscosmos	Russia
4/25/2002	5/5/2002	Marco Polo	Roberto Vittori	ESA	Italy
6/5/2002	6/19/2002	STS-111	Phillippe Perrin	ESA	France
10/30/2002	11/10/2002	Odissea	Frank De Winne	ESA	Belgium
10/18/2003	10/28/2003	Cervantes	Pedro Duque	ESA	Spain
4/19/2004	4/30/2004	Delta	André Kuipers	ESA	Netherlands
10/13/2004	10/23/2004	Expedition 10	Yuri Shargin	VKS	Russia
4/14/2005	4/24/2005	Eneide	Roberto Vittori	ESA	Italy
7/26/2005	8/9/2005	STS-114	Soichi Noguchi	JAXA	Japan
3/29/2006	4/8/2006	Soyuz TMA-8	Marcos Pontes	AEB	Brazil
7/14/2006	12/22/2006	Astrolab	Thomas Reiter	ESA	Germany
9/9/2006	9/21/2006	STS-115	Steven MacLean	CSA	Canada
12/9/2006	12/22/2006	Celsius (STS-116)	Christer Fugelsang	ESA	Sweden
8/8/2007	8/21/2007	STS-118	Dave Williams	CSA	Canada
10/23/2007	11/7/2007	STS-120	Paolo Nespoli	ESA	Italy

Acronyms:
AEB - Brazilian Space Agency (Agência Espacial Brasileira)
CSA - Canadian Space Agency
ESA - European Space Agency
JAXA - Japanese Space Agency
VKS - Russian Military Space Forces

SOURCE: Created by Kim Masters Evans for Gale, Cengage Learning, 2008

The Price Goes Up

In April 2001 NASA announced that the U.S. cost to complete the *ISS* by 2006 was going to be $4 billion more than expected. The Clinton administration responded by establishing the *ISS* Management and Cost Evaluation Task Force to assess the project. In November 2001 the task force released the *Report by the International Space Station (ISS) Management and Cost Evaluation (IMCE) Task Force to the NASA Advisory Council* (ftp://ftp.hq.nasa.gov/pub/pao/reports/2001/imce.pdf), which called for a serious downsizing of the *ISS*.

The task force recommended that the *ISS* be configured for only a three-person crew. Previous plans had called for a seven-person crew. It noted that scientists were not happy with this proposal because they feared it would "have a significant adverse impact on science." However, the task force noted that the cutback was necessary to save money and suggested that some of the research planned for the *ISS* could take place aboard space shuttle flights instead.

The task force recommended many management changes within NASA to save money and suggested that the agency prioritize its research goals for the station. One goal considered crucial was the installation of a centrifuge. A centrifuge is a machine commonly used in research to separate different substances, to remove moisture, or to simulate certain gravitational effects. The task force noted that NASA kept putting off centrifuge installation on the *ISS*, much to the disappointment of the scientific community.

The task force called for NASA to establish a specific "end state" for station construction that could be achieved within NASA's existing budget. At that point, station construction would be complete and a much cheaper operation stage could begin. The task force recommended that several planned *ISS* features be eliminated, such as a crew return vehicle, a propulsion module, and a habituation module called Node 3.

The task force issued the report only days before Bush was declared the new president by the U.S. Supreme Court. The *ISS* project had now fallen under the terms of four U.S. presidents. The Bush administration agreed with the task force's findings. The end state recommended by the report was called the core complete point. Bush appointed a new NASA administrator, Sean O'Keefe (1956–), and charged him to achieve core complete as soon as possible. NASA estimated that construction could be completed by 2004.

The United States' international partners were not happy with the plan for a smaller crew size because it meant fewer chances for their personnel to visit the station. Furthermore, many scientists were disappointed with the reduction in research potential afforded by the smaller station.

The Expeditions Continue

By the end of 2001 the station had been visited by the Expedition 3 and Expedition 4 crews, which included three members each. These crews installed Pirs, a new Russian docking and airlock module, and began construction on the truss. The truss is a long girderlike structure that is perpendicular to the row of existing modules. The truss is designed to hold the solar panels that power the station and to hold any new modules constructed in the future.

Deliveries of food, water, and supplies to the *ISS* continued to occur every few months aboard automated Russian Progress spacecraft. These vehicles were then loaded up with unneeded equipment, wastewater, and trash, which burned up with the vehicles during reentry to Earth's atmosphere.

The Russian Soyuz lifeboat docked to the *ISS* was exchanged every six months by taxi crews. In October 2001 a three-member team including two Russian cosmonauts and an ESA astronaut visited the station as part of mission Andromède. They exchanged the Russian Soyuz lifeboat and conducted a ten-day scientific experiment aboard the station. The ESA astronaut was Claudie Haigneré (1957–), the first European woman to visit the *ISS*.

In April 2002 another taxi crew visited the *ISS*. This time it included another space tourist: the South African Internet entrepreneur Mark Shuttleworth (1973–). He paid approximately $20 million to visit the space station.

After two years of negotiation, the *ISS* partners had worked out an agreement specifying who could visit the station. In November 2001 they signed the Principles Regarding Processes and Criteria for Selection, Assignment, Training, and Certification of *ISS* (Expedition and Visiting) Crewmembers (http://www.spaceref.com/news/viewsr.html?pid=4578). The agreement listed strict requirements regarding the personal character and communication skills of any visitor. It disqualified anyone found to have a drinking or drug problem, those with poor employment or military records, convicted criminals, people who had engaged in "notoriously disgraceful conduct," and anyone known to be affiliated with organizations that wished to "adversely affect the confidence of the public" in the space program. Visitors also had to speak English.

Shuttleworth passed the review process and launched aboard a Russian Soyuz rocket on April 25, 2002, with a Russian cosmonaut and an Italian flight engineer. Two days later they entered the station. Shuttleworth performed some simple scientific experiments while on board and conducted many interviews with schoolchildren. He and the taxi crew spent eight days aboard the *ISS*.

Throughout the remainder of 2002 the station was visited by the crews of Expedition 5 and Expedition 6, who continued the construction of the *ISS* truss. A Soyuz taxi flight launched in October of that year included a visiting astronaut from the ESA. Frank De Winne

(1961–) and two taxi cosmonauts spent eight days at the station before returning to Earth.

The last visitors of the year came aboard the space shuttle *Endeavour*. The orbiter docked at the *ISS* in late November to deliver the Expedition 6 crew and a new truss segment. In early December the shuttle returned safely to Earth carrying the Expedition 5 crew. It was the sixteenth American shuttle flight to the space station, and it was to be the last for a long while.

ISS Assembly Halts

On February 1, 2003, the space shuttle *Columbia* broke apart as it entered Earth's atmosphere over the western United States. The shuttle had been on a research mission and did not visit the *ISS*. The catastrophe killed the seven crewmembers and shook the U.S. space program to its core. An investigation revealed that the shuttle's thermal protection tiles were likely damaged by a foam strike shortly after launch. During reentry, hot gases seeped past the tiles into the orbiter structure, and the resulting turbulence tore it apart.

The entire shuttle fleet was grounded. The flights that were scheduled to deliver truss segments and research facilities to the *ISS* in 2003 were canceled. There was no other way to transport these heavy components to the *ISS*. The Russian Soyuz spacecraft could carry only around five thousand pounds, compared to the thirty-six-thousand-pound capacity of the space shuttle. Russia's automated Progress spacecraft could carry even less weight, only one thousand pounds. The *ISS* assembly came to a halt.

THE COST OF WAITING

The shutdown of the shuttle program had a number of operational and cost effects on the *ISS*. In September 2003 the U.S. General Accounting Office (GAO; now the U.S. Government Accountability Office) released the report *Space Station: Impact of the Grounding of the Shuttle Fleet* (http://www.gao.gov/new.items/d031107.pdf). The GAO noted that modules and other equipment already ready to fly to the *ISS* would have to be unpacked, undergo maintenance, be repacked, and retested before flight. Batteries had to be recharged due to prolonged storage. All these problems resulted in unexpected costs in NASA's *ISS* program.

Grounding the shuttle had negative effects on *ISS* research projects. NASA had planned to launch three major research facilities to the station during 2003. Onboard experiments had to be conducted using existing facilities. However, some of this equipment needed to be repaired or even replaced, particularly refrigeration and freezer units in the science section. These units had experienced a few failures. NASA had planned to replace them during 2003 with the launch of a new and larger cold-temperature facility.

The GAO found that the shuttle delay affected the safety of the *ISS*. NASA had planned to transport a new on-orbit gyro to the station in March 2003 to replace a broken unit. The station includes four gyros that maintain the structure's orbital stability and permit navigational control. NASA scientists feared that problems could arise in the station's three remaining working gyros during a prolonged delay in shuttle flights. NASA had also planned to finish installing shielding on the Zvezda module in 2003. Zvezda houses the expedition crews. The module is supposed to be covered with twenty-three shielded panels to protect it from impacts by space debris. However, at that point, only six panels had been installed. Every day that went by without the additional shielding increased the risk that the module could be struck and damaged by debris.

The shuttle delay also affected the United States' *ISS* partners. The original cost-sharing plan was worked out in the 1998 intergovernmental agreement on space station cooperation. This plan calls for NASA to pay the entire cost for ground operations and common supplies for the station. NASA is then reimbursed by the partner countries for their share, depending on their level of participation. Partner countries also fund operations and maintenance for any elements they contribute to the *ISS*, any research activities they conduct, and a share of common operating expenses. The GAO concluded that these costs would have to be adjusted as the shuttle fleet remained grounded and planned activities were canceled.

The GAO estimated that between 1985 and 2002 the United States spent $32 billion on the *ISS*.

THE EXPEDITIONS ARE DOWNSIZED

The *ISS* partners decided to downsize future station crews to only two people. This made it easier for the Russians to assume all responsibility for resupplying the crew with food, water, and other necessities. In April 2003 the two-member Expedition 7 crew flew to the station aboard a Soyuz spacecraft. Unable to proceed with assembly, they were kept busy maintaining the station and performing limited scientific research. One of the largest drawbacks to *ISS* science is the presence of only two crewmembers. The number of new and continuing experiments had to be reduced so the crews could devote more time to station maintenance and operation.

The crews of Expeditions 8 through 11 consecutively occupied the *ISS* into October 2005. The Expedition 12 crew brought along the space tourist Greg Olsen (1945–), who returned to Earth with the Expedition 11 crew. Expedition 13 included a visit by the Brazilian astronaut Marcos Pontes (1963–), the first Brazilian to visit the

space station. Another visitor, the ESA astronaut Thomas Reiter (1958–) of Germany, boarded the *ISS* during Expedition 13 and remained for more than 160 days to conduct a long-term science experiment.

The Soyuz TMA that carried the Expedition 14 crew to the station included the first woman tourist into outer space. The Iranian-American entrepreneur Anousheh Ansari (1966–) reportedly paid $20 million to Russian authorities to take the flight. Ansari is best known for her sponsorship (along with her brother-in-law) of the Ansari X Prize that awarded $10 million in 2004 to the developers of *SpaceShipOne*, the first commercially funded private spacecraft to carry a human passenger into space.

During Expeditions 14 through 16, NASA rotated its flight engineers on the *ISS* at irregular intervals, meaning that some flight engineers were members of two Expedition crews. The space tourist Charles Simonyi (1948–), a Hungarian-born businessman, accompanied the Expedition 15 crew to the *ISS*. In October 2007 space shuttle astronauts and Expedition 16 crewmembers attached the new live-in compartment called Harmony to the space station. The Italian-made compartment adds approximately twenty-five hundred cubic feet of living and working space. The Expedition 16 crew was visited by the space tourist Sheikh Muszaphar Shukor (1972–), a surgeon from Malaysia and the first practicing Muslim to visit the station.

Table 5.7 lists all the *ISS* missions flown as of December 2007. From the time that assembly began, the United States made twenty-three flights to the *ISS*, and the Russians made forty-four flights. Table 5.8 lists the major components installed on the *ISS* as of December 31, 2007.

A NEW PLAN FOR THE *ISS*

In January 2004 President Bush announced a new plan for the U.S. space program. This plan calls for retirement of the space shuttle fleet by 2010. The president also wants to end *ISS* assembly as soon as the core complete configuration is obtained and eliminate all *ISS* research projects that do not support the new plans for space travel. The core complete *ISS* would support a crew of only three people and not include some of the modules, habitat enhancements, and scientific facilities and equipment originally planned for the space station.

The plan for a downsized *ISS* was criticized by the agency's international partners and by many scientists. The small crew size was a major point of contention. According to the National Research Council of the National Academies and National Academy of Public Administration, in *Factors Affecting the Utilization of the International Space Station for Research in the Biological and Physical Sciences* (2003), at least 2.5 crew

TABLE 5.7

International Space Station (ISS) assembly missions as of December 2007

Flight no.	Launch date	Mission name	Spacecraft flying to ISS	Primary cargo	Purpose
1	11/20/98	1 A/R	Proton K	Control module FGB (Zarya)	Assembly
2	12/04/98	2A	Shuttle/STS-88	Node 1 (Unity), PMAs 1, 2	Assembly
3	05/27/99	2A.1	Shuttle/STS-96	Spacehab DM	Outfitting
4	05/19/00	2A.2a	Shuttle/STS-101	Spacehab DM	Outfitting
5	07/12/00	1R	Proton K	Service module (Zvezda)	Assembly
6	08/06/00	1P	Progress M1–3	Consumables, spares, props	Logistics
7	09/08/00	2A.2b	Shuttle/STS-106	Spacehab DM	Outfitting
8	10/11/00	3A	Shuttle/STS-92	Z1 truss, 4 CMGs, PMA 3	Assembly
9	10/31/00	2R/1S	Soyuz TM-31	Expedition 1 crew	1st crew
10	11/15/00	2P	Progress M1–4	Consumables, spares, props	Logistics
11	11/30/00	4A	Shuttle/STS-97	P6 module, PV array	Assembly
12	02/07/01	5A	Shuttle/STS-98	U.S. Destiny lab module, racks	Assembly
13	02/26/01	3P	Progress M-44	Consumables, spares, props	Logistics
14	03/08/01	5A.1	Shuttle/STS-102	Expedition 2 crew, MPLM Leonardo	2nd crew
15	04/19/01	6A	Shuttle/STS-100	SSRMS, MPLM Raffaello	Outfitting
16	04/28/01	2S	Soyuz TM-32	1st taxi (plus Tito)	New CRV
17	05/20/01	4P	Progress M1–6	Consumables, spares, props	Logistics
18	07/12/01	7A	Shuttle/STS-104	U.S. airlock, HP O2/N2 gas	Assembly
19	08/10/01	7A.1	Shuttle/STS-105	Expedition 3 crew, MPLM Leonardo	3rd crew
20	08/21/01	5P	Progress M-245	Consumables, spares, props	Logistics
21	09/14/01	4R	"Progress 301"	Docking compartment 1	Assembly
22	10/21/01	3S	Soyuz TM-33	2nd taxi	New CRV
23	11/26/01	6P	Progress M-256	Consumables, spares, props	Logistics
24	12/05/01	UF-1	Shuttle/STS-108	Expedition 4 crew, MPLM Raffaello	4th crew
25	03/21/02	7P	Progress M1-0 (257)	Consumables	Logistics
26	04/08/02	8A	Shuttle/STS-110	S0 truss segment	Assembly
27	04/25/02	4S	Soyuz TM-34	3rd taxi (plus Shuttleworth)	New CRV
28	06/05/02	UF-2	Shuttle/STS-111	Expedition 5 crew, MBS, MPLM Leonardo	5th crew
29	06/26/02	8P	Progress M-24 (246)	Consumables, spares, props	Logistics
30	09/25/02	9P	Progress M1–9 (258)	Consumables, spares, props	Logistics
31	10/07/02	9A	Shuttle/STS-112	S1 truss segment	Assembly
32	10/30/02	5S	Soyuz TMA-1 (211)	4th taxi (plus Frank DeWinne)	New CRV
33	11/23/02	11A	Shuttle/STS-113	Expedition 6 crew, P1 truss segment	6th crew
34	02/02/03	10P	Progress M-47 (247)	Consumables, spares, props.	Logistics
35	04/26/03	6S	Soyuz TMA-2 (212)	Expedition 7 crew	7th crew
36	06/08/03	11P	Progress M1–10 (259)	Consumables, spares, props	Logistics
37	08/28/03	12P	Progress M-48 (248)	Consumables, spares, props	Logistics
38	10/18/03	7S	Soyuz TMA-3 (213)	Expedition 8 crew (plus Duque)	8th crew
39	01/29/04	13P	Progress M1–11 (260)	Consumables, spares, props	Logistics
40	04/18/04	8S	Soyuz TMA-4 (214)	Expedition 9 crew (plus Kuipers)	9th crew
41	05/25/04	14P	Progress M-49 (249)	Consumables, spares, props	Logistics
42	08/11/04	15P	Progress M-50 (250)	Consumables, spares, props	Logistics
43	10/14/04	9S	Soyuz TMA-5 (215)	Expedition 10 crew (plus Shargin)	10th crew
44	12/23/04	16P	Progress M-51 (351)	Consumables, spares, props	Logistics
45	02/28/05	17P	Progress M-52 (352)	Consumables, spares, props	Logistics
46	04/14/05	10S	Soyuz TMA-6 (216)	Expedition 11 crew (plus Vittori)	11th crew
47	06/17/05	18P	Progress M-53 (353)	Consumables, spares, props	Logistics
48	07/26/05	LF-1	Shuttle/STS-114 (RTF)	MPLM Raffaello	Logistics, utilization
49	09/08/05	19P	Progress M-54 (354)	Consumables, spares, props	Logistics
50	09/30/05	11S	Soyuz TMA-7 (217)	Expedition 12 crew (plus Olsen)	12th crew
51	12/21/05	20P	Progress M-55 (355)	Consumables, spares, props	Logistics
52	03/29/06	12S	Soyuz TMA-8 (218)	Expedition 13 crew (plus Pontes)	13th crew
53	04/24/06	21P	Progress M-56 (356)	Consumables, spares, props	Logistics
54	06/24/06	22P	Progress M-57 (357)	Consumables, spares, props	Logistics
55	07/04/06	ULF1.1	Shuttle/STS-121	MPLM Leonardo; Expedition 13 crew	Logistics, outfitting, FT1

members per expedition are required to maintain and operate the *ISS*. Thus, a crew of three people would have very little time to conduct scientific experiments.

In 2005 the NASA administrator Michael D. Griffin (1949–) appeared before the U.S. House of Representative's Committee on Science and Technology to provide an update on NASA's plans for the future, including assembly of the *ISS*. Griffin stated that that the agency planned to assemble enough infrastructure on the station

to house a six-person crew and to allow "meaningful utilization" of the *ISS*.

In *NASA: Challenges in Completing and Sustaining the International Space Station* (July 24, 2007, http://legislative.nasa.gov/hearings/7-24-07%20Chaplain.pdf), Cristina T. Chaplain of the GAO outlines NASA's most recent plans for completing the assembly of the *ISS*. Chaplain notes that NASA intends to finish *ISS* assembly in 2010 and operate the station through 2016. The Space Shuttle

TABLE 5.7

International Space Station (ISS) assembly missions as of December 2007 [CONTINUED]

Flight no.	Launch date	Mission name	Spacecraft flying to ISS	Primary cargo	Purpose
56	09/09/06	12A	Shuttle/STS-115	P3/P4 trusses w/SAs, PV radiator	Assembly, FT2
57	09/18/06	13S	Soyuz TMA-9 (219)	Expedition 14 crew (plus Ansari)	14th crew
58	10/23/06	23P	Progress M-58 (358)	Consumables, spares, props	Logistics
59	12/09/06	12A.1	Shuttle/STS-116	P5 spacer truss, resupply	Assembly
60	01/17/07	24P	Progress M-59 (359)	Consumables, spares, props	Logistics
61	04/07/07	14S	Soyuz TMA-10 (220)	Expedition 15 crew (plus Simonyi)	15th crew
62	05/12/07	25P	Progress M-60 (360)	Consumables, spares, props	Logistics
63	06/08/07	13A	Shuttle/STS-117	S3/S4 trusses w/SAs, PV radiator	Assembly, crew rotation
64	08/02/07	26P	Progress M-61 (361)	Consumables, spares, props	Logistics
65	08/08/07	13A.1	Shuttle/STS-118	S5 truss, SpaceHab, CMG, etc.	Assembly
66	10/10/07	15S	Soyuz TMA-11 (221)	Expedition 16 crew (plus Shukor)	16th crew
67	10/23/07	10A	Shuttle/STS-120	Node-2 "Harmony"	Assembly, crew rotation

Acronyms:

CMG - Control moment gyro	FT - Flight test	MPLM - Multi purpose logistics module	PV - Photo voltaic
CRV - Crew return vehicle	HP - High pressure	PMA - Pressurized mating adapter	RTF - Return to flight
DM - Double cargo module	MBS - Mobile remote services base system	Props - Propellents	SA - Solar array
			SSRMS - Space station remote manipulator system

SOURCE: Adapted from "International Space Station ISS Assembly Progress," in *International Space Station*, National Aeronautics and Space Administration, November 19, 2007 http://www.hq.nasa.gov/osf/station/assembly/ISSProgress.html (accessed January 1, 2008)

TABLE 5.8

Major elements installed on International Space Station as of December 2007

Zarya	Launched Nov. 20, 1998
Unity	Attached Dec. 8, 1998
Zvezda	Attached July 25, 2000
Z1 truss	Attached Oct. 14, 2000
P6 integrated truss	Attached Dec. 3, 2000
Destiny	Attached Feb. 10, 2001
Canadarm2	Attached April 22, 2001
Joint airlock	Attached July 15, 2001
Pirs	Attached Sept. 16, 2001
S0 truss	Attached April 11, 2002
S1 truss	Attached Oct. 10, 2002
P1 truss	Attached Nov. 26, 2002
P3/P4 truss	Attached Sept. 12, 2006
P5 truss	Attached Dec. 12, 2006
S3/S4 trusses with solar arrays	Attached June 11, 2007
S5 truss	Attached August 11, 2007
Harmony	Attached October 26, 2007

SOURCE: Adapted from "Vital Statistics," in *The ISS to Date (2/22/07)*, National Aeronautics and Space Administration, March 8, 2007, http://spaceflight.nasa.gov/station/isstodate.html (accessed December 31, 2007)

Program is scheduled to end in 2010, and NASA's new spacecraft (the Ares series) will not be operational until approximately 2015. During this five-year period NASA plans to rely on commercial providers and its international partners to transport crews and supplies to the station.

Figure 5.4 gives an overall view of the *ISS* as of November 2007. Figure 5.5 names the major components that will comprise the completed station. As of December 2007 major components yet to be transported to the *ISS* include the Russian-supplied research module and multi-purpose laboratory; the ESA-supplied Columbus laboratory module, Node 3, and Cupola (an observatory to be attached to Node 3); the Japanese-supplied experiment module, pressurized module, experiment logistics module, and remote manipulator system; and the Canadian-supplied special purpose dexterous manipulator.

As of January 2008, NASA had twelve shuttle flights to the *ISS* on its flight manifest for 2008 and beyond. (See Table 4.5 in Chapter 4.) Chaplain states that if NASA's schedule gets delayed for any reason, certain elements planned for the *ISS*—specifically the Node 3 connector and the Cupola observatory—may not get delivered to the station.

ISS SCIENCE

The *ISS* was intended to be a world-class laboratory for conducting experiments under microgravity conditions. Three broad areas of research are conducted aboard the station: life sciences, biomedicine, and materials processing. The chief goal of life sciences and biomedicine research is to determine the effects of long-duration space travel on humans.

The Station's Glovebox

One of the difficulties of performing typical chemistry experiments in space is the microgravity condition. Liquids will not stay inside beakers or test tubes because they form into droplets of various sizes and float away. This could be extremely dangerous for the crew and the station's electronic components. To overcome this obstacle, NASA and

FIGURE 5.4

International Space Station structure as of November 14, 2007

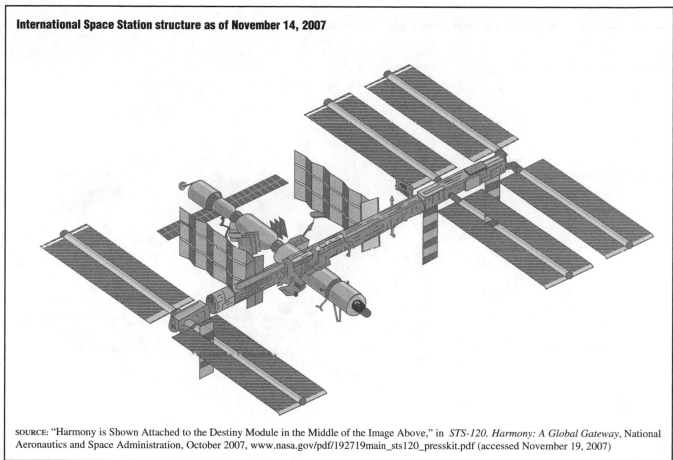

SOURCE: "Harmony is Shown Attached to the Destiny Module in the Middle of the Image Above," in *STS-120. Harmony: A Global Gateway*, National Aeronautics and Space Administration, October 2007, www.nasa.gov/pdf/192719main_sts120_presskit.pdf (accessed November 19, 2007)

ESA engineers developed an enclosed work space for the *ISS* called the microgravity science glovebox (MSG).

The MSG includes a pair of built-in gloves that crewmembers can use to handle tools and equipment within the box. The MSG was installed in the American Destiny module by the Expedition 5 crew. Figure 5.6 shows a slice of the cylindrical Destiny module. The experimental racks are positioned around the outside of the circle. An astronaut stands at the MSG research station.

The MSG is used to handle chemicals or burning or molten specimens in experiments involving fluid physics, materials science, biotechnology, and combustion science.

Materials on the International Space Station Experiment

One of the goals of space science is to determine the effect of space exposure on various materials. The *ISS* features suitcaselike containers called Materials on the International Space Station Experiment (MISSE) Passive Experiment Containers that are attached to the outside of the station. In 2006 more than eight hundred different substances were carried in MISSE containers, including samples of paints and coatings that may be used on future spacecraft. In addition, millions of basil seeds were exposed to the harsh conditions of space in the MISSE containers.

The Minus Eighty Degrees Celsius Laboratory Freezer

In 2006 *ISS* astronauts installed the station's Minus Eighty Degrees Celsius Laboratory Freezer (MELFI). The MELFI allows for fast freezing of biological and life science samples. Scientists also plan to the use the freezer to store astronauts' blood and urine samples for later analysis on Earth. In particular, researchers are interested in the effects of long-term spaceflight on levels of vitamins D and B_6 in the body. Previous research indicates that these vitamins are depleted during long space visits. The depletion is believed to be linked to the bone loss that plagues astronauts exposed to microgravity for long periods.

Bone Loss

Scientists have known for some time that human bones in the legs and feet undergo deterioration during prolonged stays in space. This was first discovered in Soviet and Russian cosmonauts who spent many months aboard space stations. Scientists believe the effect is due

FIGURE 5.5

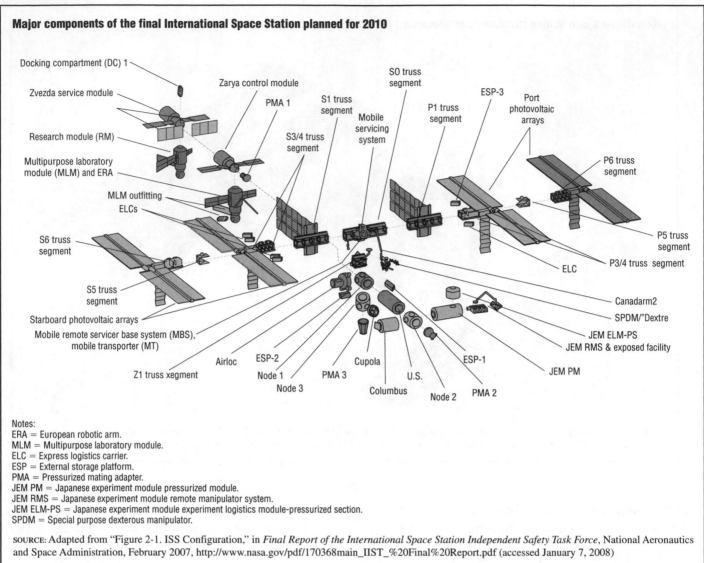

Major components of the final International Space Station planned for 2010

Docking compartment (DC) 1

Zvezda service module

Research module (RM)

Multipurpose laboratory module (MLM) and ERA

MLM outfitting

ELCs

S6 truss segment

S5 truss segment

Starboard photovoltaic arrays

Mobile remote servicer base system (MBS), mobile transporter (MT)

Z1 truss xegment

Airloc

ESP-2

Node 1

Node 3

PMA 3

Zarya control module

PMA 1

S3/4 truss segment

Cupola

Columbus

Node 2

PMA 2

S1 truss segment

Mobile servicing system

SO truss segment

P1 truss segment

ESP-1

U.S.

ESP-3

Port photovoltaic arrays

P6 truss segment

P5 truss segment

P3/4 truss segment

ELC

Canadarm2

SPDM/"Dextre

JEM ELM-PS

JEM RMS & exposed facility

JEM PM

Notes:
ERA = European robotic arm.
MLM = Multipurpose laboratory module.
ELC = Express logistics carrier.
ESP = External storage platform.
PMA = Pressurized mating adapter.
JEM PM = Japanese experiment module pressurized module.
JEM RMS = Japanese experiment module remote manipulator system.
JEM ELM-PS = Japanese experiment module experiment logistics module-pressurized section.
SPDM = Special purpose dexterous manipulator.

SOURCE: Adapted from "Figure 2-1. ISS Configuration," in *Final Report of the International Space Station Independent Safety Task Force*, National Aeronautics and Space Administration, February 2007, http://www.nasa.gov/pdf/170368main_IIST_%20Final%20Report.pdf (accessed January 7, 2008)

to the lack of mechanical loading in microgravity. Mechanical loading refers to the weight of the upper body pressing down on the lower body as a person's body is pulled toward the ground by gravity on Earth. The type of bone loss and muscle deterioration experienced by space travelers is similar to that resulting from prolonged bed rest. It has long been known that using legs and feet keeps them healthy. In a spaceship people do not experience the force of gravity or the downward load of the upper body. Also, they rarely use muscles in their legs and feet to move around. They rely much more on muscles in their arms and upper body to maneuver through hatches and accomplish tasks.

During the Russian *Mir* program, cosmonauts reported that the skin on the soles of their feet became very soft. They also lost muscle tone in their legs and feet due to lack of use. These factors caused them great difficulty

walking when they returned to Earth. Scientists incorporated exercise regimens on the *ISS* to help prevent these problems. For example, stationary bicycles help crewmembers maintain foot muscle strength. However, the exercises have had little effect on bone loss.

Historical data show that humans experience a rate of bone loss in space of approximately 1% to 2% per month. This means a bone loss of 12% to 24% per year. Scientists know that the bone loss problem has to be resolved before humans can make interplanetary journeys. A trip from Earth to Mars could take as long as six months. Crewmembers have to be able to walk on the planet's surface when they get there.

In "How Long Does It Take to Rebuild Bone Lost during Space Flight" (February 26, 2007, http://www.nasa. gov/mission_pages/station/science/subregional_bone.html), NASA reports on the results of a four-year study of the long-term effects of microgravity on sixteen *ISS* crew

FIGURE 5.6

Space station Destiny laboratory and microgravity science glovebox

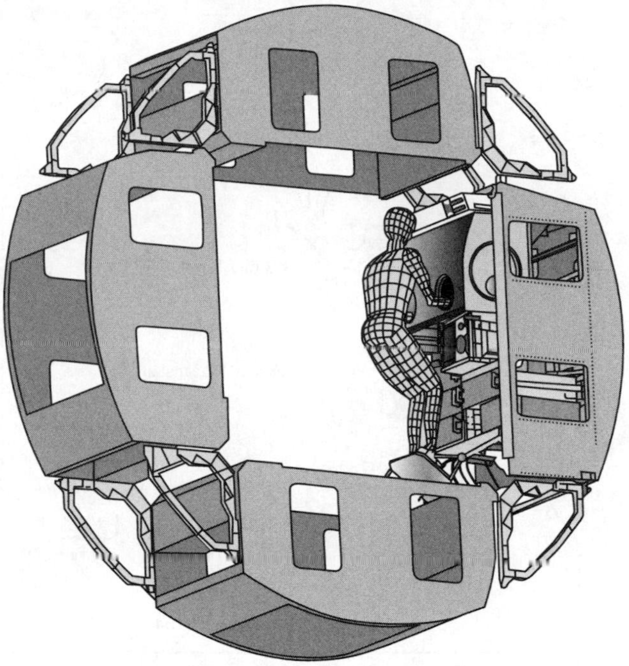

SOURCE: "This Cut-Away of the Cylindrical, Destiny Laboratory Module on the Space Station Shows How the New Microgravity Science Glovebox Fits Inside," in *NASA Fact Sheet: Microgravity Science Glovebox (MSG)*, National Aeronautics and Space Administration, Marshall Space Flight Center, March 17, 2007, http://www.nasa.gov/centers/marshall/news/background/facts/MSG.html (accessed December 31, 2007)

regrown; however, bone structure, bone density, and hip strength were not fully recovered.

ISS CREW TRAINING

The *ISS* Expedition crews undergo extensive training at facilities around the world. Figure 5.7 shows the locations of these training facilities, including:

- Johnson Space Center (JSC)—the JSC is located in Houston, Texas. This is the primary training center for Expedition crews. It features laboratories, classrooms, and simulators to prepare crewmembers for living and working aboard the *ISS*.

- Kennedy Space Center (KSC)—the KSC is located on Merritt Island, Florida, next to the Cape Canaveral Air Force Station. This is the launch site for shuttle flights. Cargo bound for the *ISS* is packed and loaded here. Crewmembers familiarize themselves with *ISS* components and practice launch procedures at the KSC.

- Canadian Space Agency (CSA) Headquarters—the CSA headquarters is located in Quebec, Canada. Canadian companies built the remote manipulator system (the robotic arm known as Canadarm2) used on the *ISS*. Expedition crewmembers undergo robotics training at this location to familiarize themselves with the Canadarm2.

- Gagarin Cosmonaut Training Center—this center is located in Zvezdny Gorodok (Star City), Russia. The training facilities are similar to those at the JSC, including classrooms, laboratories, and simulators. Expedition crewmembers learn about the Russian modules of the *ISS* and train for spacewalks in the center's Hydrolab (a forty-foot-deep pool).

- Baikonur Cosmodrome—the Cosmodrome is located in Baikonur, Kazakhstan. This is the launch site for Russian Soyuz flights to the station. Expedition crews scheduled to fly aboard Soyuz spacecraft practice launch procedures at the Cosmodrome.

members. Researchers find that astronauts in Expeditions 2 through 8 lost an average of approximately 11% of their total hip bone mass during a typical six-month mission. Bone scans performed one year after the astronauts had returned to Earth indicate that much of the bone had

FIGURE 5.7

Training locations for space expedition crewmembers

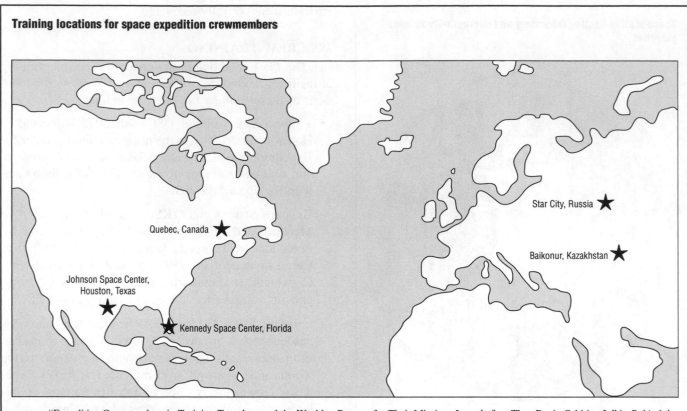

SOURCE: "Expedition Crewmembers in Training Travel around the World to Prepare for Their Missions Long before They Begin Orbiting It," in *Behind the Scenes: Training Locations*, National Aeronautics and Space Administration, August 14, 2003, http://spaceflight.nasa.gov/shuttle/support/training/isstraining/locations.html (accessed December 31, 2007)

CHAPTER 6
ROBOTIC MISSIONS IN SUN-EARTH SPACE

The Universe is an explosive, energetic and continually changing place.

—National Aeronautics and Space Administration, "Chandra's X-ray Vision" (February 19, 2004)

Sending humans into space is expensive and risky. It takes great resources to protect and sustain them every time they leave the planet. Losing a crewed spacecraft means the loss of life. This is a high price to pay to learn about the universe. This explains why robotic spacecraft are so vital to space science. Since the beginning of the space age, satellites and probes have been sent out to gather data about Earth's surroundings. The earliest ones were rather crude in their technology. People referred to them simply as unmanned spacecraft. Times changed, and technology improved significantly. In the twenty-first century, these mechanized explorers are called robotic spacecraft.

Only a handful of robotic spacecraft are sent to other planets. The vast majority of them circle Earth or the Sun. Spacecraft in Earth orbit serve commercial, military, and scientific purposes. Scientists rely on satellites to collect data about Earth's weather, climate, atmospheric conditions, sea levels, ocean circulation, and gravitational and electromagnetic fields. These satellites are not space explorers but Earth observers that reside in space.

Other satellites in Earth orbit look outward toward the cosmos. These space observatories carry high-powered telescopes that beam images back to Earth. They can detect the light and radiation of celestial objects hidden from human view. They peer into the deep, dark regions of space to explore what is out there. Scientists use the images sent back from such satellites to learn about the origins of stars and planets and unravel some of the mysteries of the universe.

Closer to Earth is the Sun. It emits radiation and heat and produces a flow of energetic particles called the solar wind that constantly blows against Earth. Gusts of solar wind can upset the planet's electromagnetic field. Every so often the Sun spits out globs of plasma and intense bursts of radiation. These, too, can have a profound effect on Earth. Investigating the Sun-Earth connection is a major goal of modern space science. Robotic spacecraft are put into Earth orbit or sent out into space to collect data about this vital connection.

For decades, robotic spacecraft have been designed for one-way trips. Eventually, their batteries give out and their radios malfunction, and then they quit reporting back to Earth. They continue silently in their orbits or are incinerated by reentry into Earth's atmosphere. During the 1990s scientists developed robotic spacecraft that can do more than report back—they can come back. These sampling ships are designed to grab samples of space particles and return safely to Earth. The first one returned in September 2005. It carried samples of solar wind collected a million miles from Earth. The spaceship's name was *Genesis*. It marked the beginning of a whole new way for humans to explore space without even leaving the planet.

NASA'S SPACE SCIENCE MISSIONS

The vast majority of robotic spacecraft are operated by the National Aeronautics and Space Administration (NASA), under the agency's Science Mission Directorate (SMD). This directorate focuses on areas of research including the origins and evolution of the universe, the nature of life, the solar system, and the relationship between Earth and the Sun. It also supports the Vision for Space Exploration by studying the formation of Mars and Earth's Moon; searching for exoplanets (planets outside the solar system), particularly those that are potentially habitable; and investigating space phenomena that could harm robotic and human explorers.

TABLE 6.1

Operating and past missions of the Science Mission Directorate as of October 2007

Earth	Sun	Solar system	Universe
Operating missions of the Science Mission Directorate			
ACRIMSAT	ACE	**Mercury**	Chandra
Aqua	AIM	MESSENGER	GALEX
Aura	Cluster-2	**Mars**	HST
CALIPSO	FAST	Mars Express	INTEGRAL
CloudSat	Geotail	Mars Rovers	RXTE
GRACE	Hinode	Mars Reconnaisance	Spitzer
	(SOLAR-B)	Orbiter	
IceSAT	Polar	Odyssey	Suzaku (Astro-E2)
Jason	RHESSI	Phoenix	SWIFT
Landsat 7	SOHO	**Saturn**	WMAP
LAGEOS 1&2	ST-6	Cassini	XMM-Newton
NMP EO-1	STEREO	**Pluto and beyond**	
QuikSCAT	THEMIS	New Horizons	
SeaWiFS	TIMED	Voyager	
SORCE	TRACE	Dawn	
Terra	Ulysses	**Comet samplers**	
TRMM	Wind	Rosetta	
		Stardust	
		Deep Impact	
Past missions of the Science Mission Directorate			
CHAMP	CRRES	Clementine	ASCA
ERBS	DE-1	CONTOUR	Astro-1
GOES L	Equator-S	Deep Space 1	Astro-2
GOES M	IMAGE	Deep Space 2	BBXRT
Meteor 3M	IMP-8	Galileo	CGRO
POES L	SAC-B	Genesis	CHIPS
POES M	SAMPEX	ISEE-3/ICE	COBE
SRTM	SNOE	Leonid MAC	DXS
TOMS-EP	Spartan	Lunar Pros.	EUVE
TOPEX/Poseidon	ST-5	Magellan	GP-B
UARS	Starshine	Mariner	HALCA
	TERRIERS	MCO	HETE-2
	TSS-1	Mars Obs.	Hipparcos
	TSS-1R	Mars Path.	IEH-3
	Yohkoh	MGS	IRTS
		MPL	ISO
		NEAR	IUE
		Pioneer 10,11	KAO
		Pioneer Venus	ORFEUS
		Ranger	ROSAT
		Surveyor	SWAS
		Viking	VLBI
			WIRE

SOURCE: Adapted from "Science Missions," in *Science Missions*, National Aeronautics and Space Administration, October 29, 2007, http://science.hq.nasa.gov/missions/phase.html (accessed January 1, 2008).

The SMD categorizes space science missions by primary research target: Earth, the Sun, the solar system, and the universe. Table 6.1 provides a categorical breakdown of the SMD's operational and past missions as of October 2007. More than fifty science missions were ongoing at that time.

The SMD also categorizes space science missions administratively, that is, by mission class and by the NASA program under which they are developed.

Mission class is characterized primarily by complexity, leadership, and cost. These elements are defined in *Summary of the Science Plan for NASA's Science Mission Directorate 2007–2016* (January 2007, http://science.hq.nasa.gov/strategy/Science_Plan_07_summary.pdf). NASA has two complexity classes: strategic and competed. Strategic missions are major complex projects that address broad science goals and have long development times and high costs. These missions are managed and led directly by NASA. Competed missions are smaller missions with narrowly focused science goals, short schedules, and relatively low-cost caps. These missions are proposed and led by entities called principal investigators (PIs). A PI can be one or more universities, research organizations, companies, or even NASA centers. Strategic missions may include components that are competed (e.g., specific science instruments onboard a spacecraft).

NASA's cost categories for space science missions are as follows:

- Small missions—life cycle costs less than approximately $300 million

- Midsize missions—life cycle costs between approximately $300 million to $700 million

- Large missions—life cycle costs more than approximately $750 million

- Flagship missions—life cycle costs more than approximately $1 billion

Major NASA programs engaged in space science include the Explorers and Discovery programs. The following describes these program in more detail.

NASA'S EXPLORERS PROGRAM

The Explorers Program includes robotic missions that conduct relatively low-cost scientific investigations with specific objectives in the fields of astrophysics and heliophysics (physics of the Sun). The program dates back to the late 1950s. The first satellite launched into space by the United States was *Explorer 1*. It was the first of a series of scientific satellites named Explorer.

In 1958 *Explorer 1* used temperature gauges and a Geiger counter to collect data in space. A Geiger counter is an instrument that detects the presence and intensity of radiation. *Explorer 1* detected radiation levels as expected during most of its orbit. However, at the highest altitudes the Geiger counter recorded no radiation. This was most puzzling. Scientists expected radiation levels to increase, not decrease, farther from Earth. Data from later Explorers and the Soviet Sputnik satellites revealed that *Explorer 1* had encountered radiation levels so high that its detector was overwhelmed.

These missions led to the discovery of the Van Allen radiation belts. These are two doughnut-shaped regions of high radioactivity that encircle Earth. The inner belt is centered approximately two thousand miles above Earth and is roughly four thousand miles thick. The outer belt lies between approximately eleven thousand and twenty-five thousand miles from Earth. All future spacecraft venturing far from Earth have to be designed to withstand the intense radiation of the Van Allen belts.

Over the next three decades the Explorers Program continued with mission series given different names, including the Atmosphere Explorer, the Electrostatic Particle Explorer, the Interplanetary Monitoring Platform, and the Solar Radiation Satellites. There were also Explorer spacecraft with colorful names such as *Hawkeye*, *Injun*, and *Uhuru*. (Uhuru means "freedom" in Swahili, an African language.)

NASA's 2007 science plan describes the Explorers missions as competed missions led by the PIs. Cost-wise, they are considered "small" missions. NASA (June 11, 2007, http://explorers.gsfc.nasa.gov/missions.html) indicates that within the Explorers Program missions are further categorized by complexity and cost as follows:

- University-class Explorer/Student Explorer Demonstration Initiative Program—total cost less than $15 million
- Small Explorer—total cost less than $120 million
- Medium-class Explorer (MIDEX)—total cost less than $180 million

NASA stopped accepting proposals for MIDEX missions in 2004. The decision was due to budget constraints, the change in NASA's focus to crewed Moon and Mars missions, and the lack of appropriate launch vehicles (mainly Delta II rockets) for spacecraft of the size typically used in MIDEX missions.

Another type of Explorer mission is the Mission of Opportunity (MO). This is a mission operated by another office within NASA or by the space agency of another country in which an SMD investigation "hitches a ride" with the mission of the other agency or country. The total cost to NASA of an MO mission cannot exceed $35 million.

Table 6.2 lists the Explorers Program's operational missions as of December 2007. Most of the spacecraft are small observatories in low Earth orbit (LEO; 125 to 1,200 miles above Earth's surface). The *Advanced Composition Explorer* and the *Wilkinson Microwave Anisotropy Probe* are positioned at Lagrange points around Earth (designated L1 and L2 in Table 6.2, respectively). These are points at which the gravitational pulls of the Sun and Earth are relatively even, meaning that a spacecraft can stay "parked" between the two heavenly bodies. Point L1 is approximately one million miles from Earth toward the Sun; point L2 is approximately one million miles from Earth in the other direction (away from the Sun). The locations of *IMP-8*, *THEMIS*, *IMAGE*, and *Integral* are given in terms of Earth radii. (Earth's radius is approximately 3,960 miles.)

As of January 2008, NASA had two full-fledged Explorer missions and two MOs scheduled for launch before the end of the decade. The full-fledged missions are the *Interstellar Boundary Explorer* (an imager designed to detect specific atoms believed to have originated outside the solar system) and the *Wide-Field Infrared Surveyor* (a miniobservatory that will image nearby stars and galaxies). The scheduled MOs are the Two Wide-Angle Imaging Neutral-Atom Spectrometers and the Coupled Ion Neutral Dynamics Investigation. Both instruments will fly on U.S. Department of Defense spacecraft.

NASA'S DISCOVERY PROGRAM

The Discovery Program was initiated in 1989 to develop missions that could be accomplished using small spacecraft at a low cost in a relatively short time to address focused scientific goals. According to NASA's 2007 science plan, Discovery missions are competed PI-led missions with a cost classification of "medium." The focus of the program is celestial bodies (mainly planets, moons, comets, and asteroids) within and outside the solar system.

The program allows scientists to conduct small space investigations that complement NASA's larger and more expensive interplanetary missions. Each Discovery mission must have a fast development time and relatively low cost. NASA calls it the "faster, better, cheaper" approach to space science. MO projects are also allowed under the program.

As of December 2007, there were ten current and past missions listed under the Discovery Program. (See Table 6.3.) Three of the missions were operational: *ASPERA-3*, *Dawn*, and *MESSENGER* (*Mercury Surface, Space Environment, Geochemistry, and Ranging*). (*ASPERA-3* and *Dawn* are described in Chapters 7 and 8, respectively.) *MESSENGER* is the only operational mission focused on Sun-Earth space. It launched on August 3, 2004, on a voyage to Mercury. The spacecraft will conduct several flybys of the planet before achieving orbit in 2011. It will be the first spacecraft to orbit that planet. NASA's *Mariner 10* flew by Mercury in the 1970s, but it captured limited images of the planet's surface. As such, much of Mercury has remained unseen territory. *MESSENGER* includes a complex suite of instruments that will capture detailed images of the planet and investigate its geology and atmosphere. (See Figure 6.1.) The payload was specially designed to endure the high-temperature environment near the Sun.

Past Discovery Missions

Seven Discovery missions (*NEAR Shoemaker*, *Sojourner*, *Lunar Prospector*, *Stardust*, *Genesis*, *CONTOUR*, and *Deep Impact*) ended their primary missions during the late 1990s or

TABLE 6.2

Explorers Program operational missions as of December 2007

Name	Long title	Launch date	Orbit location	Mission
ACE	Advanced Composition Explorer	8/25/1997	L1	Samples low-energy particles of solar origin and high-energy galactic particles
RXTE	Rossi X-ray Timing Explorer	12/30/1995	LEO	Observes black holes, neutron stars, X-ray pulsars and bursts of X-rays
IMP-8	Interplanetary Monitoring Platform	10/26/1973	35 Earth radii	Measures magnetic fields, plasmas, and energetic charged particles
Medium-class Explorers (MIDEX)				
THEMIS	Time History of Events and Macroscale Interactions	2/17/2007	10–30 Earth radii	Five satellites dispersed around Earth to monitor auroras
Swift	(Named after a small nimble bird)	11/20/2004	LEO	Multi-wavelength observatory dedicated to the study of gamma-ray burst
WMAP	Wilkinson Microwave Anisotropy Probe	6/30/2001	L2	Measures cosmic microwave background radiation over the full sky
IMAGE	Imager for Magnetopause-to-Aurora Global Exporation	3/25/2000	7.2 Earth radii	Images Earth's magnetosphere
FUSE	Far Ultraviolet Spectroscopic Explorer	6/24/1999	LEO	Uses high-resolution spectroscopy in the far-ultraviolet spectral region
Small Explorers (SMEX)				
AIM	Aeronomy of Ice in the Mesosphere	4/25/2007	373 miles	Studies Earth's high-altitude polar clouds
GALEX	Galaxy Evolution Explorer	4/28/2003	LEO	Space telescope that observes galaxies in ultraviolet light
RHESSI	Reuven Ramaty High Energy Solar Spectroscopic Imager	2/5/2002	LEO	Explore basic physics of solar flares
SWAS	Submillimeter Wave Astronomy Satellite	12/5/1998	LEO	Surveys emissions of water, O_2, C, and CO in galactic star forming regions
TRACE	Transition Region and Coronal Explorer	4/2/1998	LEO	Images the solar corona and transition region
FAST	Fast Auroral Snapshot Explorer	8/21/1996	215–2,500 miles	Investigates the plasma physics of the auroral phenomena at Earth's poles
SAMPEX	Solar Anomalous and Magnetospheric Particle Explorer	7/3/1992	LEO	Measures the composition of solar energetic particles and cosmic rays
University-Class Explorers (UNEX)/Student Explorer Demonstration Initiative Program (STEDI)				
CHIPS	Cosmic Hot Interstellar Plasma Spectrometer	1/12/2003	LEO	Conducts all-sky spectroscopy of the diffuse background
SNOE	Student Nitric Oxide Explorer	2/26/1998	LEO	Measures effects of energy on nitric oxide in the Earth's upper atmosphere
Missions of opportunity (MO)				
Suzaku	(Formerly called Astro-E2, Suzaku is a vermillion bird)	7/10/2005	LEO	Studies X-rays emitted by stars, galaxies, and black holes
Integral	International Gamma Ray Laboratory	10/17/2002	1.4–23.5 Earth radii	Gamma-ray observatory
HETE-2	High-Energy Transient Explorer	10/9/2000	LEO	Detects and localizes gamma-ray bursts

SOURCE: Adapted from "Current Missions," in *Explorers Program*, National Aeronautics and Space Administration, Goddard Space Flight Center, 2007, http://explorers.gsfc.nasa.gov/missions.html (accessed December 31, 2007)

early 2000s. The *CONTOUR* spacecraft, which was intended to encounter two comets, was lost six weeks after launch. The following describes the remaining missions. (*Sojourner* is described in Chapter 7.)

NEAR SHOEMAKER. *Near Earth Asteroid Rendezvous Shoemaker* (*NEAR Shoemaker*) was the first mission launched under the Discovery Program. The spacecraft investigated the asteroid 433 Eros. Asteroids are small celestial bodies that orbit larger ones. Most of the asteroids in the solar system are found in a massive asteroid belt that circles around the Sun between the orbits of Mars and Jupiter. 433 Eros is twenty-one miles long and has an elliptical orbit that carries it outside the Martian orbit and then in close to Earth orbit. On February 12, 2001, *NEAR* softly touched down on the asteroid. It was the first time in history that a spacecraft had landed

on an asteroid. When it happened, 433 Eros was 196 million miles from Earth.

NEAR orbited 433 Eros for nearly a year before landing and returned dozens of high-resolution photographs of the asteroid. Before it landed, the spacecraft was renamed *NEAR Shoemaker* in honor of the geologist Eugene M. Shoemaker (1928–1997). The first Discovery mission was considered an overwhelming success.

LUNAR PROSPECTOR. *Lunar Prospector* launched on January 7, 1998, and assumed an orbit around Earth's Moon to collect scientific data. On July 31, 1999, the spacecraft was purposely crashed into the lunar surface.

STARDUST. *Stardust* collected particle samples from comet Wild 2 and returned them to Earth. Wild 2 (pronounced "Vilt" 2) is a relatively small comet with a

TABLE 6.3

Discovery program mission list as of December 2007

Name	Launch date	Mission
Operational		
Dawn	9/27/2007	In flight to asteroid Vesta and dwarf planet Ceres
MESSENGER	8/3/2004	In flight to Mercury, expected to arrive in 2011
ASPERA-3[a]	6/2/2003	Analyzes interactions between solar wind and Martian atmosphere
Past		
Deep Impact	1/12/2005	Encountered comet Tempel-1 and sent probe to comet surface
CONTOUR	7/3/2002	Spacecraft failed
Genesis	8/8/2001	Returned samples of charged particles to Earth
Stardust	2/7/1999	Intercepted & sampled comet Wild 2. Returned samples to Earth.
Lunar Prospector	1/6/1998	Spent one year mapping lunar resources, gravity, magnetic fields, etc.
Sojourner[b]	12/4/1996	Roved Martian surface for 84 days
NEAR Shoemaker	2/17/1996	Flew by comets Mathilde and Eros. Landed on Eros in 2001.

[a]Mission of opportunity aboard European Space Agency (ESA) spacecraft Mars Express.
[b]Mission of opportunity aboard NASA spacecraft Mars Pathfinder.

SOURCE: Adapted from "A Look Back at the Beginning: How the Discovery Program Came to Be," in *Discovery and New Frontiers Program*, National Aeronautics and Space Administration, December 18, 2007, http://discovery newfrontiers.nasa.gov/lib/presentations/docs/HistoricalDiscoveryProgram Information.doc (accessed January 1, 2008)

FIGURE 6.1

MESSENGER spacecraft

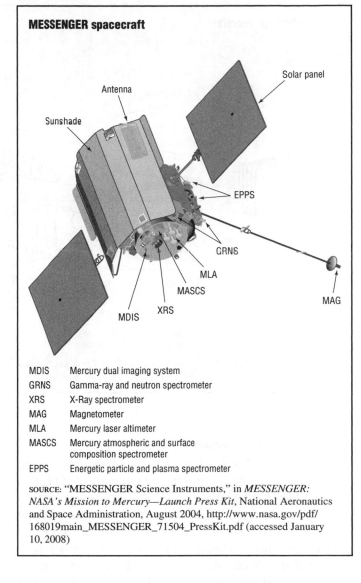

MDIS	Mercury dual imaging system
GRNS	Gamma-ray and neutron spectrometer
XRS	X-Ray spectrometer
MAG	Magnetometer
MLA	Mercury laser altimeter
MASCS	Mercury atmospheric and surface composition spectrometer
EPPS	Energetic particle and plasma spectrometer

SOURCE: "MESSENGER Science Instruments," in *MESSENGER: NASA's Mission to Mercury—Launch Press Kit*, National Aeronautics and Space Administration, August 2004, http://www.nasa.gov/pdf/ 168019main_MESSENGER_71504_PressKit.pdf (accessed January 10, 2008)

nucleus measuring about three miles in diameter. *Stardust* carried a particle collector about the size of a tennis racket that could capture and hold tiny comet dust particles. (See Figure 6.2.) It collected and analyzed interstellar dust and successfully sampled particles from the coma of Wild 2. These particles are believed to be more than 4.5 billion years old.

As the spaceship approached Earth, it released the sample-return capsule. On January 15, 2006, the capsule entered Earth's atmosphere. Parachutes were deployed, and the capsule landed safely in the Utah desert. The main spacecraft was put into orbit around the Sun and will likely be used on a future mission. As of March 2008, scientists continued to analyze the particles collected by *Stardust*.

GENESIS. *Genesis* was a revolutionary spacecraft designed to collect charged particles emitted from the Sun and return them safely to Earth. It would assume a tight orbit around L1 for 2.5 years, collect samples, and then head back to Earth. After reentering Earth's atmosphere, *Genesis* would deploy its parachutes for a slow descent toward the surface. A specially equipped helicopter was to snag the spaceship midair and carry it to land.

On September 8, 2004, *Genesis* began its descent to a Utah landing site. However, its parachutes did not open,

and the spacecraft plummeted at high speed into the ground. The capsule containing the samples split open during the crash, exposing the sample medium to the outside atmosphere. However, approximately 4 milligrams of samples were saved. As of March 2008, they were being analyzed by scientists. *Genesis* was the first spacecraft to return extraterrestrial materials to Earth since the Apollo missions.

DEEP IMPACT. On July 4, 2005, *Deep Impact* encountered the comet Tempel-1 and sent a probe into the comet's surface. The comet was discovered by the French astronomer Ernst Tempel (1821–1889) in 1867. It orbits the Sun between Mars and Jupiter with a 5.5-year orbital period. The probe relayed data to the flyby portion of the spaceship. NASA scientists are using the data to determine the physical and chemical makeup of the comet. As of March 2008, the *Deep Impact* flyby spacecraft remained in space and was expected to be used for a future Discovery MO.

FIGURE 6.2

The Stardust spacecraft

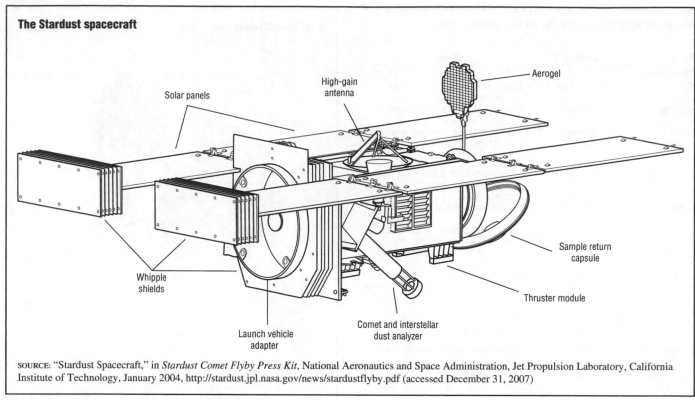

SOURCE: "Stardust Spacecraft," in *Stardust Comet Flyby Press Kit*, National Aeronautics and Space Administration, Jet Propulsion Laboratory, California Institute of Technology, January 2004, http://stardust.jpl.nasa.gov/news/stardustflyby.pdf (accessed December 31, 2007)

Future Discovery Missions

As of March 2008, future Discovery missions include one full-fledged mission called Kepler and an MO called Moon Mineralogy Mapper (M3). The *Kepler* space telescope was scheduled to launch in 2008, and will assume an Earth-trailing heliocentric orbit (an orbit behind Earth around the Sun) and survey a region of the Milky Way looking for planets similar to Earth. *Kepler* will be pointed toward the constellations Cygnus and Lyra. The primary stars in this region include Vega, Deneb, and Albireo.

The M3 is an instrument suite aboard the spacecraft *Chandrayaan-1. Chandrayaan-1* is a lunar orbit spacecraft scheduled to be launched in 2008 by the Indian Space Research Organization.

SPACE OBSERVATORIES

Celestial objects emit all kinds of radioactive waves that give clues about their shape, size, age, and location. Earth's atmosphere filters and blocks out most of this radiation, keeping it from reaching the planet's surface. This is one reason biological life is possible on planet Earth. The atmospheric shield is good for human health but bad for observing the universe.

To clearly detect all radioactive waves traveling through space, an observer has to be located above the shielding effects of Earth's atmosphere. The human eye can only detect one type of radioactive wave: visible light. These waves comprise only a small fraction of the radiation located throughout the cosmos. This is why scientists invented instruments that can detect and measure waves that are invisible to humans. These instruments are put on satellites and launched into outer space to provide a clearer "picture" of the universe.

The largest and most powerful space telescopes in the world are NASA's Great Observatories. These observatories were developed over many years. As of March 2008, NASA had four Great Observatories orbiting in space:

- *Hubble Space Telescope*
- *Chandra X-Ray Observatory*
- *Compton Gamma Ray Observatory*
- *Spitzer Space Telescope*

These observatories were designed to observe the universe across a wide range of the light energies making up the electromagnetic spectrum.

The Electromagnetic Spectrum

Scientists use a scale to describe the different types of light energies. This scale is called the electromagnetic spectrum. (See Figure 6.3.) It categorizes energy by wavelength and frequency. A radio wave is the largest type, measuring between one millimeter and one hundred

FIGURE 6.3

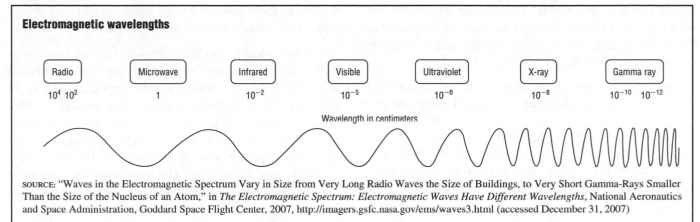

Electromagnetic wavelengths

Radio	Microwave	Infrared	Visible	Ultraviolet	X-ray	Gamma ray
10^4 10^2	1	10^{-2}	10^{-5}	10^{-6}	10^{-8}	10^{-10} 10^{-12}

Wavelength in centimeters

SOURCE: "Waves in the Electromagnetic Spectrum Vary in Size from Very Long Radio Waves the Size of Buildings, to Very Short Gamma-Rays Smaller Than the Size of the Nucleus of an Atom," in *The Electromagnetic Spectrum: Electromagnetic Waves Have Different Wavelengths*, National Aeronautics and Space Administration, Goddard Space Flight Center, 2007, http://imagers.gsfc.nasa.gov/ems/waves3.html (accessed December 31, 2007)

kilometers in length. This is a range of roughly 0.04 inches to 328,000 feet. At the other end of the scale is the gamma ray. Its length is the size of subatomic particles. Near the middle of the scale is visible light.

For most celestial objects there is a relationship between their temperature and the main type of radiation that they emit. Astronomers use the kelvin temperature scale to measure temperature. A temperature of zero kelvin is called absolute zero (the lowest possible temperature in the universe, at which all atomic activity ceases). This is equivalent to −459.7 degrees Fahrenheit.

Most stars have temperatures between thirty-five hundred and twenty-five thousand kelvin. Much of the energy they emit is visible. This explains why humans can see stars in the nighttime sky. However, stars emit radiation at other wavelengths across the spectrum, particularly at infrared.

Everything with a temperature above absolute zero emits infrared waves. This makes infrared observation an extremely important astronomical tool. There are huge clouds of dust and gas located throughout the universe. These clouds, called nebulae, can hide visible light from human sight. Scientists poetically refer to this phenomenon as the "cosmic veil." An infrared telescope is said to lift the cosmic veil by allowing humans to see through the clouds.

Many of the most mysterious objects and explosions in the cosmos are associated with extremely high temperatures and releases of gamma-ray, x-ray, and ultraviolet radiation. Space-based telescopes equipped with special instruments can detect these waves.

This is important because X-rays and gamma rays are associated with phenomena such as black holes, supernova remnants, and neutron stars. Table 6.4 defines these terms and describes other cosmic objects. According to NASA, ultraviolet observations are useful for studying

TABLE 6.4

Definitions

Term	Meaning
Black hole	Invisible celestial object believed created when a massive star collapses. Its gravitational field is so strong that light cannot escape from it.
Brown dwarf	Celestial object much smaller than a typical star that radiates energy, but does not experience nuclear fusion.
Dark matter	Hypothetical matter that provides the gravity needed to hold hot gases within a galaxy cluster.
Event horizon	The boundary of a black hole.
Galaxy cluster	Huge collection of galaxies bound together by gravity.
Nebulae	Large gas and dust clouds that populate a galaxy.
Neutron star	Hypothetical dense celestial object consisting primarily of closely packed neutrons. Believed to result from the collapse of a much larger star.
Nova	Star that suddenly begins emitting much more light than before and continues to do so for days or months before returning to its former state of illumination.
Pulsar	Celestial body emitting pulses of electromagnetic radiation at short relatively constant intervals.
Quasar	Mysterious celestial object that resembles a star, but releases a tremendous amount of energy for its size.
Superflare	Massive explosion from a young star. A superflare is thousands of times stronger than a solar flare emitted by Earth's Sun.
Supernova	Catastrophic explosion of a star.
Supernova remnant	Bubble of multimillion degree gas released during a supernova.
White dwarf	Small dying star that has used up all its fuel and is fading.

SOURCE: Created by Kim Masters Evans for Gale, Cengage Learning, 2008

the youngest, hottest, and most massive stars, besides quasars and white dwarf stars. Visible light is emitted by stars and emitted or reflected by cooler objects in the universe, including planets, nebulae, and brown dwarf stars. Radio waves are associated with cold clouds of molecules and radiation left over from celestial events that happened billions of years ago.

Telescopes as Time Machines

It takes a long time for energy waves to travel through space. Even though there are many different wavelengths of radiation, they all travel at a speed called the speed of light. The speed of light through a vacuum is 186,282 miles per second. This seems extremely fast. However, most celestial objects are so incredibly far from Earth that it takes their energy a long time to reach us despite traveling at such a high speed.

Astronomers use a unit of measure called the light-year to describe long distances in space. During one year light travels 5.9 trillion miles, so a celestial object that is 5.9 trillion miles from Earth is said to be one light-year away. The Sun is eight light-minutes from Earth. This means that it takes eight minutes for an energy wave from the Sun to reach Earth.

When a telescope captures an image of an object in the universe, the image shows what that object looked like in the past. The farther away a telescope can see, the farther back into time it looks. NASA's Great Observatories capture images of celestial objects that are extremely distant from Earth. This means that the radiation reaching the observatories left its source a long time ago. This is why NASA refers to its observatories as time machines: They allow humans to look back into time and learn about the origins of the universe.

Most astronomers believe that the universe started ten to twenty billion years ago with a massive explosion called the big bang. The energy released during this explosion would have been tremendous. Since then, the universe has been cooling and expanding. Scientists believe that most of the radiation left over from the big bang now travels throughout space as radio waves and microwaves. This is called cosmic background radiation.

Ground-Based Telescopes

Telescopes were first developed in Europe around the beginning of the 1600s. Glass lenses had been used to make eyeglasses for several centuries. The first telescopes included a series of lenses within a long slender tube that magnified distant objects. In 1610 the Italian scientist Galileo Galilei (1564–1642) popularized the telescope when he published *Sidereus Nuncius* (*Starry Messenger*). The book described Galileo's astronomical observations, including the discovery of four moons around Jupiter.

Like the human eye, optical telescopes can discern only visible light. During the 1800s scientists first developed detectors for infrared radiation coming from outer space. Because the water in Earth's atmosphere blocks out most infrared radiation, these detectors were placed atop mountains, where the air is thinner. Later, they were sent up in high-altitude balloons and even airplanes.

During the 1930s the American engineer Karl Jansky (1905–1950) built an instrument capable of detecting radio waves. His radio telescope picked up waves generated by thunderstorms and from another unknown

source in outer space. Over time, scientists constructed larger and more powerful radio telescopes to pick up the radio waves that arrived from outer space.

RADIO ARRAYS. In the 1980s dozens of radio telescopes in New Mexico were linked together to enhance their capability. This was called the Very Large Array. In 1993 the National Science Foundation created a more powerful system called the Very Long Baseline Array. It includes ten eighty-two-foot radio antennas located across the United States, from Hawaii in the west to the Virgin Islands in the east. The telescopes are connected by a computer network and provide the best radio wave images in the world.

ARECIBO OBSERVATORY. The largest single-dish radio telescope on Earth is the Arecibo Observatory in Puerto Rico. The observatory was built in the 1960s and is operated by Cornell University for the National Science Foundation. On November 16, 1974, scientists used the observatory to send a radio message out into the galaxy. The message was coded in binary, meaning that a series of zeroes and ones were transmitted by shifting frequencies. The total broadcast took less than three minutes. It was a pictorial message.

The message shows the numbers one through ten, the atomic numbers of five chemical elements, the chemical formula of deoxyribonucleic acid, information about the human form and Earth's population, a stick-figure person, the location of Earth in relation to the Sun and the other planets, a representation of the Arecibo telescope, and information about its size.

MAUNA KEA OBSERVATORIES. Mauna Kea is a fourteen-thousand-foot-high extinct volcano in Hawaii. A number of observatories have been erected atop Mauna Kea, because the thin atmosphere allows detection of near-infrared radiation. This is a narrow band of infrared radiation that lies closest to visible light in the electromagnetic spectrum.

The Keck Observatory is operated at Mauna Kea by NASA in conjunction with the California Institute of Technology and the University of California. The Subaru Telescope is a project of the National Institutes of Natural Science of Japan. The Gemini Observatory is an international collaboration between the United States, the United Kingdom, Canada, Chile, Australia, Argentina, and Brazil. Other universities and institutions from around the world also operate telescopes atop Mauna Kea.

GRAN TELESCOPIO CANARIAS. In August 2007 Spanish astronomers unveiled the largest terrestrial telescope to date: Gran Telescopio Canarias. The observatory is located on the Canary Islands off the coast of Morocco in northern Africa. NASA notes in "World's New Largest Telescope Gets Ready for Planet-Hunting" (August 2, 2007, http://planetquest.jpl.nasa.gov/news/telescopePlanetHunting.cfm)

that the new telescope is only 4% larger than the Keck I and II telescopes, the previous record holders. Gran Telescopio Canarias was expected to begin scientific operations in 2008. It will be used to search for exoplanets, brown dwarfs, nearby stars, and other celestial phenomena.

Early Space Telescopes

In 1923 the scientist Hermann Oberth (1894–1989) proposed a space telescope in "Die Rakete zu den Planetenräumen" ("The Rocket into Interplanetary Space"). Two decades later the physicist Lyman Spitzer Jr. (1914–1997) more fully outlined the scientific benefits of putting telescopes in space. At the time, space travel was not even possible.

In April 1966 NASA launched its first space telescope, the *Orbital Astronomical Observatory*. This launch was the first in a series of many satellites put into Earth orbit to detect energy sources in space. Most of these projects included NASA and international partners. In August 1975 the European Space Agency (ESA) launched *COS-B*, which provided the first complete gamma-ray map of the galaxy.

Spitzer and many other astronomers continued to urge the National Academy of Sciences and NASA to develop more powerful space telescopes for the scientific community. During the 1970s development began on the *Large Space Telescope* (*LST*). Following the Moon landings, NASA's budget was severely cut, which forced scientists to downsize the *LST* project several times. In 1975 the ESA joined the project and agreed to fund a percentage of the *LST*'s costs in exchange for a guaranteed amount of telescope time for its scientists. Two years later Congress authorized funding for the construction and assembly of the *LST*.

At the same time that the *LST* was under construction, the space shuttle was also undergoing development. *LST* planners decided to use shuttle crews to deploy and service the telescope and ultimately return it to Earth. This decision would turn out to be a fateful one. By 1985 the observatory was finished and given a new name: *Hubble Space Telescope*.

The *Hubble Space Telescope*

The *Hubble Space Telescope* (*HST*) was the first of NASA's Great Observatories. It is named after the American astronomer Edwin P. Hubble (1889–1953). The *HST* detects three types of light radiation: ultraviolet, visible, and near-infrared. It is the only one of the Great Observatories that captures images in visible light.

Figure 6.4 shows the general layout of the *HST*. It can hold eight science instruments besides the primary mirror and secondary mirrors. These instruments are powered by sunlight captured by the satellite's two solar arrays. Gyroscopes and flywheels are used to point the telescope and keep it stable.

Table 6.5 provides design, cost, and operational data about the *HST*. NASA's Goddard Space Flight Center (GSFC) in Greenbelt, Maryland, is responsible for oversight of all *HST* operations and for servicing the satellite. The Space Telescope Science Institute (STSI) in Baltimore, Maryland, selects targets for the observatory based on proposals submitted by astronomers. The STSI also analyzes the astronomical data generated by the observatory. The STSI is operated by the Association of Universities for Research in Astronomy, an international consortium of dozens of universities.

The *HST* transmits raw data to one of NASA's Tracking and Data Relay Satellites (TDRSs). There are six of these satellites in LEO. The TDRS relays the data via radio frequency communication links to a complex in White Sands, New Mexico. From there the data are relayed to the GSFC and then to the STSI.

The *HST* was originally supposed to go into space in 1986. The explosion of the space shuttle *Challenger* that year delayed the *HST*'s launch for four years. On April 24, 1990, the *HST* was carried into orbit by the space shuttle *Discovery*. One day later the astronauts deployed the satellite approximately 380 miles from Earth. It assumed an orbit that is nearly a perfect circle.

When scientists first started using the *HST*, they discovered that its images were fuzzy due to a defect in the telescope's optical mirrors. The defect had existed before the satellite was launched into space. Media publicity about the problem caused an uproar and brought harsh criticism of NASA. In December 1993 astronauts aboard the space shuttle *Endeavour* were sent to intercept the *HST* and install corrective devices. The mission was a success.

This was the first of four servicing missions conducted by shuttle crews between 1993 and 2002. During these missions astronauts performed repairs and maintenance, installed new components to enhance the *HST*'s performance, and reboosted the satellite to a higher altitude. Like all objects in LEO, the *HST* experiences some drag and gradually loses altitude. The satellite does not have its own propulsion system.

THE *HST* NEEDS SERVICING. The *HST* was originally designed for a twenty-year lifetime. Planners assumed that five shuttle servicing missions would be required over this time period to keep the observatory in orbit and functioning properly. At the end of 2002 four of these missions had been performed. A fifth servicing mission was anticipated in 2004, followed by satellite retrieval in 2010.

FIGURE 6.4

The configuration of the Hubble space telescope

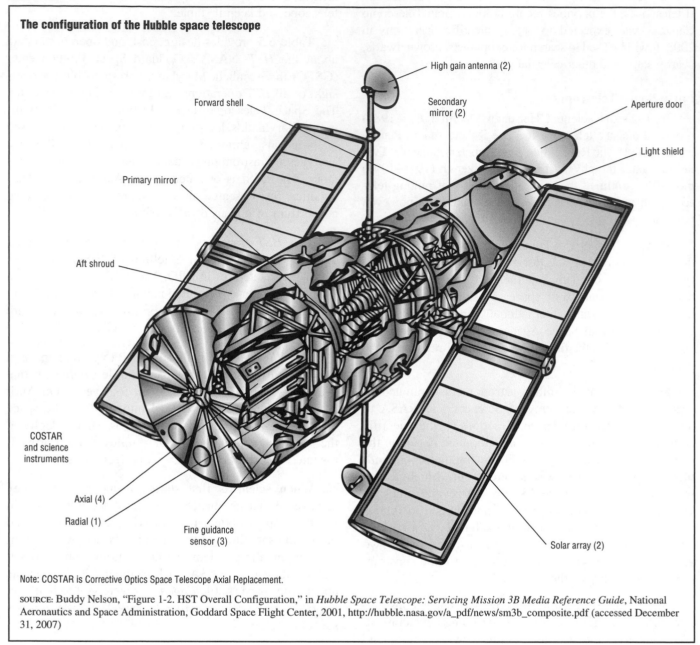

Note: COSTAR is Corrective Optics Space Telescope Axial Replacement.

SOURCE: Buddy Nelson, "Figure 1-2. HST Overall Configuration," in *Hubble Space Telescope: Servicing Mission 3B Media Reference Guide*, National Aeronautics and Space Administration, Goddard Space Flight Center, 2001, http://hubble.nasa.gov/a_pdf/news/sm3b_composite.pdf (accessed December 31, 2007)

The loss of the space shuttle *Columbia* in February 2003 altered the fate of the *HST*. The shuttle fleet was grounded while NASA examined the cause of the accident and developed ways to make shuttle flight safer. In January 2004 the NASA administrator Sean O'Keefe (1956–) announced his decision to cancel the fifth servicing mission to the *HST*. A shuttle flight to the observatory was considered too risky because the *HST* orbits far from the *International Space Station*. In the event of an emergency, the space station is the only safe haven available to shuttle astronauts.

The decision caused an uproar in the scientific community. Without a reboost, the *HST* would gradually fall out of orbit and be destroyed by reentry to Earth's atmos-phere. In October 2006 NASA announced that the agency was reinstating the *HST* servicing mission. As of March 2008, the mission had not taken place, but it was tentatively scheduled for August 2008.

In the fact sheet "Hubble Space Telescope Servicing Mission 4" (October 2006, http://www.nasa.gov/pdf/161640main_SM4-Mission_Fact%20Sheet%203.pdf), NASA describes the dire conditions aboard the *HST* in 2006. At that time, scientists had been operating the *HST* for two years with only two gyroscopes, the minimum necessary to accurately point the telescope at its target. Only four of the *HST*'s six original gyroscopes were still operational. Two of the four were shut down to hold in reserve as a backup. NASA estimated that the existing

TABLE 6.5

The Hubble space telescope at a glance

Hubble's name:	NASA named the world's first space-based optical telescope after American astronomer Edwin P. Hubble (1889–1953). Dr. Hubble confirmed an "expanding" universe, which provided the foundation for the Big Bang theory.
Launch:	April 24, 1990, from space shuttle Discovery (STS-31)
Deployment:	April 25, 1990
Mission duration:	Up to 20 years
Servicing mission 1:	December 1993
Servicing mission 2:	February 1997
Servicing mission 3A:	December 1999
Servicing mission 3B:	February 2002
Length:	43.5 ft (13.2 m)
Weight:	24,500 lb (11,110 kg)
Maximum diameter:	14 ft (4.2 m)
Cost at launch:	$1.5 billion
Orbit:	At an altitude of 380 statute miles (612 km), inclined 28.5 degrees to the equator (low-Earth orbit)
Time to complete one orbit:	97 minutes
Speed:	17,500 mph (28,000 kph)
Hubble can't observe:	The Sun or Mercury, which is too close to the Sun
Sensitivity to light:	Ultraviolet through near infrared (110–2,500 nanometers)
First image:	May 20, 1990: Star Cluster NGC 3532
Data stats:	Each day the telescope generates enough data—3 to 4 gigabytes—to fill six CD-ROMs. The orbiting observatory's observations have amounted to more than 7 terabytes of data. Hubble's digital archive delivers 10 to 20 gigabytes of data a day to astronomers all over the world.
Power mechanism:	Two 25-foot solar panels
Power usage:	3,000 watts. In an average orbit, Hubble uses about the same amount of energy as 30 household light bulbs.
Pointing accuracy:	In order to take images of distant, faint objects, Hubble must be extremely steady and accurate. The telescope is able to lock onto a target without deviating more than 7/1000th of an arcsecond, or about the width of a human hair seen at a distance of 1 mile. Pointing the Hubble Space Telescope and locking onto distant celestial targets is like holding a laser light steady on a dime that is 200 miles away.
Primary mirror	
Diameter:	94.5 in (2.4 m)
Weight:	1,825 lb (828 kg)
Secondary mirror	
Diameter:	12 in (0.3 m)
Weight:	27.4 lb (12.3 kg)
Power storage	
Batteries:	6 nickel-hydrogen (NiH)
Storage capacity:	Equal to 20 car batteries

SOURCE: "Hubble at a Glance," in *About Hubble*, National Aeronautics and Space Administration and Space Telescope Science Institute, Undated, http://hubblesite.org/newscenter/news_media_resources/reference_center/about_hubble/glance.php (accessed December 31, 2007)

gyroscopes on the telescope would allow it to operate only through the end of 2008. In addition, NASA was concerned about the satellite's deteriorating batteries and outside heat shielding. In 2004 the *HST*'s Space Telescope Imaging Spectrograph (STIS) quit working when its power supply failed. In January 2007 the Advanced Camera for Surveys (ACS) suffered a similar failure. The loss of the ACS was particularly troublesome, because it has supplied many of the most sensitive and dramatic images captured by the *HST* over the years. NASA's plans for the servicing mission include replacing all of the *HST*'s batteries and gyroscopes and installing new external thermal protection sheets.

These modifications are expected to extend the *HST*'s useful life through 2013. Repairs of the STIS and the ACS and the installation of two new instruments were also planned for the servicing mission.

During its mission the *HST* has captured more than seven hundred thousand images of celestial objects throughout the universe, including nebulae, galaxies, stars, and even some bodies believed to be planets. In late 2005 NASA began using the telescope to search Earth's Moon for oxygen-bearing minerals. Scientists hope to find a potential source of oxygen for use by future astronauts visiting the lunar surface. The *HST* provided the first-ever high-resolution ultraviolet images of the Moon.

The *Compton Gamma Ray Observatory*

The *Compton Gamma Ray Observatory* (*CGRO*) was the second of NASA's Great Observatories. It was designed to detect high-energy gamma rays, the most powerful type of energy in the electromagnetic spectrum. The observatory was named after the American physicist Arthur Holly Compton (1892–1962).

On April 5, 1991, the *CGRO* was launched into space aboard the space shuttle *Atlantis*. The satellite was deployed at an orbit altitude of 280 miles above Earth. It was equipped with four highly sensitive detecting instruments and a pair of solar arrays. (See Figure 6.5.) The satellite also had a small propulsion system and three gyroscopes that were used to point the telescope and maintain flight stability. The propulsion system was not powerful enough to boost the *CGRO* to higher altitudes.

The original plan was for a five-year mission. However, the observatory proved to be much more durable than expected and remained in space for nine years.

In early 2000 NASA learned that one of the *CGRO*'s gyroscopes had failed. Even though the observatory's instruments were still in working order, NASA decided to purposely deorbit the satellite. Scientists feared that if left to reenter on its own, the *CGRO* could rain pieces down on populated areas. This was of particular concern because the satellite was unusually massive at seventeen tons and included a fair amount of titanium in its components. Titanium is not easily disintegrated during atmospheric reentry.

On June 4, 2000, the *CGRO*'s propulsion system was used to guide the satellite to a safe reentry over a deserted area of the Pacific Ocean.

The *CGRO* program included participation by scientists from Germany, the Netherlands, the United Kingdom, and the ESA. During its mission the observatory investigated high-energy phenomena associated with black holes, novas, supernovas, quasars, pulsars, solar flares, cosmic rays, and gamma-ray bursts. Gamma-ray bursts are sudden short flashes of gamma rays that do not seem to occur at

FIGURE 6.5

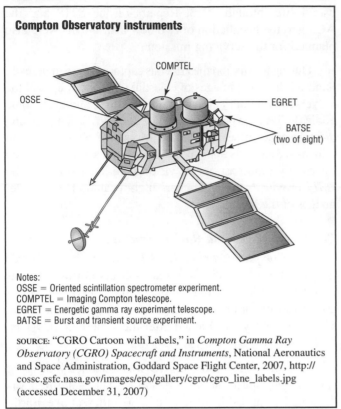

Compton Observatory instruments

OSSE

COMPTEL

EGRET

BATSE
(two of eight)

Notes:
OSSE = Oriented scintillation spectrometer experiment.
COMPTEL = Imaging Compton telescope.
EGRET = Energetic gamma ray experiment telescope.
BATSE = Burst and transient source experiment.

SOURCE: "CGRO Cartoon with Labels," in *Compton Gamma Ray Observatory (CGRO) Spacecraft and Instruments*, National Aeronautics and Space Administration, Goddard Space Flight Center, 2007, http:// cossc.gsfc.nasa.gov/images/epo/gallery/cgro/cgro_line_labels.jpg (accessed December 31, 2007)

predictable locations. The *CGRO* recorded more than twenty-five hundred gamma-ray bursts, far more than had ever been detected before. It also mapped hundreds of gamma-ray sources.

The *Chandra X-Ray Observatory*

The *Chandra X-Ray Observatory* (*CXRO*) is the third of NASA's Great Observatories and the world's most powerful x-ray telescope. It was named after the Indian-American scientist Subrahmanyan Chandrasekhar (1910–1995). The *CXRO* can detect x-ray sources that are billions of light-years from Earth.

On July 23, 1999, the *CXRO* was launched into space by the shuttle *Columbia*. The *CXRO* was equipped with a rocket called an Inertial Upper Stage (IUS). The shuttle crew released the satellite and then moved a safe distance away. The IUS was fired for four minutes to move the satellite into a temporary orbit high above Earth.

At that point, the *CXRO*'s twin solar wings were unfolded and began converting sunlight into electrical power. Figure 6.6 shows a diagram of the spacecraft. Important design information is included in Table 6.6. Solar power is used to run the *CXRO*'s equipment and charge its batteries.

The *CXRO* circles Earth once every sixty-four hours. The satellite's orbit is highly elliptical. At its closest point the observatory is 6,214 miles from Earth, and at its farthest point it is 86,992 miles. (See Table 6.6.) This is nearly one-third of the distance to the Moon. The *CXRO*'s flight path carries it through the Van Allen radiation belts that encircle Earth. When the satellite is in or near this highly radioactive area of space, its sensitive electronic instruments are turned off.

Scientists around the world are using *CXRO* images to create an x-ray map of the universe. They hope to use this map to learn more about black holes, supernovas, superflares, quasars, extremely hot gases at the center of galaxy clusters, and the mysterious substance known as dark matter. In May 2007 the *CXRO* imaged the brightest stellar explosion ever recorded. The supernova known as SN 2006gy is in the galaxy NGC 1260, which is approximately 240 million light-years from Earth.

The *CXRO* was designed for a five-year mission. As of March 2008, the telescope had been operating for more than eight years and was expected to remain in service for up to seven more years. The satellite will likely continue to orbit for decades after that.

The *CXRO* is managed by the Marshall Space Flight Center for NASA's Office of Space Science. NASA's Jet Propulsion Laboratory in Pasadena, California, provides communications and data links. The Smithsonian Astrophysical Observatory in Cambridge, Maryland, controls science and flight operations. NASA's High-Energy Astrophysics Science Archive collects and maintains all astronomy data obtained from the *CXRO* and NASA's smaller gamma-ray, x-ray, and extreme ultraviolet observatories.

The *Spitzer Space Telescope*

The *Spitzer Space Telescope* is the fourth of NASA's Great Observatories and detects infrared radiation. When it was originally conceived during the 1970s, the observatory was called the *Shuttle Infrared Telescope Facility* (*SIRTF*). Its planners hoped to carry the telescope into space as a science payload on many space shuttle missions. In 1983 NASA decided the telescope needed to be in continuous orbit and able to fly alone. The *SIRTF* was renamed the *Space Infrared Telescope Facility*.

During the 1990s NASA's science programs suffered harsh budget cuts. The *SIRTF* was redesigned several times and downsized from a large $2 billion telescope with many capabilities to a modest telescope costing less than half a billion dollars.

On August 25, 2003, the telescope was launched into orbit atop a Delta rocket. It was the only Great Observatory not carried into space by a space shuttle. Figure 6.7 shows the components of the two-stage launch vehicle. The telescope was housed inside a protective case called a fairing that fell away when the satellite reached orbit. Figure 6.8 shows details of the observatory's structure.

FIGURE 6.6

The Chandra X-Ray Observatory

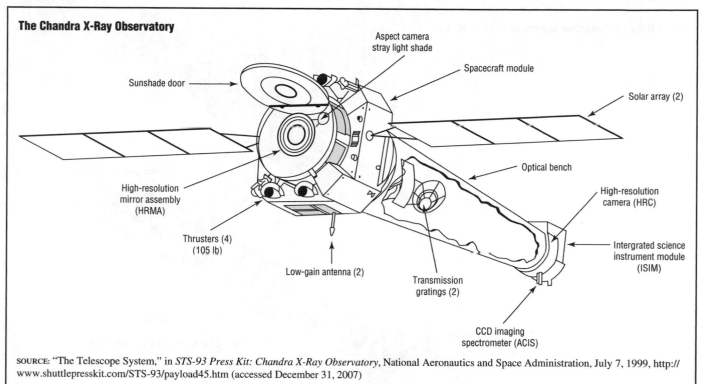

SOURCE: "The Telescope System," in *STS-93 Press Kit: Chandra X-Ray Observatory*, National Aeronautics and Space Administration, July 7, 1999, http://www.shuttlepresskit.com/STS-93/payload45.htm (accessed December 31, 2007)

TABLE 6.6

The Chandra Observatory at a glance

Mission duration

Chandra science mission	Approx 5 years
Orbital activation & checkout period	Approx 2 months

Orbital data

Inclination	28.5 degrees
Altitude at apogee	86,992 statute miles
Altitude at perigee	6,214 statute miles
Orbital period	64 hours
Observing time per orbital period	Up to 55 hours

Dimensions

Length—(Sun shade open)	45.3 feet
Length—(Sun shade closed)	38.7 feet
Width—(solar arrays deployed)	64.0 feet
Width—(solar arrays stowed)	14.0 feet

High resolution mirror assembly

Configuration	4 sets of nested, grazing incidence araboloid/hyperboloid mirror pairs
Mirror weight	2,093 pounds
Focal length	33 feet
Outer diameter	4 feet
Length	33.5 inches
Material	Zerodur
Coating	600 angstroms of iridium

Science instruments

Charged coupled imaging spectrometer (ACIS)
High resolution camera (HRC)
High energy transmission grating (HETG)
Low energy transmission grating (LETG)

SOURCE: Adapted from "Chandra at a Glance," in *STS-93 Press Kit: Chandra X-Ray Observatory*, National Aeronautics and Space Administration, July 7, 1999, http://www.shuttlepresskit.com/STS-93/payload45.htm (accessed December 31, 2007)

The dark circle at the top of the observatory is actually a door that opens to expose the telescope to space.

In December 2003 NASA chose a new name for the *SIRTF* from thousands of names suggested during a naming contest. More than seven thousand people from around the world entered the contest. Some of the most frequently proposed names were Red Eye, Sagan (after the scientist Carl Sagan [1934–1996]), Herschel (after the scientist John Herschel [1792–1871], who in 1800 discovered infrared radiation), and Roddenberry (after the science-fiction writer Gene Roddenberry [1921–1991], the creator of the *Star Trek* television show). In the end NASA chose the name Spitzer to honor the late American physicist. It was Spitzer's groundbreaking work in the 1940s that inspired astronomers to build space telescopes.

The *Spitzer Space Telescope* is unique among the Great Observatories because it orbits the Sun instead of Earth in an Earth-trailing heliocentric orbit. This orbit was chosen for several reasons. It allows the spacecraft to avoid interference from Earth's infrared-absorbing atmosphere. The orbit also provides a colder environment for the telescope than would an Earth orbit. Space infrared telescopes must be maintained at an extremely cold temperature to operate properly. Everything with a temperature emits infrared radiation. The spacecraft must be kept as cold as possible to prevent heat within it from interfering with its own detection equipment. The relatively cold Earth-trailing heliocentric orbit was selected

FIGURE 6.7

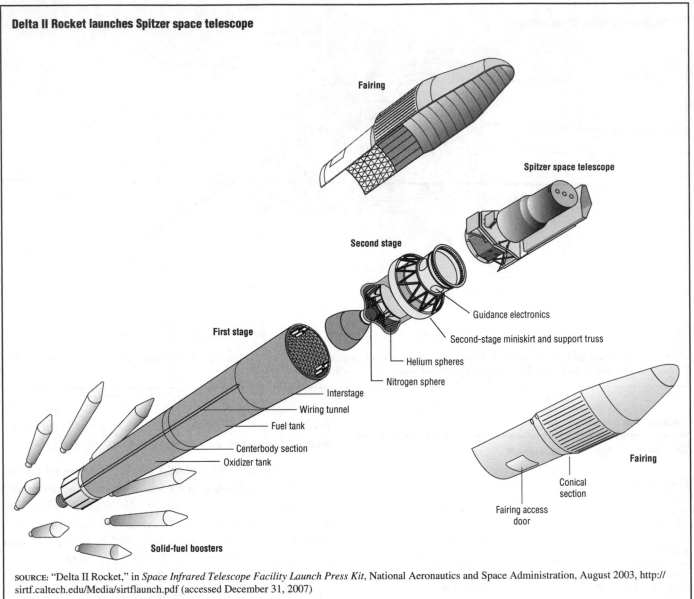

Delta II Rocket launches Spitzer space telescope

Fairing

Spitzer space telescope

Second stage

First stage

Guidance electronics

Second-stage miniskirt and support truss

Helium spheres

Nitrogen sphere

Interstage

Wiring tunnel

Fuel tank

Centerbody section

Oxidizer tank

Fairing

Conical section

Fairing access door

Solid-fuel boosters

SOURCE: "Delta II Rocket," in *Space Infrared Telescope Facility Launch Press Kit*, National Aeronautics and Space Administration, August 2003, http://sirtf.caltech.edu/Media/sirtflaunch.pdf (accessed December 31, 2007)

to minimize the amount of liquid helium required onboard to keep the telescope cool.

Spitzer can detect infrared energy with wavelengths of 3 to 180 microns. A micron is one-millionth of a meter. Detection of infrared waves at these lengths allows the telescope to image celestial objects hidden by dense clouds of dust and gas. During its first few months of operation, *Spitzer* provided images of galaxies and nebulae up to three billion light-years away. In January 2004 NASA released colorful *Spitzer* images of massive newborn stars at the core of the Tarantula Nebula. This nebula is a known star-forming region 179,000 light-years from Earth.

In early 2005 the telescope captured the first-ever infrared images of two exoplanets. The two large gas planets, known as HD 209458b and TrES-1, orbit close to their respective suns. This makes them impossible to

image directly with visible light telescopes. HD 209458b circles a yellow sun 150 light-years from Earth in the constellation Pegasus. TrES-1 is located five hundred light-years from Earth in the constellation Lyra.

In October 2005 NASA released infrared images of the spiral galaxy Messier 31, which is commonly called Andromeda. The galaxy is about 2.5 million light-years from Earth. *Spitzer* recorded nearly eleven thousand separate snapshots of the galaxy that were pieced together to form a dramatic mosaic. The images reveal old giant stars at Andromeda's center and a system of arms spiraling out to a prominent ring of stars.

Humans cannot see infrared radiation. The energy data that *Spitzer* collects are transformed into visible pictures by assigning different colors to different energy levels. The resulting pictures are called false-color

FIGURE 6.8

Exterior of the Spitzer Space Telescope

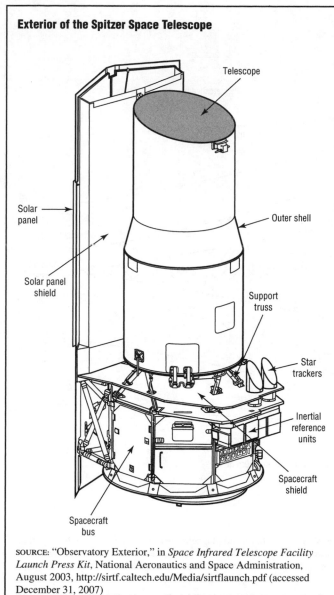

SOURCE: "Observatory Exterior," in *Space Infrared Telescope Facility Launch Press Kit*, National Aeronautics and Space Administration, August 2003, http://sirtf.caltech.edu/Media/sirtflaunch.pdf (accessed December 31, 2007)

images. Scientists either choose colors to highlight a specific area of scientific interest or to make a celestial object appear realistic to the human eye. For example, coloring the high-energy areas of an image with white or red indicates brightness and heat to a human looking at the picture. Likewise, low-energy regions are shaded with darker colors to indicate relative coolness.

Spitzer is managed by NASA's Jet Propulsion Laboratory, a division of the California Institute of Technology in Pasadena, California. The university also includes the Spitzer Science Center, which conducts science operations for the telescope. According to John R. Stauffer et al., in *The Spitzer Warm Mission Science Prospects* (2007, http://ssc.spitzer.caltech.edu/mtgs/warm/wp/003stauffer.pdf), *Spitzer*'s cryogenic helium supply will be depleted by mid-2009, and its primary mission will end. Because some of

the instruments will continue to operate, astronomers hope to conduct limited astronomical observations during a so-called warm mission that could last up to five years.

The Next Great Observatory

As of 2008, NASA's next Great Observatory was under development and scheduled for launch in 2013. It is called the *James Webb Space Telescope* (*JWST*) in honor of James Edwin Webb (1906–1992), the NASA director of flight operations during the Apollo program. The *JWST* will detect infrared radiation from its orbit location at L2 approximately one million miles from Earth in the direction away from the Sun.

When it is stationed at the L2 point, the *JWST* will make a small circle called a halo orbit around the L2 point. This point will not only provide the *JWST* with a relatively cold location in space but will also make it easier to shield the telescope from the massive infrared radiation coming from the Sun, Earth, and Moon. The *JWST* will look outward into space.

Other Space Observatories

Besides the Great Observatories, NASA operates a number of smaller space observatories in Sun-Earth orbits. These spacecraft were funded and built under NASA's Explorers Program. (See Table 6.2.) The projects are conducted with the help of scientists from academic institutions and/or foreign space agencies.

The ESA operates two observatories of its own: the *X-ray Multimirror Mission* (*XMM-Newton*) and the *International Gamma Ray Astrophysics Laboratory* (*INTEGRAL*). *XMM-Newton* was named after Isaac Newton (1642–1727). This powerful telescope is similar to one of NASA's Great Observatories. The *XMM-Newton* is the largest science satellite ever built in Europe and includes three x-ray telescopes. It was launched into space on December 10, 1999, by an Ariane rocket. *XMM-Newton* was expected to have a ten-year lifetime. Its images have provided crucial information to scientists researching black holes and the formation of galaxies.

INTEGRAL was launched in October 17, 2002, and images celestial gamma-ray sources. It orbits Earth once every three days. In "Five Years of INTEGRAL" (October 17, 2007, http://sci.esa.int/science-e/www/object/index.cfm?fobjectid=41414), the ESA summarizes the major findings of the observatory. Scientists are using *INTEGRAL* data to study black holes, explosive stars, and other objects in the Milky Way and in other galaxies.

THE SUN-EARTH CONNECTION

One of NASA's primary research goals is to learn about the Sun-Earth connection. The Sun bathes Earth with life-sustaining warmth. It also emits radiation, charged particles, and other substances that can disrupt

FIGURE 6.9

The Earth and the magnetosphere

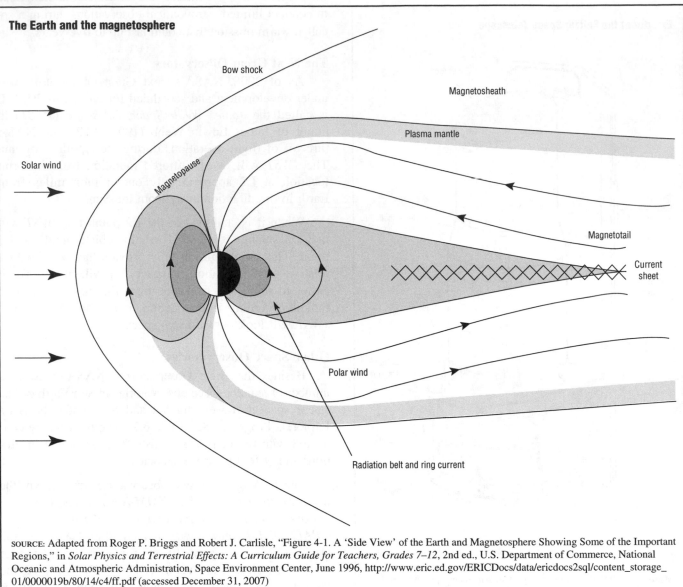

SOURCE: Adapted from Roger P. Briggs and Robert J. Carlisle, "Figure 4-1. A 'Side View' of the Earth and Magnetosphere Showing Some of the Important Regions," in *Solar Physics and Terrestrial Effects: A Curriculum Guide for Teachers, Grades 7–12*, 2nd ed., U.S. Department of Commerce, National Oceanic and Atmospheric Administration, Space Environment Center, June 1996, http://www.eric.ed.gov/ERICDocs/data/ericdocs2sql/content_storage_01/0000019b/80/14/c4/ff.pdf (accessed December 31, 2007)

electrical systems and electronic equipment vital to modern societies. Since the beginning of the space age scientists have put satellites in Earth orbit to monitor the Sun and its effects on Earth. During the 1990s NASA begin sending spacecraft even farther out into space to investigate solar phenomena that directly affect planet Earth.

Solar Wind

The solar wind is a constant flow of charged particles from the Sun into space. It moves away from the Sun at a speed of two hundred to four hundred miles per second and flows across the solar system reaching just past Pluto. The region of outer space exposed to the solar wind is called the heliosphere.

The solar wind constantly pushes and shapes Earth's magnetosphere. This is the region of space around Earth dominated by the planet's magnetic field.

(See Figure 6.9.) The magnetosphere helps protect Earth from dangerous electromagnetic radiation moving through space. The outer boundary of Earth's magnetosphere is called the bow shock.

The speed, composition, density, and magnetic field strength of the solar wind are not constant but vary depending on conditions on the Sun. A gust of solar wind can energize Earth's magnetosphere, producing beautiful auroras, but wreaking havoc on sensitive electronics.

Sunspots

Sunspots look like dark blemishes on the surface of the Sun. They are actually areas of plasma that are slightly cooler than their surroundings due to magnetic activity. Sunspots can be enormous in size, even bigger than planet Earth. Sunspots can appear, change size, and disappear. Each typically lasts from a few hours to a

FIGURE 6.10

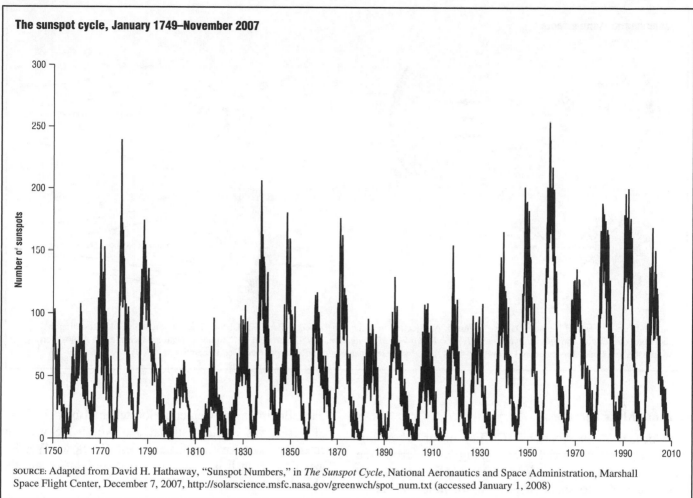

The sunspot cycle, January 1749–November 2007

SOURCE: Adapted from David H. Hathaway, "Sunspot Numbers," in *The Sunspot Cycle*, National Aeronautics and Space Administration, Marshall Space Flight Center, December 7, 2007, http://solarscience.msfc.nasa.gov/greenwch/spot_num.txt (accessed January 1, 2008)

few months. Most sunspots are visible only through telescopes.

In 1826 the amateur German astronomer Samuel H. Schwabe (1789–1875) began keeping detailed records of the number of sunspots he observed every day. After nearly two decades of doing this, he noticed a cyclical pattern to the data. By the early 1900s scientists knew that the number of sunspots peaks approximately every eleven years and then drops off dramatically. (See Figure 6.10.) This is called the solar cycle. The period of peak sunspot activity is called the solar maximum, and the period of lowest activity is called the solar minimum.

In 1952 the International Council of Scientific Unions proposed that scientists around the world cooperate in conducting extensive earth science investigations between July 1957 and December 1958. This was the next expected solar maximum. Scientists hoped to collect large amounts of data on the relationship between sunspots and solar activity and the resulting effects on Earth's magnetic fields. This research remained a priority throughout the space age. The most recent solar maximum occurred in 2000–01. The next peak is expected in 2011–12.

Solar Flares

Solar flares are sudden energy releases that burst out from the Sun near sunspots. They are most common during the solar maximums. Solar flares emit electromagnetic radiation, and can include energy particles and bulk plasma. They can last from minutes to hours.

Solar flares that erupt in Earth's direction can shower the planet with energetic particles within thirty minutes. Solar flares are associated with auroras and magnetic storms on Earth and can cause radio interference if large amounts of x-ray radiation are released.

Solar Prominences

Solar prominences are giant clouds of dense plasma suspended in the Sun's corona (outermost atmosphere). They are usually calm, but occasionally erupt and snake out from the Sun along magnetic field lines. Prominences can break away from the Sun and hurtle through space carrying large amounts of solar material.

FIGURE 6.11

Geomagnetic storm effects

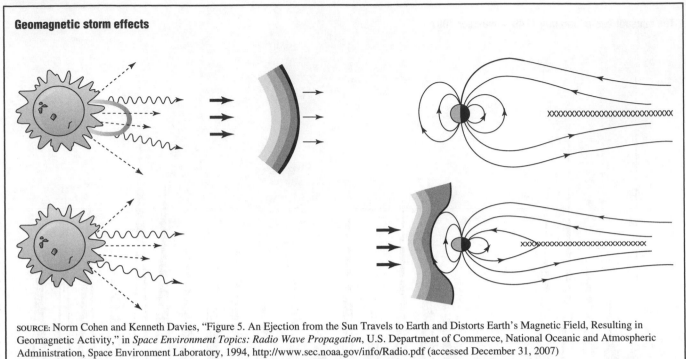

SOURCE: Norm Cohen and Kenneth Davies, "Figure 5. An Ejection from the Sun Travels to Earth and Distorts Earth's Magnetic Field, Resulting in Geomagnetic Activity," in *Space Environment Topics: Radio Wave Propagation*, U.S. Department of Commerce, National Oceanic and Atmospheric Administration, Space Environment Laboratory, 1994, http://www.sec.noaa.gov/info/Radio.pdf (accessed December 31, 2007)

Coronal Mass Ejections

Coronal mass ejections (CMEs) occur when billions of tons of particles are slung away from the Sun by broken magnetic field lines. CMEs move away from the Sun into space at millions of miles per hour. These ejections happen frequently and are most common during the solar maximum, when they can occur several times a day. CMEs are known informally as solar storms.

When a CME blasts toward Earth, the planet's magnetosphere is hit within two to four days by a cloud of electrically charged particles. This cloud distorts the entire magnetosphere. (See Figure 6.11.) The resulting disturbance is called a geomagnetic storm. These storms can harm satellites and disrupt telecommunications and electric power generation around the world.

Space Weather

The term *space weather* was created by scientists to refer to the overall effects of solar activities on the space around Earth (or geospace). Space weather encompasses all the solar phenomena (solar wind, sunspots, flares, prominences, and CMEs) and the resulting conditions in Earth's magnetosphere and upper atmosphere.

The National Oceanic and Atmospheric Administration (NOAA) monitors space weather and issues warnings about geomagnetic and solar radiation storms (increases in the number of energy particles in geospace). NOAA's

Space Environment Center is located in Boulder, Colorado. It serves as the national and worldwide warning center for space weather disturbances. The Space Weather Operations branch is jointly operated by NOAA and the U.S. Air Force.

The monitoring of space weather is important. A major solar event such as a CME can cause a tremendous inflow of electrical energy into Earth's atmosphere. This is disruptive to electrical power grids and telecommunication systems on the ground and dangerous for Earth-orbiting satellites. NASA also worries about possible harmful exposure of astronauts to excessive radiation levels during solar storms.

Ongoing Solar Exploration Missions

NASA and other space agencies operate a number of missions dedicated to studying the Sun-Earth connection. Table 6.7 describes the major missions as of December 2007. Most of these spacecraft are stationed in Earth orbit and study the effects of solar activity on the magnetosphere or upper atmosphere. Some of the spacecraft are in orbits far from Earth or on other paths designed for optimal study of the Sun-Earth connection.

INTERNATIONAL SOLAR-TERRESTRIAL PHYSICS PROGRAM. During the 1990s NASA teamed with the ESA and the Japan Aerospace Exploration Agency in the project known as the International Solar-Terrestrial Physics Science Initiative. The purpose of this project is to combine international resources to conduct long-term investiga-

TABLE 6.7

Ongoing solar missions as of December 2007

Name	Primary mission sponsors	NASA science program	Launch date	Location in space	Mission
Cluster	ESA	Sun-Earth Connection	07/16/00 and 08/09/00	Earth orbit	Includes 2 pair of two satellites that study the solar wind and its interaction with Earth's magnetospheric plasma
Geotail	NASA, JAXA	International Solar-Terrestrial Physics	07/24/1992	Earth orbit	Studying the dynamics of the Earth's magnetotail
Hinode (or Solar-B) Hinode means sunrise in Japanese	JAXA, NASA	Solar Terrestrial Probes	09/22/2006	Earth orbit	Three-year mission to explore the sun's magnetic fields and gather data on the solar atmosphere and solar eruptions
Polar	NASA	International Solar-Terrestrial Physics	02/24/1996	Earth orbit	Images the aurora and measures the entry of plasma into the polar magnetosphere and the geomagnetic tail, the flow of plasma to and from the ionosphere, and the deposition of particle energy in the ionosphere and upper atmosphere
SOHO (Solar and Heliospheric Observatory)	NASA, ESA	Sun-Earth Connection	12/02/1995	L1 orbit	Solar observatory studying the Sun's internal structure, heating of its extensive outer atmosphere, and the origin of the solar wind
STEREO (Solar TErrestrial RElations Observatory)	NASA	Solar Terrestrial Probes	10/25/2006	Solar orbit	Two satellites trace the flow of energy and matter from the Sun to Earth and reveal the 3-D structure of coronal mass ejections. Also provide alerts for Earth-directed solar ejections.
TIMED (Thermosphere, Ionosphere, Mesosphere Energetics and Dynamics)	NASA, John Hopkins University Applied Physics Laboratory	Solar Terrestrial Probes	12/07/2001	Earth orbit	Studying solar influences on Earth's mesosphere and lower thermosphere/ionosphere
Ulysses	NASA, ESA	Sun-Earth Connection	10/06/1990	Solar orbit	An observatory in polar solar orbit that studies the solar wind throughout the heliosphere
Wind	NASA	International Solar-Terrestrial Physics	11/01/1994	Traveling a path with multiple loops around L1, Earth, and L2	Investigating solar phenomena and their effects on Earth's magnetosphere. Provides almost continuous monitoring of the solar wind.

Notes:
ESA - European Space Agency.
JAXA - Japanese Space Agency.

SOURCE: Created by Kim Masters Evans for Gale, Cengage Learning, 2008

tions of the Sun-Earth space environment. The program includes both ground-based studies and space missions. The space activities fall into two categories: terrestrial (Earth directed) and solar (Sun directed).

Terrestrial space missions rely on satellites in Earth orbit that gather data about the Sun's effects on the planet. This effort is supported by two other U.S. federal agencies: NOAA and the Los Alamos National Laboratory.

CHAPTER 7
MARS

Mars moves through our skies in its stately dance, distant and enigmatic, a world awaiting exploration.

—Carl Sagan, "Mars: A New World to Explore" (December 1967)

Mars has been a mystery to humans for thousands of years. Even though much is known about it, there is still much more to learn. Mars is the fourth planet from the Sun, and the planet most like Earth in the solar system. It is named after the mythical god of war whom the Romans called Mars and the Greeks called Ares. Mars is also known as the Red Planet, because it looks reddish from Earth. Mars is a dusty, cold world. The average temperature is −64 degrees Fahrenheit. Rays of ultraviolet radiation beat down on the surface continuously. The atmosphere is nearly all carbon dioxide.

People on Earth have always been fascinated with the idea of life on Mars. Ancient people could see Mars as a pale reddish light in the nighttime sky. They believed that it was stained with the blood of fallen warriors. Once telescopes were invented, people had a better view of the planet, but many still thought it was inhabited. Patterns of straight lines could be seen on the surface. To some, these were evidence of water canals dug into the ground by hard-working Martians. The notion lingered for decades in the public imagination.

At the dawn of the space age, humans sent robotic probes to Mars to settle the question once and for all. These probes found a frozen wasteland of fine powdery dust. Neither canals nor Martians could be located. There was some water vapor in the atmosphere and some frozen water at the planet's poles. Where there is water, there is the potential for life similar to that found on Earth. Scientists continue to send probes to search for water and life.

In January 2004 President George W. Bush (1946–) proposed that astronauts travel to Mars and explore the planet. It will be expensive and difficult. It takes six months to fly to Mars. The United States will need new rockets and spacecraft and some clever ways to keep astronauts healthy and happy on such a long journey. These are great challenges, but the idea is tantalizing—humans standing on another planet. Finally, there would be some life on Mars.

EARLY TELESCOPIC VIEWS OF MARS

The Italian astronomer Galileo Galilei (1564–1642) was probably the first to see Mars through a telescope. He noticed that sometimes it appeared larger than at other times. He believed that its distance from Earth was changing over time. During the seventeenth century Johannes Kepler (1571–1630) studied Mars's movement for years. His observations helped him to develop the laws of planetary motion for which he would become famous.

As telescopes improved, astronomers reported seeing dark and light patches on Mars that also varied in size over time. Some people thought these were patches of vegetation changing in response to the changing seasons. Others believed that they represented contrasting areas of land and sea.

In 1659 the Dutch astronomer Christiaan Huygens (1629–1695) recorded his Mars observations and noticed an odd-shaped feature that came to be called the hour-glass sea. Huygens kept an eye on the location of the sea over time and determined that the Martian day lasts about twenty-four hours. The same conclusion was reached independently by the French astronomer Giovanni Cassini (1625–1712).

During the 1700s astronomers performed more detailed observations of the light and dark patches on Mars, particularly the whitish spots at the north and south poles. They could see that the spots changed in size over time, but they did not guess that these were polar ice caps. It was commonly believed that Mars was inhabited by some kind of beings. In 1774 the English astronomer William Herschel (1738–1822) speculated that Martians lived on a world much like Earth, with oceans on the surface and clouds flying overhead.

GIOVANNI SCHIAPARELLI

During the late 1800s Mars became the topic of a debate that would go on for decades. The controversy was sparked by the observations of the Italian astronomer Giovanni Schiaparelli (1835–1910). He created some of the first maps of the planet and assigned names to prominent features. Schiaparelli's naming system relied on place names taken from the Bible and ancient mythology.

Schiaparelli said he saw straight lines on the Martian surface and called them *canali*. In Italian *canali* can mean either "channels" or "canals." Many people interpreted the word to mean that there were artificial canals on Mars. The Suez Canal had recently been constructed in Egypt to connect the Mediterranean Sea to the Red Sea. Obviously, if there were artificial canals on Mars, they had been built by Martians.

Some other Mars observers also reported seeing the canals and claimed they connected light and dark patches on the planet. This reinforced the mistaken idea that the patches were areas of land and water.

ASAPH HALL

In August 1877 the American astronomer Asaph Hall (1829–1907) discovered that Mars has two moons. Centuries before him, Kepler guessed that Mars had two moons, but this had never been verified.

Hall reported that the moons were small and orbited close to the planet's surface, which made them difficult to observe. He made the discovery using a powerful new telescope recently installed at the U.S. Naval Observatory in Washington, D.C. He named the moons Phobos (meaning fear) and Deimos (meaning flight or panic). These are two characters mentioned in ancient Greek mythology as being servants to the god Mars.

PERCIVAL LOWELL

Percival Lowell (1855–1916) was a mathematician and amateur astronomer who greatly popularized the idea that Mars was inhabited by intelligent beings.

In 1894 he founded the Lowell Observatory in Flagstaff, Arizona. Perched at an altitude of seven thousand feet, the observatory provided one of the best views yet of the cosmos, including Mars. For fifteen years Lowell studied the Red Planet and wrote about his observations. He was convinced that there were artificial canals on Mars, because he could see hundreds of straight lines on the surface that intersected large patches of contrast-

ing colors. Lowell argued that the canals must have been built to move water from the melting polar ice caps toward the desert regions near the planet's equator.

Lowell publicized his theories in many articles and three popular books: *Mars* (1895), *Mars and Its Canals* (1906), and *Mars as the Abode of Life* (1908). In 1901 he constructed a globe of Mars showing large geological features crisscrossed by a network of lines that intersected at certain points around the planet. Lowell called these intersections oases, because he imagined they were fertile green areas amid the desert.

In a series of articles published during 1895 in the *Atlantic Monthly*, Lowell explained his theories in detail. He believed that Mars had a thin air-based atmosphere containing lots of water vapor and that fresh water flowed from the polar ice caps through irrigation canals built by the highly intelligent Martians.

INHABITED OR NOT?

Lowell's ideas were not shared by most astronomers of the time. In 1908 the distinguished journal *Scientific American* noted that "Lowell is practically alone in the astronomical world in believing that he has proven that Mars is inhabited."

Scientists pointed out that artificial canals would have to be hundreds of miles wide to be visible from Earth. Furthermore, Mars was believed to be extremely cold, because of its great distance from the Sun. This made it even more unlikely that open flowing water was present on the planet's surface. Agnes Mary Clerke (1842–1907) was a science writer trained in astronomy who wrote well-respected books about astronomical discoveries. She called Lowell's idea "hopelessly unworkable."

Lowell did have his supporters. The French astronomer Camille Flammarion (1842–1925) also believed that the lines on Mars were artificial canals built by an advanced civilization. Flammarion insisted that the reddish appearance of Mars was due to the growth of red vegetation on the planet.

In 1907 the natural scientist Alfred Russel Wallace (1823–1913) wrote the book *Is Mars Habitable?*, which examined Lowell's claims one by one and attacked them with scientific data and reasoning. The book is considered a pioneering work in the field of exobiology (the investigation of possible life beyond Earth).

Wallace argued that Mars was a frozen desert and that the polar caps were probably frozen carbon dioxide, instead of water ice. Wallace ended the book with the following definitive statement: "Mars, therefore, is not only uninhabited by intelligent beings such as Mr. Lowell postulates, but is absolutely UNINHABITABLE."

Many astronomers of the time admitted seeing fine lines on the Martian surface. Most believed that these lines were either natural geological features or an optical illusion. The astronomer William H. Pickering (1858–1938) believed the lines to be cracks in Mars's volcanic crust. He speculated that hot gases and water escaped through the cracks and supported vegetative growth. This explained the appearance of different colored splotches on the planet. The general public and science-fiction writers much preferred Lowell's explanation.

MARS IN SCIENCE FICTION

Around the turn of the nineteenth century Mars became a popular topic of science fiction. Before that time there is little mention of the Red Planet. One notable exception is a fanciful story published in 1726 by the Irish writer Jonathan Swift (1667–1745). *Gulliver's Travels* mentions the discovery of two Martian moons by astronomers living on the fictional island of Laputa. Oddly enough, Mars does have two moons, but they were not discovered until 151 years after the book was published.

After Schiaparelli and Lowell popularized the idea of intelligent life on Mars, science-fiction writers gleefully embraced the notion. In 1898 Herbert George Wells (1866–1946) portrayed Martians as lethal invaders in *War of the Worlds*. The insectlike creatures come to Earth looking for water and leave destruction in their path. They are finally wiped out by a common Earth germ to which they do not have immunity. The story was famously adapted for radio in 1938 and for film more than once, most recently in 2005.

Beginning in 1910 Edgar Rice Burroughs (1875–1950) wrote a series of adventure books in which an Earth man battles and romances his way around Mars. In his books the planet is called Barsoom by its exotic inhabitants. They come in various shapes, sizes, and colors.

In 1924 the motion picture *Aelita: Queen of Mars* debuted in the Soviet Union. It featured an engineer who takes a spaceship to Mars and falls in love with the planet's beautiful queen. At the end of the film, he wakes up and discovers the journey was just a dream.

Three decades later Martians became popular characters in American media. Ray Bradbury (1920–) published a series of stories called *The Martian Chronicles* in which well-intentioned humans travel to Mars and accidentally spread deadly Earth germs among the Martian population. It was an interesting twist on the theme introduced by Wells a half-century before.

Evil invaders from Mars were common villains in low-budget horror movies of the 1950s. Historians now believe these sinister creatures symbolized the threat that Americans felt from the Soviet Union during the cold war. During the early 1960s the television show *My Favorite Martian* featured a friendly and wise Martian who crash lands on Earth and befriends a newspaper reporter.

SCIENTIFIC FACTS ABOUT MARS

Mars is a small planet. Its diameter is about half that of Earth. Mars is twice as large as Earth's Moon.

A Martian day lasts twenty-four hours and thirty-nine minutes and is called a sol. It takes Mars 687 days to travel around the Sun. The planet has different seasons throughout its orbit, because it is tilted, just like Earth. During a Martian winter, the temperature at the poles can drop to −200 degrees Fahrenheit. At the equator during the summer, the temperature can reach 80 degrees Fahrenheit.

The force of gravity is much weaker on Mars than it is on Earth. An astronaut standing on Mars would feel only 38% as much gravity as on Earth.

Martian Geology and Atmosphere

Mars is called a terrestrial planet, because it is composed of rocky material, like Mercury, Venus, and Earth. Mars has some of the same geological features as Earth, including volcanoes, valleys, ridges, plains, and canyons.

Most Martian features have two-word names. One of the words is a geological term, and is usually from Latin or Greek, for example, *mons* for "mountain," *planitia* for "plains," and *vallis* for "valley." The other word comes from the classical naming system begun by Schiaparelli during the 1800s or from later astronomers. Beginning in 1919 the International Astronomical Union (IAU) became the official designator of names for celestial objects and the features on them. Only the IAU has this authority.

There are two particularly prominent features on Mars. The first is the volcano Olympus Mons that is about seventeen miles high. This is three times higher than Mount Everest on Earth. In English Olympus Mons means Mount Olympus. This was the home of the gods in ancient Greek mythology. The other notable geological feature on Mars is the canyon Valles Marineris (Mariner Valleys). This enormous canyon is twenty-five hundred miles long by sixty miles wide and up to six miles deep in places. It was named after the Mariner spacecraft that photographed it during the 1960s.

The surface of Mars is covered with a fine powdery dust with a pale reddish tint. This is due to the presence of oxidized iron minerals (like rust) on the planet's surface. The Martian atmosphere is thin and contains more than 95% carbon dioxide. There is a tiny amount of oxygen, but not enough for humans to breathe. It is windy on Mars. Strong winds sometimes engulf the planet in dust storms that turn the atmosphere a hazy yellowish-brown color. The wind also blows clouds around the sky.

The Martian poles are covered by solid carbon dioxide (dry ice) layered with dust and water ice. These polar caps change in size as the seasons change. Sometimes during the summer the uppermost dry ice evaporates away, only to re-form again when the weather turns cold.

Martian Moons

The two Martian moons Phobos and Deimos are not round spheres like Earth's Moon. They are shaped like lopsided potatoes. Phobos is seventeen miles long and twelve miles wide and is approximately fifty-eight hundred miles from Mars; Deimos is ten miles long and six miles wide and is nearly fifteen thousand miles away.

The Martian moons are small compared to other moons in the solar system. Many scientists believe that Phobos and Deimos are actually asteroids that wandered too close to Mars and were captured by its gravity. There is a large asteroid belt located between the orbits of Mars and Jupiter. This could be where Phobos and Deimos originated.

Mars in Orbit and Opposition

Because their orbital paths are different, Earth and Mars each take a different amount of time to complete an orbit around the Sun. This means that Mars and Earth are constantly changing position in relation to each other. At their most distant point the two planets are 233 million miles apart. At their closest point they are less than thirty-five million miles apart. This explains why in some years Mars looks closer to Earth than in others. During August 2003 Mars was only 34.7 million miles from Earth. It will not be this close again until 2287.

About every twenty-six months the Sun, Earth, and Mars line up in a row with Earth lying directly in the middle. This configuration is called Mars in opposition. It means that Mars is closer to Earth than usual and is easier to observe. Most of the historic discoveries about Mars occurred when the planet was in opposition. This was particularly true for the 1877 opposition associated with the findings of Schiaparelli and Hall. Scientists now know that Mars was only thirty-five million miles from Earth during that opposition.

The most recent Mars opposition occurred in December 2007. The next one will be in January 2010. Oppositions are the best times to send spacecraft to Mars.

MISSIONS TO MARS

After the Moon the planet Mars was the destination of choice during the early days of space travel. The Soviet Union was particularly eager to reach the Red Planet before the United States. A historical log of all Mars missions from 1960 to 2007 is presented in Table 7.1.

Many Failures

Historically, spacecraft have had a difficult time making it to Mars in working order and staying that way. More than half of the missions intended for Mars have failed for one reason or another. (See Table 7.1.) Some were plagued by launch problems, whereas others suffered malfunctions during flight, descent, or landing.

Mars missions undertaken during the 1960s by the former Soviet Union were particularly trouble-prone. All six of them failed. Even though the next decade showed some improvement, little usable data were obtained from the spacecraft that reached their destination. The one attempt to reach Mars by the Russian Space Agency, in 1996, failed when the spacecraft was unable to leave Earth orbit.

In contrast to the Soviet Union's Mars attempts, most of the National Aeronautics and Space Administration's (NASA) Mars missions conducted during the 1960s achieved their objectives. There was also notable success over the next decade with the Viking spacecraft. After the Viking mission, there was a long lull in NASA's Mars exploration program.

During the 1990s NASA launched five separate spacecraft to Mars: *Mars Observer* (1992), *Mars Global Surveyor* (1996), *Mars Pathfinder* (1996), *Mars Climate Orbiter* (1998), and *Mars Polar Lander* (1999). Only two of the spacecraft were successful (*Mars Global Surveyor* and *Mars Pathfinder*). The other spacecraft were lost on arrival.

NASA lost contact with the *Mars Observer* just before it was to go into orbit around Mars. It is believed that some kind of fuel explosion destroyed the spacecraft as it began its maneuvering sequence. The *Mars Observer* carried a highly sophisticated gamma-ray spectrometer designed to map the Martian surface composition from orbit. Failure of the mission resulted in a loss estimated at $1 billion. This was by far the most expensive of NASA's failed Mars missions.

In September 1999 the *Mars Climate Orbiter* was more than sixty miles off course when it ran into the Martian atmosphere and was destroyed. The loss of the $85 million spacecraft was particularly embarrassing for NASA, because it was due to human error. An investigation revealed that flight controllers had made mistakes doing unit conversions between metric units and English units. This resulted in erroneous steering commands being sent to the spacecraft. Outside investigators complained that the problem was larger than some mathematical errors. They blamed overconfidence and poor oversight by NASA management during the mission.

NASA's embarrassment deepened a few months later when the *Mars Polar Lander* was lost. The loss was attributed to a software problem that caused the spacecraft

TABLE 7.1

Historical log of Mars expeditions, 1960–2007

Mission	Sponsor	Launch date	Purpose	Results
Korabl 4	USSR	10/10/1960	Mars flyby	Did not reach Earth orbit
Korabl 5	USSR	10/14/1960	Mars flyby	Did not reach Earth orbit
Korabl 11	USSR	10/24/1962	Mars flyby	Achieved Earth orbit only
Mars 1	USSR	11/1/1962	Mars flyby	Radio failed at 65.9 million miles (106 million km)
Korabl 13	USSR	11/4/1962	Mars flyby	Achieved Earth orbit only
Mariner 3	U.S.	11/5/1964	Mars flyby	Shroud failed to jettison
Mariner 4	U.S.	11/28/1964	First successful Mars flyby 7/14/65	Returned 21 photos
Zond 2	USSR	11/30/1964	Mars flyby	Passed Mars but radio failed, returned no planetary data
Mariner 6	U.S.	2/24/1969	Mars flyby 7/31/69	Returned 75 photos
Mariner 7	U.S.	3/27/1969	Mars flyby 8/5/69	Returned 126 photos
Mariner 8	U.S.	5/8/1971	Mars orbiter	Failed during launch
Kosmos 419	USSR	5/10/1971	Mars lander	Achieved Earth orbit only
Mars 2	USSR	5/19/1971	Mars orbiter/lander arrived 11/27/71	No useful data, lander destroyed
Mars 3	USSR	5/28/1971	Mars orbiter/lander, arrived 12/3/71	Some data and few photos
Mariner 9	U.S.	5/30/1971	Mars orbiter, in orbit 11/13/71 to 10/27/72	Returned 7,329 photos
Mars 4	USSR	7/21/1973	Failed Mars orbiter	Flew past Mars 2/10/74
Mars 5	USSR	7/25/1973	Mars orbiter, arrived 2/12/74	Lasted a few days
Mars 6	USSR	8/5/1973	Mars orbiter/lander, arrived 3/12/74	Little data return
Mars 7	USSR	8/9/1973	Mars orbiter/lander, arrived 3/9/74	Little data return
Viking 1	U.S.	8/20/1975	Mars orbiter/lander, orbit 6/19/76–1980, lander 7/20/76–1982	Combined, the Viking orbiters and landers returned 50,000+ photos
Viking 2	U.S.	9/9/1975	Mars orbiter/lander, orbit 8/7/76–1978, lander 9/3/76–1980	Combined, the Viking orbiters and landers returned 50,000+ photos
Phobos 1	USSR	7/7/1988	Mars/Phobos orbiter/lander	Lost 8/88 en route to Mars
Phobos 2	USSR	7/12/1988	Mars/Phobos orbiter/lander	Lost 3/89 near Phobos
Mars Observer	U.S.	9/25/1992	Orbiter	Lost just before Mars arrival 8/21/93
Mars Global Surveyor	U.S.	11/7/1996	Orbiter, in orbit 9/12/97–2006	Conducted prime mission of science mapping
Mars 96	Russia	11/16/1996	Orbiter and landers	Launch vehicle failed
Mars Pathfinder	U.S.	12/4/1996	Mars lander and rover, landed 7/4/97	Last transmission 9/27/97
Nozomi (Planet-B)	Japan	7/4/1998	Mars orbiter	Could not achieve Martian orbit due to propulsion problem
Mars Climate Orbiter	U.S.	12/11/1998	Orbiter	Lost on arrival at Mars 9/23/99
Mars Polar Lander/Deep Space 2	U.S.	1/3/1999	Lander/descent probes to explore Martian south pole	Lost on arrival 12/3/99
Mars Odyssey	U.S.	4/7/2001	Orbiter, arrived 10/24/2001	Currently conducting prime mission of science mapping
Mars Express	Europe	6/2/2003	Orbiter and lander, arrived 12/24/2003	Orbiter currently collecting planetary data. Beagle 2 lost during descent.
Mars Exploration	U.S.	6/10/03 (Spirit) and 7/7/03 (Opportunity)	Two rovers: Spirit, landed 1/4/2004, and Opportunity, landed 1/25/2004	Rovers landed in January 2004. Currently exploring planet surface.
Mars Reconnaissance Orbiter	U.S.	8/12/2005	Orbiter, arrived 3/10/2006	Currently photographing the planet, identifying surface minerals, and studying how dust and water are transported in the Martian atmosphere
Phoenix Mars Lander	U.S.	8/4/2007	Lander will use robotic arms to sample Mars's icy northern pole	Scheduled to land in May 2008

SOURCE: Adapted from "Historical Log," in *NASA's Mars Exploration Program*, National Aeronautics and Space Administration, Jet Propulsion Laboratory, California Institute of Technology, November 6, 2007, http://marsprogram.jpl.nasa.gov/missions/log/ (accessed January 1, 2008)

to think it had touched down on the surface even though it had not. The computer apparently shut down the engines during descent and let the spacecraft plummet at high speed into the ground, where it was destroyed. The cost of the failed spacecraft was estimated at $120 million.

THE MARINER PROGRAM

The Mariner program included a series of spacecraft launched by NASA between 1962 and 1973 to explore the inner solar system (Mercury, Venus, and Mars). These were relatively low-cost missions conducted with small spacecraft launched atop Atlas-type rockets. Each spacecraft weighed between four hundred and twenty-two hundred pounds. They were designed to operate for several years and collect specific scientific data about Earth's nearest planetary neighbors.

Six of the Mariner spacecraft were scheduled for Mars missions. Two of these spacecraft failed. In 1964 *Mariner 3* malfunctioned after takeoff and never made it to Mars. In 1971 *Mariner 8* failed during launch. This left four successful Mariner Mars spacecraft: *Mariner 4*, *Mariner 6*, *Mariner 7*, and *9*.

Mariner 4

In July 1965 *Mariner 4* achieved the first successful flyby of Mars. A planetary flyby mission is one in which a spacecraft is put on a trajectory that takes it near enough to a planet for detailed observation, but not close enough to be pulled in by the planet's gravity.

During its flyby, *Mariner 4* took twenty-one photos, the first close-ups ever obtained of Mars. They showed a world pockmarked with craters, probably from meteor strikes.

Mariner 6 and *7*

In 1969 *Mariner 6* and *Mariner 7* conducted a dual mission to Mars. Both spacecraft flew by the planet, and together sent back 201 photos. These photos revealed that the features once thought to be canals were not canals after all. Instead, it appears that a number of small features or shadows on Mars only looked like they were aligned when viewed through Earth-based telescopes. The illusion was perpetuated by a human tendency to see order in a random collection of shapes. The mystery of the *canali* had finally been solved.

Mariner 9

Mariner 9 turned out to be the most fruitful of the Mariner missions. In November 1971 the spacecraft went into orbit around Mars after a five-and-a-half-month flight from Earth. It was the first artificial satellite ever to be placed in orbit around the planet.

When it first arrived, *Mariner 9* found the entire planet engulfed in a massive dust storm. The spacecraft remained in orbit for nearly a year and returned 7,329 photos of the planet's surface. For the first time scientists got a good look at Mar's surface features, such as volcanoes and valleys. *Mariner 9* showed geological features that looked like dry flood channels. It also captured the first close-up photos of Phobos and Deimos.

Scientists learned from Mariner data that Mars had virtually no magnetic field and was bombarded with ultraviolet radiation. Earth's extensive magnetic field (or magnetosphere) helps protect the planet from dangerous electromagnetic radiation traveling through space. Scientists knew that lack of such protection on Mars would make it exceedingly difficult for life to exist on the planet.

THE VIKING MISSION

Within only four years NASA went from orbiting Mars to landing on the planet. In 1976 the Viking mission was the first American spacecraft to land safely on Mars. For the mission NASA built two identical spacecraft, each containing an orbiter and lander. The two spacecraft entered orbit around Mars and released their landers to descend to the planet's surface.

The spacecraft were launched only weeks apart during the summer of 1975. It took them nearly a year to

reach Mars. On July 20, 1976, the *Viking 1* lander set down on the western slope of Chryse Planitia (Plains of Gold). On September 3, 1976, the *Viking 2* lander set down at Utopia Planitia (Plains of Utopia).

The landers provided NASA with constant weather reports. They detected nitrogen in the atmosphere. Scientists reported that a thin layer of water frost formed on the ground during the winter near the *Viking 2* lander. Temperatures varied between −184 degrees Fahrenheit in the winter to 7 degrees Fahrenheit in the summer at the lander locations.

The orbiters mapped 97% of the Martian surface and observed more than a dozen dust storms. Scientists examined Viking images and decided that some geologic features on Mars could have been carved out millions of years ago by flowing water. The *Viking 2* orbiter continued functioning until July 1978, and its lander ended communications in April 1980. The *Viking 1* orbiter was powered down in August 1980, and its lander continued to make transmissions to Earth until November 1982.

The landers were unique because they were powered by generators that created electricity from heat released during the natural decay of plutonium, a radioactive element. This method of power generation was selected because NASA feared that sunlight on the planet would not be consistent enough to provide solar power.

The Viking orbiters carried high-resolution cameras and were able to map atmospheric water vapor and surface heat from orbit. The landers included cameras and a variety of scientific instruments designed to investigate seismology, magnetic properties, meteorology, atmospheric conditions, and soil properties. They also tested for the presence of living microorganisms in the soil, but found no clear evidence of them. They did learn that the surface of Mars contains iron-rich clay. The Viking images revealed that Mars has a light yellowish-brown atmosphere due to the presence of airborne dust. In other words, the Red Planet is actually more the color of butterscotch.

Many scientists associated with the Viking project concluded that Mars is self-sterilizing. This means that the natural planetary conditions are such that living organisms cannot form. The high radiation levels and the unique soil chemistry are actually destructive to life. The Martian soil was found to be extremely dry and oxidizing. Oxidizing agents destroy organic chemicals considered necessary for life to form. The self-sterilizing theory is not universally accepted, however, and remains controversial.

ALH84001

On December 27, 1984, a meteorite hunter found a four-pound rock on the Allan Hills ice field in Antarctica. The rock was grayish-green and covered with pits and gouges. It was given the designation ALH84001.

The National Science Foundation (NSF) conducts annual searches in Antarctica looking for meteorites (rocks that have traveled through space to Earth). Each possible candidate is collected and assigned a tracking code. The letters in the tracking code represent the location of the find (Allan Hills). The first two numbers indicate the year of the find (1984), and the last three digits indicate the order in which the rock was processed by the NSF that year. ALH84001 was recognized immediately as a significant find, so it was the first rock investigated during that sampling year. In fact, the article "X. ALH84001" (Charles Meyer, comp., *The Mars Meteorite Compendium*, 2003) notes that the person who found it wrote "Yowza-Yowza" across the field notes.

Scientists also got excited when they examined the rock, because they found gas trapped within it that matched the known atmosphere of Mars. They concluded that the rock formed on Mars 4.5 billion years ago. About sixteen million years ago an asteroid probably slammed into the planet and sent the rock hurtling through space. Scientists believe the rock arrived on Earth thirteen thousand years ago.

The rock contains a small amount of carbonate (a carbon-containing compound). Some scientists believe that the carbonate formed inside the rock in the presence of liquid water. This would mean that liquid water existed on Mars billions of years ago. However, the exact origin of the carbonate is still under debate.

Rocks determined to be meteorites are kept in special laboratories at NASA or the Smithsonian Institution. NASA reports in "Meteorites from Mars" (March 26, 2007, http://curator.jsc.nasa.gov/antmet/marsmets/index.cfm) that there have been thirty-one known Martian meteorites found on Earth since 1815. ALH84001 is the oldest meteorite in the collection.

MARS GLOBAL SURVEYOR

More than twenty years passed between the launch of the highly productive Viking mission and another successful mission to Mars. In November 1996 the *Mars Global Surveyor* (*MGS*) took off from the Cape Canaveral Air Station in Florida atop a Delta II rocket. The spacecraft arrived near the planet ten months later. To save on fuel, the *MGS* was put into its final Martian orbit very slowly through a process called aerobraking.

During aerobraking a spacecraft is repeatedly skimmed through the thin upper atmosphere surrounding a planet. Each skim reduces the speed of the craft due to frictional drag. Aerobraking eliminates the need for extra fuel to do a retro-burn to slow down a spacecraft.

The *MGS* was put through a long series of gentle skims for a year and a half. Generally, aerobraking does not take this long. However, flight controllers were extremely careful with the *MGS* because one of its solar panels did not fully deploy during flight. Scientists were afraid that aggressive skimming might put too much stress on the panel.

In March 1999 the spacecraft began its mapping mission. This continued for one Martian year (687 days). The most significant finding during mapping was images of gullies and other flow features that scientists believe may have been formed by flowing water. The *MGS* also captured close-up photographs of Phobos. The images reveal that the moon is covered with at least three feet of powdery material.

In April 2002 the *MGS* began performing data relay and imaging services for other NASA spacecraft carrying out missions at Mars. In November 2006 NASA lost contact with the *MGS* and assumed that its batteries had finally failed. The spacecraft operated for nine years and fifty-two days, the longest Mars mission to record.

MARS PATHFINDER

Mars Pathfinder was a mission conducted as part of NASA's Discovery Program. This was the agency's "faster, better, cheaper" approach to space science. The mission was developed in only three years and cost $265 million. On December 4, 1996, the spacecraft launched atop a Delta II rocket from the Cape Canaveral Air Station in Florida. The *Pathfinder* traveled for seven months before entering into the gravitational influence of Mars.

On July 4, 1997, the spacecraft was ordered to begin its descent to the planet's surface. The landing craft separated from the spacecraft shell and began to drop. A giant parachute released to slow its fall. Eight seconds before hitting the ground the lander's air bags deployed around it like a cocoon to cushion its impact on the surface. The lander ball bounced and rolled for several minutes before coming to a stop more than half a mile from where it first impacted. It was in the rocky flood plain Ares Vallis (Valley of Ares).

After the successful landing, NASA renamed the lander the Carl Sagan Memorial Station, in memory of the astronomer Carl Sagan (1934–1996). He died while *Pathfinder* was en route to Mars. The lander unfolded three hinged solar panels onto the ground. (See Figure 7.1.) It released a small six-wheeled rover named *Sojourner* that began exploring the nearby area. The name resulted from a NASA contest in which schoolchildren proposed names of historical heroines for the mission. The winning entry suggested Sojourner Truth (1797?–1883), an African-American woman who crusaded for human rights during the 1800s.

For two and a half months the *Sojourner* collected data about Martian soil, radiation levels, and rocks. The rover weighed twenty-three pounds and could move at a

FIGURE 7.1

The Pathfinder spacecraft

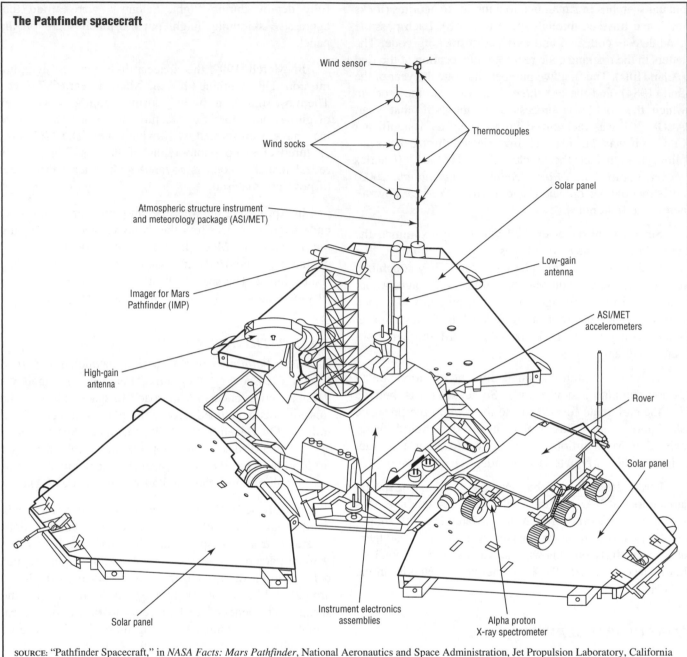

Wind sensor

Wind socks

Thermocouples

Atmospheric structure instrument
and meteorology package (ASI/MET)

Solar panel

Low-gain
antenna

Imager for Mars
Pathfinder (IMP)

ASI/MET
accelerometers

High-gain
antenna

Rover

Solar panel

Solar panel

Instrument electronics
assemblies

Alpha proton
X-ray spectrometer

SOURCE: "Pathfinder Spacecraft," in *NASA Facts: Mars Pathfinder*, National Aeronautics and Space Administration, Jet Propulsion Laboratory, California Institute of Technology, May 1999, http://www.jpl.nasa.gov/news/fact_sheets.cfm (accessed December 31, 2007)

top speed of two feet per minute. It was powered by a flat solar panel that rested atop its frame. (See Figure 7.2.)

Meanwhile, the lander collected images and relayed data back to Earth. It also measured the amount of dust and water vapor in the atmosphere. The lander's forty-inch mast held little wind socks at different heights to determine variations in wind speed near the planet's surface. Magnets were mounted along the lander to collect dust particles for analysis. Scientists learned that airborne Martian dust is magnetic and may contain the mineral maghemite, a form of iron oxide.

The *Pathfinder* returned more than seventeen thousand images and performed fifteen chemical analyses. Scientists studying this data concluded that Mars might have been warm and wet sometime in the past with a thicker, wetter atmosphere. In late September 1997 *Pathfinder* sent its last message home.

2001 MARS ODYSSEY

In "Mars. I. Atmosphere" (*Atlantic Monthly*, vol. 75, May 1895), Lowell said, "If Mars be capable of supporting life, there must be water upon his surface; for to all

FIGURE 7.2

The Sojourner rover

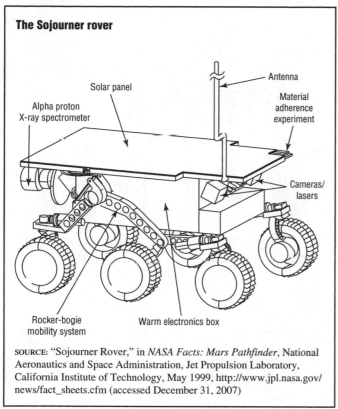

SOURCE: "Sojourner Rover," in *NASA Facts: Mars Pathfinder*, National Aeronautics and Space Administration, Jet Propulsion Laboratory, California Institute of Technology, May 1999, http://www.jpl.nasa.gov/news/fact_sheets.cfm (accessed December 31, 2007)

forms of life water is as vital a matter as air. To all organisms water is absolutely essential. On the question of habitability, therefore, it becomes all-important to know whether there be water on Mars."

A century later this same issue drove NASA to conduct it most extensive program of missions to the Red Planet: the Mars Exploration Program. This is a long-term program in which robotic explorers are used to investigate Mars in support of four science objectives:

- Determining whether life ever existed on Mars

- Characterizing the climate of Mars

- Characterizing the geology of Mars

- Preparing for future human exploration of Mars

The overall motto of the Mars Exploration Program (March 22, 2006, http://mars.jpl.nasa.gov/overview/) is "Follow the Water." In other words, the mission scientists hope that the discovery of liquid water on Mars will lead them to any microscopic life forms that exist on the planet or were ever present.

The *2001 Mars Odyssey* mission falls under NASA's Mars Exploration Program. The mission was named after the hit 1968 movie *2001: A Space Odyssey*, based on a short story by the science-fiction writer Arthur C. Clarke (1917–2008).

On April 7, 2001, *Odyssey* was launched toward Mars atop a Delta II rocket. The spacecraft reached Mars

six months later. To conserve fuel *Odyssey* was placed in Martian orbit via aerobraking.

In February 2002 *Odyssey* reached its final orbit and began mapping the planet's surface. The mission was intended to last for at least one Mars year. In early January 2004 *Odyssey* completed one Mars year in service. As of March 2008, NASA (http://marsprogram.jpl.nasa.gov/odyssey/) reported that the spacecraft was still operational and functioning well.

A schematic of the spacecraft is shown in Figure 7.3. It includes three scientific instruments: a thermal imaging system, a gamma-ray spectrometer, and the Mars Radiation Environment Experiment (MARIE).

The thermal imaging system collects surface images in the infrared portion of the electromagnetic spectrum. Everything that has a temperature above zero kelvin (the lowest possible temperature in the universe, at which all atomic activity ceases; equivalent to −459.7 degrees Fahrenheit) emits infrared radiation. Scientists use *Odyssey*'s images to identify and map minerals in the surface soils and rocks. This work is being coordinated with the mineral mapping being performed by the *Mars Global Surveyor*.

Odyssey's gamma-ray spectrometer can detect the presence of various chemical elements on the planet's surface. This is particularly useful for finding water ice buried beneath the surface and for detecting salty minerals. *Odyssey* data indicate the presence of large amounts of water ice just beneath the surface in the polar regions. The MARIE instrument collects radiation data that will be useful to planning any future Mars expeditions by humans.

Odyssey's telecommunications system performs a dual role. It transmits to NASA data collected by the spacecraft itself and data collected by other NASA spacecraft conducting Mars missions.

THE PERIHELIC OPPOSITION OF 2003

Scientists knew that 2003 was going to be a good year to go to Mars, because Mars would be in opposition to Earth. On August 28, 2003, the Sun, Earth, and Mars were going to line up in a row. This happens every twenty-six months.

The opposition of 2003 was special, because it was going to occur while Mars was at its closest point to the Sun. This configuration is known as a perihelic opposition. When Mars is in perihelic opposition, it is much closer to Earth than usual. This means that less fuel and flight time are required to send a spacecraft from Earth to Mars near the time of a perihelic opposition.

Perihelic oppositions happen every fifteen to seventeen years. During the late 1990s the Japan Aerospace

FIGURE 7.3

Scientific instruments on the Mars Odyssey Orbiter

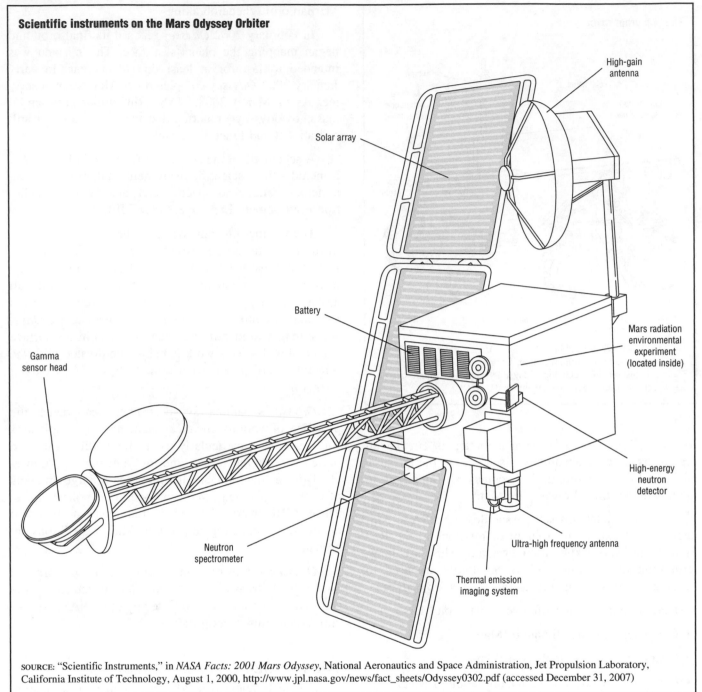

High-gain antenna

Solar array

Battery

Gamma sensor head

Mars radiation environmental experiment (located inside)

High-energy neutron detector

Neutron spectrometer

Ultra-high frequency antenna

Thermal emission imaging system

SOURCE: "Scientific Instruments," in *NASA Facts: 2001 Mars Odyssey*, National Aeronautics and Space Administration, Jet Propulsion Laboratory, California Institute of Technology, August 1, 2000, http://www.jpl.nasa.gov/news/fact_sheets/Odyssey0302.pdf (accessed December 31, 2007)

Exploration Agency, the European Space Agency (ESA), and NASA began planning Mars missions to coincide with the perihelic opposition of 2003. The Japanese *Nozomi* spacecraft suffered radiation damage during its flight and never made it to Mars.

MARS EXPRESS

The *Mars Express* mission is the first mission to Mars by the ESA. It was timed to put the spacecraft in flight near the time of Mars's perihelic opposition.

In June 2003 the spacecraft was launched toward Mars from the Baikonur launch pad in Kazakhstan. A Russian Soyuz-Fregat rocket was used as the launch vehicle. The spacecraft included two parts: an orbiter and a lander named *Beagle 2*. The lander name was chosen in honor of the ship on which Charles Darwin (1809–1892) traveled during the 1830s while exploring South America and the Pacific region.

In late November 2003 the *Mars Express* reached the planet's vicinity and prepared to go into orbit. On December

19, 2003, the *Beagle 2* was released from the orbiter. Six days later the lander entered the Martian atmosphere on its way to a landing site at Isidis Planitia (Plains of Isis). The ESA lost contact with *Beagle 2* as it descended toward the planet. Repeated attempts to reestablish contact were made over the next few months, but were not successful.

The *Mars Express* orbiter achieved orbit to begin its mission of collecting planetary data. As of March 2008, the ESA (http://www.esa.int/esaMI/Mars_Express/index.html) reported that the orbiter was still operating. The orbiter carries seven instruments designed to investigate the Martian atmosphere and geological structure and to search for subsurface water. One of the instruments (*ASPERA-3*) was supplied by NASA.

MARS EXPLORATION ROVERS

Another Mars mission began in 2003 with the launch of NASA's twin Mars Exploration Rovers (MERs). Each spacecraft carried a lander to Mars. Inside each lander was a golf cart–sized rover that was designed to explore the Martian surface.

The rovers were named *Spirit* and *Opportunity*. The names were the winning entries in a naming contest NASA held in 2002. The winning entry came from a third-grade student living in Scottsdale, Arizona. She was born in Russia and adopted by an American family. She chose the names to honor her feelings about the United States.

NASA selected seven specific objectives for the MER missions:

- Find and sample rocks and soils that could reveal evidence of past water on the planet

- Characterize the composition of rocks, soils, and minerals near the landing sites

- Look for evidence of geological processes (such as erosion or volcanic activity) that could have shaped the Martian surface

- Use the rovers to verify data reported by the orbiters regarding Martian geology

- Probe for minerals containing iron or water or minerals known to form in water

- Analyze rocks and soils to characterize their mineral content and morphology (form and structure)

- Seek out clues about the geological history of the planet to determine whether watery conditions could have supported life

The Launches

Spirit launched first on June 10, 2003. *Opportunity* launched several weeks later on July 7, 2003. The launch dates were chosen to put the spacecraft in flight near the time of Mars's perihelic opposition.

Both spacecraft were launched atop Delta II rockets from the Cape Canaveral Air Station in Florida. Figure 7.4 shows a drawing of a rover spacecraft being released by its rocket to make the journey to Mars.

Landing on Mars

Figure 7.5 shows the various parts of the spacecraft that traveled to Mars. Each rover was nestled inside a landing vehicle protected by an aeroshell connected to the cruise stage of the spacecraft. The cruise stage contained fuel tanks, solar panels, and the propulsion system for trajectory corrections during flight. The aeroshell included two parts: a back shell and a heat shield. The back shell carried a deceleration instrument to ensure that the parachute was deployed at the right altitude above the Martian surface. It also had some small rockets to stabilize the spacecraft as it fell. The heat shield protected the lander-rover package from the heat generated by entering the Martian atmosphere.

The stages of entry, descent, and landing are shown in Figure 7.5. At twenty-one minutes before landing, the cruise stage separated from the rest of the spacecraft. Fifteen minutes later the spacecraft entered the atmosphere about seventy-four miles above the surface. The parachute deployed at an altitude of five miles when the craft was traveling nearly three hundred miles per hour. Seconds later the heat shield was jettisoned away. Eight seconds before hitting the ground the spacecraft deployed its air bags to cushion its impact with the ground. Retrorockets were fired to slow its descent. Three seconds later the parachute line was cut. The spacecraft ball bounced and rolled until it finally came to a stop. About an hour after landing the airbags were deflated and retracted so the lander could open its petal and release the rover.

On January 4, 2004, the *Spirit* MER landed on Mars. It was just after 8:30 p.m. at the mission control center in California. The landing site was in Gusev Crater, which was named in honor of the Russian astronomer Matvei Gusev (1826–1866). The crater is about one hundred miles in diameter and lies at the end of a long valley known as Ma'adim Vallis. This translates as Mars Valley, because *Ma'adim* is Hebrew for "Mars." Major valleys on the Red Planet are named after Mars in different Earth languages.

On January 25, 2004, the *Opportunity* MER set down near Mars's equator in an area called Meridiani Planum, which is considered the site of zero longitude on Mars. This is the longitude arbitrarily selected by astrogeologists to be the prime meridian for the rest of the planet. *Opportunity*'s landing site was nearly half way around Mars from Gusev Crater.

FIGURE 7.4

Mars Exploration Rover spacecraft released by Delta II rocket

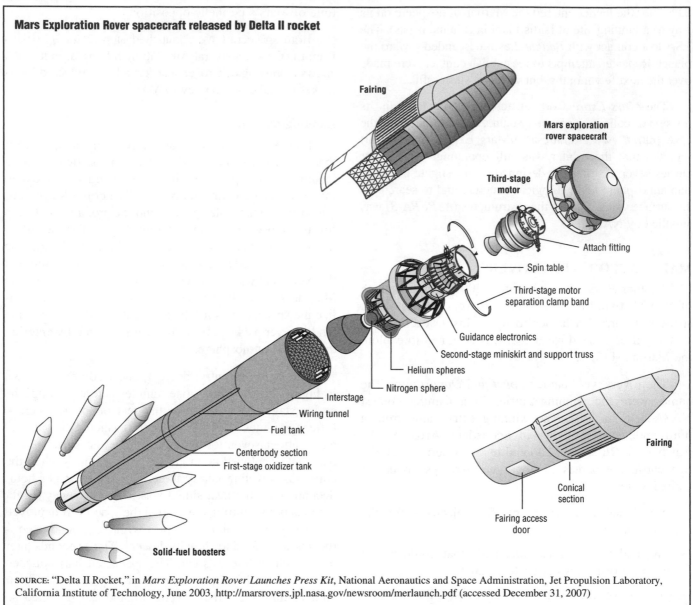

SOURCE: "Delta II Rocket," in *Mars Exploration Rover Launches Press Kit*, National Aeronautics and Space Administration, Jet Propulsion Laboratory, California Institute of Technology, June 2003, http://marsrovers.jpl.nasa.gov/newsroom/merlaunch.pdf (accessed December 31, 2007)

Both landing sites were chosen for their flat terrain. Gusev Crater is of interest to scientists because they believe it could be a dried-up lakebed. The Meridiani Planum is thought to contain a layer of hematite beneath the surface. Hematite is a gray iron-ore mineral similar to red rust that on Earth usually only forms in a wet environment. Both landing sites were considered prime locations to look for evidence of ancient water.

Roving *Spirit* and *Opportunity*

The components of an MER are labeled in Figure 7.6. The rovers are just over five feet long and weighed about 380 pounds on Earth. The panoramic cameras sit about five feet above the ground atop a mast.

Each rover carries a package of science instruments called an Athena science payload. Each payload includes two survey instruments, three instruments for close-up investigation of rocks, and a tool for scraping off the outer layer of rocks. The rovers were designed to move at a top speed of two inches per second. An average speed of 0.4 inches per second was expected when a rover was traveling over rougher terrain.

The rovers were designed to operate independently of their landers. Each rover carries its own telecommunications equipment, camera, and computer. The electronic equipment receives power from batteries that are repeatedly recharged by solar arrays. It was late summer on Mars when the rovers began their mission. Scientists expected that power generation would taper off after about ninety sols (or ninety-two Earth days) and eventually stop as the arrays became too dust-coated to harness solar power. However, scientists were pleasantly

FIGURE 7.5

Mars Exploration Rover flight system

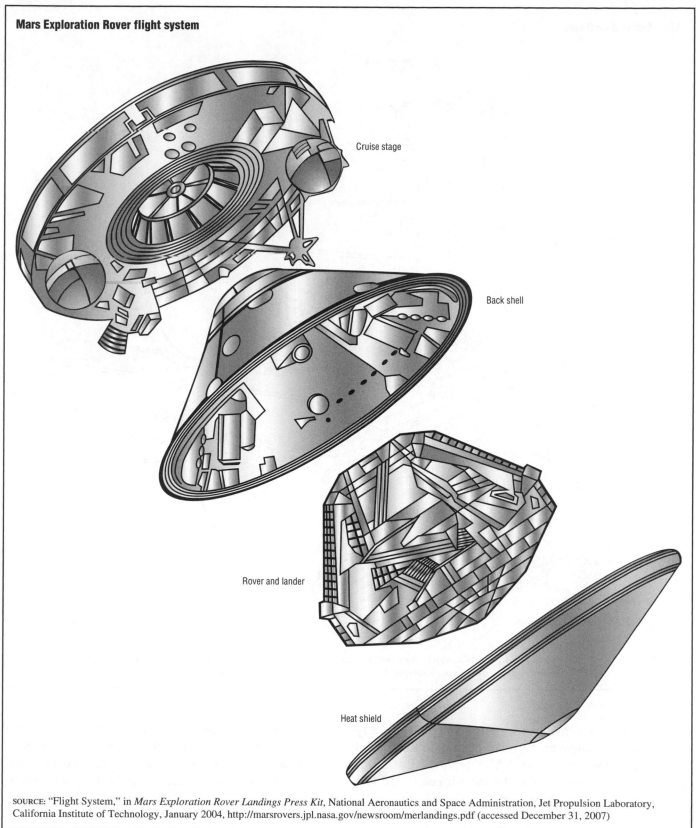

Cruise stage

Back shell

Rover and lander

Heat shield

SOURCE: "Flight System," in *Mars Exploration Rover Landings Press Kit*, National Aeronautics and Space Administration, Jet Propulsion Laboratory, California Institute of Technology, January 2004, http://marsrovers.jpl.nasa.gov/newsroom/merlandings.pdf (accessed December 31, 2007)

surprised when dust devils kept sweeping by the rovers and blowing the dust off the arrays. These periodic cleanings have allowed the rovers to keep operating for much longer than expected.

The rovers completed their prime missions in April 2004. Since that time they have investigated dozens of additional sites. In May 2005 *Opportunity* became stuck in a small sand dune when its wheels sank into soft sand

FIGURE 7.6

Mars Exploration Rover

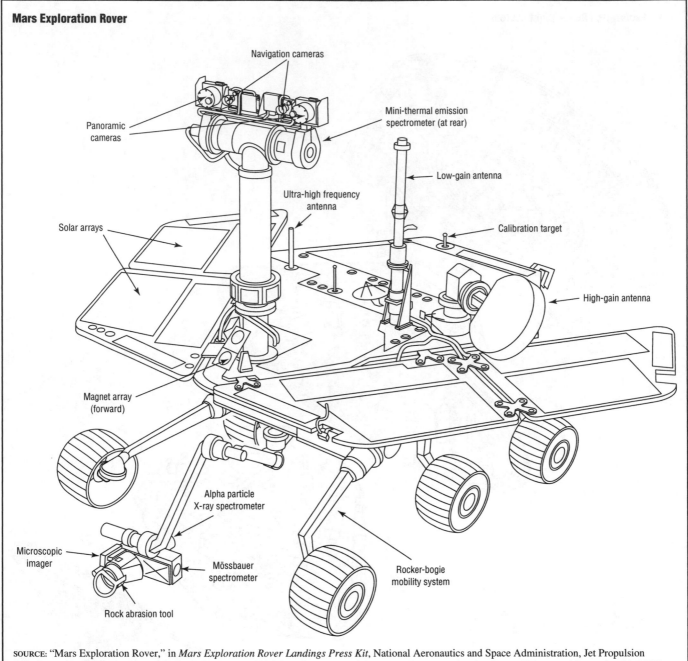

Navigation cameras

Panoramic cameras

Mini-thermal emission spectrometer (at rear)

Low-gain antenna

Ultra-high frequency antenna

Solar arrays

Calibration target

High-gain antenna

Magnet array (forward)

Alpha particle X-ray spectrometer

Microscopic imager

Mössbauer spectrometer

Rocker-bogie mobility system

Rock abrasion tool

SOURCE: "Mars Exploration Rover," in *Mars Exploration Rover Landings Press Kit*, National Aeronautics and Space Administration, Jet Propulsion Laboratory, California Institute of Technology, January 2004, http://marsrovers.jpl.nasa.gov/newsroom/merlandings.pdf (accessed December 31, 2007)

and could not gain traction. Scientists worked for nearly five weeks to maneuver the rover back onto more solid ground. In September 2005 NASA reported that *Spirit* had reached the summit of a Martian hill nearly 350 feet higher than where the rover landed. The hill was tentatively named Husband Hill in honor of Rick D. Husband (1957–2003), the commander of the doomed space shuttle *Columbia*. Scientists used the panoramic pictures captured from this vantage point to map out future exploration routes for the rover.

In January 2008 both rovers reached their four-Earth-year anniversary on Mars. At that time, *Spirit* had traveled more than 4.5 miles and *Opportunity* just over 7 miles from their respective landing site. NASA scientists believe the rovers will operate indefinitely as long as their solar arrays continue to be cleaned by Mars's dust devils. Thus far, the planet has not experienced a global-wide dust storm during the MER missions. However, such storms do occur on Mars and could render the rovers inoperable.

The Name Game

Only the IAU has the authority to assign official names to planetary features. Major features, such as mountains, valleys, and large craters, have already been named. The IAU naming process can take many months and even years to accomplish. NASA scientists handling images from the MERs have to quickly assign temporary working names to the many new smaller features being revealed. The evolution of this process is described in the article "Naming Mars: You're in Charge" (*Astrobiology Magazine*, June, 20, 2004).

Most of the names are picked arbitrarily by whatever scientist first views an incoming image. Features are named after people, places, sailing ships, or other things the scientist fancies. *Opportunity* landed within a tiny crater dubbed Eagle Crater in honor of the *Apollo 11* spacecraft that carried the first men to Earth's Moon. When *Spirit* landed in January 2004, it captured images of seven hilltops about two miles in the distance. Scientists dubbed them the Columbia Hills in honor of the seven shuttle *Columbia* astronauts who perished during 2003. Each hill was named after one of the astronauts. NASA hopes that the IAU will choose to make these names official.

Water and Blueberries

On March 2, 2004, NASA scientists announced that *Opportunity* had uncovered strong evidence that the Meridiani Planum had been "soaking wet" in the past.

The claim was based on examination of the chemical composition and structure of rocks found in an outcrop in the area. The rocks contained minerals, such as sulfate salts, that are known to form in watery areas on Earth. The rocks also had niches in which crystals appear to have grown in the past. These empty niches are called vugs and are a strong indicator that the rocks sat in water for some time. Finally, there are round particles embedded in the rock that are about the size of ball bearings. Scientists have nicknamed them blueberries. The iron-rich composition of the blueberries and the way they are embedded in the rocks hints that water acted against the rocks in the past.

In 2005 NASA published a series of reports in *Earth and Planetary Science Letters* (vol. 240, no. 1, November 2005) detailing the latest findings from *Opportunity*. Scientists believe that ancient conditions in the Meridiani Planum region were "strongly acidic, oxidizing, and sometimes wet." These harsh conditions are considered unlikely to have allowed Martian life to develop at that time in the planet's history.

Mission Costs

The total cost of the MER missions has been estimated at $825 million. Each spacecraft cost about $325 million to develop, build, and equip with scientific instruments. Another $100 million was spent launching the spacecraft, and $75 million was devoted to operations and science costs.

MARS RECONNAISSANCE ORBITERR

On August 12, 2005, NASA launched the *Mars Reconnaissance Orbiter* (*MRO*) toward the Red Planet. The spacecraft was approximately twenty-one feet by forty-five feet in size and weighed more than two tons. A powerful Atlas V two-stage rocket was used to hoist the heavy *MRO* into space.

The *MRO* includes sophisticated radar, mineralogy, and atmospheric probes designed to investigate the atmosphere, terrain, and subsurface of the planet. (See Figure 7.7.) It also carries a high-resolution camera to provide detailed images of the Martian surface. NASA calls the spacecraft its "eyes in the sky." The *MRO* entered Mars orbit on March 10, 2006, and, following several months of aerobraking, took up an orbiting position 160 to 190 miles from the surface of the planet to begin its science mission. That mission is scheduled to last for one Martian year. In May 2007 NASA announced that the *MRO* had returned eleven terabits of scientific data about Mars. The orbiter is expected to operate at least through 2010 and return a total of thirty-four terabits of scientific data.

Beginning in late 2008 the *MRO* will act as a communications relay satellite for future Mars missions. The total price of the MRO mission has been estimated at approximately $720 million.

FIGURE 7.7

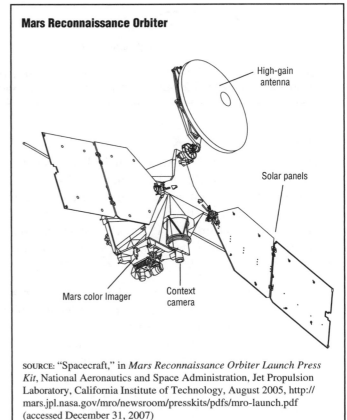

Mars Reconnaissance Orbiter

High-gain antenna

Solar panels

Mars color Imager

Context camera

SOURCE: "Spacecraft," in *Mars Reconnaissance Orbiter Launch Press Kit*, National Aeronautics and Space Administration, Jet Propulsion Laboratory, California Institute of Technology, August 2005, http://mars.jpl.nasa.gov/mro/newsroom/presskits/pdfs/mro-launch.pdf (accessed December 31, 2007)

FIGURE 7.8

Phoenix Mars Lander launch vehicle

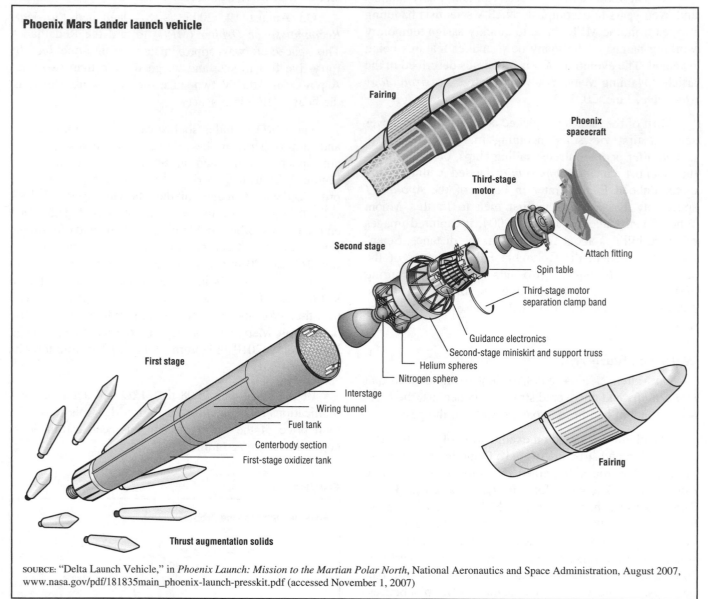

SOURCE: "Delta Launch Vehicle," in *Phoenix Launch: Mission to the Martian Polar North*, National Aeronautics and Space Administration, August 2007, www.nasa.gov/pdf/181835main_phoenix-launch-presskit.pdf (accessed November 1, 2007)

PHOENIX MARS LANDER

On August 4, 2007, NASA launched the *Phoenix Mars Lander* aboard a Delta II rocket. (See Figure 7.8.) The *Lander* will set down on Mars' northern polar region in May 2008. The planned landing site is in Vastitas Borealis (Northern Plains), a relatively flat landscape believed to contain water ice close to the surface.

The *Lander* carries seven science instruments, including a robotic arm for digging and collecting soil and ice samples. (See Figure 7.9.) Samples will be analyzed by onboard instruments for water and carbon-containing compounds. The *Lander* also includes a stereoscopic imager to record full-color panoramic views of the environment, gas and soil analyzers, a meteorological station to track daily and seasonal weather changes, and a descent imager that will photograph Mars during the

spacecraft's descent. The primary mission duration is projected to be 90 to 150 sols (approximately 92 to 154 Earth days). The *Lander* will cease operations when winter sets in, because there will be no sunlight to capture on the solar arrays and recharge the spacecraft's batteries. The *Lander* is expected to be buried by ice during the polar Martian winter.

THE FUTURE OF MARS EXPLORATION

NASA plans to launch the *Mars Science Laboratory* during the Mars opposition of 2009. This rover will collect soil and rock samples and subject them to detailed chemical analysis using onboard instruments. Both NASA and the ESA had considered launching robotic Mars missions during the Mars opposition of 2011, but as of March 2008, both missions had been postponed until at least 2013.

FIGURE 7.9

Configuration of Phoenix Mars Lander after landing

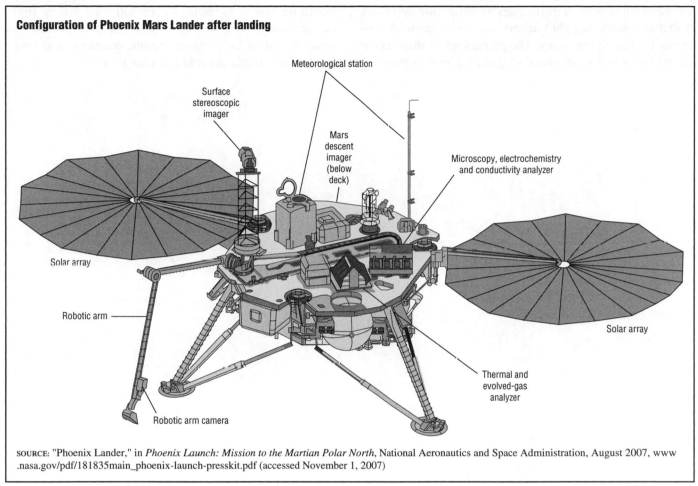

SOURCE: "Phoenix Lander," in *Phoenix Launch: Mission to the Martian Polar North*, National Aeronautics and Space Administration, August 2007, www .nasa.gov/pdf/181835main_phoenix-launch-presskit.pdf (accessed November 1, 2007)

In November 2007 the International Mars Architecture for Return Samples (IMARS) committee met in Washington, D.C., to discuss preliminary plans for an international mission to Mars to collect and return Martian soil samples to Earth. Representatives from NASA, the ESA, the Canadian Space Agency, and the Japan Aerospace Exploration Agency attended the meeting. According to Ker Than, in "Global Group Aims to Return Martial Soil to Earth" (*New Scientist*, December 11, 2007), the committee believes multiple spacecraft will be involved in the mission, which is tentatively scheduled to take place in the late 2010s. A Martian sample return mission is expected to be extremely expensive, but is considered a key precursor to any human missions to Mars.

Human Missions to Mars

Human exploration missions will probably not be possible until the 2030s. There are several major obstacles that must be overcome to make these missions feasible. Most of the problems lie within bioastronautics (the field of biology concerned with the effects of space travel on humans).

Scientists worry that radiation exposure poses a major health risk to astronauts traveling in deep space (beyond Earth's magnetosphere). A solar flare while they are in flight or on Mars could be particularly hazardous. Mars has no magnetosphere of its own, and its atmosphere is thin, with little shielding effect. The radiation levels around Mars are two to three times higher than around Earth. Special protective clothing and materials will have to be developed to protect the astronauts from the radiation hazards.

Bone loss due to long-term weightlessness is also a major concern. A trip to Mars takes about six months with current propulsion technology. They might have to spend a long time on the planet. It is considered likely that the astronauts would make their flights to and from Mars near the times of Mars oppositions, which occur twenty-six months apart. Thus, it is possible that an entire Mars mission could last around two years. Scientists know that humans lose 1% to 2% of their bone mass per month while in space. This bone loss would pose a serious health threat to the astronauts during such a long mission.

The psychological pressures of long space missions have not been well studied. A trip to Mars would require astronauts to live and work in tight quarters and under stressful conditions for one to two years. The psychological strain could prove to be a major problem during such a long journey.

Another obstacle facing astronauts on a Mars mission would be access to medical care. On such a long flight the astronauts would have to have doctors aboard and some means of performing remote diagnosis and treatment of any medical problems that arose.

CHAPTER 8
THE FAR PLANETS AND BEYOND

The farther we penetrate the unknown, the vaster and more marvelous it becomes.

—Charles A. Lindbergh Jr., *Autobiography of Values* (1978)

Beyond Mars lie the far planets: Jupiter, Saturn, Uranus, and Neptune. Even though they are a great distance from the Sun, they are not even close to the edge of the solar system. Beyond Neptune is a large icy area called the Kuiper Belt that extends outward seven billion miles. Within it there are untold numbers of celestial bodies orbiting the Sun. One of these Kuiper Belt Objects is Pluto, formerly a full-fledged planet, but now considered a dwarf planet. Figure 8.1 shows the relative locations of the far planets and Pluto. They are far from the Sun, in a cold and dark part of the solar system.

In ancient times people noticed that some lights in the sky followed odd paths around the heavens. The Greeks called them *asteres planetos* (wandering stars). Later, they would be called planets. The ancients could see only two of the far planets in the nighttime sky: Jupiter and Saturn.

Jupiter was named for the mythical Roman god of light and sky. He was the supreme god also known as Jove or *dies pater* (shining father). His counterpart in Greek mythology was named Zeus. Saturn was named after the god of agriculture, who was also Jupiter's father. His Greek counterpart was called Kronos.

Following the invention of the telescope, Uranus, Neptune, and Pluto were discovered. Uranus was named for the father of the god Saturn. Neptune was the god of the sea and Jupiter's brother in Roman mythology. Pluto was named after the Greek god of the underworld.

When the space age began, humans sent robotic spacecraft to investigate the far planets. They returned images of strange and marvelous worlds composed of gas and slush instead of rock. Many new moons were revealed. Some of these moons are covered with ice and have atmospheres. There could be liquid water beneath that ice teeming with life. This possibility is particularly appealing to space scientists and to all people who wonder if life extends beyond Earth.

THREE CENTURIES OF DISCOVERY

It took three centuries for humans to uncover the far planets in the solar system. In the 1600s the telescope opened up new opportunities for observation. People learned that Jupiter and Saturn had moons and that Saturn had rings. The telescope also showed that wandering stars were not stars at all, because they did not generate their own light, but reflected light from the Sun.

No new planets were discovered during the 1600s. The far planets were still too distant and fuzzy to be recognized for what they were. Uranus was discovered in the late 1700s. Another century passed before the discovery of Neptune. Pluto was discovered in 1930.

Astronomers categorize planets based on geology and composition. Mercury, Venus, Earth, and Mars are called the terrestrial planets, because they are made of rock and metal. Jupiter, Saturn, Uranus, and Neptune are called the gas giants. Some scientists think they may have solid cores, but the exterior of these planets consists of huge clouds of gas. These planets are also known as the Jovian planets (after Jove or Jupiter). All of them have ring systems.

Pluto is a different story. It is a small ice world. For decades astronomers argued whether it was even a planet. In 2006 the debate was ended by a decision from the International Astronomical Union (IAU), the body responsible for naming celestial objects. On August 24, 2006, the IAU proclaimed that Pluto will from now on be called a dwarf planet. By official definition, a dwarf planet is planetlike in that it orbits the Sun and has

FIGURE 8.1

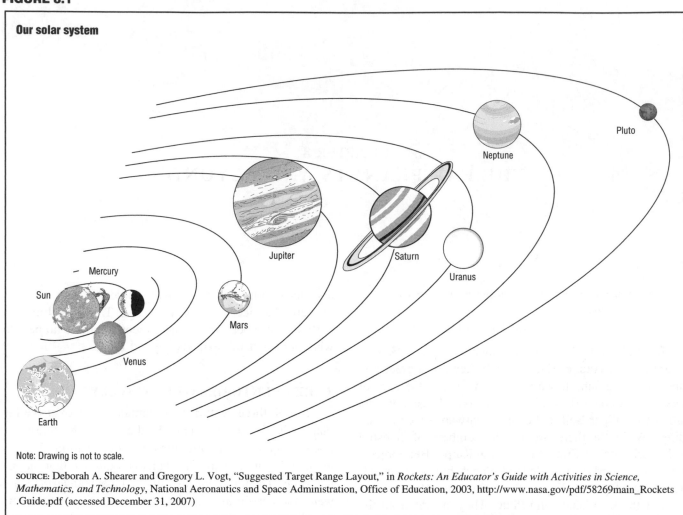

Our solar system

Note: Drawing is not to scale.

SOURCE: Deborah A. Shearer and Gregory L. Vogt, "Suggested Target Range Layout," in *Rockets: An Educator's Guide with Activities in Science, Mathematics, and Technology*, National Aeronautics and Space Administration, Office of Education, 2003, http://www.nasa.gov/pdf/58269main_Rockets .Guide.pdf (accessed December 31, 2007)

sufficient mass and self-gravity to be nearly round in shape. However, the IAU explains in the press release "IAU 2006 General Assembly: Result of the IAU Resolution Votes" (August 24, 2006, http://www.iau.org/ iau0603.414.0.html) that unlike a planet, a dwarf planet "has not cleared the neighbourhood around its orbit."

JUPITER

Jupiter is the fifth planet from the Sun and the largest planet in the solar system. It takes the planet nearly twelve Earth years to make one orbit around the Sun. Jupiter is eleven times larger than Earth. The planet is bright enough to be seen with the naked eye and appears yellowish from Earth. It is similar in composition to a small star and has an incredibly powerful magnetic field that stretches out millions of miles. The poles experience dazzling auroras many times more powerful and bright than the aurora borealis (northern lights) on Earth.

Jupiter's atmosphere is 90% hydrogen, and the remaining 10% is mostly helium, with traces of methane, water, and ammonia. Its sky is streaked with clouds and often with lightning. A gigantic hurricane-like storm has

raged on the planet for hundreds of years, if not longer. It is a cold high-pressure area that is two to three times wider than Earth. The storm is nicknamed the Great Red Spot. The red color is probably due to the presence of certain chemical elements within the storm.

Scientists believe that Jupiter's surface is not solid, but slushy. The planet has dozens of moons. They are named for the lovers and children of Jupiter or Zeus. Jupiter also has a thin ring of material that orbits the planet.

Galileo Is First to Discover Jupiter's Moons

On January 7, 1610, the Italian astronomer Galileo Galilei (1564–1642) was looking through his homemade telescope and discovered four celestial objects near Jupiter. At first he thought they were stars. After watching them for a week, he realized they were satellites in orbit around Jupiter. Two months later Galileo published his findings in *Sidereus Nuncius* (*Starry Messenger*).

That same year the German astronomer Simon Marius (1573–1624) published *Mundus Iovialis* (*The Jovian World*), in which he claimed that he discovered the satellites before Galileo. Marius did not provide any observational data in his book, and Galileo was better respected. The credit was given to Galileo.

In his book Marius proposed the names Io, Europa, Ganymede, and Callisto for the satellites. In Greek mythology these characters were lovers of Zeus. Marius said that fellow astronomer Johannes Kepler (1571–1630) suggested the names to him. Galileo referred to the moons as the Medician stars (to honor the family that ruled his Italian province) and numbered them from one to four. This naming convention was used for two centuries.

Renaming Jupiter's Moons

During the 1800s astronomers decided that a numbering system was too complicated for the moons of planets. More and more of the satellites were being discovered as telescopes improved. It was decided to name moons after literary characters from myths, legends, plays, and poems. Galileo's Medician moons were renamed Io, Europa, Ganymede, and Callisto as Marius had suggested.

More Jupiter Moons

In the years since Galileo's discovery, other observers have discovered many smaller moons around Jupiter. The pace of these discoveries accelerated greatly in the late twentieth and early twenty-first centuries as better equipment was developed. In 2003 astronomers at an observatory atop Mauna Kea in Hawaii spotted twenty-three previously unknown moons around Jupiter. These moons have been named after the lovers, favorites, or descendants of Zeus in accordance with IAU guidelines. NASA notes in "Planetary Satellite Discovery Circumstances" (December 28, 2007, http://ssd.jpl.nasa.gov/?sat_discovery) that Jupiter has sixty-two known moons.

SATURN

Saturn is the sixth planet from the Sun and the second largest planet in the solar system. It takes 29.5 Earth years to orbit around the Sun. Saturn's atmosphere is mostly hydrogen, with traces of helium and methane. It is a hazy yellow color. The planet is very windy, with wind speeds reaching one thousand miles per hour.

Saturn is flat at the poles. The planet is surrounded by several thin rings of orbiting material that circle near its equator. Saturn has dozens of moons. They are named after various characters from Greek and Roman mythology (mainly Saturn's siblings, the titans) and after giants from Gallic, Inuit, and Norse legends.

Galileo Sees Saturn's Handles

In 1610, when Galileo first saw Saturn through his telescope, its rings appeared to him to be two dim stars on either side of the planet. He described these stars as "handles." In 1612 Galileo reported that he could no longer see the dim stars. Much to his amazement, they had disappeared.

In the following years other astronomers saw the strange shapes around Saturn. They were variously described as ears or arms extending from the planet's surface. It would take an improvement in telescopic power before their true nature was revealed.

Huygens Finds a Moon and a Ring

Christiaan Huygens (1629–1695) was a Dutch astronomer who became famous for his observations of Saturn. He and his brother Constantyn built new and more powerful telescopes that were greatly admired by astronomers of the time.

In 1655 Huygens discovered a satellite around Saturn. This turned out to be the planet's largest moon. In 1656 he wrote about his discovery in *De Saturni Luna Observatio Nova* (*The Discovery of a Moon of Saturn*). Huygens referred to his discovery as simply Saturn's Moon. Later, it would be called Titan.

Huygens also figured out that the mysterious shapes near Saturn were not stars, arms, or ears, but a ring of material around the planet. Huygens mistakenly thought the ring was one solid object. In 1659 he published his observations in *Systema Saturnium* (*The Saturn System*).

Ring Plane Crossings

Huygens explained that the ring around Saturn was difficult to view because it is extremely thin. Every fourteen to fifteen years Earth moved into the same plane as the ring. If someone tried to observe Saturn from Earth at this time, Huygens said, he or she would be viewing the outer edge of the ring head-on, making it virtually invisible. This explained why Galileo was unable to see the handles around Saturn in 1612. It was a year in which Earth passed through Saturn's ring plane.

There are several planetary alignments that cause Saturn's rings to be invisible to Earth observers. One of these is when Earth passes into the Saturn ring plane. A similar effect occurs when the Sun passes through Saturn's ring plane and when the Sun and Earth are on opposite sides of the ring plane. The next Saturn ring plane passage will occur in August and September 2009. Throughout history ring crossings have been the best times to discover new moons around Saturn.

More Moons of Saturn

Giovanni Cassini (1625–1712) was born in Italy but lived in France. He was the first director of the Royal Observatory in Paris. During the late 1600s he discovered four more of Saturn's moons. The first two he observed

FIGURE 8.2

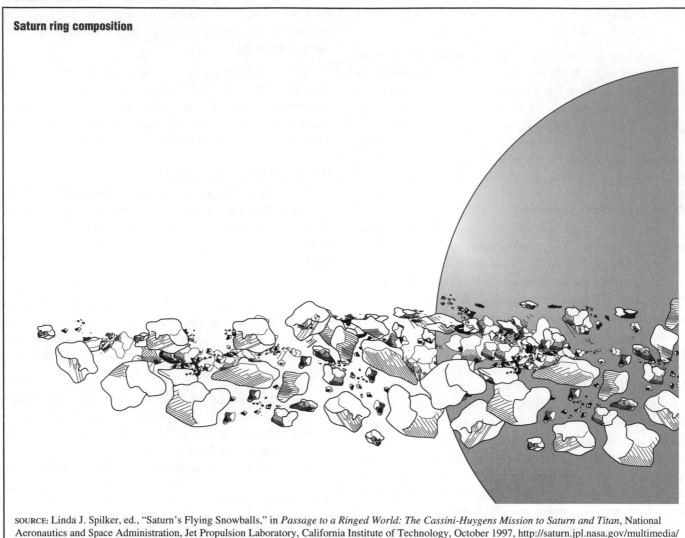

Saturn ring composition

SOURCE: Linda J. Spilker, ed., "Saturn's Flying Snowballs," in *Passage to a Ringed World: The Cassini-Huygens Mission to Saturn and Titan*, National Aeronautics and Space Administration, Jet Propulsion Laboratory, California Institute of Technology, October 1997, http://saturn.jpl.nasa.gov/multimedia/products/pdfs/ptarw.pdf (accessed December 31, 2007)

during the ring crossing of 1671–72. The second pair he discovered just before the ring crossing of 1685.

Over the next three centuries many more Saturn moons were discovered. In December 2004 astronomers at the Mauna Kea observatory in Hawaii found twelve previously unknown moons around Saturn. The latest discovery occurred in July 2007, when NASA reported that the *Cassini* spacecraft orbiting Saturn had captured an image of a new moon. According to NASA, in "Planetary Satellite Discovery Circumstances," this discovery is the sixtieth moon found around Saturn.

Cassini and Saturn's Rings

During the 1600s Cassini discovered a major gap in the ring around Saturn. This proved that the structure was not one solid object as Huygens had thought. The gap would later be called the Cassini Division. Cassini believed that Saturn's rings were composed of millions of small particles. This view was shared by the French

astronomer Jean Chapelain (1595–1674). However, it was not generally accepted until the eighteenth century.

Modern astronomers believe the rings are composed of chunks of ice. These chunks range in size from tiny particles to as large as automobiles. (See Figure 8.2.) Saturn's ring system is actually many ringlets of different sizes nestled within each other with gaps between ring systems. Scientists use letters to designate distinct ring systems around the planet. (See Table 8.1.)

URANUS

Uranus is the seventh planet from the Sun and the third largest planet in the solar system. It looks featureless through even the most powerful telescopes. Scientists believe the planet is shrouded in clouds that hide it from view. The presence of methane in the upper atmosphere is believed to account for the planet's light blue-green color. It takes eighty-four Earth years for Uranus to orbit around the Sun. Uranus is unique in the solar sys-

TABLE 8.1

The rings of Saturn

Ring	Distance, kilometers*	Width, kilometers
D	66,970	7,500
C	74,500	17,500
B	92,000	25,400
A	122,170	14,610
F	140,180	50
G	170,180	8,000
E	180,000	300,000

*Distance from Saturn to closest edge of ring.

SOURCE: Linda J. Spilker, ed., "The Rings of Saturn," in *Passage to a Ringed World: The Cassini-Huygens Mission to Saturn and Titan*, National Aeronautics and Space Administration, Jet Propulsion Laboratory, California Institute of Technology, October 1997, http://saturn.jpl.nasa.gov/multimedia/products/pdfs/ptarw.pdf (accessed December 31, 2007)

tem, because its axis is tilted so far from its orbital plane. The planet lies on its side as it orbits with a pole pointed toward the Sun.

Herschel Discovers Uranus and Two of Its Moons

The astronomer William Herschel (1738–1822) was born in Germany, but lived and worked in Britain. In 1781 he was searching the sky with his telescope when he discovered Uranus. Herschel wanted to name the planet Georgium Sidus in honor of King George III (1738–1820) of England. However, the name Uranus was selected from ancient mythology.

A few years later, in 1787, Herschel was the first to spot satellites around the planet. He discovered the two largest moons: Titania and Oberon.

More Moons

During the mid-1800s two more moons were discovered around Uranus by the amateur British astronomer William Lassell (1799–1880). It was another century before the next moon, Miranda, was found by the American astronomer Gerrit P. Kuiper (1905–1973) in 1948. During the 1980s and 1990s more than a dozen new moons were added to the list. In 2003 three additional moons were discovered by the *Hubble Space Telescope* and astronomers at the Mauna Kea observatory in Hawaii: Margaret, Mab, and Cupid.

In "Planetary Satellite Discovery Circumstances," NASA states that Uranus has twenty-seven known satellites. They are named after characters from the plays of William Shakespeare (1564–1616) and from the poem "The Rape of the Lock" by Alexander Pope (1688–1744).

NEPTUNE

Neptune is the eighth planet from the Sun. The planet is far from Earth and extremely difficult to observe. It has

a distinctive bluish hue when viewed through a telescope. It orbits around the Sun once in 165 Earth years.

NASA indicates in "Planetary Satellite Discovery Circumstances" that Neptune has thirteen moons. They are named after characters associated with Neptune or Poseidon (his Greek counterpart) or other sea-related individuals in ancient mythology.

Neptune's Controversial Discovery

Neptune's discovery is a twisted tale of mathematics, bureaucrats, and international competition. Following the discovery of Uranus in 1781, astronomers watched the planet for several decades. They were puzzled because its orbit did not follow the expected path. Some astronomers began to suspect that there might be another planet beyond Uranus. The effect of its gravity would explain the irregularities that astronomers saw in Uranus's orbit.

During the 1840s John Couch Adams (1819–1892) of Britain and Urbain Le Verrier (1811–1877) of France used mathematics to plot the location of this mystery planet. Adams presented his theory to George Airy (1801–1892), the Astronomer Royal of England. For some reason, Airy failed to pursue the matter and look for the unknown planet. Le Verrier submitted his theory to Johann Galle (1812–1910), the director of the Berlin Observatory. On the night of September 23, 1846, Galle used Le Verrier's notes to locate the planet in the sky.

When Le Verrier and Galle publicized the discovery, Airy complained that Adams had described the location of the planet months before Le Verrier. It turned into a heated argument between France and England. Astronomers decided to split the credit for the planet's discovery between Adams and Le Verrier. Galle is considered the first to observe the planet. However, a review of Galileo's notes from the 1600s revealed that Galileo actually spotted the planet centuries before, but he thought it was a fixed star.

Lassell Discovers a Moon around Neptune

Only weeks after Neptune's discovery its first moon was discovered. In early October 1846 Lassell spotted the moon. It was named Triton, after the son of Poseidon, the sea god. The name was suggested by the French astronomer Camille Flammarion (1842–1925).

More Moons of Neptune

In 1949 Kuiper found another moon around Neptune. In 1989 images from the spacecraft *Voyager 2* revealed six previously unknown moons. The most recent discoveries occurred in 2002 and 2003, when five new moons were added to the list, bringing the total to thirteen.

DWARF PLANETS

Dwarf planets are a new category of celestial bodies. The designation was created in 2006 by IAU resolution.

Even though Pluto is the best-known dwarf planet, it was not the first one discovered. This distinction goes to Ceres, a small world named after a Roman goddess. Ceres was discovered in 1801 by the Italian astronomer Giuseppe Piazzi (1746–1826). He found it in the massive asteroid belt lying between Mars and Jupiter. Another dwarf planet is Eris. It was discovered in July 2005 by astronomers at the California Institute of Technology in Pasadena, California. Like Pluto, Eris is a trans-Neptunian object, meaning it lies beyond Neptune. Eris is named after a Greek goddess.

Tombaugh Discovers Pluto

Clyde Tombaugh (1906–1997) is credited with discovering the dwarf planet Pluto. Tombaugh made the discovery on February 18, 1930, while working at the Lowell Observatory in Flagstaff, Arizona. This famous observatory was founded in the 1890s by Percival Lowell (1855–1916). For years, Lowell had searched for a planet believed by some astronomers to lie beyond Neptune. Following Lowell's death the observatory continued the search. Tombaugh found Pluto after diligently photographing the sky for many nights and studying the photographs for objects that changed position relative to the fixed stars.

The Naming of Pluto

Lowell's widow wanted to name the planet after her late husband. This was not allowed, because it would have broken the tradition of using names from Greek and Roman mythology. The name Pluto was finally selected from many suggestions made by the public.

Pluto was the Greek god of the underworld and was able to make himself invisible. The name seemed appropriate for the darkest planet in the solar system that had been so difficult to find. Also, the first two letters of the name matched the initials of Percival Lowell. The name Pluto was originally suggested by an eleven-year-old British girl named Venetia Burney.

Pluto's Moons

Pluto's primary moon is Charon. It is named after a character in Greek mythology who ferried the souls of the dead across the river Styx to the underworld. On June 22, 1978, Charon was discovered by James W. Christy (1938–) at the U.S. Naval Observatory in Washington, D.C. Christy was studying photographs of the planet when he noticed an odd shape in some of the images. After comparing photographs, he realized that the shape moved over time when compared to Pluto and the fixed stars. When the discovery was made public, Christy suggested the name that was assigned to the moon. In November 2005 images from the *Hubble Space Telescope* revealed that Pluto has two additional moons orbiting far from the planet. In 2006 the IAU gave the new

moons the names of Nix (after Nyx, the mother of Charon) and Hydra (a mythical serpent associated with Pluto in Greek mythology).

Facts about Pluto

It takes Pluto 248 Earth years to circle the Sun. It has a highly elliptical orbit, in that sometimes it is closer to the Sun than Neptune. This last occurred between 1979 and 1999.

Pluto is believed to be a dark and icy world with a surface of frozen nitrogen, methane, and carbon dioxide. It has been observed and photographed only from great distances. No spacecraft have ever been near the dwarf planet. In January 2006 NASA launched the robotic probe *New Horizons* that should reach Pluto in 2015. It will provide the first-ever detailed images of the distant dwarf planet.

THE FAR PLANETS IN SCIENCE FICTION

The far planets have not been as popular as the Moon and Mars in science-fiction stories. One of the first mentions of Jupiter occurs in *A Journey in Other Worlds: A Romance of the Future* (1894) by the American capitalist and inventor John Jacob Astor (1864–1912). In this story Jupiter is similar to a prehistoric Earth. *Skeleton Men of Jupiter* was an unfinished story by the American writer Edgar Rice Burroughs (1875–1950). It appeared in print during the 1940s. The story referred to a Jupiter-like world called Sasoom, and it was inhabited by creatures that looked like human skeletons. In Arthur C. Clarke's (1917–2008) novel *2001: A Space Odyssey* (1968), the exploration of the solar system reaches Saturn, whereas in the Stanley Kubrick (1928–1999) film of the same name, much of the story takes place near Jupiter.

Advances in telescopes and astronomy made it clear that Jupiter and the other far planets were gaseous worlds without solid surfaces. This made them much less appealing as home worlds for aliens. During the 1990s scientists learned that larger moons in the outer solar system may have thick atmospheres and some organic chemicals in their composition. This increases the chances that life could exist there. These moons became popular home worlds for seafaring creatures in science-fiction stories.

PIONEER

During the early 1970s the United States began a series of interplanetary missions designed to explore the far planets. The first of these missions was aptly named Pioneer.

Pioneer spacecraft were the first to investigate Jupiter and Saturn. The missions were managed by NASA's Ames Research Center in Moffett Field, California, for the agency's Office of Space Science. The two spacecraft involved were *Pioneer 10* and *Pioneer 11*. The total cost of their mission was approximately $350 million.

On each spacecraft was mounted a six-inch by nine-inch metal plaque with greetings from Earth. The plaque included illustrations of a human man and woman, the spacecraft's silhouette, and some mathematical, chemical, and astronomical data represented in binary code symbols. An image of the solar system at the bottom of the plaque shows a Pioneer spacecraft leaving Earth and passing between Jupiter and Saturn on its way out of the solar system. The scientists who designed the plaque hoped the images and symbols would serve as a viable means of communication, should any intelligent life form happen to encounter the spacecraft.

Pioneer 10

On March 3, 1972, *Pioneer 10* was launched atop an Atlas-Centaur rocket from Cape Canaveral Air Station in Florida. It was the first mission ever sent to the outer solar system. Ultimately, it became the first human-made object to leave the solar system for interstellar space.

Pioneer 10 was the first spacecraft to travel through the asteroid belt between Mars and Jupiter. Scientists had feared that this would be a dangerous area of space. They learned that the asteroids in the belt are spread far apart and do not pose a significant hazard to spacecraft flying through.

In December 1973 *Pioneer 10* was the first spacecraft to investigate Jupiter. Its closest approach came within 124,000 miles of the planet. *Pioneer 10* carried various instruments to study the solar wind, magnetic fields, cosmic radiation and dust, and hydrogen concentrations in space. Its Jupiter studies focused on the planet's magnetic effects, radio waves, and atmosphere. The atmospheres of Jupiter's satellites (particularly Io) were also investigated.

On June 1983 *Pioneer 10* became the first human-made object to leave the solar system. Over the years the instruments aboard the spacecraft began to fail or were turned off by NASA to conserve power. In 1997 NASA ceased routine tracking of the spacecraft due to budget reasons. The spacecraft was the most distant human-made object in space until February 1998, when it was passed by an even faster spacecraft called *Voyager 1*. NASA last detected a signal from *Pioneer 10* in January 2003. It was approximately 7.6 billion miles away from Earth.

As of March 2008, *Pioneer 10* was more than eight billion miles from Earth and was heading toward the star Aldebaran (the eye in the constellation Taurus), which is eighty-two light-years away. It will take the spacecraft over two million years to reach the star.

Pioneer 11

On April 6, 1973, the *Pioneer 11* spacecraft was launched into space by an Atlas-Centaur rocket. A year and a half later it flew by Jupiter on its way to Saturn. The spacecraft approached within twenty-one thousand miles of Jupiter. It was the first spacecraft to observe the planet's polar regions. It also returned detailed images of the Great Red Spot. Like its sister spacecraft, *Pioneer 11* investigated solar and cosmic phenomena and interplanetary and planetary magnetic fields during its journey.

In September 1979 *Pioneer 11* flew within thirteen thousand miles of Saturn and returned the first close-up pictures of the planet and its rings. It continued past the planet toward the edge of the solar system. In 1995 routine missions operations were ended, and NASA received its last transmission from the spacecraft. By the end of that year, *Pioneer 11* was approximately four billion miles from Earth.

Pioneer and Plutonium

The Pioneer spacecraft were built with special power systems based on radioisotope thermoelectric generators (RTGs). RTGs generate electricity from the heat released during the natural radioactive decay of a plutonium pellet. Even though sending plutonium into space is controversial, NASA has used this power source on all of its missions to the far planets. The planets are too far from the Sun to make solar power a feasible and reliable choice for these spacecraft.

VOYAGER

In 1977 NASA began another bold mission to investigate Jupiter and Saturn. The program was called Voyager and included twin robotic spacecraft named *Voyager 1* and *Voyager 2*. An illustration of a Voyager spacecraft is shown in Figure 8.3.

The various instruments on board were designed to detect and measure the solar wind and other charged particles, cosmic radiation, magnetic field intensities, and plasma waves. The original five-year Voyager mission was so successful that it was extended to include flybys of Uranus and Neptune. The total cost of Voyager's planetary explorations was $865 million.

The Missions

Both spacecraft were launched into space atop Titan rockets. *Voyager 2* was the first to launch, on August 20, 1977. It was followed on September 5, 1977, by *Voyager 1*. Both spacecraft traveled for two years to fly by Jupiter. They made many scientific observations as they passed Jupiter and continued on to Saturn. *Voyager 1* was on a faster trajectory than *Voyager 2* and reached the planet first. *Voyager 2* was directed to fly by Uranus and Neptune. It was the first spacecraft to do so.

The Voyager spacecraft proved to be so hardy after completing their planetary journeys that they were sent on a new mission called the Voyager Interstellar Mission

FIGURE 8.3

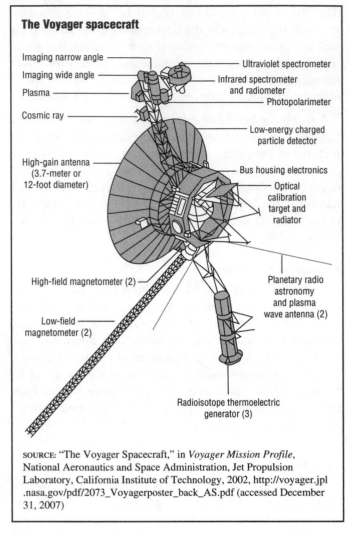

The Voyager spacecraft

Imaging narrow angle
Imaging wide angle
Plasma
Cosmic ray
High-gain antenna
(3.7-meter or
12-foot diameter)
High-field magnetometer (2)
Low-field
magnetometer (2)

Ultraviolet spectrometer
Infrared spectrometer
and radiometer
Photopolarimeter
Low-energy charged
particle detector
Bus housing electronics
Optical
calibration
target and
radiator
Planetary radio
astronomy
and plasma
wave antenna (2)
Radioisotope thermoelectric
generator (3)

SOURCE: "The Voyager Spacecraft," in *Voyager Mission Profile*, National Aeronautics and Space Administration, Jet Propulsion Laboratory, California Institute of Technology, 2002, http://voyager.jpl .nasa.gov/pdf/2073_Voyagerposter_back_AS.pdf (accessed December 31, 2007)

(VIM). The purpose of the VIM is to use the instruments on the spacecraft to explore the outermost edge of the heliosphere. This is the region of space dominated by energy effects from the Sun.

Planetary Achievements

The Voyager missions were two of the most successful in NASA's history. The spacecraft revealed a number of discoveries about the gas giants in the outer solar system:

- Jupiter, Uranus, and Neptune have faint ring systems.
- Jupiter has a complicated atmosphere in which lightning storms and aurora are common.
- Jupiter's moon Io has active volcanoes.
- Jupiter's moon Europa has a smooth surface composed of water ice.
- The radiation levels experienced during the Jupiter flyby were one thousand times stronger than what is lethal to humans.
- Saturn's rings consist of thousands of strands (ringlets).

- Saturn's ringlets are not as uniform and separate as expected—some are kinked or braided together, and additional gaps between rings were discovered.
- Saturn's weather is relatively tame compared to that on Jupiter.
- Saturn's largest moon, Titan, has a dense smoggy atmosphere that contains nitrogen and carbon-containing compounds.
- Saturn's moon Mimas has a massive impact crater.
- Neptune's moon Triton has a thin atmosphere.

The mission also uncovered twenty-two previously unknown moons (three around Jupiter, three around Saturn, ten around Uranus, and six around Neptune). The discovery of water ice on the surface of Europa was particularly exciting, because it raises the possibility that there is liquid water underneath.

Voyager Interstellar Mission

In February 1998 *Voyager 1* became the most distant human-made object in space when it reached a distance of 6.5 billion miles from the Sun, surpassing the record of *Pioneer 10*. It continues to travel at a speed of nearly one million miles per day. *Voyager 2* is a little slower than its sister ship.

Figure 8.4 shows the locations of the spacecraft in December 2003. *Voyager 1* crossed into the heliosheath in December 2004. *Voyager 2* did likewise in August 2007. Solar wind emanates from the Sun and forms a long "wind sock" that moves with the Sun as it journeys through space. The heliosheath is the outer layer of the heliosphere. The heliopause is the boundary between the heliosphere and interstellar space. It lies more than thirteen billion miles from Earth.

In August 2007 scientists celebrated the thirtieth anniversaries of the launches of the Voyager spacecraft, both of which were still returning data to Earth and described by NASA as "healthy." At that time *Voyager 1* was 9.7 billion miles and *Voyager 2* was 7.8 billion miles from the Sun.

Messages from Earth

The Voyager spacecraft carry written and recorded messages from Earth, in case they come across any intelligent life. Attached to each spacecraft is a twelve-inch gold-plated copper disk inside a protective aluminum case. The cover of the protective case has symbolic instructions for playing the disc and a diagram of Earth's location in the solar system carved into it. The disks contain recorded greetings in fifty-five different languages and various other sounds, including bits of music and natural and human-made sounds. There are 115 images encoded in analog form on the disks of various

FIGURE 8.4

Locations of Voyager 1 and Voyager 2 as of December 2003

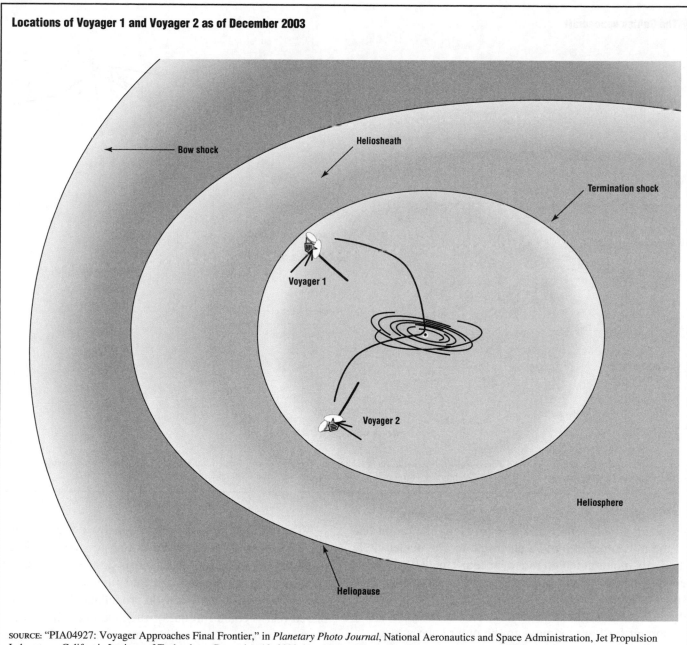

SOURCE: "PIA04927: Voyager Approaches Final Frontier," in *Planetary Photo Journal*, National Aeronautics and Space Administration, Jet Propulsion Laboratory, California Institute of Technology, December 12, 2003, http://www.jpl.nasa.gov/images/voyager/voyager-interstellar-browse.jpg (accessed January 11, 2008)

Earth scenes. These include pictures of people, objects, and places from around the world. The disks carry printed messages from President Jimmy Carter (1924–) and Kurt Waldheim (1918–2007), the secretary general of the United Nations.

GALILEO

NASA's *Galileo* mission was the first to put a spacecraft in orbit around one of the far planets. The $1.4 billion mission to Jupiter included a scientific probe that left the orbiter and plunged into the planet's atmosphere. See Figure 8.5 for a diagram of the spacecraft including the descent probe. The mission was operated by NASA's Jet Propulsion Laboratory in Pasadena, California.

On October 18, 1989, the space shuttle *Atlantis* lifted off from Kennedy Space Center in Florida with the *Galileo* spacecraft on board. The shuttle astronauts released *Galileo* in Earth orbit, then the craft used its two-stage inertial upper stage rocket to boost itself toward Venus.

The spacecraft swung by Venus once and Earth twice as part of gravity assist maneuvers. These are maneuvers in which a spacecraft flies in close enough to a planet to get a boost from the orbital momentum of a planet traveling around the Sun. NASA compares a gravity assist to

FIGURE 8.5

The Galileo spacecraft

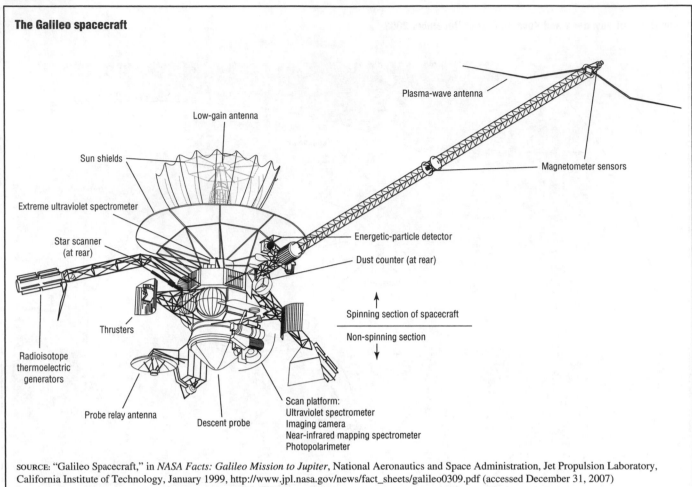

Plasma-wave antenna

Low-gain antenna

Sun shields

Magnetometer sensors

Extreme ultraviolet spectrometer

Star scanner (at rear)

Energetic-particle detector

Dust counter (at rear)

Thrusters

Spinning section of spacecraft

Non-spinning section

Radioisotope thermoelectric generators

Scan platform:
Ultraviolet spectrometer
Imaging camera
Near-infrared mapping spectrometer
Photopolarimeter

Probe relay antenna

Descent probe

SOURCE: "Galileo Spacecraft," in *NASA Facts: Galileo Mission to Jupiter*, National Aeronautics and Space Administration, Jet Propulsion Laboratory, California Institute of Technology, January 1999, http://www.jpl.nasa.gov/news/fact_sheets/galileo0309.pdf (accessed December 31, 2007)

throwing a table tennis ball to skim along the top of one of the moving blades of an electric fan. The blades circle the fan's motor at a high rate of speed. The ball gets close enough to one of the blades to pick up momentum and shoot off in a different direction. Using gravity assists during space flight saves on fuel. This is particularly important for long journeys to the outer solar system.

By July 1995 *Galileo* was nearing Jupiter. It released the probe, which was about four feet in diameter and three feet long, and the probe began a five-month plunge toward the planet. On December 7, 1995, the orbiter was in position when the probe began its final descent at more than 105,000 miles per hour. For nearly an hour the heavily protected probe transmitted data about Jupiter's atmosphere, temperature, and weather. It was finally destroyed by the intense heat and pressure surrounding the planet. It had penetrated 124 miles into the violent atmosphere.

The orbiter spacecraft spent the next eight years in orbit around Jupiter. It conducted many flybys of the moons Europa, Ganymede, and Callisto and used its eleven scientific instruments to collect data about radiation, magnetic fields, charged particles, and cosmic dust.

The *Galileo* orbiter was originally designed for a two-year mission. It ended up lasting for fourteen years. In September 2003 NASA scientists destroyed the spacecraft by purposely plunging it into Jupiter's atmosphere. The orbiter was running low on propellant. The scientists feared that it could run out of fuel and crash into one of Jupiter's moons. This could contaminate environments that might contain water and life forms.

The *Galileo* mission was hugely successful. The spacecraft traveled more than 2.8 billion miles during its long journey. It flew by two asteroids, Gaspra and Ida, on its way to the planet and watched Comet Shoemaker-Levy 9 impact Jupiter while it was in orbit there. *Galileo* captured thousands of detailed images of the planet and its largest moons and collected a wealth of data about these celestial objects.

Major findings attributed to, or confirmed by, the *Galileo* mission include:

- There is an intense radiation belt around Jupiter.

- The surface of Io is constantly being reshaped by heavy volcanic activity.

- There is evidence of liquid water oceans beneath the icy surface of Europa and possibly Callisto.

- Ganymede has its own magnetosphere and probably its own magnetic field.

- Ganymede is heavily cratered from impacts of comets and asteroids and has icy plains, mountains, and basins likely caused by geologic forces.

- Ganymede has a thin ionosphere (electrically charged atmosphere).

- Ganymede, Europa, and Io all appear to have metallic cores.

CASSINI

In 1997 NASA collaborated with the European Space Agency (ESA) and the Agenzia Spaziale Italiana (Italian Space Agency) to launch the *Cassini* mission to Saturn. (See Figure 8.6.) It was designed for a four-year orbit of the planet and to release a probe to land on Titan, Saturn's largest moon. Specific mission objectives are to investigate Saturn's magnetosphere and atmosphere, determine the structure and behavior of its rings, and characterize the composition, weather, and geological history of its moons.

On October 15, 1997, the spacecraft was launched atop a Titan IV rocket from the Kennedy Space Center. Over the next three years it received two gravity assists from Venus and one each from Earth and Jupiter. *Cassini* arrived at Saturn in July 2004, becoming the first spacecraft ever to orbit the planet.

The *Cassini* orbiter is equipped with twelve scientific instruments. It also carried the *Huygens* probe with six instruments of its own. (See Figure 8.7.) The probe was released on December 25, 2004, and began its three-week journey to the surface of Titan. It penetrated the thick cloud cover that hides the moon and touched down on January 14, 2005. The probe sampled Titan's atmosphere and provided the first photographs ever of its surface. It was active for nearly two and half hours during its descent and another hour and twelve minutes after landing before its battery power ceased. The orbiter continued to circle Saturn and conducted flybys of Titan and the smaller moons Enceladus, Hyperion, Dione, Rhea, Iapetus, and Phoebe.

FIGURE 8.6

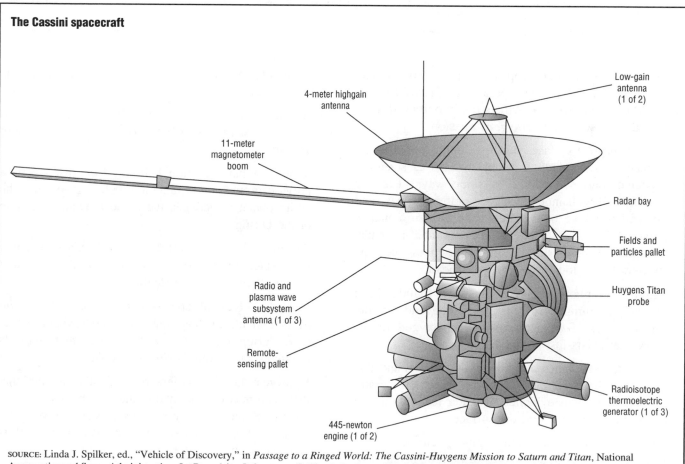

The Cassini spacecraft

Low-gain antenna (1 of 2)

4-meter highgain antenna

11-meter magnetometer boom

Radar bay

Fields and particles pallet

Huygens Titan probe

Radio and plasma wave subsystem antenna (1 of 3)

Remote-sensing pallet

445-newton engine (1 of 2)

Radioisotope thermoelectric generator (1 of 3)

SOURCE: Linda J. Spilker, ed., "Vehicle of Discovery," in *Passage to a Ringed World: The Cassini-Huygens Mission to Saturn and Titan*, National Aeronautics and Space Administration, Jet Propulsion Laboratory, California Institute of Technology, October 1997, http://saturn.jpl.nasa.gov/multimedia/products/pdfs/ptarw.pdf (accessed December 31, 2007)

FIGURE 8.7

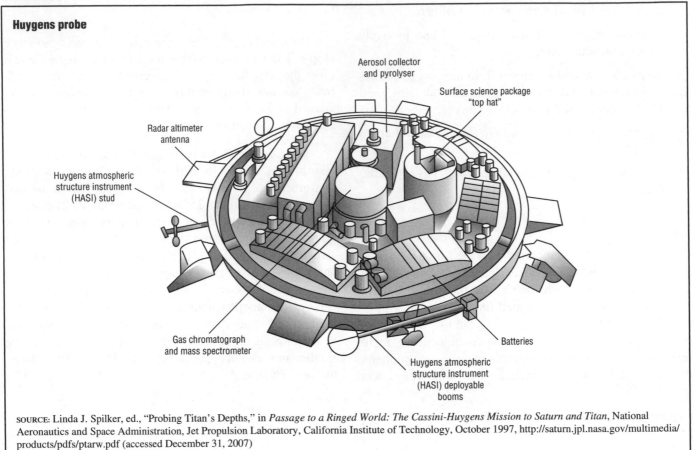

Huygens probe

Aerosol collector
and pyrolyser

Surface science package
"top hat"

Radar altimeter
antenna

Huygens atmospheric
structure instrument
(HASI) stud

Gas chromatograph
and mass spectrometer

Batteries

Huygens atmospheric
structure instrument
(HASI) deployable
booms

SOURCE: Linda J. Spilker, ed., "Probing Titan's Depths," in *Passage to a Ringed World: The Cassini-Huygens Mission to Saturn and Titan*, National Aeronautics and Space Administration, Jet Propulsion Laboratory, California Institute of Technology, October 1997, http://saturn.jpl.nasa.gov/multimedia/products/pdfs/ptarw.pdf (accessed December 31, 2007).

In "Cassini-Huygens Top 10 Science Highlights" (July 15, 2005, http://saturn.jpl.nasa.gov/news/features/feature20050715.cfm), NASA lists ten important discoveries made by the *Cassini-Huygens* mission:

- Titan's surprise surface and organic atmosphere—the surface does not include global oceans as scientists expected, but is Earthlike in some ways. There is evidence of volcanoes, erosion, craters, dunes, and dry and wet lake beds. Titan's atmosphere contains organic chemicals, such as benzene and methane. Scientists believe the moon experiences methane showers from clouds sweeping overhead.

- Saturn's complex rings—the rings were found to have "strawlike clumps" several miles long and rotating ring particles. *Cassini* discovered an oxygen atmosphere that exists just above the rings.

- First detailed images of Phoebe—*Cassini* found this tiny moon battered and scarred by many large crater strikes. There was evidence of water ice and silicate and organic materials on the surface.

- Saturn's colorful and violent atmosphere—scientists were surprised to find that the northern hemisphere of the planet appeared deep blue, rather than hazy yellow like the rest of the world. Also, violent lighting storms

were detected in enormous thunderstorms nearly the size of Earth.

- Enceladus may have an atmosphere—magnetic field data suggest this small icy moon has an atmosphere around it.

- Saturn's inner radiation belt—*Cassini* discovered a previously unknown radiation belt that circles the entire planet in between the cloud tops and the edge of the D ring.

- Dynamic ring-moon relationships—images revealed unexpected interactions between Saturn's rings and moons, such as particle stealing.

- Saturn's rotational speed—comparisons of *Cassini* measurements to those made by the Voyager spacecraft during the early 1980s suggest that Saturn's internal rotation rate is slowing down.

- Massive mountains on Iapetus—scientists learned that there is a massive mountain range on the dark side of Iapetus. Some of the mountains exceed twelve miles in height. For comparison, Mount Everest on Earth is approximately 5.5 miles high.

- Cracks in Dione—*Cassini* images reveal that the moon's terrain is creased with giant fractures.

Later in 2005 *Cassini* captured new images during flybys of the moons Mimas, Tethys, Hyperion, and Dione. In September 2007 the spacecraft flew within one thousand miles of Iapetus. Scientists call it "the two-faced moon," because its surface appears snowy white in some places and dark black in others. *Cassini*'s images reveal that the moon is heavily cratered and has a mountain ridge along its equator. A similar flyby of Titan the following month provided new radar images of many hydrocarbon lakes and seas in the moon's polar regions.

In October 2007 NASA celebrated the ten-year anniversary of *Cassini*'s launch. That same month Miodrag Sremčević et al. reported in "A Belt of Moonlets in Saturn's A Ring" (*Nature*, vol. 44, October 25, 2007) that images taken by *Cassini* indicate the presence of a moonlet belt in Saturn's A ring. The moonlets, which are described as the size of large boulders, are believed to have originated from a moon that once orbited the planet and was demolished by asteroid impacts.

As of March 2008, the orbiter continued its journey around Saturn conducting detailed studies of the planet, its rings, and its moons.

FUTURE MISSIONS TO THE FAR PLANETS

NASA's next planned mission to a far planet is the *Jupiter Polar Orbiter* (*Juno*). *Juno* will assume a polar orbit and study the planet's geology, atmosphere, and climate. It is scheduled to launch in 2010 and arrive at Jupiter in 2016. Other Jupiter missions in the conceptual stage for the late 2010s through early 2030s include the *Europa Geophysical Explorer*, a Jupiter flyby, and the *Europa Astrobiology Lander*. NASA also has plans for three Saturn missions during this same time period: a Saturn flyby and orbiters around Saturn's moons Enceladus and Titan.

PLUTO AND THE KUIPER BELT

As mentioned earlier, the Kuiper Belt consists of many icy worlds in a vast region that lies beyond Neptune in the solar system. Astronomers refer to celestial bodies in this region as Kuiper Belt Objects (KBOs). Since the first discovery of a KBO in 1992, scientists have determined that there are many thousands of these objects. Pluto is now considered a KBO, as are the recently discovered worlds Eris, Quaoar, Orcus, and Varuna. These objects lie far from Earth, and little is known about them.

New Horizons

New Horizons was launched on January 19, 2006, aboard an Atlas V rocket. More than a year later the spacecraft passed by Jupiter. *New Horizons* is scheduled to reach Pluto in late 2016 or early 2017. Following this encounter it will move into the Kuiper Belt and explore there through 2022.

The spacecraft includes seven scientific instruments designed to assess the geology and atmosphere of Pluto and its primary moon Charon and map their surface compositions. Charon is of particular interest to scientists, because it is believed to be covered by water ice. Following these encounters, *New Horizons* will perform flybys of objects in the Kuiper Belt.

New Horizons was conceived in 2001 and is the first mission to be conducted under NASA's New Frontiers Program. The spacecraft is operated for NASA by the Johns Hopkins University Applied Physics Laboratory in Laurel, Maryland.

CHAPTER 9
PUBLIC OPINION ABOUT SPACE EXPLORATION

We will build new ships to carry man forward into the universe, to gain a new foothold on the moon, and to prepare for new journeys to worlds beyond our own.

—President George W. Bush, January 14, 2004

How will a country at war and in deficit pay for such things?

—*Harvard Independent Newsmagazine*, February 12, 2004

Humans seem to have an inherent desire to surmount great obstacles and push into new frontiers. There have always been brave people willing to risk their lives on bold and dangerous journeys into uncharted territory. They have climbed Mount Everest, traversed wild jungles, crossed barren deserts, and sailed stormy seas. Successful explorers become popular heroes. Their achievements thrill and delight people who do not have the ability, resources, or courage to go themselves.

The U.S. space program taps into this spirit of adventure. Astronauts became the heroic explorers of the twentieth century. They opened new frontiers and set foot on the Moon. These successes were achieved at a high price. They cost the country human lives and billions of dollars that some critics say could have been spent feeding the poor, healing the sick, and housing the homeless. Was it worth it?

Space exploration is appealing on a psychological level. It is awesome, daring, and closely associated with American can-do optimism and patriotic pride. A robust space program also showcases and strengthens U.S. capabilities in science, engineering, and technology. These are powerful motivations to keep venturing out into space.

However, the United States faces a number of expensive problems: incurable diseases, crime, poverty, pollution, unemployment, and war. People concerned with poor social conditions resent the billions spent on exploring outer space. Within the scientific community many respected researchers would rather see scarce funds devoted to Earth-related research than space science. There are promising scientific and medical frontiers on this planet that still need to be explored.

In a democratic society the public gets to weigh the relative costs and benefits of national goals and decide which ones to pursue. Public opinion polls show that most Americans have an uneasy devotion to the nation's space travel agenda. They love the idea, but hate paying the bill. Sometimes they wonder if money spent on space exploration might be better spent on Earth-based issues. It is a debate that has raged since the earliest days of space exploration and probably always will be a primary issue in space exploration.

IS SPACE EXPLORATION IMPORTANT TO SOCIETY?

In November 1999, as the century came to a close, Frank Newport, David W. Moore, and Lydia Saad of the Gallup Organization asked people to rank eighteen specific events of the twentieth century in order of importance and reported the results in *The Most Important Events of the Century from the Viewpoint of the People* (December 6, 1999, http://www.gallup.com/poll/3427/Most-Important-Events-Century-From-Viewpoint-People.aspx). Landing a man on the Moon ranked seventh in importance. (See Table 9.1.) This put it behind major events associated with World War I (1914–1918), World War II (1939–1945), and important social milestones that granted rights to women and minorities. Fifty percent of those asked believed that landing a man on the Moon was the most important event of the century.

A second space-travel milestone also made the top eighteen list. Ranked fourteenth was the launching of the Russian Sputnik satellites during the 1950s. (See Table 9.1.) Twenty-five percent of those asked rated this as one of the most important events of the century. Charles A. Lindbergh

TABLE 9.1

Public opinion on the most important events of the twentieth century, 1999

1. World War II
2. Women gaining the right to vote in 1920
3. Dropping the atomic bomb on Hiroshima in 1945
4. The Nazi Holocaust during World War II
5. Passage of the 1964 Civil Rights Act
6. World War I
7. Landing a man on the moon in 1969
8. The assassination of President Kennedy in 1963
9. The fall of the Berlin Wall in 1989
10. The U.S. Depression in the 1930s
11. The breakup of the Soviet Union in the early 1990s
12. The Vietnam War in the 1960s and early 1970s
13. Charles Lindbergh's transatlantic flight in 1927
14. The launching of the Russian Sputnik satellites in the 1950s
15. The Korean War in the early 1950s
16. The Persian Gulf War in 1991
17. The impeachment of President Bill Clinton in 1998
18. The Watergate scandal involving Richard Nixon in the 1970s

SOURCE: Adapted from Frank Newport, David W. Moore, and Lydia Saad, "The 18 Events Were Then Rank-Ordered Based on the Percentage of Americans Who Placed Each in the Top Category as 'One of the Most Important Events of the Century,'" in *The Most Important Events of the Century from the Viewpoint of the People*, The Gallup Organization, December 6, 1999, http://www.gallup.com/poll/3427/Most-Important-Events-Century-From-Viewpoint-People.aspx (accessed January 8, 2008). Copyright © 1999 by The Gallup Organization. Reproduced by permission of The Gallup Organization.

FIGURE 9.1

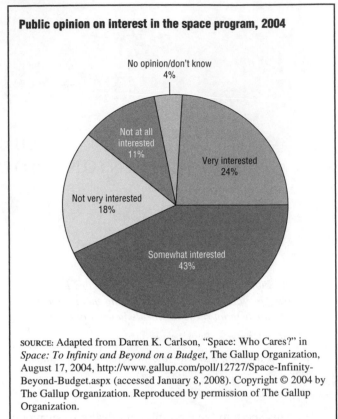

Public opinion on interest in the space program, 2004

SOURCE: Adapted from Darren K. Carlson, "Space: Who Cares?" in *Space: To Infinity and Beyond on a Budget*, The Gallup Organization, August 17, 2004, http://www.gallup.com/poll/12727/Space-Infinity-Beyond-Budget.aspx (accessed January 8, 2008). Copyright © 2004 by The Gallup Organization. Reproduced by permission of The Gallup Organization.

Jr.'s (1902–1974) historic flight across the Atlantic in 1927 also made the list, coming in at number thirteen.

In *Space: To Infinity and Beyond on a Budget* (August 17, 2004, http://www.gallup.com/poll/12727/Space-Infinity-Beyond-Budget.aspx), Darren K. Carlson of the Gallup Organization reports on a poll conducted between June and July 2004, which found that a majority of people were interested in the space program: 24% were "very interested" and another 43% were "somewhat interested." (See Figure 9.1.) Only 11% reported they were "not at all interested." More men (34%) than women (15%) indicated they were "very interested" in the space program. Interest was also higher among respondents aged fifty to sixty-four years old. When provided with five possible reasons for space exploration, 29% chose that it is "human nature to explore." (See Figure 9.2.) Another 21% believed that space exploration is primarily performed to help maintain the nation's status as an international leader in space. Nearly as many respondents (18%) thought the main reason is to provide benefits on Earth. Small percentages believed that Americans explore space to ensure national security (12%) or inspire people and motivate children (10%).

SHOULD SPACE TRAVEL BE A NATIONAL PRIORITY?

History shows that space travel was a national priority during the 1960s. President John F. Kennedy (1917–1963) and Vice President Lyndon B. Johnson (1908–1973) were convinced that putting a man on the Moon was vital to U.S. political interests during the cold war. They convinced Congress to devote billions of dollars to the effort. At the time, the public was not enthusiastic about the idea. According to the Gallup Organization, most polls it conducted during the 1960s showed that less than 50% of Americans considered the endeavor worth the cost.

In *Where Do We Go from Here: Chaos or Community?* (1967), the civil rights leader Martin Luther King Jr. (1929–1968) said, "Without denying the value of scientific endeavor, there is a striking absurdity in committing billions to reach the moon where no people live, while only a fraction of that amount is appropriated to service the densely populated slums." King's sentiment sums up a moral question that has plagued the space program since its inception. Is it right for a nation to spend its money on space travel while there are people suffering on Earth?

The National Aeronautics and Space Administration (NASA) would argue that its budget comprises only a tiny fraction of the nation's total spending. Figure 2.1 in Chapter 2 shows that in 2007 NASA received less than 1% of the federal budget and has been near this level since the end of the Apollo program in 1972. Nevertheless, recent polls indicate that Americans do not favor

FIGURE 9.2

Public opinion on what drives American space exploration, 2004

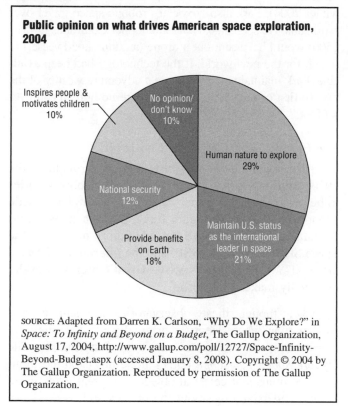

SOURCE: Adapted from Darren K. Carlson, "Why Do We Explore?" in *Space: To Infinity and Beyond on a Budget*, The Gallup Organization, August 17, 2004, http://www.gallup.com/poll/12727/Space-Infinity-Beyond-Budget.aspx (accessed January 8, 2008). Copyright © 2004 by The Gallup Organization. Reproduced by permission of The Gallup Organization.

TABLE 9.2

Public opinion on government spending on the space program, selected years, 1984–2006

	Increased	Present levels	Reduced	Ended altogether	No opinion
	%	%	%	%	%
2006 Jun 23–25	17	48	28	5	2
2003 Aug 4–6	24	51	17	7	1
2003 Feb 7–9	25	49	17	7	2
1999 Dec 9–12	16	49	24	10	1
1999 Jul 13–14	18	45	26	8	3
1998 Nov 20–22	21	47	26	4	2
1993 Dec 17–19	11	42	38	8	1
1993 Sep 13–15	9	37	41	10	3
1991 May 2–5	21	44	28	3	4
1989 Jul 6–9	27	42	22	4	5
1986 Jan 29–30	26	50	14	5	5
1984 Jan 30–Feb 6	21	48	23	5	4

SOURCE: Joseph Carroll, "Now I'd Like to Ask You about Government Spending on NASA. In Answering, Please Bear in Mind That Sooner or Later All Government Spending Has to Be Taken out of the Taxes That You and Other Americans Pay. Do You Think Spending on the U.S. Space Program Should Be Increased, Kept at the Present Level, Reduced, or Ended Altogether?" in *Public Divided over Money Spent on Space Shuttle Program*, The Gallup Organization, June 30, 2006, http://brain.gallup.com/content/default.aspx?ci=23545 (accessed November 6, 2007). Copyright © 2006 by The Gallup Organization. Reproduced by permission of The Gallup Organization.

increasing NASA's budget. Gallup polling conducted from 1984 to 2006 regarding government spending on NASA sheds some light on Americans' opinions. In June 2006 nearly half (48%) of those asked said that NASA's budget should remain at its present level. (See Table 9.2.) Another 28% believed the agency's budget should be reduced. Only 17% thought NASA's budget should be increased. Gallup has been asking this same poll question since 1984. The percentage of people wanting to increase NASA's budget has varied between 9% and 27% over time. Consistently, the largest group of people (37% to 51%) advocated maintaining the agency's budget at its existing level.

Two different polls conducted in 2006 and 2007 indicate that the American public assigns little value to government spending on the space program. The University of Chicago's National Opinion Research Center conducts the annual poll General Social Survey (GSS). The GSS covers a variety of subjects, including the nation's spending priorities. The 2006 GSS asked respondents to indicate their level of support for twenty-two national spending priorities. The list included specific programs, such as welfare and social security, and more generic priorities, such as environment, crime, health, and space exploration. The results of the polling were reported by Tom W. Smith in "Trends in National Spending Priorities, 1973–2006" (January 10, 2007, http://www.norc.org/). Smith notes that in 2006 space exploration ranked twenty-first out of the twenty-two categories. Only for-

eign aid received a lower spending priority. In "Closing the Budget Deficit: U.S. Adults Strongly Resist Raising Any Taxes Except 'Sin Taxes' or Cutting Major Programs" (April 10, 2007, http://www.harrisinteractive.com/harris_poll/index.asp?PID=746), HarrisInteractive reports on a March 2007 poll that it conducted. People were asked to choose two programs out of a list of eleven national programs that they would favor cutting if federal spending had to be cut to reduce the federal deficit. The space program received the largest percentage of votes with 51%. This compares to 28% favoring welfare spending cuts, 28% for defense spending cuts, 24% for cuts in farm subsidies, and 16% for cuts in environmental spending.

SHOULD SPACE TRAVEL BE A SCIENCE PRIORITY?

In the 1960s television show *Star Trek*, space was called "the final frontier." While this may be true from a philosophical viewpoint, it does not apply as well to the realm of science. Geneticists, oceanographers, geologists, and biologists maintain that there are still many scientific and medical frontiers to be explored on Earth.

Since 1998 the marine biologist Sylvia Earle (1935–) has been an explorer-in-residence at the National Geographic Society. That same year *Time* magazine named her a "hero for the planet." In "Mars Critics Wonder If Billions Aren't Better Spent Elsewhere" (Associated Press, March 8, 2004), Joseph B. Verrengia asks Earle about

NASA's discovery that water once existed on Mars. Earle states that "the resources going into the investigation of our own planet and its oceans are trivial compared to investment looking for water elsewhere in the universe.... Real oceans need scientific attention more than the dried-up remnants on Mars." She states that she does not want to cut funding for space science, but notes that "we have better maps of Mars than our own ocean floor. That's just not right."

Verrengia notes that Amitai Etzioni (1929–), a sociologist at George Washington University and a long-time critic of the U.S. space program, believes that the scientific community should focus more attention on Earth's oceans because of their potential to yield new energy and food sources or medical breakthroughs that would benefit humanity. Etzioni also criticizes the money spent looking for water on Mars and asks, "So what if there is water up there? What difference does it make to anyone's life? Will it grow any more food? Cure a disease? This doesn't even broaden our horizons." Etzioni believes that any crewed space missions should be financed by private investors, not with taxpayers' dollars.

CREWED VERSUS ROBOTIC MISSIONS?

In 1964 Etzioni published *The Moon-Doggle*, which questions the scientific value of putting astronauts on the Moon and criticizes NASA for favoring expensive manned missions over cheaper, more productive robotic missions. This complaint has been a common one in the scientific community since the 1960s.

It is extremely expensive to send explorers into space, particularly human ones. Robotic spacecraft can accomplish more for less money, but they lack the glamour of human explorers. Machines do not give television interviews from space or get ticker tape parades when they return. Astronauts do. Human explorers inspire young people to be astronauts and encourage voters and politicians to keep funding space travel. NASA knows that machines simply do not reap the same public relations benefits as human astronauts.

James Van Allen (1914–2006) and Robert L. Park have been highly critical of the plan presented by President George W. Bush (1946–) in 2004 to send astronauts to the Moon and Mars. Van Allen, an astrophysicist, is credited with discovering the Van Allen radiation belts around Earth. Park is a physics professor at the University of Maryland.

In "Bush's New Space Program Criticized over Costs & Nuclear Fears" (January 15, 2004, http://www.democracynow .org/2004/1/15/bushs_new_space_program_criticized_over), Allen explains his opinion of human spaceflight: "I'm a critic of it in terms of the yield of either scientific results or any results from the human space flight program that's been very

meager." In "The Virtual Astronaut" (*New Atlantis*, no. 4, winter 2004), Park also advocates robotic space travel over astronauts. He speculates that Christopher Columbus (1451–1506) would have sent out a drone (an unmanned vessel) to search for the new world, if the technology had been available. Park maintains that "the great adventure worthy of the twenty-first century is to explore where no human can ever set foot."

The *Hubble Space Telescope* Controversy

Astronomers and physicists fought throughout the 1970s and 1980s for large, sophisticated observatories to be put in space to gather data about solar and galactic phenomena. Time and again funding for their programs was slashed, because NASA needed more money for the Space Shuttle Program (SSP) and the *International Space Station* (*ISS*). However, NASA's Great Observatories did eventually make it into orbit.

Even though these observatories are smaller and weaker than what scientists originally wanted, they are considered some of space science's greatest triumphs. The *Hubble Space Telescope* (*HST*) alone has captured thousands of images of celestial objects and greatly advanced human understanding about the origins and workings of the universe.

However, in 2004 NASA announced it would let the *HST* fall out of orbit before the end of its useful life. The observatory needed an altitude boost that only a space shuttle mission could give it, but NASA was reluctant to risk astronaut lives for such a purpose. Since the 2003 space shuttle *Columbia* disaster the agency has shown heightened concern about shuttle safety issues. Also, NASA has switched its focus to President George W. Bush's new space travel mandate. This plan calls for devoting shuttle missions to finishing the *ISS* as soon as possible and then retiring the shuttle fleet in 2010. Bush wants NASA to concentrate on developing new spacecraft for long-distance flights to the Moon and Mars.

The *HST* decision met with fierce disapproval from many astronomers and space scientists who were once again disappointed to see human missions given priority over robotic ones. In 2006 NASA relented to pressure and agreed to reinstate the *HST* servicing mission. However, as of March 2008 this mission had not taken place.

AMERICANS RATE NASA'S PERFORMANCE

In June 2006 Gallup asked Americans to rate NASA's performance. Seventeen percent of those asked rated its performance as "excellent" and 40% said it was "good." (See Table 9.3.) Nearly a third (30%) of those asked said that NASA's performance was "only fair," and 7% gave the agency a "poor" rating.

TABLE 9.3

Public opinion on the performance of NASA, selected years, 1990–2006

	Excellent	Good	Only fair	Poor	No opinion
	%	%	%	%	%
2006 Jun 23–25	17	40	30	7	6
2005 Aug 5–7	16	44	29	8	3
2005 Jun 24–26	11	42	34	6	7
2003 Sep 8–10	12	38	36	10	4
1999 Dec 9–12	13	40	31	12	4
1999 Jul 13–4	20	44	20	5	11
1998 Nov 20–22	26	50	17	4	3
1998 Jan 30–Feb 1	21	46	21	4	8
1994 Jul 15–17	14	43	29	6	8
1993 Dec 17–19	18	43	30	7	2
1993 Sept 13–15	7	36	35	11	11
1991 May 2–5	16	48	24	6	6
1990 July 19–22	10	36	34	15	5

SOURCE: Joseph Carroll, "How Would You Rate the Job Being Done by NASA—The U.S. Space Agency? Would You Say It Is Doing an Excellent, Good, Only Fair, or Poor Job?" in *Public Divided over Money Spent on Space Shuttle Program*, The Gallup Organization, June 30, 2006, http://brain.gallup.com/content/default.aspx?ci=23545 (accessed November 6, 2007). Copyright © 2006 by The Gallup Organization. Reproduced by permission of The Gallup Organization.

Gallup has asked this same question about NASA's performance since July 1990. The highest approval (76%) was in November 1998, when 26% said it was "excellent" and 50% said it was "good." (See Table 9.3.) This was shortly after John Glenn's (1921–) flight aboard the space shuttle *Discovery*. The next three polls saw NASA's rating slip dramatically, reaching 50% in September 2003, when 12% said it was "excellent" and 38% said it was "good." This was a few months after the *Columbia* shuttle disaster. NASA's image has improved slightly since then.

Mary Lynne Dittmar reports in "Engaging the 18–25 Generation: Educational Outreach, Interactive Technologies, and Space" (2006, http://www.dittmar-associates.com/Publications/Engaging%20the%2018-25%20Generation%20Update~web.pdf) that in 2006 young people aged eighteen to twenty-five were questioned about the relevance of NASA to their life. A majority (51%) of young adults deemed NASA "irrelevant or very irrelevant." Less than a third (32%) of the respondents said NASA was "relevant or very relevant" to their life. Another 17% had neutral opinions on the subject. When pressed for more detail about their negative viewpoints, 39% of the young people agreed with the statement "nothing useful has come out of NASA." A large majority (72%) felt that government spending on NASA should be diverted to other priorities, particularly employment and defense programs.

Focus on the SSP

NASA's most horrific failures occurred in 1986 and 2003, when space shuttles were lost in accidents. Seven astronauts died each time. In *Americans Want Space Shuttle Program to Go On* (February 3, 2003, http://www.gallup.com/poll/7708/Americans-Want-Space-Shuttle-Program.aspx), Frank Newport of the Gallup Organization notes that days after each disaster the public's confidence in NASA's ability to avoid similar accidents in the future was assessed. Following the loss of *Challenger* in 1986, 79% (38% had "a great deal" and 41% had a "fair amount") of respondents expressed confidence that another shuttle loss could be avoided. When the *Columbia* shuttle was destroyed during reentry in 2003, this confidence proved to be misplaced. Interestingly enough, the public's confidence level actually increased to 82% (38% had "a great deal" and 44% had a "fair amount") after the second accident. These polls suggest that Americans remain optimistic about NASA's competency in regards to the SSP.

Jeffrey M. Jones of the Gallup Organization notes in *Support for Space Program Funding High by Historical Standards* (August 19, 2003, http://www.gallup.com/poll/9082/Support-Space-Program-Funding-High-Historical-Standards.aspx) that in August 2003 Gallup surveyed 1,003 adults regarding their expectations about the risks associated with the SSP. Most respondents (43%) believed that a fatal crash every one hundred missions was an "acceptable price to pay" to advance U.S. space exploration goals. In reality, the shuttle program has experienced two crashes during 120 missions. This is an average of one fatal crash every sixty missions.

Seventeen percent of those asked expressed the belief that a successful SSP should experience no fatal crashes at all. However, the vast majority (75%) accepted the loss of human lives as a regrettable, but expected, price to pay to advance the nation's space program.

Recent polls show support may be waning for the SSP. For example, in *Americans Express Confidence in NASA* (July 11, 2005, http://www.gallup.com/poll/17224/Americans-Express-Confidence-NASA.aspx), Jeffrey M. Jones indicates that Gallup polled adults about their opinions on shuttle missions shortly after the *Challenger* and *Columbia* space shuttle disasters. More than 80% of the people asked in each poll thought the SSP should continue. The same question was asked in June 2005 (before the first return-to-flight mission). Nearly three-quarters (74%) of those asked said the SSP should continue, whereas 21% said the program should not continue.

In "Public up in Air on Shuttle" (CBS News, August 3, 2005), a poll that was conducted in August 2005 during the shuttle return-to-flight mission, support for the SSP was down compared to years past. The poll indicates that 59% of respondents thought the SSP was worth continuing. This value was down from 75% in 2003 and 72% in 1999.

A June 2006 poll conducted by Gallup found Americans evenly split on the financial worthiness of the SSP.

FIGURE 9.3

Public opinion on the value of the space shuttle program, 2006

WHICH COMES CLOSER TO YOUR VIEW: THE MONEY THE U.S. HAS SPENT ON THE SPACE SHUTTLE PROGRAM WOULD HAVE BEEN BETTER SPENT IN SOME OTHER WAY (OR) THE SPACE SHUTTLE PROGRAM HAS BEEN WORTH THE MONEY THE U.S. HAS SPENT ON IT?

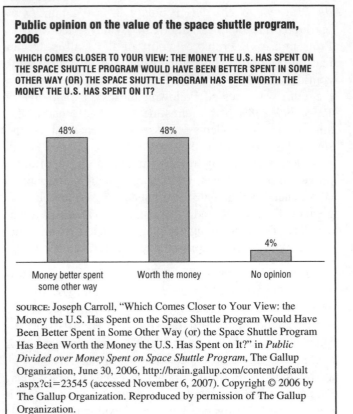

SOURCE: Joseph Carroll, "Which Comes Closer to Your View: the Money the U.S. Has Spent on the Space Shuttle Program Would Have Been Better Spent in Some Other Way (or) the Space Shuttle Program Has Been Worth the Money the U.S. Has Spent on It?" in *Public Divided over Money Spent on Space Shuttle Program*, The Gallup Organization, June 30, 2006, http://brain.gallup.com/content/default.aspx?ci=23545 (accessed November 6, 2007). Copyright © 2006 by The Gallup Organization. Reproduced by permission of The Gallup Organization.

FIGURE 9.4

Public opinion on support for President Bush's plan for space exploration, 2004

THIS YEAR, A NEW PLAN OR GOAL FOR SPACE EXPLORATION WAS ANNOUNCED. THE PLAN INCLUDES A STEPPING-STONE APPROACH TO RETURN THE SPACE SHUTTLE TO FLIGHT, COMPLETE ASSEMBLY OF THE SPACE STATION, BUILD A REPLACEMENT FOR THE SHUTTLE, GO BACK TO THE MOON, AND THEN ON TO MARS AND BEYOND. IF NASA'S BUDGET DID NOT EXCEED 1% OF THE FEDERAL BUDGET, TO WHAT EXTENT WOULD YOU SUPPORT OR OPPOSE THIS NEW PLAN FOR SPACE EXPLORATION? WOULD YOU STRONGLY SUPPORT IT, SUPPORT IT, OPPOSE IT, OR STRONGLY OPPOSE IT?

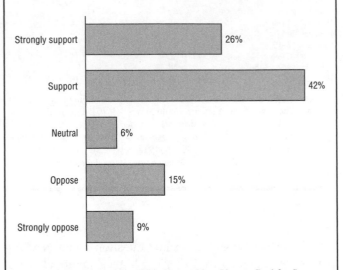

SOURCE: Darren K. Carlson, "This Year, a New Plan or Goal for Space Exploration Was Announced. The Plan Includes a Stepping-Stone Approach to Return the Space Shuttle to Flight, Complete Assembly of the Space Station, Build a Replacement for the Shuttle, Go Back to the Moon, and Then on to Mars and Beyond. If NASA's Budget Did Not Exceed 1% of the Federal Budget, to What Extent Would You Support or Oppose This New Plan for Space Exploration? Would You Strongly Support It, Support It, Oppose It, or Strongly Oppose It?" in *Space: To Infinity and Beyond on a Budget*, The Gallup Organization, August 17, 2004, http://www.gallup.com/poll/12727/Space-Infinity-Beyond-Budget.aspx (accessed January 8, 2008). Copyright © 2004 by The Gallup Organization. Reproduced by permission of The Gallup Organization.

Forty-eight percent of those asked felt the program had been worth the cost, whereas an equal portion thought the money would have been better spent elsewhere. (See Figure 9.3.)

PUBLIC OPINION ABOUT FUTURE SPACE PROGRAMS TO THE MOON AND MARS

In January 2004 President Bush proposed a new agenda for the nation's space program called the Vision for Space Exploration, which focuses on sending astronauts to the Moon and Mars. During the summer of 2004 Gallup polled Americans about their level of support for this new space exploration plan. The pollsters described the plan in general terms and noted that it was to be assumed that NASA's budget would not exceed 1% of the total federal budget. A majority (26% "strongly support" and 42% "support") of those asked supported the plan. (See Figure 9.4.) Another quarter (15% "oppose" and 9% "strongly oppose") were opposed to the plan, and 6% expressed a neutral opinion.

However, a Gallup poll conducted later indicated that Americans provide somewhat different viewpoints when this question is phrased in a different manner. In *Americans Express Confidence in NASA*, Jones notes that a June 2005 poll asked people if they favored or opposed the United States "setting aside money" for a project to land an astronaut on Mars. He notes that 58% of those asked opposed the idea, whereas 40% were in favor of it.

The NASA administrator Michael D. Griffin (1949–) publicly criticized the wording of this poll question. In an interview televised on *Meet the Press* (July 31, 2005, http://www.nasa.gov/pdf/123993main_meet_the_press_trans.pdf), Griffin said the question should have been phrased to ask Americans how best to spend the budget that NASA was going to be allocated in future years. Griffin believed that, given a choice between shuttle missions in low Earth orbit and more adventuresome plans, Americans will choose the bolder undertaking.

Dittmar reports that in 2004, 55% of young people supported the Vision for Space Exploration, whereas 30% opposed it. Overall, young men were far more supportive than young women. By 2006 support for the plan had dropped among young people, with only 45% favoring the plan and 40% opposing it. Dittmar notes that when asked about specific measures within the plan, the respond-

FIGURE 9.5

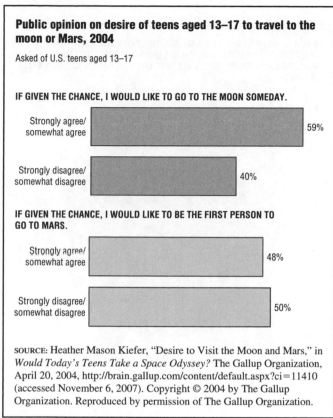

Public opinion on desire of teens aged 13–17 to travel to the moon or Mars, 2004

Asked of U.S. teens aged 13–17

IF GIVEN THE CHANCE, I WOULD LIKE TO GO TO THE MOON SOMEDAY.

Strongly agree/somewhat agree — 59%

Strongly disagree/somewhat disagree — 40%

IF GIVEN THE CHANCE, I WOULD LIKE TO BE THE FIRST PERSON TO GO TO MARS.

Strongly agree/somewhat agree — 48%

Strongly disagree/somewhat disagree — 50%

SOURCE: Heather Mason Kiefer, "Desire to Visit the Moon and Mars," in *Would Today's Teens Take a Space Odyssey?* The Gallup Organization, April 20, 2004, http://brain.gallup.com/content/default.aspx?ci=11410 (accessed November 6, 2007). Copyright © 2004 by The Gallup Organization. Reproduced by permission of The Gallup Organization.

ents showed greater enthusiasm for a crewed Moon mission (34% support) than for a crewed Mars mission (18% support). A large majority (77%) was opposed to sending astronauts to Mars because of its irrelevance, high costs, or other concerns. Young people were much more enthused about the prospects of commercial space travel and opportunities for space tourism offered by private companies. Sixty-one percent of the respondents said these endeavors were relevant to their life.

In *Would Today's Teens Take a Space Odyssey?* (April 20, 2004, http://www.gallup.com/poll/11410/Would-Todays-Teens-Take-Space-Odyssey.aspx), Heather Mason Kiefer of the Gallup Organization reports on a poll that asked teenagers aged thirteen to seventeen about their desires to visit the Moon and Mars. A majority (59%) of teens indicated they would like to go to the Moon someday. (See Figure 9.5.) A smaller percentage (48%) wanted to be the first person to go to Mars. Mason Kiefer notes that responses varied widely by gender, with 74% of boys and only 43% of girls indicating a desire to go to the Moon. Likewise, 64% of boys and only 31% of girls wanted to be the first astronaut on Mars.

PRACTICAL BENEFITS OF SPACE TRAVEL

Even though it is widely acknowledged that space travel has psychological and scientific benefits to society, it is more difficult to point to everyday products that have directly resulted from the nation's space program. Certainly satellites have brought about great changes in telecommunications, navigation, military operations, and weather prediction. All of these developments do affect American lives. The technologies associated with space exploration have advanced the fields of robotics, computer programming, and cryogenics (the physics of extremely cold temperatures). In addition, improvements based on NASA technologies have been incorporated into diverse products such as memory foam mattresses, medical imaging devices, eyeglass lenses, golf balls, baby food, pacemakers, and life rafts.

One of the mandates of the 1958 National Aeronautics and Space Administration Act is that the agency (and its contractors) must publicize any new developments significant to commercial industry. NASA accomplishes this through four publications: the newsletter *Technology Innovation*; a monthly magazine for engineers, managers, and scientists called *NASA Tech Briefs* that briefly describes new technologies; *Technical Support Packages*, which describe in detail the technologies presented in *NASA Tech Briefs*; and *Spinoff*, an annual publication describing successfully commercialized NASA technology.

In *NASA Hits: Rewards from Space—How NASA Improves Our Quality of Life* (2004, http://www.nasa.gov/externalflash/hits2_flash/index_noaccess.html), NASA describes many practical benefits associated with its work in space flight, space science, Earth science, and aeronautical research and development, including:

- Communications satellite technology
- Medical monitoring systems used in intensive care units
- The Hazard Analysis and Critical Control Point system for ensuring food safety
- The NASTRAN software system for computerized design
- Space-based beacon locators used in satellite-based search-and-rescue systems
- Use of thin grooves in concrete airport runways and highways to improve drainage and reduce hydroplaning
- Advances in hydroponics (growing crops using water rather than soil to support plants)
- Improved hurricane forecasting and wildfire tracking using Earth-observing satellites
- Developments in microelectromechanical systems (extremely small devices and sensors about the diameter of a human hair)
- Combustion research that has improved the performance of jet engines
- Suspension techniques used by animal researchers

- A new light source now used to improve chemotherapy treatment for cancer patients

- Needle-based biopsies used in breast cancer diagnosis

- Bioreactors (devices used to turn cell cultures into functional tissue)

- Lifeshears (a hand-held shearing tool used by rescue workers to free people trapped in cars or underneath rubble)

NASA also discusses patents and Nobel prizes associated with NASA-funded research and development.

In 1988 NASA and the Space Foundation, a private organization, established the Space Technology Hall of Fame. Each year a handful of space-based technologies are selected for induction into the Hall of Fame. Inductees are honored at an annual conference held in Colorado Springs, Colorado, called the National Space Symposium. Previous Hall of Fame winners familiar to consumers include satellite radio technology and the DirecTV satellite system.

Douglas A. Comstock and Daniel Lockney of NASA trace in "NASA's Legacy of Technology Transfer and Prospects for Future Benefits" (2007, http://www.ip.nasa.gov/documents/aiaa_space_2007.pdf) the development of NASA's practices for sharing technology and describe significant commercial products that have resulted. These include Teflon-coated fiberglass, which was used in astronaut spacesuits in the 1970s. The product is now used extensively in roofing materials. Another spacesuit innovation—a liquid cooling system—is reportedly "one of the most widely used spinoffs in NASA history" with applications in a variety of medical devices. Another major NASA-developed technology in widespread use evolved from the light-weight breathing apparatuses created for astronauts. This technology has played a crucial role in the development of breathing apparatuses for firefighters. During the 1990s NASA techniques for the robotic servicing of spacecraft were adapted into robotic devices that perform laparoscopic surgery. In 2002 NASA technology led to the commercial development of innovative parachute systems capable of carrying small aircraft safely to the ground in the event of catastrophic engine failure while in the air.

The Public Speaks Out

Polls were conducted on the tenth, twenty-fifth, and thirtieth anniversaries of the *Apollo 11* Moon landing to quiz the public regarding the benefits of the U.S. space program.

In *Landing a Man on the Moon: The Public's View* (July 20, 1999, http://www.gallup.com/poll/3712/Landing-Man-Moon-Publics-View.aspx), Frank Newport explains that in each poll the participants were asked whether they

FIGURE 9.6

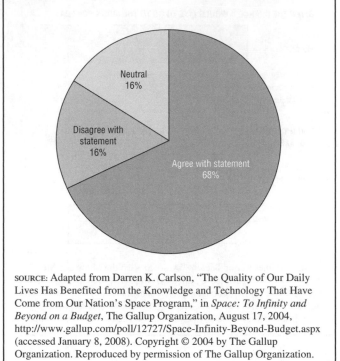

Public opinion on benefits of the space program, 2004

DO YOU AGREE, DISAGREE, OR HAVE NEUTRAL FEELINGS ABOUT THIS STATEMENT: THE QUALITY OF OUR DAILY LIVES HAS BENEFITED FROM THE KNOWLEDGE AND TECHNOLOGY THAT HAVE COME FROM OUR NATION'S SPACE PROGRAM.

Neutral 16%

Disagree with statement 16%

Agree with statement 68%

SOURCE: Adapted from Darren K. Carlson, "The Quality of Our Daily Lives Has Benefited from the Knowledge and Technology That Have Come from Our Nation's Space Program," in *Space: To Infinity and Beyond on a Budget*, The Gallup Organization, August 17, 2004, http://www.gallup.com/poll/12727/Space-Infinity-Beyond-Budget.aspx (accessed January 8, 2008). Copyright © 2004 by The Gallup Organization. Reproduced by permission of The Gallup Organization.

believe the space program has benefited the country enough to justify its costs. Newport notes that a 1979 poll conducted by NBC News and the Associated Press found that only 41% of respondents considered the benefits worth the costs. A majority (53%) thought the expense was not worth what was accomplished. In a 1994 Gallup poll Americans were evenly split on the issue, with 47% taking each side. By 1999 the space program had earned a bit more respect. Newport indicates that 55% of those asked believed the space program's benefits justified its cost, whereas 40% did not.

In 2004 Gallup asked Americans whether they agreed or disagreed with the statement: "The quality of our daily lives has benefited from the knowledge and technology that have come from our nation's space program." (See Figure 9.6.) Sixty-eight percent of those asked agreed with this statement, whereas 16% disagreed. Another 16% were neutral on the subject.

NASA WOOS THE AMERICAN PUBLIC

NASA employs a number of public relations tools designed to interest and excite people about space travel. Since its inception the agency has recognized that public support is crucial to fostering a successful long-term space program.

Television

Throughout the space age NASA has used television as a publicity tool to try to spark greater interest in the space program. Television turned out to be one of the greatest public relations tools of the Apollo program. In 1968 the *Apollo 7* astronauts conducted the first live television interview from space. All the remaining Apollo flights carried television cameras. The worldwide television audience for the *Apollo 11* Moon landing was estimated at half a billion people.

Newport notes in *Landing a Man on the Moon* that in July 1999 Americans were polled about their memories of the first manned lunar landing by *Apollo 11*. The survey found that 76% of people aged thirty-five and over claimed to have watched the event on television as it happened.

NASA's Web Site

NASA's Web site (http://www.nasa.gov/) includes thousands of mission photographs and millions of documents related to the nation's space endeavors. The Web site provides detailed information about NASA facilities, programs, and missions. There are a variety of multimedia features, including interactive displays, video and audio downloads, and spectacular images of Earth and space captured by NASA spacecraft. Furthermore, it provides access to historical archives that include documentation dating back to the earliest days of space travel.

According to NASA, the Web site is visited millions of times each day. The number of "hits" increases dramatically during highly publicized missions. For example, NASA reports in the press release "NASA Portal Makes a Little Bit of Mars Available to Everyone on Earth" (February 19, 2004, http://www.nasa.gov/home/hqnews/2004/feb/HQ_04064_portal.html) that it received over 6.5 billion hits between January 4 and February 19, 2004. This period coincides with the highly successful landings of the Mars Exploration rovers on Mars.

SIGHTING OPPORTUNITIES. One of the ways that NASA tries to engage public interest in space travel is by posting sighting opportunities for its satellites, particularly the *ISS* and any ongoing shuttle missions. The NASA Web site instructs people how and where to look in the nighttime sky to see the spacecraft as it is passing overhead. Figure 9.7 shows a set of instructions for viewing the *ISS* at a particular location, assuming that skies are clear enough.

This listing identifies the exact date and time at which the *ISS* should become visible to observers on the ground and how long it will remain visible. It also gives information about the station's location in the sky based on direction (north, south, east, or west) and angle of elevation compared to the horizon. A spacecraft flying directly overhead would be at 90-degree maximum elevation.

FIGURE 9.7

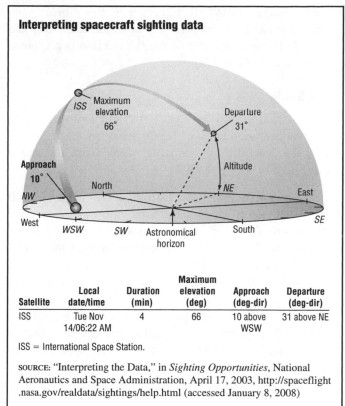

Interpreting spacecraft sighting data

Satellite	Local date/time	Duration (min)	Maximum elevation (deg)	Approach (deg-dir)	Departure (deg-dir)
ISS	Tue Nov 14/06:22 AM	4	66	10 above WSW	31 above NE

ISS = International Space Station.

SOURCE: "Interpreting the Data," in *Sighting Opportunities*, National Aeronautics and Space Administration, April 17, 2003, http://spaceflight.nasa.gov/realdata/sightings/help.html (accessed January 8, 2008)

In the example shown, the *ISS* will appear in the west-southwest direction approximately 10 degrees above the horizon. (See Figure 9.7.) It will then climb to a maximum elevation of 66 degrees above the horizon and travel out of sight heading toward the northeast. It should disappear from view about 31 degrees above the horizon.

In *Sighting Opportunities* (April 17, 2003, http://spaceflight.nasa.gov/realdata/sightings/help.html), NASA explains that a spacecraft looks like "a steady white pinpoint of light moving slowly across the sky." Viewers are urged to observe spacecraft with the naked eye or through binoculars. The speed at which spacecraft move makes telescope viewing impractical.

NASA's Web site provides links to sighting data for hundreds of cities around the world. People at locations not listed can use an applet (a small application program) called SkyWatch to enter their latitude and longitude and receive viewing information for numerous orbiting satellites.

NTV

NASA operates its own television network called NASA TV (NTV). NTV broadcasts via satellite and cable and is streamed over the Internet. It features live coverage of NASA activities and missions, video of events for the news media, and educational programming for teachers and students.

The show *NASA Education Hour* plays at 8:00 a.m. eastern standard time (EST) every weekday morning and is rebroadcast at regular intervals throughout the day and night. Hour-long coverage of the *ISS* mission is presented live at 11 a.m. EST daily.

Ham Radio

Ham radios vary in signal strength and capability. The strongest stations can reach operators on the other side of the world by bouncing signals off the upper atmosphere or using satellites.

In November 1983 the astronaut Owen K. Garriott (1930–) carried a small ham radio with him aboard the space shuttle *Columbia*. During his spare time he used the radio to contact fellow ham operators around the world. This was the first of more than twenty-four shuttle missions that carried ham radio equipment so astronauts could communicate with their families and other ham operators worldwide and perform interviews for schoolchildren. The program was called the Space Amateur Radio Experiment (SAREX). The Soviet space agency operated a similar ham radio program for cosmonauts aboard the *Mir* space station.

In September 2000 the crew of the space shuttle *Atlantis* carried a ham radio to the *ISS* for use by Expedition crews. The SAREX program was given the new name of Amateur Radio on the International Space Station (ARISS). Under the ARISS program, *ISS* crewmembers can communicate with ham radio operators all over the world.

Educational Programs

NASA's strategic plan says that one of the agency's primary goals is to "inspire the next generation of explorers." To accomplish this goal, NASA operates an extensive student education program designed to encourage young people to pursue studies in science, mathematics, technology, and engineering and careers in aeronautics and space science. NASA reports in *National Aeronautics and Space Administration: FY 2008 Budget Estimates* (February 5, 2007, http://www.nasa.gov/pdf/168653main _NASA_FY08_Budget_Summary.pdf) that the program's proposed budget for 2008 was $153.7 million. NASA prides itself on its educational programs and the partnerships it establishes with schools, museums, libraries, and science centers around the nation to reach as many young people as possible.

NASA EXPLORER SCHOOLS. The NASA Explorer School program was started in 2003 for educators teaching grades four through nine. Each year NASA selects fifty schools for the program and enters into a three-year partnership agreement with them. The schools are eligible for grants and summer training courses for science and mathematics teachers. The courses are provided at

NASA centers around the country and present new teaching resources and tools to better educate students.

TEACHER RESOURCE CENTERS. Teacher Resource Centers (TRCs) are offices maintained at NASA facilities around the country. The TRCs serve as libraries that loan educational materials including lesson plans, audio and video tapes, slides, and miscellaneous print publications to teachers.

ASTRONAUT INTERVIEWS VIA AMATEUR RADIO. One of the most innovative ways that students can interact with astronauts in orbit is via ARISS, which is sponsored by NASA in conjunction with the American Radio Relay League and the Radio Amateur Satellite Corporation. Volunteers set up ham radio stations at schools so students can interview *ISS* crewmembers.

CURRICULUM DEVELOPMENT. In 2004 NASA announced a new partnership with Pearson Scott Foresman (PSF), a leading publisher of educational products for elementary schools. The PSF will draw on publications in the NASA archives to create new science textbooks and other learning materials for the classroom. According to NASA, in "A Learning Adventure" (March 17, 2006, http://www .nasa.gov/audience/foreducators/informal/features/F_Zathura _Learning_Adventure.html), the goal of the program is to "spark student imagination, encourage interest in space exploration, and enhance elementary science curricula."

Art Program

In 1962 the NASA administrator James Edwin Webb (1906–1992) established the NASA Art Program to encourage and collect works of art about aeronautics and space. As of 2008, the NASA art collection included over eight hundred works of art in a variety of media, including paintings, drawings, poems, and songs. NASA has donated more than two thousand of its art works (including a number by Norman Rockwell [1894–1978]) to the National Air and Space Museum in Washington, D.C. Other famous artists who have participated in the program include Annie Leibovitz (1949–), William Wegman (1942–), Andy Warhol (1927–1987), and Jamie Wyeth (1946–).

Over two hundred artists have provided art works to the program. Many of the pieces are displayed at art galleries and museums around the country. NASA centers, particularly the Kennedy Space Center in Florida, also display the art works in their visitor areas.

Astronauts

Astronauts have always been NASA's greatest public relations agents. The early astronauts became instant heroes during the 1950s and 1960s. They were flooded with fan mail and held up by the media as sterling role models of what was great and daring about the United States. However, after the first Moon landing in 1969, public interest in the space program began to fade. The astronauts of later decades were still admired and respected, but they were not treated to the same level of hero worship as their predecessors.

During the early 1980s NASA decided to include a new type of astronaut on space shuttle flights to catch the public's attention. The agency began the Educator in Space program. NASA hoped that sending a teacher into space would excite the nation's schoolchildren and foster goodwill toward the space program. The schoolteacher Christa McAuliffe (1948–1986) was selected and trained for a mission aboard the space shuttle *Challenger*. She was killed with the other six crew members in 1986 when the shuttle exploded soon after liftoff.

NASA's public relations experiment turned into a nightmare. The catastrophe brought harsh criticism of the agency. The shuttle program was found to have serious management and safety problems. The loss seemed even more poignant to the public because a teacher, an everyday kind of person, had been one of the victims. NASA decided that space travel was not routine enough to risk the lives of private citizens as goodwill ambassadors.

In 1998 NASA relented somewhat and allowed Glenn, a former Mercury astronaut, to ride aboard the space shuttle *Discovery*. At the time Glenn was a seventy-seven-year-old senator from Ohio. NASA said the mission would reveal new knowledge about the effects of weightlessness and bone loss in older people. Critics complained that it was nothing more than a publicity stunt. Whatever the motivation, the event did greatly improve NASA's image. The public was entranced by the idea of an old hero traveling back into space.

Tourist Attractions

Many NASA facilities have become popular tourist attractions. This is particularly true for centers associated with the Apollo program and the SSP. Most NASA facilities operate their own visitor centers for which admission is free. The Johnson Space Center (Houston, Texas), the Kennedy Space Center (Cape Canaveral, Florida), and the Marshall Space Flight Center (Huntsville, Alabama) have privately operated tourist centers that charge a fee for admittance.

Contests and Gimmicks

One relatively new way that NASA engages the public in space travel is by holding spacecraft-naming contests. During the 1990s NASA held contests that chose the names for the Mars Pathfinder mission's *Sojourner* rover and the *Magellan* spacecraft.

In 1998 the agency asked people to suggest names for an x-ray telescope to be launched as part of the Great Observatories Program. Each entry had to be supported by a short essay justifying why the name was appropriate.

More than six thousand people entered the contest, representing every state in the country and sixty-one other nations. Two winning essays were selected. Both suggested the name Chandra, in honor of the Indian-American scientist Subrahmanyan Chandrasekhar (1910–1995). The winners were a high-school student from Laclede, Idaho, and a high-school teacher from Camarillo, California.

In 2001 a similar contest was held to name an infrared telescope intended for the Great Observatories Program. Over seven thousand entries were received from people around the world. NASA chose the name Spitzer in honor of the American physicist Lyman Spitzer Jr. (1914–1997). The winning essay came from a Canadian astronomy enthusiast.

In 2002 NASA held a contest for children to name the planned Mars rover craft. The contest was held in partnership with the Planetary Society and the Lego Company. A nine-year-old girl from Scottsdale, Arizona, wrote the winning essay, which suggested the names *Spirit* and *Opportunity*. Hers was one of nearly ten thousand entries in the contest.

Another public relations device used by NASA is to ask people to submit their names for inclusion on CDs or DVDs carried by spacecraft. Numerous NASA missions conducted since the 1990s have included electronic disks carrying the names of millions of people. In 1999 the *Mars Polar Lander* carried a CD containing the names of one million schoolchildren from around the world. The spacecraft was lost before it landed on Mars.

The highly successful Mars Explorer rovers *Spirit* and *Opportunity* carried mini-DVDs including the names of more than 3.5 million people. A DVD library has been compiled to fly aboard the *Phoenix Mars Lander*, which was scheduled for launch in 2008. The DVD includes a list of individual names, messages from space enthusiasts, and other works, including poems and stories.

PUBLIC KNOWLEDGE ABOUT SPACE TRAVEL

In *Landing a Man on the Moon*, Newport states that respondents were asked about the number of astronauts who have actually walked on the Moon. Only 5% of those asked correctly answered that twelve different men have walked on the Moon. (See Figure 9.8.) A vast majority (77%) of the respondents guessed too low. Another 11% guessed too high, and 7% had no opinion.

According to Newport, only 50% of the people asked correctly named Neil A. Armstrong (1930–) as the first person to walk on the Moon. (See Table 9.4.) Newport notes that young people aged eighteen to twenty-nine were the most likely to give the correct answer, despite the fact that the event occurred before they were born. Other astronauts receiving votes included Glenn, who received 13%; Alan B. Shepard Jr. (1923–1998), 4%; and Edwin E. (Buzz)

FIGURE 9.8

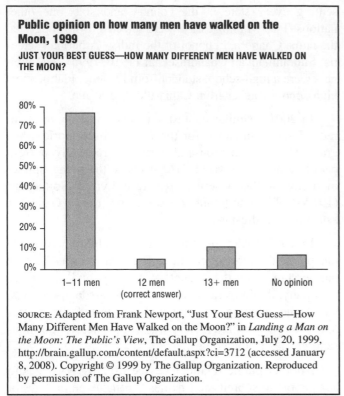

Public opinion on how many men have walked on the Moon, 1999

JUST YOUR BEST GUESS—HOW MANY DIFFERENT MEN HAVE WALKED ON THE MOON?

SOURCE: Adapted from Frank Newport, "Just Your Best Guess—How Many Different Men Have Walked on the Moon?" in *Landing a Man on the Moon: The Public's View*, The Gallup Organization, July 20, 1999, http://brain.gallup.com/content/default.aspx?ci=3712 (accessed January 8, 2008). Copyright © 1999 by The Gallup Organization. Reproduced by permission of The Gallup Organization.

TABLE 9.4

Poll respondents' identification of the first person to walk on the Moon, 1989 and 1999

DO YOU HAPPEN TO KNOW WHO WAS THE FIRST PERSON TO WALK ON THE MOON?

	99 Jul 13–14	89 Jul 6–9
Neil Armstrong	50%	39%
John Glenn	13	
Alan Shepard	4	
Buzz Aldrin	2	
Other	3	
No opinion	28	61*
	100%	100%

*Incorrect; don't know.

SOURCE: Frank Newport, "Do You Happen to Know Who Was the First Person to Walk on the Moon?" in *Landing a Man on the Moon: The Public's View*, The Gallup Organization, July 20, 1999, http://brain.gallup.com/content/default.aspx?ci=3712 (accessed January 8, 2008). Copyright © 1999 by The Gallup Organization. Reproduced by permission of The Gallup Organization.

the project. Amazingly, 32% of the respondents "were completely unaware that there is an ISS."

OPINIONS ABOUT SPACE TOPICS

Extraterrestrial Life

In *Life on Mars?* (February 27, 2001, http://www.gallup.com/poll/1957/Life-Mars.aspx), Darren K. Carlson explains that Americans were surveyed in 1996 and 1999 about the possible existence of extraterrestrial (not Earth-related) life. Each time a strong majority of poll participants expressed the opinion that some form of life does exist on other planets in the universe. Belief in extraterrestrial life declined somewhat from 72% in 1996 to 61% in 1999.

Carlson notes that according to several Gallup polls conducted between 1973 and 1999, Americans are less convinced in the possibility of extraterrestrial human life. Only 38% to 51% of poll participants agreed that there could be "people somewhat like ourselves" living elsewhere in the universe. The latest poll, taken in 1999, reflects the greatest skepticism for the idea of extraterrestrial people. For the first time, a majority (54%) of those asked did not believe that such people exist.

According to Linda Lyons of the Gallup Organization, in *Paranormal Beliefs Come (Super)Naturally to Some* (November 1, 2005, http://www.gallup.com/poll/19558/Paranormal-Beliefs-Come-SuperNaturally-Some.aspx), in the summer of 2005 Gallup asked people in the United States, Canada, and Great Britain about their beliefs in various supernatural or paranormal phenomena. Twenty-four percent of the Americans polled believed that extraterrestrial beings have visited Earth at some time in the past. Slightly smaller percentages of Canadians (21%) and Britons (19%) held the same belief.

Aldrin Jr. (1930–), 2%. More than a quarter (28%) of the people asked could not come up with an answer.

Newport states that Gallup asked this same question back in July 1989, on the twentieth anniversary of the first human lunar landing. At that time only 39% of respondents gave the correct answer. The other 61% either did not know the answer or gave an incorrect answer.

Jeffrey M. Jones reports in *Support for Space Program Funding High by Historical Standards* (August 19, 2003, http://www.gallup.com/poll/9082/Support-Space-Program-Funding-High-Historical-Standards.aspx) that in August 2003, 534 adults were asked whether there were any U.S. astronauts in space at that time or not. Exactly half of the people said there were no U.S. astronauts in space at that time. Another 35% believed that U.S. astronauts were in space, and 15% had no opinion or did not know. In reality, there was one U.S. astronaut in space at the time: Edward Tsang Lu (1963–) was aboard the *ISS*. Since 2000 the *ISS* has been continually inhabited by at least one American astronaut.

According to Dittmar, in 2006 less than a third (32%) of respondents aged eighteen to twenty-five expressed "meaningful awareness" about the *ISS*. A much higher percentage (61%) indicated awareness of the Mars rover projects. Only 28% of the young people correctly answered "basic" questions about the *ISS* regarding where in space the station orbits and which countries are partnered with the United States on

A Moon Hoax?

One of the most offbeat conspiracy theories of the space age is that the U.S. government faked the Apollo Moon landings. In 2001 the FOX television network broadcast the show *Conspiracy Theory: Did We Land on the Moon?* Guests on the show claimed that the Apollo program never actually put a man on the Moon but faked the lunar landing for television cameras. The theory continues to be supported on various Web sites on the Internet.

Advocates of the hoax theory rely on several key points to support their position. Chief among these are:

- NASA's Moon photographs do not show stars in the background behind the astronauts.

- The American flag supposedly planted on the Moon by *Apollo 11* astronauts is rippling in a breeze, yet there is no atmosphere on the Moon.

- There is no blast crater beneath the lunar lander.

- Humans could not have survived exposure to the intense radiation of the Van Allen belts lying between Earth and the Moon.

In general, NASA ignores the hoax claims and does not address them publicly. However, the NASA Web site does include one article of rebuttal: "The Great Moon Hoax" (February 23, 2001, http://science.nasa.gov/headlines/y2001/ast23feb_2.htm). In it Tony Phillips addresses questions about Moon photographs and the rippling flag. He points out that the exposure on the Moon cameras had to be adjusted to tone down the dazzling brightness of the astronauts' sunlit spacesuits. This caused the background stars to be too faint to appear in the photographs. The rippling flag is explained by the wire inserts built into the fabric and by the twisting motion the astronauts used to push the flagpole into the lunar ground.

Phillips notes that Moon rocks are the best evidence that astronauts visited the Moon. The astronauts brought back 841 pounds of these rocks, and these rocks have been investigated by researchers from all over the world. Moon rocks differ greatly in mineral and water content from any rocks found on Earth. They also contain isotopes created by long-term exposure to high-energy cosmic rays on the lunar surface.

In "Ask an Astrophysicist" (December 1, 2005, http://imagine.gsfc.nasa.gov/docs/ask_astro/answers/970630a.html), Laura Whitlock addresses the hoax issue concerning

TABLE 9.5

Public opinion on whether the government faked the Apollo Moon landing, 1995 and 1999

THINKING ABOUT THE SPACE EXPLORATION, DO YOU THINK THE GOVERNMENT STAGED OR FAKED THE APOLLO MOON LANDING, OR DON'T YOU FEEL THAT WAY?

	Yes, staged	No	No opinion
1999 Jul 13–14	6%	89	5
1995 Jul 19–20	6%	83	11

SOURCE: "Thinking about the Space Exploration, Do You Think the Government Staged or Faked the Apollo Moon Landing, or Don't You Feel That Way?" in *Did Men Really Land on the Moon?* The Gallup Organization, February 15, 2001, http://brain.gallup.com/content/default.aspx?ci=1993 (accessed January 8, 2008). Copyright © 2001 by The Gallup Organization. Reproduced by permission of The Gallup Organization. 1995 data from Time/CNN/Yankelovich Partners, Inc. Poll.

the Van Allen radiation belts, which are regions of highly energized ionized particles trapped within the geomagnetic fields surrounding Earth. Whitlock explains that early NASA researchers were also worried about the radiation belts. Scientists at the Oak Ridge National Laboratory (ORNL) in Oak Ridge, Tennessee, devised experiments in which bacteria and blood cells were sent aboard unmanned probes into space and returned to Earth. Animal experiments were also performed. The ORNL used the resulting data to design special radiation shields for the Apollo spacecraft. The shields utilized materials left over from nuclear testing performed during the 1950s. Whitlock also notes that the Apollo spacecraft traveled so fast that the astronauts were exposed to Van Allen radiation for only a short time.

In a survey conducted in July 1999, Gallup asked poll participants their view about a possible Moon-landing hoax. The vast majority (89%) of those interviewed did not believe that the government staged the Apollo Moon landing. (See Table 9.5.) Only 6% agreed that the landing was a hoax. Another 5% had no opinion. The results closely match those of a poll taken in 1995 by Time, CNN, and Yankelovich Partners, Inc. That poll also found that 6% of the respondents believed the Moon landing was staged. Most people (83%) did not.

However, Dittmar notes that in 2006, 27% of eighteen-to twenty-five-year-olds were doubtful to some degree that astronauts had traveled to the Moon. Ten percent of the young people indicated that it was "highly unlikely" that the Moon landings occurred at all.

IMPORTANT NAMES AND ADDRESSES

Amateur Radio on the International Space Station
ARRL Headquarters
SuitSat QSL
225 Main St.
Newington, CT 06111-1494
URL: http://www.rac.ca/ariss/

American Institute of Aeronautics and Astronautics
1801 Alexander Bell Dr., Ste. 500
Reston, VA 20191-4344
(703) 264-7500
1-800-639-2422
FAX: (703) 264-7551
URL: http://www.aiaa.org/

Ames Research Center
Moffett Field, CA 94035
(650) 604-5000
URL: http://www.nasa.gov/centers/ames/

Arecibo Observatory
HCO 3 Box 53995
Arecibo, PR 00612
(787) 878-2612
FAX: (787) 878-1861
URL: http://www.naic.edu/

Canadian Space Agency
John H. Chapman Space Centre
6767 Route de l'Aéroport
Saint-Hubert, Quebec, Canada J3Y 8Y9
(450) 926-4800
FAX: (450) 926-4352
URL: http://www.space.gc.ca/asc/eng/

Columbia Accident Investigation Board
2900 S. Quincy St., Ste. 800
Arlington, VA 22206
URL: http://caib.nasa.gov/

Dryden Flight Research Center
PO Box 273
Edwards, CA 93523-0273
(661) 276-3311
URL: http://www.nasa.gov/centers/dryden/

European Space Agency
8-10 rue Mario Nikis
75738 Paris, France Cedex 15
011-33-1-5369-7654
FAX: 011-33-1-5369-7560
E-mail: contactesa@esa.int
URL: http://www.esa.int/esaCP/index.html

Fédération Aéronautique Internationale
Avenue Mon-Repos 24
Lausanne, Switzerland CH-1005
011-41-1-21-345-1070
URL: http://www.fai.org/

Glenn Research Center
21000 Brookpark Rd.
Cleveland, OH 44135
(216) 433-4000
URL: http://www.nasa.gov/centers/glenn/

Goddard Space Flight Center
Mail Code 130, Public Inquiries
Greenbelt, MD 20771
(301) 286-2000
URL: http://www.nasa.gov/centers/goddard/

International Astronomical Union
98-bis, Blvd. Arago
F-75014 Paris, France
011-33-1-43-25-83-58
FAX: 011-33-1-43-25-26-16
E-mail: iau@iap.fr
URL: http://www.iau.org/

Japan Aerospace Exploration Agency
7-44-1 Jindaiji, Higashi-Machi, Chofu
Tokyo, Japan 182
011-81-4-2244-3551
FAX: 011-81-4-2242-1371
URL: http://www.jaxa.jp/index_e.html

Jet Propulsion Laboratory
4800 Oak Grove Dr.
Pasadena, CA 91109
(818) 354-4321
URL: http://www.jpl.nasa.gov/

John F. Kennedy Space Center
Kennedy Space Center, FL 32899
(321) 867-5000
URL: http://www.nasa.gov/centers/kennedy/

Keck Observatory
California Association for Research in Astronomy
65-1120 Mamalahoa Hwy.
Kamuela, HI 96743
(808) 885-7887
FAX: (808) 885-4464
URL: http://www.keckobservatory.org/

Langley Research Center
Hampton, VA 23681-2199
(757) 864-1000
URL: http://www.nasa.gov/centers/langley/

Los Alamos National Laboratory
Community Programs Office
1619 Central Ave., MS A117
Los Alamos, NM 87545
(505) 665-4400
1-888-841-8256
FAX: (505) 665-4411
E-mail: community@lanl.gov
URL: http://www.lanl.gov/

Lowell Observatory
1400 W. Mars Hill Rd.
Flagstaff, AZ 86001
(928) 774-3358
E-mail: friends@lowell.edu
URL: http://www.lowell.edu/

Lyndon B. Johnson Space Center
2101 NASA Pkwy.
Houston, TX 77058
(281) 483-0123
URL: http://www.nasa.gov/centers/johnson/

Marshall Space Flight Center
Bldg. 4200, Rm. 120
MSFC
Huntsville, AL 35812
URL: http://www.nasa.gov/centers/marshall/

National Aeronautics and Space Administration
Ste. 5K39
Washington, DC 20546-0001
(202) 358-0001
FAX: (202) 358-3469
URL: http://www.nasa.gov/home/

National Oceanic and Atmospheric Administration
1401 Constitution Ave. NW, Rm. 6217
Washington, DC 20230
(202) 482-6090
FAX: (202) 482-3154
URL: http://www.noaa.gov/

National Science Foundation
4201 Wilson Blvd.
Arlington, VA 22230
(703) 292-5111
1-800-877-8339
URL: http://www.nsf.gov/

Office for Outer Space Affairs
United Nations Office at Vienna
Vienna International Centre
A-1400 Vienna, Austria
011-43-1-260-60-4950
FAX: 011-43-1-260-60-5830
E-mail: oosa@unvienna.org
URL: http://www.unoosa.org/

Planetary Society
65 N. Catalina Ave.
Pasadena, CA 91106-2301
(626) 793-5100
FAX: (626) 793-5528
E-mail: tps@planetary.org
URL: http://www.planetary.org/

Scaled Composites
1624 Flight Line
Mojave, CA 93501
(661) 824-4541
FAX: (661) 824-4174
URL: http://www.scaled.com/

Space Adventures
8000 Towers Crescent Dr., Ste. 1000
Vienna, VA 22182
(703) 524-7172
1-888-857-7223
FAX: (703) 524-7176
E-mail: info@spaceadventures.com
URL: http://www.spaceadventures.com/

Space Telescope Science Institute
3700 San Martin Dr.
Baltimore, MD 21218
(410) 338-4700
E-mail: help@stsci.edu
URL: http://www.stsci.edu/resources

Space Weather Prediction Center
W/NP9
325 Broadway
Boulder, CO 80305
URL: http://www.sec.noaa.gov/

Stennis Space Center
Stennis Space Center, MS 39529
(228) 688-2211
URL: http://www.nasa.gov/centers/stennis/

U.S. Alliance
1150 Gemini
Houston, TX 77058
(281) 212-6200
URL: http://www.unitedspacealliance.com/

U.S. Geological Survey Astrogeological Program
2255 N. Gemini Dr.
Flagstaff, AZ 86001
URL: http://astrogeology.usgs.gov/

U.S. Government Accountability Office
441 G St. NW
Washington, DC 20548
(202) 512-3000
E-mail: contact@gao.gov
URL: http://www.gao.gov/

U.S. Strategic Command
901 SAC Blvd., Ste. 1A1
Offutt Air Force Base, NE 68113-6020
(402) 294-4130
FAX: (402) 294-4892
E-mail: pa@stratcom.mil
URL: http://www.stratcom.mil/

Virgin Galactic
URL: http://www.virgingalactic.com

Wallops Flight Facility
Wallops Island, VA 23337
URL: http://www.wff.nasa.gov/

White Sands Test Facility
PO Box 20
Las Cruces, NM 88004
URL: http://www.wstf.nasa.gov/

X Prize Foundation
1441 Fourth St., Ste. 200
Santa Monica, CA 90401
(310) 587-3355
FAX: (310) 393-4207
URL: http://www.xprizefoundation.com/

RESOURCES

The National Aeronautics and Space Administration (NASA) is the premier resource for information about the U.S. space program. NASA headquarters operates an informative Web site (http://www.nasa.gov/). There are links to all the facilities operated by NASA around the country. Many of these links were consulted for this book. In addition, some specific NASA publications proved to be useful, including *Suited for Spacewalking: A Teacher's Guide with Activities for Technology, Education, Mathematics, and Science* (1998), *Space Transportation System* (August 2000), *Basics of Space Flight* (May 2001), *Rockets: An Educator's Guide with Activities in Science, Mathematics, and Technology* (2003), *CAIB Report: Volume 1* (August 2003), *NASA's Implementation Plan for Space Shuttle Return to Flight and Beyond* (October 2003), *NASA Hits: Rewards from Space—How NASA Improves Our Quality of Life* (2004), *The Vision for Space Exploration* (February 2004), *Fiscal Year 2005 Performance and Accountability Report* (2005), *Final Report of the Return to Flight Task Group* (July 2005), *Statement of Michael D. Griffin, Administrator, National Aeronautics and Space Administration, before the Committee on Science, House of Representatives: November 3, 2005* (November 2005), *National Aeronautics and Space Administration 2006 Strategic Plan* (2006), *Passage to a Ringed World* (2006), *Final Report of the International Space Station Independent Safety Task Force* (February 2007), *National Aeronautics and Space Administration: FY 2008 Budget Estimates* (February 2007), *Phoenix Launch: Mission to the Martian Polar North* (August 2007), *STS-120: Harmony: A Global Gateway* (October 2007), and *Exploring the NASA Workforce* (December 2007).

NASA's History Office (http://www.hq.nasa.gov/office/pao/History) maintains an extensive collection of historical documents. This collection includes the complete text of books written for NASA about space activities of previous decades. Online books valuable to this project include *This New Ocean: A History of Project Mercury* (Loyd S. Swenson Jr., James M. Grimwood, and Charles C. Alexander, 1989), *On the Shoulders of Titans: A History of Project Gemini* (Barton C. Hacker and James M. Grimwood, 1977), *Apollo by the Numbers: A Statistical Reference* (Richard W. Orloff, 2000), *Chariots for Apollo: A History of Manned Lunar Spacecraft* (Courtney G. Brooks, James M. Grimwood, and Loyd S. Swenson Jr., 1979), and *The Human Factor: Biomedicine in the Manned Space Program to 1980* (John A. Pitts, 1985).

NASA publishes a press kit for each space shuttle mission and for major missions of the robotic space program. These press kits contain key information on mission objectives, spacecraft design, crewmembers, and science experiments. Another important NASA series is *NASA Facts*. This series provides data about missions and space science and biographies of historical figures key to the U.S. space program. The quarterly NASA newsletter *Discovery Dispatch* describes the progress of ongoing robotic missions. The series *Technology Innovation* discusses businesses and technologies related to NASA's Innovative Partnerships Program.

The National Oceanic and Atmospheric Administration's Space Environment Center publishes a series of educational brochures called *Space Environment Topics*. Informative brochures in the series include "Radio Wave Propagation" (Norm Cohen and Kenneth Davies, 1994), "Navigation" (Joe Kunches, 1995), "Aurora" (Larry Combs and Rodney Viereck, 1996), "The Ionosphere" (Dave Anderson and Tim Fuller-Rowell, 1999), "Solar Maximum" (Gary Heckman, 1999), and "Satellite Anomalies" (Dave Speich and Barbara Poppe, 2000). Another excellent publication from the Space Environment Center is *Solar Physics and Terrestrial Effects: A Curriculum Guide for Teachers, Grades 7–12* (June 1996).

The Congressional Research Service (CRS) is the public policy research arm of Congress. CRS publications useful to this book were *China's Space Program: An Overview* (Marcia S. Smith, October 2005), *Space Stations* (Marcia S. Smith, January 2006), and *U.S. Space Programs: Civilian, Military, and Commercial* (Patricia Moloney Figliola, Carl E. Behrens, and Daniel Morgan, June 13, 2006).

The U.S. Government Accountability Office (GAO) is the investigative arm of Congress. GAO publications used in this book include *Space Transportation: Challenges Facing NASA's Space Launch Initiative* (September 2002), *Space Station: Impact of the Grounding of the Shuttle Fleet* (September 2003), *NASA: Shuttle Fleet's Safe Return to Flight Is Key to Space Station Progress* (Allen Li, October 2003), *Space Shuttle: Further Improvements Needed in NASA's Modernization Efforts* (January 2004), *Space Shuttle: Actions Needed to Better Position NASA to Sustain Its Workforce through Retirement* (March 2005), *Defense Space Activities: Management Guidance and Performance Measures Needed to Develop Personnel* (September 2005), *National Aeronautics and Space Administration: Long-Standing Financial Management Challenges Threaten the Agency's Ability to Manage Its Programs* (Gregory D. Kutz, October 2005), *NASA: Challenges in Completing and Sustaining the International Space Station* (Cristina T. Chaplain, July 2007), *NASA Supplier Base: Challenges Exist in Transitioning from the Space Shuttle Program to the Next Generation of Human Spaceflight Systems* (July 2007), and *Space Based Infrared System High Program and Its Alternative* (September 2007).

Other government agencies with online publications about space activities include the U.S. Army at Redstone Arsenal, the U.S. Air Force Space Command, the U.S. Naval Observatory, the National Science Foundation, the National Academy of Sciences, the U.S. Department of Energy's Los Alamos National Laboratory, and the U.S. Geological Survey Astrogeology Research Program.

Information about international space programs and missions was obtained from the Web sites of the Canadian Space Agency, the China Aerospace Science and Technology Corporation, the European Space Agency, the Japan Aerospace Exploration Agency, and the Russian Federal Space Agency. The United Nations Office for Outer Space Affairs operates a Web site that describes international space law and treaties.

Private companies and organizations engaged in space-related enterprises and educational programs include the American Radio Relay League, the Google Lunar X Prize, Mojave Aerospace Ventures, the Planetary Society, Scaled Composites, Space Adventures, and the X Prize Foundation. Breaking news about space activities is available from online news services, including *Environmental News Network*, *National Geographic News*, *Space.com*, and *Spaceflight Now*.

The Smithsonian Institution operates the National Air and Space Museum in Washington, D.C. The museum's Web site (http://www.nasm.si.edu) provides information about the history of airplane flight and space flight. Many thanks to the Gallup Organization for its polls and surveys about American attitudes regarding programs and missions conducted throughout the space age.

INDEX

S